THE ELUSIVE PROPHET

OUDTESTAMENTISCHE STUDIËN

NAMENS HET OUDTESTAMENTISCH WERKGEZELSCHAP IN NEDERLAND EN BELGIË

UITGEGEVEN DOOR

JOHANNES C. DE MOOR
KAMPEN

ADVISORY BOARD

HARRY VAN ROOY
POTCHEFSTROOM

MARC VERVENNE
LEUVEN

DEEL XLV

THE ELUSIVE PROPHET

THE ELUSIVE PROPHET
The Prophet as a Historical Person, Literary Character
and Anonymous Artist

PAPERS READ AT THE ELEVENTH JOINT MEETING OF

THE SOCIETY FOR OLD TESTAMENT STUDY

AND

HET OUDTESTAMENTISCH WERKGEZELSCHAP
IN NEDERLAND EN BELGIË

HELD AT SOESTERBERG 2000

EDITED BY
JOHANNES C. DE MOOR

Society of Biblical Literature
Atlanta

THE ELUSIVE PROPHET

Copyright © 2001 by Koninklijke Brill NV, Leiden,
The Netherlands

This edition published under license from Koninklijke Brill NV, Leiden, The Netherlands by the Society of Biblical Literature.

All rights reserved. No part of this work may be reproduced or transmitted in any form or by any means, electronic or mechanical, including photocopying and recording, or by any means of any information storage or retrieval system, except as may be expressly permitted by the 1976 Copyright Act or in writing from the Publisher. Requests for permission should be addressed in writing to the Rights and Permissions Department, Koninklijke Brill NV, Leiden, The Netherlands.

Authorization to photocopy items for internal or personal use is granted by Brill provided that the appropriate fees are paid directly to The Copyright Clearance Center, 222 Rosewood Drive, Suite 910, Danvers, MA 01923, USA. Fees are subject to change.

Library of Congress Cataloging-in-Publication Data

Joint Meeting of the Society for Old Testament Study and the Oudtestamentisch Werkgezelschap in Nederland en België (11th : 2000 : Soesterberg, Netherlands)
    The elusive prophet : the prophet as a historical person, literary character, and anonymous artist / edited by Johannes C. de Moor.
        p. cm. – (Oudtestamentische studiën, ISSN 0169-7226 ; d. 45)
"Papers read at the eleventh joint meeting of the Society for Old Testament Study and het Oudtestamentisch Werkgezelshap in Nederland en België, held at Soesterberg 2000."
    Originally published: Leiden ; Boston : Brill, 2001.
    Includes index.
    ISBN-13: 978-1-58983-196-4 (paper binding : alk. paper)
    ISBN-10: 1-58983-196-9 (paper binding : alk. paper)
    1. Prophets–Congresses. 2. Bible. O.T. –Criticism, interpretation, etc. –Congresses. I. Moor, Johannes Cornelis de, 1935- II. Title. III. Series.

BS1198.J65 2000
224'.06–dc22
                                              2005029536

Printed in the United States of America
on acid-free paper

Contents

Introduction vii

A.A. ABELA, When the Agenda of an Artistic Composition Is
   Hidden: Jonah and Intertextual Dialogue with Isaiah 6,
   the 'Confessions of Jeremiah' and Other Texts 1

A.G. AULD, From King to Prophet in Samuel and Kings 31

P.C. BEENTJES, Prophets in the Book of Chronicles 45

U. BERGES, Personifications and Prophetic Voices of Zion
   in Isaiah and Beyond 54

C. BULTMANN, A Prophet in Desperation?
   The Confessions of Jeremiah 83

T.A. COLLINS, Threading as a Stylistic Feature of Amos 94

M. DIJKSTRA, 'I am neither a prophet nor a prophet's pupil':
   Amos 7:9-17 as the Presentation of a Prophet like Moses 105

T.L. FENTON, Israelite Prophecy: Characteristics of the First
   Protest Movement 129

A.G. HUNTER, Jonah from the Whale:
   Exodus Motifs in Jonah 2 142

W. JOHNSTONE, The Portrayal of Moses as Deuteronomic
   Archetypal Prophet in Exodus and its Revisal 159

H. LEENE, Blowing the Same Shofar: An Intertextual
   Comparison of Representations of the Prophetic Role in
   Jeremiah and Ezekiel 175

A. MEIN, Ezekiel as a Priest in Exile 199

L.J. DE REGT, Person Shift in Prophetic Texts: Its Function
   and its Rendering in Ancient and Modern Translations ... 214

K. SPRONK, Deborah, a Prophetess: The Meaning and
   Background of Judges 4:4-5 232

Abbreviations 244

Index of Authors 245

Index of Texts 250

Introduction

The essays here published were read during the Eleventh Joint Meeting of the 'Oudtestamentisch Werkgezelschap in Nederland and België' and the Society for Old Testament Study, held at Soesterberg, The Netherlands, from 27 to 30 August 2000. The theme of the conference was 'Person or Personage? The Prophet as a Historical Person and/or a Literary Character'. The meeting was hosted by Professor Henk Leene and Dr Lénart de Regt, respectively, President and Secretary of the 'Oudtestamentisch Werkgezelschap'.

Personifications are common to all literature. But the form in which they occur may differ. Sometimes entirely fictive characters are presented as historical persons, in other cases historical persons are almost completely hidden behind an opaque screen of fiction, in still other cases personifications are deliberately made recognisable as literary fiction. Since no human being is able to describe any other person realistically in an absolute sense, any literary character is to some extent a personification.

One of the best-known personifications in the Old Testament is Lady Zion/Jerusalem. In this volume Ulrich Berges traces her role from the beginning of the Book of Isaiah where she is still the militant defender of her children via the faithful female Ebed in Second Isaiah to the new Zion of Trito-Isaiah who accepts her prophetic mission as defender of the rights of the poor, and finally the grieving post-exilic Zion hoping for consolation not in this world, but in the world to come.

Here we have a personification with prophetic traits. But who were the prophets themselves? The (auto)biographic details about their lives and experiences as found in the Bible are hardly ever accepted as authentic anymore. The moving so-called Confessions of Jeremiah, for example, are often seen as later additions to the book bearing his name, made up only to make his role as a prophet of doom more or less acceptable. Christoph Bultmann, however, argues that we should not prematurely exclude the possibility that a prophet could also find relief from his anguish in composing 'precious words', poetry liberating him to some extent from the burden of his prophetic office.

Basing himself on Ugaritic parallels, Klaas Spronk proposes a new interpretation of Judges 4:4-5. Originally Deborah would have been a woman involved in necromancy, not unlike the woman in 1 Sam. 28. When this type of soothsaying became unacceptable, a later editor called her a 'prophetess', thus masking her real activities. Spronk concludes that Israelite prophecy only gradually broke free from the mantic practices common in the Ancient Near East.

Indeed, it has been claimed that the historical phenomenon of prophecy is not typically Israelite. Scholars have pointed out parallels in e.g. Egypt, Mari, Emar, Deir 'Allah and Assyria. Terry Fenton disagrees. In his opinion Israelite prophecy was unique in that it became a first protest movement which distanced itself deliberately from prophetic frenzy and gradually developed a sophisticated poetic literary genre of its own.

Several contributions concentrate on the artistic qualities of prophetic literature. Terry Collins explores the stylistic feature of 'threading' – a term from the Internet vocabulary denoting messages related to the same line of thought – in the seemingly inconsequential collection of oracles constituting the Book of Amos. Words and their semantic cognates appear to form webs of information spreading throughout the book.

Lénart de Regt demonstrates that sudden switches in person are attested in so many prophetic texts that they cannot be ascribed to errors or clumsy redactional activity. They must be seen as a rhetorical device intended to draw the audience's attention. As such they often occur at the beginning of paragraphs, especially in the Book of Hosea. Ancient as well as modern translations show a tendency to homogenise the alternating grammatical persons which is understandable, but should be curbed in order not to loose the rhetorical impact of the source text.

Obviously the destruction of the Solomonic temple and the ensuing exile necessitated a rethinking of the role of leadership in the pre-exilic period. Kings, priests, judges and officers were criticised severely, and the people for following their leaders blindly. Much of this criticism was inserted into already existing prophetic traditions. However, with regard to the prophets themselves the post-exilic theologians had the difficult task to distinguish between 'good' and 'bad' prophets. This task being so difficult that it could not be performed without risking grave errors, prophecy itself became increasingly controversial in the exilic and post-exilic periods.

This phenomenon is what William Johnstone studies in his article 'The Portrayal of Moses as Deuteronomic Archetypal Prophet in Exodus and its Revisal'. According to the D-version of Exodus, Moses becomes the uniquely privileged mediator of God's revelation, no other is needed. Other prophetic spokesmen may have succeeded him, but they were subordinated to this one great prophet. The P-layer in Exodus, however, tries to revise this picture by putting Aaron on a par with Moses and even making him the 'prophet' on whom Moses had to rely. Also Moses' prophetic role as an intercessor is clearly profiled in the D-version in Exodus, but again is corrected by P who is trying to minimise the importance of prophecy to the point of redundancy.

Further exploring the consequences of his theory about a Book of Two Houses as the source of the material shared by Samuel–Kings on the one hand and Chronicles on the other, Graeme Auld reads the narrative of the death of Eli as a prefiguration of the end of the houses of Saul and David. So the characters in this narrative are not what they seem to be, they also play roles. Samuel is depicted as the true 'servant of the LORD' who unites the traditions of king, priest and prophet.

Henk Leene scrutinises the roles attributed to prophets in the Books of Jeremiah and Ezekiel. Here too the struggle to distinguish between true and 'false' prophecy may be discerned. Jeremiah and Ezekiel 'blow the same shofar' in as far as both see the legitimate prophet as a watchman, but Leene is convinced that, contrary to prevailing opinion, priority has to be given to Ezekiel for whom the misleading prophet is the person who neglects his duty as a watchman. The 'biographic' details indicate that the true prophet in Ezekiel is probably a historical person, but is a literary personage in Jeremiah. This means that seemingly historical events like those described in Jer. 28 and 29 must be viewed as rather late theological reflections on history, not as biography.

Andrew Mein, however, is rather sceptical with regard to the possibility to recover the historical Ezekiel. Yet, the way in which the prophet is described in the Book of Ezekiel may give us some insight into the way the historical Jewish community in Babylonia looked upon the status of a priest in exile. Being far removed from the temple, he could not participate in sacrificial ritual or make atonement, but concern for ritual purity and the possibility to teach the Law are indications that he did not need to give up his priestly role entirely.

In Amos 7 a 'biographical' narrative interrupts the 'autobiographically' phrased visionary reports. Meindert Dijkstra argues in favour of an original unity of vv. 9-17 and the independent provenance of the story which may have belonged to a set of conspiracy stories in which the prophet who announced the downfall of Jehu's dynasty was involved. He regards the story as a late pre-exilic prophetic legend, influenced by the Deuteronomistic historians who made Amos a prophet not by profession but by virtue of his special calling, like Moses. The authenticity of the word against Jeroboam II (7:11) need not be questioned, but this is about the only element going back to the historical Amos.

The Book of Jonah can be read as a post-exilic reflection on prophecy, a phenomenon already fading from history by that time. There is a broad scholarly agreement that Jonah himself is a literary invention, even though 2 Kgs 14:25 may have suggested a historical person to many readers in the past. Intertextual links with other passages in the Old Testament indicate deliberate transformations intended to underline what a real prophet should be: a person moved by the pathos of God (so Anthony Abela). Starting from intertextual connections between the psalm in Jonah 2 and other parts of the Old Testament, Alastair Hunter argues that the poem is influenced by what might called epic motifs, the river ordeal and the Exodus escape through the sea.

Pancratius Beentjes draws attention to the remarkable circumstance that Chronicles omits almost all narratives describing prophets as historical persons in the Deuteronomistic History. On the other hand, the Chronicler 'invents' many new prophetic characters, 'literary personages'. Their speeches reveal the Chronicler's view on prophecy in general and are meant to revitalise the word of God for the post-exilic community.

Whereas modern methods of literary analysis have brought the artistic qualities of the Books of the Prophets increasingly into focus during the past century, various modes of deconstruction have made the historical prophets themselves an ever more elusive phenomenon. To a large extent this theme was inspired by the influential work of a great scholar who passed away too soon: Robert P. Carroll, whose sudden death came as a terrible shock for all of us during the preparations for the Joint Meeting 2000.

The Editor,

Johannes C. de Moor

Anthony Abela *Zejtun - Malta*

When the Agenda of an Artistic Composition Is Hidden

Jonah and Intertextual Dialogue with Isaiah 6, the 'Confessions of Jeremiah', and Other Texts

1 Introductory Remarks

There is one item on this conference general agenda that seems to have been adequately discussed by scholarship, and definitively closed: 'Person or Personage? The Prophet as a Historical Person and/or a Literary Character'. The issue as to whether the Book of Jonah is strictly biography and history dominated the scene in some academic quarters during the middle decades of the 20th century.[1] And yet circles claiming historicity for this narrative still voice their protest to the current overwhelming consensus. Jack M. Sasson's cautious advice would suffice to dry up any interest for this track: 'Scholars who insist that Jonah is recording history risk equating what is plausible with what really has happened in the past. This approach ignores the fact that plausibility and verisimilititude are also goals for imaginative writing, resulting in "historical fiction" (in which historical personalities are placed within nonhistorical contexts) or "fictional history" (in which fictitious happenings are set within a historical event)'.[2] Of course, the metaphorical or allegorical character of this 'parable-like story'[3] or 'short story'[4] would not preclude the situation or institution it addresses from being historical, however difficult or hypothetical its scientific reconstruction remains.

---

[1] Cf. P.L. Trible, *Studies in the Book of Jonah*, defended in 1963), 127-43; E.J. Bickermann, *Four Strange Books of the Bible: Jonah, Daniel, Koheleth, Esther*, New York 1967, 1-49; M. Burrows, 'The Literary Category of the Book of Jonah', in: H.T. Frank, W.L.Reed (eds), *Translating and Understanding the Old Testament: Essays in Honor of Herbert Gordon May*, Nashville 1970, 80-9; L. Alonso Schökel, J.L. Sicre Diaz, *Profetas: Commentario*, vol. 2, Madrid 1980, 1007-8; B. Vawter, *Job and Jonah: Questioning the Hidden God*, New York 1983, 96-102; J.M.Sasson, *Jonah*, (AncB, 24), New York 1990, 327-8.

[2] Sasson, *Jonah*, 327.

[3] B.S. Childs, *Introduction to the Old Testament as Scripture*, London 1979, 421-2.

[4] J.S. Ackermann, 'Jonah', in: R. Alter, F. Kermode (eds), *The Literary Guide to the Bible*, Cambridge, MA 1987, 234.

Working Hypothesis

The present author endorses Sasson's claim that 'there are many reasonable readings and interpretations' of the Book of Jonah as a whole.[5] This hermeneutical multiplicity ultimately rests upon the writer's strategy not to formulate the narrative's focus clearly[6] so that theodicy,[7] the universal nature of religious salvation,[8] prophecy,[9] and the troubled relationship of the prophet with his God,[10] have often been identified as the main or as important themes.[11] This paper proposes as a working hypothesis that Jonah is a prophetic writing involved in metalinguistic discourse on prophecy itself. And that with this discourse its anonymous author is involved in intertextual dialogue with other writings during the post-exilic period.

2 Some Methodological Considerations

a) An adequate hermeneutical exercise on the Book of Jonah has to account for every literary feature in this short but dense composition. Failure to consider even an apparently insignificant detail may lead to an unbalanced interpretation. As an illustration we shall mention Ernst R. Wendland's splendid discussion of 'five key aspects of style in Jonah' namely, repetition, variation, irony, structure, and enigma; and yet in this study Wendland fails to give due consideration to the dissonance between the 'psalm of thanksgiving' in Jonah and its current narrative framework. The result is that his overall analysis of the book tends to dilute its contents: 'The central issue concerns that age-old question: "Who is my neighbour?" in relation to the Kingdom of God (Jon. 4:10-11; compare Lk. 10:29). The answer to this crucial query is not given directly. Rather, it is strongly implied through the

---

[5] Sasson, *Jonah*, 326.

[6] Cf. S. Frolov, 'Returning the Ticket: God and his Prophet in the Book of Jonah', *JSOT* 86 (1999), 85.

[7] Cf. J. Blenkinsopp, *A History of Prophecy in Israel: From the Settlement in the Land to the Hellenistic Period*, Philadelphia 1983, 268-73; D.N. Freedman, 'Did God Play a Dirty Trick on Jonah at the End?', *BR* 6/4 (1990), 31.

[8] Alonso Schökel, Sicre Diaz, *Profetas*, 1011-3; E.M. Good, *Irony in the Old Testament* (BiLiSe, 3), Sheffield 1981, 39-55; P.R. House, *The Unity of the Twelve* (JSOT.S, 97), Sheffield 1990, 82-3; E.R. Wendland, 'Five Key Aspects of Style in Jonah and (Possibly) How to Translate Them', *BiTr* 48 (1997), 309.

[9] Cf. Blenkinsopp, *ibid.*; J.C. Holbert, ' "Deliverance belongs to the LORD!": Satire in the Book of Jonah', *JSOT* 21 (1981), 50-81, reproduced in P. Davies (ed.), *The Prophets: A Sheffield Reader* (BiSe, 42), Sheffield 1996, 334-54.

[10] Cf. Frolov, *ibid.*

[11] Cf. Bickermann, *ibid.*; J.D. Magonet, *Form and Meaning: Studies in the Literary Techniques in the Book of Jonah*, Bern 1976.

LORD's dealings with his prophet Jonah, which reach a climax in the divine word at the very end of the book(Jon. 4:10-11)'.[12] But is the universality of religious salvation the real 'central issue' of the book? It is certainly an important theme; but I do not think this theme can account for the entry of this 'pamphlet' within the group of prophetic writings that were probably going through the canonization process somewhere in the post-exilic period (*pace* House). Gerhard von Rad's strictures to the speculative nature of the 'universalistic' interpretation that sees the Book of Jonah somehow in contestation of the cultic reforms of Esdra and Nehemiah, which among other things led a strong campaign against mixed marriages, are still valid: 'We have no knowledge of any "universalistic" opposition to the "particularist" measures taken by Ezra and Nehemiah, and the book itself contains no evidence to support such theory'.[13]

b) Essential to any exhaustive interpretation of the Book of Jonah remains accounting for the embedding of the 'psalm of thanksgiving' within its current narrative context.[14] Traditionally, historical critical approaches resorted to the explanation of diverse authorship for the two parts, so that the relationship of the psalm to the narrative is seen to be redactional rather than organic.[15] Since George Landes famous 1967 essay,[16] though, scholarship refrains from reading the Book of Jonah *with* and *without* the prophet's psalm in the fish's belly as if the poem is secondary to the story which could thus be adequately understood without Jonah's prayer. The two need each other from the very beginning.[17] Unfortunately, the question as to whether the psalm is diachronically posterior to the rest of the composition cannot be definitively answered. Even if the convention of organically insetting poetry within narrative frameworks had wide acceptance in the Middle East (Watts), this would not exclude the possibility that an editor met an already established narrative and thought it germane to embed this psalm within the/his story because he found it fitting the situation of the main character in the story. All this leads

---

[12] Wendland, 'Five Key Aspects of Style', 309.

[13] G. von Rad, *The Message of the Prophets*, London 1962, 1975, 256.

[14] Cf. J.W. Watts, *Psalm and Story: Inset Hymns in Hebrew Narrative* (JSOT.S, 139), Sheffield 1992.

[15] Cf. Childs, *Introduction*, 417-26; Good, *Irony*, 39-55. For criticism of this explanation, cf. K.M. Craig, Jr., 'Jonah and the Reading Process', *JSOT* 62 (1994), 106-7.

[16] G. Landes, 'The Kerygma of the Book of Jonah: The Contextual Interpretation of the Jonah Psalm,' *Interp.* 21 (1967), 3-31.

[17] Cf. Holbert, 'Satire'; Craig, 'Reading Process'; Sasson, *Jonah*; Frolov, 'Returning the Ticket'.

to the conclusion that the investigation into the mutual relationship of psalm and narrative in the Book of Jonah is an obligatory path in the hermeneutical process.

c) There are six features of the literary dimension of the Book of Jonah which the exegete has to give an account of. One may call them 'aspects of style' or 'poetic features' and they may well be formulated as questions:

1. If, as acknowledged by tradition and scholarship, the Book of Jonah belongs to prophecy, how are we to explain that it has no superscription like most other prophetic books, and it employs none of the more important prophetic technical terms like נביא and חשה?

2. As the book is predominantly narrative and is presumably following literary conventions current in Israelite/Jewish tradition, what narrative techniques is the author employing to construct the human main character, יונה?

3. How are we to explain the dissonance between the narrative framework and the embedded psalm in Jon. 2? In other words, what is the narratological function of Jonah's prayer וַיִּתְפַּלֵּל (Jon. 2:2) in the big fish's belly within the overall structure of the composition?

4. What relationship passes between the Book of Jonah's 'Exposition' in 1:1-3 and what looks like being the climax of the Jonah narrative in 4:10-11?

5. Following the narrator's intimations for internal demarcation of the text (Wendland), and uncovering the structure that subsists beneath the narrative as a literary unity, can we identify the author/narrator's agenda for telling this story of Jonah?

6. What are we to make of the intertextual reality of this prophetic book, a reality that is widely recognized by commentators of varied backgrounds, and yet hardly ever globally explained?

We cannot hope in this essay to answer one and all six queries as formulated above. We shall limit ourselves to only considering three of these issues, which, it is hoped, will give a reasonable understanding of the Book of Jonah.

3 Answering Difficult Questions

3.1 I am no נָבִיא and no בֶּן־נָבִיא

While in a normal 'reading process' the reader is safely guided by the narrator to fill in informational gaps and to make sense of an evolving narrative he/she has chosen to follow,[18] the narrator in the Book of Jonah chooses to misdirect the reader on more than one count. 'The opening scene, Crouch warns us, shapes the expectations of the reader';[19] and the manner the narrator chooses to introduce the reader/listener into narrated reality 'programmes' him/her to expect a story about a well known personage called 'Jonah'. The narrator opens his narrative with a phrase that is 'inconfundiblemente profética' (Alonso Schökel, Sicre Diaz):

(1:1) וַיְהִי דְּבַר־יְהוָה אֶל־יוֹנָה בֶן־אֲמִתַּי לֵאמֹר

As early as 1934, O. Grether[20] has investigated the use of what constitutes the nucleus of the above clause, the phrase דְּבַר־יְהוָה, and concluded that it is nearly everywhere the technical terminology for the opening of prophetic messages, whether before or after the exilic period.[21] And yet in Jonah we meet none of the classical prophetic terms like נָבִיא, חֹזֶה, or אִישׁ הָאֱלֹהִים, even though this writing is currently being chronologically situated in the post-exilic period(s), when, according to Prof. A. Graeme Auld's chronology of lexical use in prophetical literature, the title נָבִיא, for instance, should have been popular.[22] Besides, the clause in Jon. 1:1 seems to have had the syntactical function within prophetic corpora of indicating that the addressee of the divine communication registered in the clause was not utterly unknown to the reader/listener.[23] So that, the reader, 'consciously,

---

[18] M. Sternberg, *The Poetics of Biblical Narrative: Ideological Literature and the Drama of Reading*, Bloomington 1987, 186-90.

[19] W.B. Crouch, 'To Question an End, to End a Question: Opening the Closure of the Book of Jonah', *JSOT* 62 (1994), 104.

[20] O. Grether, *Name und Wort Gottes im alten Testament* (BZAW, 64), Giessen 1934.

[21] Cf. Sasson, *Jonah*, 67.

[22] A.G. Auld, 'Prophets through the Looking Glass: Between Writings and the Moses,' *JSOT* (1983), 2-23, reproduced in Davies (ed.), *The Prophets*, 22-42. For this reference, cf. pp. 24-6. The writer of this paper believes that on the issue of prophetic terminology one should also consult both the debate which Prof. Auld's essay gave rise to and which is reproduced in the same volume edited by Prof. Davies, pp. 22-127, as well as D.L. Petersen, *The Roles of Israel's Prophets* (JSOT.S, 17), Sheffield 1981.

[23] Cf. Sasson, *Jonah*, 67.

laboriously, hesitantly engaged in gap-filling' as the narrative builds up, is furtively, through lexicography and syntax, fed the information that the hero of the narrative is a 'prophet'; that this hero is entrusted with a 'prophetic mission' (Jon. 1:2); and it is the reader who has to provide the labelling of 'prophetic' to both hero and mission since the narrator for some reason chooses not to provide this labelling. Besides, the narrator offers another clue to the reader: as soon as the Deity commissions the hero with going to Nineveh with the prophetic message, Jonah, the hero, seeks to escape (ברח) from the LORD's presence (מִלִּפְנֵי יְהוָה) (Jon. 1:3).

This means that already in what may be considered as the 'Exposition' of the Jonah narrative,[24] the narrator's strategy gives rise to a number of important questions: if the protagonist Jonah is being depicted as a prophet, why does he never receive the title נָבִיא or its equivalents? Some commentators suggested that this strategy of the narrator implies that the Book of Jonah is not dealing with prophecy.[25] This explanation, however, runs counter to at least two facts: a) A superficial examination of the literary texture would be enough to show that the narrative focuses on the prophet himself and his troubled relationship to יְהוָה אֱלֹהָיו (Jon. 2:2). b) The Book of Jonah, at some point in its history (surely before its translation into Greek (LXX) or at least to its textual reproduction(s) for the 'Qumran Library',[26] found itself inserted within an editorial collection of prophetic writings by time to be labelled 'the Book of the Twelve'.[27] Given its sharp divergence in literary genre from the other members

---

[24] For this narratological term cf. R. Alter, *The Art of Biblical Narrative*, New York 1981, 80-89; S. Bar-Efrat, *Narrative Art in the Bible* (JSOT.S, 70), Sheffield 1989, 111-21; J.L. Ska, *'Our Fathers Have Told Us': Introduction to the Analysis of Hebrew Narrative* (SubBi,13), Rome 1990, 21-5.

[25] Cf. H.W. Wolff, *Dodekapropheton, 3: Obadja und Jona*, Neukirchen-Vluyn 1977; T.E. Fretheim, 'Jonah and Theodicy', *ZAW* 90 (1978), 227-37.

[26] Cf. R. Fuller, 'The Form and Formation of the Book of the Twelve: The Evidence from the Judean Desert', in: J.W. Watts, P.R. House (eds), *Forming Prophetic Literature: Essays on Isaiah and the Twelve in Honor of John D.W. Watts* (JSOT.S, 235), Sheffield 1996, 86-101.

[27] There is a whole discussion on the editorial dynamics that went into the formation of this collection, cf. House, *The Unity of the Twelve*; J.D. Nogalski, *The Literary Precursors of the Book of the Twelve* (BZAW, 217), Berlin 1993; Idem, *Redactional Processes in the Book of the Twelve* (BZAW, 218), Berlin 1993; Idem, 'Intertextuality in the Twelve', in: Watts, House (eds), *Forming Prophetic Literature*, 102-24; B.A. Jones, *The Formation of the Book of the Twelve: A Study in Text and Canon* (SBL.DS, 149), Atlanta 1995; E. Ben Zvi, *A Historical-Critical Study of the Book of Obadia* (BZAW, 242), Berlin 1996; Idem, 'Twelve Prophetic Books or "The Twelve": A Few Preliminary Considerations', in: Watts, House, *Forming Prophetic Literature*, 125-57.

of the collection, one has to explain its insertion into this 'anthology of prophetic writings' by its thematic relevance to the collection as whole. Admittedly, this statement may implicate all 'themes' and 'sub-themes' in Jonah. But this clamorous absence of the 'expected terminology' may be hinting to the narrator's strategy of dealing with the subject-matter of his composition in an indirect manner, through narrative rather then through expository literature which the normal prophetic genres constitute. One may consider this absence of the label נָבִיא for the protagonist as one of the narrator's 'techniques of indirection'[28] through which positive statements are made by the narrator as he/she highlights the absence of an expected constituent of the phrase. The same happens when Amos underlines his prophetic call by denying that he was a prophet or a son of a prophet (Amos 7:14).[29]

4 Strategies for Building the Persona 'Jonah'

The narrator[30] employs the main character 'Jonah' to express his point of view; characterization techniques used in this narrative, therefore, are essential to study for whosoever wishes to penetrate into the message of the Book of Jonah.[31] Scholarship has been divided as to

---

[28] Cf. Holbert, 'Satire', 338 for this terminology.

[29] Could this statement in Amos 7:14 have influenced the adoption of this narrative strategy in Jon. 1:1? Both texts have appeared in the Book of the Twelve Prophets, with Jonah constantly following Amos though their position within the list was never contiguous (see Fuller, 'Form and Formation'). We do not know much about the dynamics of the editorial process that dictated the order of each prophetic writing within this collection (cf. Ben Zvi, 'Twelve Prophetic Books'). May be the chronological principle shaped the traditional order(s); but the 'contents principle' could also have been influential (cf. House, *Unity*). As we lack definitive proof to sustain such line of argumentation we can never be sure; but this also means that we may not exclude the possibility that Amos which always preceded Jonah within the Book of the Twelve could have influenced Jonah. Of course, this would imply that Jonah could have been composed in the later stages of the editorial process that gave us this collection.

[30] For this narratological figure in biblical narratives cf. S. Chatman, *Story and Discourse: Narrative Structure in Fiction and Film*, London 1978, 147-51; P. Pugliatti, *Lo sguardo nel racconto: Teorie e prassi del punto di vista*, Bologna 1985, 26-32; Ska, *'Our Fathers Have Told Us'*, 43-54.

[31] For characterization techniques in biblical narratives cf. among others Alter, *Art*, 114-130; A. Berlin, *Poetics and Interpretation of Biblical Narrative* (BiLeSe, 9), Sheffield 1983, 23-42; Sternberg, *Poetics*, 321-366; Bar-Efrat, *Narrative Art*, 93-140; Ska, *'Our Fathers Have Told Us'*, 83-94; B. Green, 'The Determination of Pharaoh: His Characterization in the Joseph Story (Genesis 37-50)', in: P.R. Davies, D.J.A. Clines (eds), *The World of Genesis: Persons, Places, Perspectives*, Sheffield 1998, 150-71.

how the narrator is looking at his hero; some would say that the narrator is caricaturing Jonah (Good, Holbert); others that he deals with him sympathetically (Frolov).³² But of course before the reader jumps to conclusions as to how the narrator perceives his protagonist, he/she needs to go through the entire reading process, linking the various elements for reading provided by the narrator, patiently constructing networks, and modifying his/her understanding 'in the light of the later stages of the reading' (Sternberg).

This exegetical rule of reading a biblical story in its entirety and of balancing the narrative function of one piece of information with that of another, does not seem to have been respected by at least two recent studies of the Book of Jonah: that of John C. Holbert first printed in 1981³³ and the other of Serge Frolov printed in 1999.³⁴ We shall have a closer look at these two attempts at understanding the Book of Jonah, each taking a different point of departure.

a) Holbert considers the Book of Jonah as an attack on 'Hebrew prophetic hypocrisy'; he admits though that no historical group can be identified as the sure object of this attack. 'Do not all religions bring forth "hypocritical prophets" who claim great substance and unique callings but who ultimately are found empty of substance, save their real anger at those who do not agree with them?' (p. 354). This interpretative slant required that the Book of Jonah be read above all as a satire aimed at the prophet himself, Jonah who embodies the figure of the hypocritical prophet (p. 348). Holbert dedicates the first few pages of his essay to discuss what satire is, and how it functions (pp. 334-9). He then applies these insights to Jonah 1-2 where 'the grotesque, so characteristic of satire' appears 'in profusion' (p. 342). 'The attack on Jonah is indeed indirect in that we see him for what he is with the help of his interaction with characters with whom we find great sympathy' (p. 348). Actually, this 'Tendenz of the text' (p. 342) has been programmed in the book's introduction, or rather in the protagonist's own name יוֹנָה בֶן־אֲמִתַּי (Jon. 1:1). 'He is "Dove, the son of faithfulness or fidelity." By choosing this name, the author establishes the expectation in the mind of the reader that God has got the right man for the job. Like the dove of Noah (Gen 8:8-12), this

---

³²Cf. D. Payne, 'Jonah from the Perspective of its Audience', *JSOT* 13 (1979), 3-12 reproduced in P. Gordon (ed.), *The Place Is Too Small for Us: The Israelite Prophets in Recent Scholarship*, Winona Lake, Indiana 1995, 263-74, here p. 266.

³³J.C. Holbert, ' "Deliverance belongs to the LORD!" Satire in the Book of Jonah', *JSOT* 21 (1981), 50-81.

³⁴S. Frolov, 'Returning the Ticket: God and his Prophet in the Book of Jonah', *JSOT* 86 (1999), 85-105.

dove will perform his duty. And because he is the "son of faithfulness," we can expect nothing but obedience to the call of God' (p. 341). In the second half of his essay, Holbert tries to show how satire, which 'is the hallmark of the narrative art of the book,' is extended into 'the controversial psalm of ch 2' (p. 348).

Three remarks may be made concerning this contribution:

1) While a satirical reading of the prophet Jonah cannot be excluded,[35] one of the essential characteristics of satire listed by Holbert has not been fulfilled by the author of the Book of Jonah: 'Satire has a definite target which must be familiar enough to make the assault meaningful and memorable'.[36] Pseudoprophecy or what was perceived as pseudoprophecy was a constant theme in prophetic literature (cf. Jer. 23); however, the object of criticism in the prophetic harangues against false prophets would normally be the validity of their message, דָּבָר (cf. Jer. 18:18 for this designation of prophetic messages) rather than the behaviour of the pseudoprophets themselves. On the other hand, according to Holbert's reconstruction, satire in the Book of Jonah was directed towards the hypocrisy of presumably authentic prophets who chose to attack people that disagreed with them. Is this exegete reading too much into the text of the book?

2) Holbert limits his analysis to the first two chapters of the Book of Jonah. But Chapter 3 which narrates the ministry of Jonah at Nineveh, and Chapter 4 which tells of the final dialogue scene between יְהוָה and יוֹנָה, cannot be left out if we want to understand the message of the book.[37] Unless satire proves to be the best reading also of these two parts of the story, it cannot be taken to be the best interpretative key of the Book of Jonah as a whole but simply as a possible feature of parts of the same.

3) A technical objection may be raised to the satiric interpretation. This reading makes much of the presumed contrast between the programme set by the name chosen for the protagonist in the story's Exposition (1:1-3) and his subsequent behaviour which ill-fits that of a faithful servant of the LORD. This name was programmed to create in the readers/listeners the expectation of an obedient hero who would carry the LORD's message to the intended addressees. Instead, Jonah, 'son of faithfulness' immediately shatters these expectations by fleeing westward, 'away from the presence of the LORD'. One should

---

[35] Good, *Irony*, 39-55; Ackerman, 'Jonah'. For a contrary view cf. Frolov, 'Returning the ticket'; U. Simon, *Jonah*, (trans. Lenn Schramm), Philadelphia 1999.
[36] Holbert, 'Satire,' 339.
[37] Cf. Crouch, 'To Question an End'.

note though that Jonah's escape to Tarshish does not form part of the complication of the plot[38] and does not come within the 'body' of the story, but it is part and parcel of the Exposition. This can be deduced from the use of syntactical inversion in verse 4. The theme of the Book of Jonah therefore, is not 'What happens when the LORD gives an order to a prophet to bring a message to a place and he/she, who is supposed to be obedient, escapes from the presence of the LORD?' but another one. But this means that the satirical reading of the protagonist's behaviour cannot be considered as the primary item on the narrator's agenda.

b) Serge Frolov is quite sceptical about the prevalent scholarly consensus that sees the human main character of the Book of Jonah as a 'predominantly negative figure' (p. 87). 'Such impressive unanimity of writers[39] with quite different backgrounds, agendas and hermeneutic preferences is suspicious enough per se: if divergent premises and methodologies produce strikingly convergent results, it may be due to replacement of sound reasoning by uncritically assimilated stereotypes. One should also remember that undisputable villains hardly ever play pivotal roles in biblical narratives; the "strange" book of Jonah may be unique in this repsect as well, but it is not enough just to postulate this without checking other possibilities and comparing different hypotheses' (p. 87). In his stimulating essay, Frolov suggests 'an alternative approach to Jonah both as person and as a book' (*ibid.*). He focuses on the 'suicidal motif' very much visible in chapters 1 and 4 of the book, and concludes that the prophet's death desire as such was not aimed at sabotaging the Nineveh mission. 'Rather, he (Jonah) foresaw that for him the successful implementation of this plan would be a personal disaster, that it was going to damage his life beyond repair, making it less attractive than death .... In other words, he was trying to defend his own future, not an abstract theological doctrine' (p. 90). The 'main conflict' in the Book of Jonah is neither the mission to Nineveh nor prophecy as such; rather this main conflict concerns Jonah's relationship to God. 'Jonah's interaction with God who is shown not only the ultimate source of this prophecy, but also as the playwright and the director of Jonah's tragedy as a whole' (p. 92). And יְהוָה is presented in the Book of Jonah as ruthless in his use of his

---

[38] The 'complication' of the story takes place when the LORD sees the signs of repentance of the Ninevites and appears to Jonah to change his plans concerning his threat to destroy 'the great city', a threat that is contained in his original message to Jonah (1:2). This change of heart on the part of the LORD is not in Jonah's plans, and complicates his life (4:2).

[39] He lists a number of authors spanning from 1926 to 1995.

prophet whom he sent to an 'unbearable mission' and shows himself totally indifferent to the prophet's own personal agenda. 'He treats Jonah as an impersonal device, a useful but expendable flesh-and-blood robot; when this robot refuses to obey, troubleshooting measures are taken, but not of a verbal nature ... Jonah's "word" of refusal to which he alludes in 4:2 ... falls on deaf ears, so that in the final dialogue with God Jonah has to reproduce it' (pp. 92-3). The LORD becomes ever harsher with Jonah as the plot develops: 'YHWH is a source of terror, not of care' for the prophet (p. 93). Jonah is denied even the 'privilege of charitable death (probably his only hope to preserve his dignity)', and the fleeing Jonah becomes Yahweh's prisoner in the big fish's belly.[40] In the context of this strained relationship between Jonah and 'his God', the 'psalm of thanksgiving and praise' (p. 94) becomes at one time Jonah's act of surrender but also an act of defiance; the canticle may well be read as almost blasphemous. As instances of Frolov's reading of this psalm we may tarry on what he says on v. 10. This promise of Jonah sounds 'vague and ambiguous': 'As far as Jonah's quarrel with God was not about temple sacrifices and the former had never made any vows, this extraordinary promise-without-promise could be understood only as a suspicious attempt to avoid addressing the heart of the matter and expressing genuine submissiveness' (p. 95). 'Driven by the deity's renewed command, Jonah reaches Nineveh and destroys his own life, pronouncing the prophecy he knows to be false (3:1-3)' (p. 95). In the remaining part of his study Frolov examines 'the theological significance of the prophet's fate' (pp. 95-105).

Frolov's interpretation gives great importance to two factors: 1) A 'literal' interpretation of Jonah's mission to Nineveh (Jon. 1:2) seen in the light of the Deuteronomic principle for authentic prophecy: Deut. 18:21-22; 2) The semantics of Jonah's name (יוֹנָה = turtle-dove).

יְהוָה and Jonah both knew from the start that on the first signs of repentance from the addressees of the prophetic message, a message of doom, the LORD could 'repent' and would not fulfil the threat of destruction contained in the message. This would necessarily mean that the prophet would make a poor show, would appear as a lunatic. In other words, Frolov's Jonah understood the LORD's commission in Jon. 1:2 as 'an unconditional prophecy of doom' which contemplated no conversion on the part of the addressees and no consequent change of heart on the part of יְהוָה versus the Ninevites. This would throw light on Jonah's strange behaviour, who, on accomplishing his preach-

---

[40] Cf. also A. Berlin, 'A Rejoinder to John A. Miles, Jr., With Some Observation on the Nature of Prophecy', *JQR* 66 (1976), 228.

ing mission, and after his protest to the LORD (Jon. 3:10–4:4), went out of the city to have a better view of what was going to happen to Nineveh (Jon. 4:5). But the LORD, according to Frolov, planned to sacrifice the good name of his prophet from the beginning and it is this that Jonah suspected, and hence his attempt to escape (Jon. 1:3). For Frolov, therefore, the message Jonah was sent to take to Nineveh was deceptive, for the unconditionally sounding message was in fact conditional, so that the ruin of Jonah's professional life as a prophet was guaranteed or rather was part of the plan: 'From this time on, no one is likely to be "frightened" by his word, and a prophet without a scared audience is just a pitiable lunatic. Jonah has nothing to live for. God's life-bestowing grace towards Nineveh is a murderous disgrace for him' (pp. 91-2). 'Jonah's disgrace is shown in the book' as 'the *conditio sine qua non* of Nineveh's salvation' (p. 96). And this is what the semantics of the prophet's name confirms: 'For the ancient Israelites יוֹנָה was first and foremost a sacrificial species' (p. 97). This means that for the author of the Book of Jonah and his/her intended readers 'the meaning encoded in Jonah's name was not "a fickle, capricious and timid winged creature that moans and laments when in distress" (as suggested by many scholars), but a 'suitable animal for atonement' (p.97). Frolov is convinced 'that it is possible to read the book of Jonah as a story of the sacrifice of its main protagonist. Accordingly, Jonah's behaviour may also be seen in a new light. Picked as guilt offering and dealt with as such, he is ready to do everything, even to die, in order to defend his dignity and to prove that he is not to be treated as a sacrificial turtle-dove' (p. 97). And Jonah's arguments that he did not merit to be sacrificed on behalf of Nineveh are cogent enough (p. 98).

So, what is the message behind such a story? Frolov suggests that the author of the Book of Jonah could be reacting to the official theology in the post-exilic period, which saw the suffering of Israel as a vicarious sacrifice on behalf of the Gentile world (pp. 101-4). 'The author of Jonah may be tentatively characterized as a post-exilic dissident who sought to counter the official ideology by showing that Israel's misery should not be understood as atonement for sins of other peoples, for salvation of the wicked at the expence of the righteous is nonsensical' (p. 104). Frolov does not say whether an alternative has been offered in the Book of Jonah for this post-exilic official theology.

It is not easy to adequately critique this well written and cogently argued interpretation of the Book of Jonah. But perhaps a few remarks may be made:

1) It would seem that Frolov has let his Holocaust theology shape his reading of Jonah's prophecy. For instance, one may grant that Frolov's semantics of Jonah's name cannot be excluded; but may one say that this item of Jonah as a sacrificial victim was on the author's agenda since this theme fails to surface on the literary dynamics of the book? Again, Frolov's interpretation of יְהוָה's commissioning of Jonah as a prophet betray the influence of the Holocaust Theology which posits the participation of an 'oppressor'; Frolov thinks he found this 'oppressor' in an 'absurd deity' who is prepared to sacrifice his faithful servant to achieve the salvation of the wicked Nineveh. And Jonah the prophet escapes in order to safeguard 'his dignity as a human being.' In this perspective, the theme of prophecy becomes secondary, a function, in the service of the wider theme of Jonah's relationship with his deity.

2) One wonders whether Frolov's interpretation of the LORD's commissioning of Jonah in 1:2 with an unconditional message of doom is tenable. Conversion of the addressees of prophetic messages was generally the first item on the agenda. And Jonah knew this (Jon. 4:2). Only he would object to this item for some reason he does not specify. This would defend the Deity against the accusation of having sent Jonah with a 'deceptive message'. The traditions articulated in Deut. 18:21-22 could have been on the mind of our author's Jonah, and may have been the source of his misgivings when the LORD sent him with the message. As a matter of fact, Jonah was proved wrong: his addressees did not take him for 'just a pitiable lunatic'. Rather his message of doom was accepted very seriously and the Ninevites' conversion was indeed sincere and radical. What Jonah was not prepared to accept was the full agenda of prophetic mission.

Having discussed two contributions that pay attention to the building of Jonah's character, we return to the original question of the paragraph: what strategies does the narrator employ to construct the protagonist of this prophetic writing? On a superficial level, one may accede to the majority's satirical reading that posits that Jonah is being contrasted to the secondary characters featuring in the story like the sailors in Scene One (Jon. 1:4-16) and the Ninevites in Scene Three (Jon. 3:1–4:4).[41] Both groups of characters though are more like 'functionaries'[42] or 'agents',[43] that is, *personae* created to serve the plot. May be, they were meant to embody certain qualities which

---

[41] Cf. Good, *Irony*; Ackerman, 'Jonah'; and Holbert, 'Satire'.
[42] Cf. Ska, *'Our Fathers Have Told Us'*, 87.
[43] Cf. Berlin, *Poetics*, 23.

Jonah as the LORD's prophet should have shown to possess: a proper appreciation of Jonah's behaviour in fleeing from the presence of the LORD (Jon. 1:10); or a quick and radical obedience to the LORD's word as brought by the LORD's intermediary; or faith in God's gracious kindness (Jon. 3:9). But I wonder whether the narrator meant to compare Jonah to the sailors or the Ninevites in order to poke fun at him or to paint him negatively. These secondary characters remain nameless participants in the action, and hardly take part in the main action which is the debate between Jonah and 'his God'. One may not compare the frantic behaviour of the sailors as they attempt to negotiate with their gods for their safety with Jonah's passive reaction to what was going on around him; the narrator is not comparing their efforts to Jonah's 'irresponsible' falling asleep with no good prayer to 'his God' for the safety of his ship mates. His 'falling asleep' (וַיֵּרָדַם, Jon. 1:5) is theologically marked in tradition in that it was supposedly induced by the LORD himself (cf. Gen. 2:21; 15:12). Jonah's slumber is being seen by the narrator as an action of God that came in response to the prophet's escaping from the LORD's presence. 'In stories about prophets, however, "deep sleep" is said to overtake a prophet only *after* signs and wonders of God's presence become manifest (Ps. 76:7; Dan. 10:9)'.[44] If one wishes to look at this sleeping from the point of view of the prophet's psychology, one may see Jonah's falling asleep as an act of surrender before the violent reaction of יהוה.[45] If a contrast exists in the Book of Jonah, this is between Jonah and his God, the way they seem to be looking at the subject matter of the debate, the mission to Nineveh, and ultimately prophecy itself.

Another means of characterisation used in the Book of Jonah is direct speech by the main character himself, that is, all the occasions in which Jonah speaks about himself (Jon. 1:9, 12), his beliefs (Jon. 1:9), his own point of view (Jon. 4:2-3) concerning the event being narrated, and his anxieties (Jon. 4:3, 9). In this context the most important outpouring of Jonah's spirit is his 'prayer' (וַיִּתְפַּלֵּל) in Jon 2. The methodological question one has to ask concerns the way this psalm fits the general theme enunciated in the Exposition (1:1-3). Is the psalm 'narrating' Jonah's downward thrust as he fathoms the ocean in his living submarine? Or is the psalm metaphorically describing another experience which the main character considers as being one of 'submersion' and 'salvation', both movements being piloted by the LORD? If prophecy is the theme of the Book of Jonah, is it being depicted as such kind of experience? Why is prophecy perceived

---

[44] Sasson, *Jonah*, 102.
[45] Sasson, *ibid*.

as being an experience of 'death and resurrection'? Probably, these questions cannot be answered unless we examine the Book of Jonah in its intertextual relationships.

But before passing on to the issue of intertextuality, we should first consider another technique employed by the narrator for building the character of Jonah. Relatively often, the narrator himself gives information about the prophet by directly passing remarks about his reactions and, in a few instances, through secondary characters, or through direct speech of the Deity. A few instances. By using the enveloping technique in Jon. 1:3 (cf. Wendland) to frame Jonah's attempted escape from going to Nineveh, the narrator aptly gives an insight into the prophet's motivation: לִבְרֹחַ ... מִלִּפְנֵי יְהוָה. We are told that Jonah seeks to escape from the presence of the LORD; that's why he goes westwards rather than eastwards. However, we are not informed yet why Jonah has chosen to escape from the presence of the LORD. But could Jonah escape the LORD's presence? From tradition, Jonah, as well as the narrator and reader, knew that this was an impossible enterprise (Ps. 139:7-10).[46] What kind of man, therefore, is this Jonah who embarks on a 'mission impossible'? Through the sailors and their captain, we discover not merely that Jonah cannot pray (Jon. 1:6), but that his attempt at fleeing from his God is perceived as a serious offence: מַה־זֹּאת עָשִׂיתָ (Jon. 1:10). An offence that merit the death penalty (Jon. 1:14). Jonah himself recognizes this and asks to be thrown overboard. Only when the LORD provides for his safety in an unexpected manner can Jonah bring himself to pray (וַיִּתְפַּלֵּל) (Jon. 2:2).

The narrator himself intervenes once again at Jon. 4:1 in order to report Jonah's reaction to the LORD's change of heart towards the Ninevites as they took the prophet's call for repentance seriously (Jon. 3:10): וַיֵּרַע אֶל־יוֹנָה רָעָה גְדוֹלָה וַיִּחַר לוֹ. There and then Jonah prays once more, giving his explanation for fleeing towards Tarshish (Jon. 4:2-3). The LORD answers with a rhetorical question concerning the thanatic urges Jonah gives vent to (Jon. 4:4); Jonah opts not to answer this question. The concluding scene (Jon. 4:5-11) takes us outside the city of Nineveh. Jonah constructs a refuge to protect himself from the heat of the sun as he waits to see what will happen to the city: no doubts he expected disaster. The LORD takes some initiatives aimed at making Jonah talk and reflect. The narrator gets us into the main character's psychology as he tells us of Jonah's overjoy at the creation of the קִיקָיוֹן (Jon. 4:6) but also of his utter distress when through the LORD's

---

[46] Cf. Magonet, *Form and Meaning*, 82-4; Sasson, *Jonah*, 76-8.

own agency this plant dies immediately (Jon. 4:7). Once Jonah starts feeling the effects of the plant's sudden death, the prophet starts lamenting, and his thanatic desires return with vehemence (Jon. 4:9). יְהוָה's concluding remarks (Jon. 4:10-11) open Jonah's, as well as the reader's eyes to the prophet's shallow spirituality and humanity, and brings the underlying discussion to its climactic point. What is Jonah throughout the story reacting to? What is he refusing? What has he failed to understand? The discussion of the text's intertextuality will provide us with the clues for answering such questions.

4.1 The Book of Jonah and its Intertextual Links

A methodological clarification is here in order. What does the present writer mean by 'intertextuality'? Generally speaking there seem to be two kinds of intertextual approaches to a text: 'reader-oriented' and 'authorial intention oriented'. As an example of the former approach one may cite Fokkelien van Dijk-Hemmes' analysis of the Song of Songs and Hosea 2.[47] In her essay, Van Dijk-Hemmes investigates how the author of Hosea 2 employs motifs in the Song of Songs in order to convey his/her own message, and 'why Hosea's call for justice is "packaged" in a specific sexual metaphorical language' (p. 278). She claims that her analysis is based on 'a gender-specific narratological and intertextual approach to the texts' (p. 279). By 'intertextuality' Van Dijk-Hemmes means 'studying of concrete relationships between texts as the reader perceives them. These relationships can be described as transformations, which can be classified as "repetition", "addition", "deletion" and "substitution" (p. 281). It is not this kind of intertextuality that we mean to study in this paper. Instead, we shall adopt James D. Nogalski's definition of what we are terming 'authorial intention oriented' intertextuality. 'Here, "intertextuality" means the interrelationship between two or more texts which evidence suggest (1) was deliberately established by ancient authors/editors or (2) was presupposed by those authors/editors'.[48] In intertextual analyses 'safeguards should be established to avoid ideosyncratic recreations which do not exhibit some reasonable likelihood of having actually occurred'.[49] Nogalski's agenda was to probe into intertextu-

---

[47] F. van Dijk-Hemmes, 'The Imagination of Power and the Power of Imagination: An Intertextual Analysis of Two Biblical Love Songs: The Song of Songs and Hosea 2', *JSOT* 44 (1989), 75-88, reproduced in Davies (ed.), *The Prophets*, 278-91.

[48] J.D. Nogalski, 'Intertextuality in the Twelve', in: Watts, House (eds), *Forming Prophetic Literature*, 102.

[49] Nogalski, 'Intertextuality', 103.

ality within the 'Book of the Twelve' in order to establish whether it was a positive element in the compositional process behind this collection of prophetical writings. For the purpose of this paper we are interested only in Nogalski's theoretical discussion of some types of intertextual relationships: quotations, allusions, catchwords, motifs, and framing devices. Of course, we shall refrain from investigating whether all these types of intertextual relationships between the Book of Jonah and other writings exist. In this section of the essay we shall a) try to establish the reality of intertextuality in this prophetic writing; b) speculate about its significance; and c) investigate whether intertextuality will not help us understand better this literary composition. These three aims will not be reached separately in different paragraphs but altogether as we discuss three different kinds of intertextual links of the Book of Jonah with tradition.

4.1.1 Citations and Allusions

a) The hermeneutical tradition has found no difficulty linking the manner the author of the Book of Jonah identifies the hero of his story to the personage hurriedly referred to in 2 Kgs 14:25. The main character in the Book of Jonah is identified as יוֹנָה בֶן־ אֲמִתַּי while the barely visible prophetic figure in what has been called the 'Deuteronomistic History'[50] or the 'Primary History'[51] is identified as יוֹנָה בֶן־ אֲמִתַּי הַנָּבִיא אֲשֶׁר מִגַּת הַחֵפֶר (2 Kgs 14:25). The texts raises a number of important issues:

1. Are the texts in any redactional relationship? That is, can we say that one of the two texts assumes the existence of the other, and that the author of the more recent of the two employed the chronologically older text as his/her source? There is of course the possibility that neither text was employed as source for the other: both drew instead from a common document or tradition. But while this possibility has to be recognized, the hypothesis that Jon. 1:1 and 2 Kgs 14:25 are related redactionally has for the present writer greater plausibility. One should notice that both form part of 'the Prophets' though they are found in different subsections of this group of canonical texts.[52] Naturally, we are still faced with the issue of the two texts' relative chronology. There are at least two arguments that would favour the

---

[50] M. Noth, *Überlieferungsgeschichtliche Studien*, Tübingen 1943, repr. 1957.

[51] A. Abela, 'Shifting Paradigms in Theorizing about the Composition of the Pentateuch', in: *Bibele: Raksti Teksts Kulturvide*, Riga 1999, 30-53.

[52] Cf. R. Beckwith, *The Old Testament Canon of the New Testament Church*, London 1985, 138-66, for a theoretical reconstruction of הנביאים.

hypothesis that Jonah followed 2 Kings in time and that the former employed the latter as its source. Regarding personal details on the Jonah figure in the two texts, 2 Kings is much richer; and it is more logical to deduce that the author of Jonah selected the details from his source that suited his personage rather than that the author of 2 Kings expanded the material in his source if this source were the Book of Jonah. So one may hypothetically say that there exists an intertextual relationship between Jon. 1:1 and 2 Kgs 14:25 in that the author of the opening verse in Jonah knew of and presumably used the half verse in 2 Kgs 14:25.

2. What type of intertextuality do we find between the two texts? The author of the Book of Jonah is *quoting* 2 Kgs 14:25. 'The use of a pre-existing *phrase, sentence,* or *paragraph* which is taken from another source constitutes a quotation' (italics his).[53] 'An author may "quote" another text inexactly. An author may work from memory and simply record a slightly different version of the text, or an author may also deliberately alter the quotation to fit the context or to make a different point. One should attempt to make a decision regarding these alternatives since the presupposition of an intentional change or an oversight can directly impact how one interprets the function of the quotation'.[54]

Jonah differs from 2 Kgs 14:25 on several scores: a) While in both texts we are dealing with prophecy, the act of communicating the message by the deity is differently expressed. In 2 Kings the message 'is spoken' (דִּבֶּר) through (בְּיַד) 'his servant' the prophet. In the Book of Jonah the message is communicated only to (אֶל) Jonah while the final recipients are indicated in the message itself. b) The deity in 2 Kings is identified as יְהוָה אֱלֹהֵי יִשְׂרָאֵל; in Jon. 1:1 the source of the message received by Jonah is יְהוָה who as the story evolves becomes Jonah's אֱלֹהִים (Jon. 2:2). c) The first addressee of the LORD's message in the Book of Kings, later to become his messenger, is given the title of the LORD's עֶבֶד to which is put in apposition the entire phrase יוֹנָה בֶן־אֲמִתַּי הַנָּבִיא אֲשֶׁר מִגַּת הַחֵפֶר. Of this descriptive phrase only the nucleus appears in Jonah: יוֹנָה בֶן־אֲמִתַּי.

3. Given our premises in sub-paragraph 1, one may hardly be allowed to view these dissimilarities as unintentional. They may

---

[53] Nogalski, 'Intertextuality,' 103.
[54] Nogalski, 'Intertextuality,' 104.

be regarded rather as 'transformations'. Remarkably missing from the Book of Jonah are the two semantic units עֶבֶד and נָבִיא as well as any reference to Israel not only from the Exposition of the story (Jon. 1:1-3) but also from the story itself (though see Jon. 1:9). Why is the author of Jonah α) clearly avoiding any reference to Israel; β) dropping two important terms linked to the deuteronomistic view of prophecy? One may speculatively answer query α) by saying that, given his project, the narrator tries to diminish the strength of a clearly historical implausibility: that of the 'God of Israel' sending 'his prophet' on a preaching mission to Nineveh; or perhaps he operates with the presupposition that the prophet's point of departure was Jerusalem from where he could have 'gone down' (וַיֵּרֶד) to Joppa. The answer for β) lies in the narrator's design or strategy. That means that the narrator has chosen to leave out the two qualifications because this was required by the nature of his story.

From the Exposition (Jon. 1:1-3) one may already articulate the theme discussed in this prophetic writing as follows: can one escape from a prophetic commissioning from יְהוָה? What happens when one tries to escape from such a commissioning? How will יְהוָה react? What does a prophetic commissioning involve? The nature of this theme dictated the amount of marking the narrator could offer his protagonist. Instead of marking him as עֶבֶד or נָבִיא which would have allowed no room for compromises over blind obedience to the LORD (for how could a 'prophet' or a 'servant of the LORD' attempt to escape the LORD's presence?), the narrator preferred an opaque outlining of his hero who for some unknown reasons could afford to disobey the LORD and attempt to flee away from his presence. In this manner the narrator could build his story as he/she did, in which he discusses actually what being a prophet means. How is the prophet supposed to react when יְהוָה confronts him with a mission that appears paradoxical, even absurd? His citation from 2 Kgs 14:25 provided the author of the Book of Jonah with the possibility of contextualizing the story in the 8th century BCE when Nineveh was yet not heaps of ruin but a terrifying enemy, a menace to territorial and political intergrity of the Northern Kingdom.[55] Biographical details are few in both 2 Kgs 14:25 and Jon. 1:1 with the latter being even more selective. From the spate of details offered in his source, the author of the Book of Jonah

---

[55] Cf. M. Noth, *The History of Israel*, London ²1960, 253-69; J.A. Soggin, *A History of Israel: From the Beginnings to the Bar Kochba Revolt, AD 135*, London 1984, 189-230.

selects only the name and the patronym. And the way he uses this information opens the door for allegorical interpretations.[56] This author only hints that his hero is to be regarded as a prophet; this strategy allowed him to weave a story about the relationship of a prophet with 'his God' יְהוָה. As the story evolves, the prophet attempting his escape soon realizes that becoming a fugitive from the 'presence of the LORD' is an impossibility. Just like the psalmist in Psalm 139. The prophet has to carry out his mission even if it appears absurd. And especially if the LORD has to renew the commission (שֵׁנִית, Jon. 3:1). Why is the LORD's demand perceived by the prophet as being absurd? And why does יְהוָה persists in his demand notwithstanding the protests of his emissary? What was the personal cost to be paid by the prophet of the LORD's sending Jonah on what is being seen as absurd? This seems to be the subject-matter of the Book of Jonah.

b) The author of the Book of Jonah could perhaps claim originality in creating this intriguing story that takes the cue, it seems, from 2 Kgs 14:25. But would he/she be justified if he/she were to make the same claim for the psalm in Jon. 2:3-10? We have postulated organic unity for the psalm to its narrative framework;[57] but this would not exclude that the author is purposely echoing 'tradition'. Jonah's song from inside the belly of the great fish 'takes the form of a typical (individual) "psalm of thanksgiving". It features an elaborate recycling of three basic structure-functional elements that are characteristic of this particular lyric genre – namely: a description of the *crisis* (in conventionalized poetic terms); the *means* of dealing with the problem (through appeal to the LORD); and the providential *result* (divine deliverance). Another common component is added here, that is, a personal *response*, for example, a vow of sacrificial action or a promise to worship and praise Yahweh in his "holy temple" ' (italics his).[58] 'The prayer of Jonah is a veritable catena of traditional phrases from the Psalter. Jonah prays in the stereotypical language of the psalms which every faithful Jew had always used. He first describes the threat to his life in the language of the complaint psalm, which, however, because of the context of the ongoing narrative works to provide a new and remarkable dimension of historical specificity ... '[59] These two scholarly witnesses are enough to show how Jonah's psalm is seen as

---

[56]Cf. A. Hauser, 'Jonah: In Pursuit of the Dove', *JBL* 104 (1985), 21-37.

[57]Cf. also Alonso Schökel, Sicre Diaz, *Profetas*, 1021-4; G. Landes, 'The Kerygma of the Book of Jonah: The Contextual Interpretation of the Jonah Psalm', *Interp.* 21 (1967), 3-31.

[58]Wendland, 'Five Key Aspects,' 315-6.

[59]Childs, *Introduction*, 423.

an original composition which strongly echoes if not cites tradition.⁶⁰ How may we define these contacts of Jonah's psalm to what we are terming 'tradition'?

We may define these contacts of Jon. 2:3-10 with such 'more or less fossilized conventions, often found in Hebrew liturgical texts'⁶¹ as a case of an 'external allusion'. 'An allusion consists of one or more words whose appearance intends to elicit the reader's recollection of another text (or texts) *for a specific purpose*. In practice, various types of allusions appear with some frequency in exegetical treatments, but exegetes should approach each of these with care to evaluate the likelihood of intentionality and/or cognizance by the author/redactor ...' (italics his)⁶² Nogalski distinguishes between 'internal allusions' when their 'literary horizon focuses on another part of the same writing' and 'external allusions' 'which anticipate or reach back to another text'.⁶³

The question to tackle now regards the author's motivations for adopting through allusion thoroughly known conventions in tradition. May one speculate that the author of the Book of Jonah could have made use of the Psalter in some redactional form? Probably one may, and this may lead to the reconstruction of the possible 'edition' had by our author. But perhaps this line of thought goes beyond what interests us in this essay. It would appear that what the author of the Book of Jonah was keen in alluding to was not a particular liturgical 'text' but a liturgical and spiritual 'tradition' which could help articulate the main character's experience of going through distress and being therefrom liberated through יְהוָה's agency. Alonso Schökel and Sicre Diaz's comments upon the psalm are illuminating: 'En el relato total este capitulo impone una pausa narrativa, llena un tiempo y analiza poéticamente la reacción del profeta y el sentido de los hechos. Sin este salmo, el relato no bajaría a su profundidad significativa .... El salmo describe un movimiento de bajada e inicia un movimiento de subida, lo señalan algunos verbos y algunos sostantivos ... '⁶⁴ The problem is identifying the real nature of the prophet Jonah's distress. What was causing Jonah so much distress and anxiety as to desire death? On the surface level of the narrative, it was finding himself in the big fish's belly that provoked Jonah's prayer. But the dissonance of the psalm with the literary context into which it is inset clamours

---

⁶⁰One should read Alonso Schökel, Sicre Diaz, *Profetas*,1022-3; Sasson, *Jonah*, 161-215, for how each each phrase reflects this tradition.
⁶¹Frolov, 'Returning the Ticket', 94.
⁶²Nogalski, 'Intertextuality', 109.
⁶³Nogalski, 'Intertextuality', 110.
⁶⁴Alonso Schökel, Sicre Diaz, *Profetas*, 1022-3.

for an allegorical interpretation of the psalm. And as the narrative framework was seen to focus on the meaning of prophetic ministry and on its effects on the life of the prophet, one may well speculate that for the author of the Book of Jonah the divinely piloted downward/upward movement metaphorically and mythically described in the psalm, stands for the sensation of being 'annihilated' and then 'resurrected' that prophecy seems to have procured for some subjects in tradition.

And tradition did offer paradigms of prophecy experienced as an 'annihilation' and a 'resurrection' of the subject of prophecy. By the time the Book of Jonah was composed, tradition had probably already canonised the prophetic figures of the 8th century Isaiah and of the 6th century Jeremiah. Both prophets voiced their suffering protests to the demands upon their lives of their prophetic ministry. To the LORD's sending Isaiah לָעָם הַזֶּה with a message that is immediately perceived by the prophet to be paradoxical(Isa. 6:9-10), the prophet replies with a question which has seemed simply rhetorical:

עַד־מָתַי אֲדֹנָי (Isa. 6:11)
How long, O LORD? (NRSV)
Signore, fino a quando accadrà questo? (BLC)
Jusques à quand, Seigneur (TOB)[65]

God had decreed the destruction of his own people and decided to use the prophet and his word as tools of destruction.[66] This question reflects Isaiah's reaction to this tragic mission entrusted to him by the LORD. The greater part of commentators on the other hand would exclude any psychological connotations in this question of the prophet to the LORD.[67] In Isa. 6, however, the personal and the emotional are not at all alien to the text;[68] v. 11 cannot be seen simply as a rhetorical question that helps link the enunciation of the threat enigmatically

---

[65] *New Standard Revised Version* (1989); *La Bibbia in Lingua Corrente* (1985); *La Bible: Traduction Oecuménique* (1995).

[66] Cf. Von Rad's commentary on this text in: *Message of the Prophets*, 122-6.

[67] Cf. Childs, *Introduction*, 331.

[68] For most scholars Isaiah would not allow the personal to transpire in his poetry. Luis Alonso Schökel's statement made in the influential *The Literary Guide to the Bible*, edited by Robert Alter and Frank Kermode, Cambridge, MA 1987, is representative of current ideas on the issue: 'Although the poetry of Isaiah is objective, in that it does now seek to express personal emotions, it is intensely rhetorical poetry. The prophet wants his words to create a particular reaction in his listeners: he wants to affect them, shake them, motivate them by confronting them with transcendental issues' (p. 166). The present author wonders whether this statement is not in need of some revision.

formulated (Isa. 6:9-10) and the time/sign of its fulfilment (Isa. 6:11b-13). One may also read it as an emotionally sensitive reaction of the prophet as he recoils in front of the horrible implication of his mission. 'Le prophète ne veut pas accepter que la condemnation soit definitive' (says the apposit note of *La Bible de Jerusalem*). In their commentary on prophets Alonso Schökel and Sicre Diaz qualify Isaiah's mission or call as 'destino tragico';⁶⁹ and a tragic destiny it was if this perception of his mission was with the historical Isaiah from the very beginning of his ministry.⁷⁰ According to biblical tradition, a prophet may never remain neutral in the sense that he is an ambassador who *non porta pena*, who is absolutely distinct from the one who sends him. He is personally deeply involved in his act of prophesying. And it is this message that Jonah the prophet, as he is depicted in the homonymous book, needed to understand.

Jeremiah is the other figure in tradition who is pictured as reacting even more vigorously to the demands made of him by his prophetic calling. Jeremiah excelled all his predecessors in articulating both the core of prophecy as essentially a personal relationship with יהוה, the God of Israel, as well as the level of involvement by the prophet in psychological and spiritual terms. Just a short abstract from the so-called 'confessions of Jeremiah'⁷¹ will suffice to make this point clear:

> O LORD, you have enticed me, and I was enticed;
> you have overpowered me, and you have prevailed.
> I have become the laughingstock all day long;
> everyone mocks me.
> For whenever I speak, I must cry out,
> I must shout, 'Violence and destruction!'
> For the word of the LORD has become for me
> a reproach and derision all day long.
> If I say, 'I will not mention him,
> or speak anymore in his name,'

---

⁶⁹ Alonso Schökel, Sicre Diaz, *Profetas*, 142.

⁷⁰ Cf. Von Rad, *Message of the Prophets*, 122; *contra* K. Koch, *The Prophets*, vol. 1: The Assyrian Period, London 1982, 113.

⁷¹ The present writer is of course aware that in speaking of Jeremiah one must recall the distinction between 'Historical Figure' and 'Personage'; he is also aware of the complex redactional history of this 'book'. On this cf. among others J. Bright, *Jeremiah: A New Translation with Introduction and Commentary* (AncB, 21), New York 1965; R.P. Carroll, *From Chaos to Covenant: Uses of Prophecy in the Book of Jeremiah*, London 1981; Idem, 'Dismantling the Book of Jeremiah and Deconstructing the Prophet', in: M. Augustin, K.-D. Schunck (eds), *'Wünschet Jerusalem Frieden': Collected Communications to the XII*ᵗʰ *Congress of the International Organization for the Study of the Old Testament*, Jerusalem 1986, Frankfurt a. M. 1986, 291-302.

> then within me there is something like a burning fire
> shut up in my bones;
> I am weary with holding it in, and I cannot ...
>
> (20,7-9, NRSV)

We cannot hope to comment adequately on these confessions in this essay. And it is not our task to discuss the issues that these confessions give rise to.[72] Instead we shall depend upon Gerhard von Rad's theological commentary which we shall cite only in part:

> The confessions are central for the interpretation of Jeremiah. They must be understood as a written testimony to an intercourse between Yahweh and his prophet that is both striking and unique. The external circumstance of the order in which they appear in itself outlines a road which leads step by step into ever greater despair ... The passages all point alike to a darkness which the prophet was powerless to overcome, and this makes them a unity. It is a darkness so terrible – it could also be said that it is something so absolutely new in the dealings between Israel and her God – that it constitutes a menace to very much more than the life of a single man: God's whole way with Israel hereby threatens to end in some kind of metaphysical abyss ... It is still Jeremiah's secret how, in the face of growing scepticism about his own office, he was able to give an almost superhuman obedience to God, and, bearing the immense strains of his calling, was yet able to follow a road which led ultimately to abandonment. Never for a moment did it occur to him that this mediatorial suffering might have a meaning in the sight of God. Again, if God brought the life of the most faithful of his ambassadors into so terrible and utterly uncomprehended a night and there to all appearances allowed him to come to utter grief, this remained God's secret.[73]

It would appear that it is to escape from 'so terrible and utterly uncomprehended a night' that the 'prophet' of the Book of Jonah sought to escape. But he failed miserably because he had to go through the experience of darkness and light and to re-establish he relationship which he broke when he sought to 'flee from the presence of the LORD'.

c) The author of the Book of Jonah must have had some 'text' when he wrote Jonah's lament in Jon. 4:2. By 'text' here we do not understand

---

[72] The paper read during this seminar by Dr Christoph Bultmann, entitled 'A Prophet in Desperation? The Confessions of Jeremiah', offered a very good discussion of these issues and also a bibliography.

[73] Von Rad, *Message of the Prophets*, 173-5.

that this writer was employing 'written material'. It could simply have been a 'crystallized tradition' or a 'liturgical formula' which the author then adopted *in toto* or *in parte* to suit his literary project. Jack M. Sasson criticises the *New English Bible* and others for parsing the second כִּי-clause in Jon. 4:2 as a citation: '*Kî* does not introduce citations'.[74] May be he is correct. But G. Vanoni 1978's analysis[75] which Sasson reproduces in his own commentary[76] makes it clear that Jonah is at least partly reproducing and may be partly transforming a known 'text', whether written or otherwise:

כִּי אַתָּה

(a) אֵל־חַנּוּן וְרַחוּם
(b) אֶרֶךְ אַפַּיִם וְרַב־חֶסֶד
(c) וְנִחָם עַל־הָרָעָה

Some form-critical comments: 1) In unit (a) qualifying the nominal אֵל, God, there are two adjectives in coordination. 2) Asyndeton separates (b) from (a). 3) Element (b) of the quotation consists of a pair of phrases, each with a 'head' which is an adjective and a qualifying noun in construct state. 4) One wonders whether element (c) is not meant to be part of element (b); syntactically speaking it constitutes the climax of the quotation and of the unit (b) and (c) together if they were taken by the narrator to be one unit rather than two; the coordinating waw with נִחָם gives this impression. 5) One should note also that while elements (a) and (b) have not lexical echoes in the context, element (c) seems to owe its existence to Jon. 3:10 which are the narrator's words and not Jonah's. 6) The entire citation is object of another כִּי-clause: כִּי יָדַעְתִּי.

One cannot be absolutely sure whether the version we find in Jonah (as well as that in Joel 2:13) is not a transformation of a longer citation fully represented in Exod. 34:6-7. It may be that the latter edition is itself a transformation of a version that feeded both. In case Jon. 4:2 is chronologically posterior (as it probably is) and redactionally dependent (as it plausibly is) upon Exod. 34:6-7, the transformation that was operated was directed to emphasise the LORD's compassionate love towards the weak, the innocent, and even sinners. However, one cannot be completely certain whether the narrator meant to be satirical of Jonah's behaviour.

The text raises three questions which require an answer: 1) Why has the author adopted traditional theological expressions, possibly

---

[74] Sasson, *Jonah*, 279.
[75] G. Vanoni, *Das Buch Jona*, St. Ottilien 1978.
[76] Sasson, *Jonah*, 279-83.

culled from the liturgy, to describe יְהוָה? 2) What is the reason for making Jonah reveal his motivation for escaping to Tarshish at this juncture of the story? 3) How is this confession of faith in the LORD's mercifulness contributing to the overall message of the Book of Jonah? In the remaining part of this essay we shall try to answer these queries globally.

We have to read Jon. 4:2 within the overarching structure of the book, if such structure exists. In the standard editions of the Hebrew text, Jonah's confession forms part of Ch. 4 and hence apparently of the final scene in the story. Unfortunately, this division of the book into chapters has not respected the narrative dynamics of the story, and has ignored the narrator's boundary marks. It would seem from the positioning of the *setumah*[77] before Jon. 4:4 that the Masoretes themselves misunderstood the narrator's paragraphing in this text. But it is clear that Jonah's lament in 4:2-3 and the LORD's rhetorical question in 4:3 belong to the ministry Scene which opens at Jon. 3:1.

In 3:1 we are told by the narrator that the LORD speaks to Jonah a second time (שֵׁנִית), and commissions him with a message for the population of Nineveh, 'the great city' (Jon. 3:2). Jonah obeys (Jon. 3:3), and starts his missionary activity that consists essentially of preaching a message of doom (Jon. 3:4). This ministry was successful indeed since the entire population, and their domestic animals, believed God (וַיַּאֲמִינוּ בֵּאלֹהִים) and expressed their conversion in liturgical terms and rites (Jon. 3:5-8). Their hope was that God would notice their change of heart and alter his plans concerning Nineveh (Jon. 3:9). The narrator then tells us that God did notice their sincere change of ways and 'repented' concerning the disaster he had threatened them with (Jon. 3:10). This complicates the plot for somehow Jonah got to know God's change of plan:[78] 'This outcome was so terribly upsetting to Jonah that he was dejected' (Sasson's translation of Jon. 4:1); Jonah lamented that afterall he was right in believing that God will not be consistent with his threat of utter destruction of Nineveh because, as it well known, he is so compassionate and good that he would not

---

[77]For this punctuation mark cf. E. Würthwein, *The Text of the Old Testament*, (trans. E.F. Rhodes), Michigan 1979, 21; J.M. Oesch, *Petucha und Setuma: Untersuchungen zu einder überlieferten Gliederung im hebräischen Text des Alten Testaments*, Göttingen 1979.

[78]From the narratological point of view this looks like being a defect. Was God discussing with Jonah the change of behaviour of the Ninevites? Do we have here an instance of the principle formulated in Amos 3:7 which BHS considers as an addition? But cf. F.I. Andersen, D.N. Freedman, *Amos*(AncB, 2,4A), New York 1989, 391-2).

carry such threats to their logical end (Jon. 4:2). This situation makes Jonah desire death (Jon. 4:3). But יְהוָה intervenes with a rhetorical question:

הַהֵיטֵב חָרָה לָךְ (Jon. 4:4)

to which Jonah has no answer to give, and the scene comes to an end.

Scene Four (Jon. 4:5-11) opens in narration; the narrator informs us that Jonah changes venue, in that he leaves the city itself to move outside, to the east (Jon. 4:5). Jonah's motivation for his choice of location is stated just as it has been for Jonah's attempt to escape from the LORD (Jon. 1:3). Notwithstanding the mysterious communication of God's new design concerning Nineveh, Jonah was still expecting that something spectacular would happen to the population of the city. He settles at a safe distance away from Nineveh עַד אֲשֶׁר יִרְאֶה מַה־יִּהְיֶה בָּעִיר (Jon. 4:5). But in this Scene Four we have another personage who participates actively in the action through his 'creative word'. This other character is at times called (הָ)אֱלֹהִים, other times יְהוָה, and even יְהוָה־אֱלֹהִים. Strictly speaking he does not 'enter the scene' but participates in the action by 'speaking from outside'. He 'appoints' (וַיְמַן) creatures to perform various tasks that would somehow affect Jonah; in this way God provokes Jonah to participate in the debate that interests God, and the author. What breaks Jonah is the death of the קִיקָיוֹן which provided him with shade from the blistering sun. The net result of these provocations of God is that Jonah asks to be killed (Jon. 4:8). Again, the LORD queries the prophet whether he was justified in desiring death, and Jonah gives a positive answer (Jon. 4:8). And it is this answer that provides the LORD with the occasion to put the rhetorical question with which the story comes to an abrupt end. Jonah is given no time for an answer.[79] The point of the story has been made.

So between Scene Three (Jon. 3:1–4:4) and Scene Four (Jon. 4:5-11) there do exist a number of structural parallels which are hermeneutically relevant:

Scene Three	Scene Four
a) An event in which the LORD takes part provokes Jonah to anger/dejection (Sasson): the decision to pardon the Ninevites after their sincere signs of genuine conversion (Jon. 3:10–4:1)	a) An event in which the LORD takes part provokes Jonah to dejection: the creation and destruction of the protecting קִיקָיוֹן (Jon. 4:6-8).

---

[79] W.B. Crouch, 'To Question an End, to End a Question: Opening the Closure of the Book of Jonah', *JSOT* 62 (1994), 101-112.

b) A rhetorical question by Jonah which serves him to explain his previous behaviour when he attempted to escape from the presence of the LORD in Scene One (Jon. 4:2).

b) A rhetorical question by the LORD in order to explain his behaviour when he pardoned the Ninevites in the third Scene (Jon. 4:10-11).

c) יוֹנָה desires to die (Jon. 4:3).

c) יוֹנָה asks that his life be taken as death is preferable to life (Jon. 4:8).

d) The LORD asks Jonah whether he feels he was justified in desiring death (Jon. 4:4). Jonah gives no answer and moves outside Nineveh.

d) The LORD asks Jonah whether he considers himself justified in asking for death on account of the קִיקָיוֹן; Jonah answers he was justified.

One should notice that while the listed elements in Scene Four exhaust the whole scene, in Scene Three there are other elements which are not included in these lists. This means that the two scenes are not perfectly parallel from the structural point of view. Besides, the order of the component parts of each scene changes according, it seems, to specific needs of the context. One important variation concerns the rhetorical question in each scene. In Scene Three Jonah's question/statement (Jon. 4:2) comes as the second element; יְהוָה's question/statement features as the concluding element in Scene Four and the climatic point of the story as a whole. The two scenes hint to a chiastic arrangement. This different position within the respective scene of element (b) perhaps reflects the different narrative function they are made to play. Jonah's statement is not the conclusion of Scene Three. It has a question by Yahweh (Jon. 4:4) which orientates the narrative to the next scene so that Scene Three presupposes the existence of Scene Four. Jonah has shown by his statement that his point of view differs from that of the LORD and shows that he still needs instruction. He has not drawn all the implications of his belief in יְהוָה's compassionate love. As Jonah's confession in Jon. 1:9 may sound hollow (Holbert) and contradictory, Jonah's professed faith in the LORD's love may be interpreted almost as blasphemous (Frolov). Jonah seems to have truly believed neither the Ninevites's profession of repentance nor the LORD's readiness to forgive them and to avert the disaster which their former wickedness had brought about. He still needed the lesson to be imparted by the LORD in his final question (Jon. 4:10-11) which marries compassion to justice (cf. Gen. 18:20-33).

All this boils down to saying:

1) That in Jon. 4:2 Jonah repeats tradition about the character of Yahweh as a compassionate God; this tradition could have been found by the writer of Jonah already written or in oral form.

2) That Jonah's profession of faith in Jon. 4:2, which is recited as a justification for his behaviour in Jon. 1:1-3, has to be read together with Scene Four, especially with the LORD's concluding statement formulated as a question in Jon. 4:10-11, where יְהוָה insists that he could not punish Nineveh in view of the presence in it of many innocent people.

3) The LORD's final statement in Scene Four (Jon. 4:10-11) throws light upon his commissioning in Jon. 1:2. The LORD admits that within Nineveh not all inhabitants were evil, and therefore the personal pronoun attached to רָעָה in his message entrusted to Jonah has to be nuanced. But this means that Jonah's message to the inhabitants of Nineveh could not be understood as an unconditional message of doom, but only as a conditional threat. On the other hand, in Jon. 3:4 we are given the impression that Jonah preached a sermon of unconditional destruction, which explains the surprising show of repentance on the part of the people of Nineveh. Jonah in this prophetic writing seems to be misunderstanding his own God. Something may have gone wrong.

4) What went wrong was Jonah's understanding of what a prophet is. If Jonah's perspective differed so sharply from that of יְהוָה, it means that he was not, to say it with Abraham J. Heschel, the *homo sympathetikos* that he was supposed to be. The Polish Jewish scholar suggested some decades ago that we read the figure of the prophet through the category of sympathy.[80] 'In contrast to the Stoic sage who is a *homo apathetikos*, the prophet may be characterized as a *homo sympathetikos*. For the phenomenology of religion the prophet represents a type *sui generis*. The pathos of God is upon him. It moves him. It breaks out in him like a storm in the soul, overwhelming his inner life, his thoughts, feelings, wishes, and hopes. It takes possession of his heart and mind, giving him the courage, to act against the world ...In prophetic sympathy, man is open to the presence and emotion of the transcendent Subject. He carries within himself the awareness

---

[80]'Sympathy is a state in which a person is open to the presence of another person. It is a feeling which feels the feeling to which it reacts – the opposite of emotional solitariness', A.J. Heschel, *The Prophets* (Harper Torchbooks), vol. 2, New York 1962, 89.

of what is happening to God ...'[81] And this is what Jonah has not yet understood before the LORD puts him in front of the naked truth. He opted to escape his mission to Nineveh because he could not bear the 'pathetic' in prophecy. But through this negative figure of Jonah the author of the book is telling us what a prophet is.

5 Partial Conclusions

The present writer thinks that he has reached only 'partial' conclusions concerning the Book of Jonah because not all the elements mentioned in paragraph 2 (c) have been taken into due consideration in this paper:

1. The Book of Jonah is a narrative about prophecy written somewhere in the post-exilic period as a contribution for the understanding of this religious phenomenon which was perhaps disappearing from the historical horizon.[82]

2. It is quite possible that the writer was in intertextual dialogue with written texts; surely he/she was in discussion with religious tradition which was canonical in some sense, especially with the figures of Isaiah and Jeremiah.

3. The author of the Book of Jonah underlines the aspect of 'pathos' in prophecy as being constitutive to Israelite prophecy.

---

[81] Heschel, *The Prophets*, 88-9.
[82] Cf. Blenkinsopp, *History of Prophecy*, Chapters v and vi.

Graeme Auld *Edinburgh – United Kingdom*

From King to Prophet in Samuel and Kings

1   Personae at the Beginning of Samuel

The characters in the opening chapters of Samuel are not just what they seem, or even what they are said to be. They also play other roles: they take on other πρόσωπα or *personae*. Eli for example is introduced explicitly (1 Sam. 1:9) as 'the priest'; and we have already been told (1 Sam. 1:3) that his two sons were 'priests of Yahweh'. However, when we meet him first, we find him seated on a כִּסֵּא – and that appears throughout the Bible to be exclusively a royal 'throne'. No one else in 1 Samuel, neither Samuel nor Saul, will sit on a כִּסֵּא. And as we leave Eli, he is lying dead, fallen backward from off his כִּסֵּא at the news of the taking of the ark (1 Sam. 4:18). We are told, in retrospect, that 'he had judged Israel forty years'. He is introduced as a priest of Yahweh, and left dead as the one who had long judged Israel – and at both points we see on stage the significant 'prop' that denotes the royal persona.

The impression intended by this silent indicator is confirmed by two, and perhaps three features of the language used of Eli by Yahweh, as reported by the anonymous 'man of God'.

The first is 'I chose [your father] out of all the tribes of Israel to be my priest' (1 Sam. 2:28) – and בָּחַרְתִּי מִכֹּל־שִׁבְטֵי יִשְׂרָאֵל is language used elsewhere within Samuel-Kings of the divine choice of Jerusalem and David (1 Kgs 8:16, resumed in 2 Kgs. 21:7).[1] Then the unique and difficult אִישׁ לֹא־אַכְרִית לְךָ in 1 Sam. 2:33 will be adapted from לֹא־יִכָּרֵת לְךָ אִישׁ in 1 Kgs 8:25 and 9:5.[2] Yahweh's promise in Kings is stated in passive terms: that 'there shall not be cut off a man of yours', of David's line (that is), from sitting on the royal כִּסֵּא. Yahweh's threat in Samuel to the Eli who has already been seen sitting on a כִּסֵּא is stated in active terms, and makes his priestly role explicit: 'I shall not cut off a man of yours from near my altar, wearing out his eyes and grieving his heart, but all the greater part of your house shall die by the sword of men.'

Thirdly, כָּבוֹד (however that is to be rendered: 'honour, glory, wealth'?) is associated with only one human in the synoptic chapters

---

[1] The same formula is used of priestly election in Deut. 18:5; but I hold that that will depend on 1 Sam. 2, rather than the other way round.

[2] This phrase has no close counterpart in Deuteronomy.

of Samuel-Kings. Solomon is told in his vision at Gibeon that he will receive כָּבוֹד from Yahweh. The same is not straightforwardly said of Eli. However, on the analogy of the phrases just discussed, two or three things which are said about him may be distortions of Solomon's כָּבוֹד: he was 'heavy' (כָּבֵד – 1 Sam. 4:18); he honoured his sons rather than Yahweh (1 Sam. 2:29); by so doing, he was unable to meet the succinct divine challenge מְכַבְּדַי אֲכַבֵּד ('who honour me I will honour' – 1 Sam. 2:30).

I have been interested for many years now in the so-called synoptic material shared by Samuel-Kings and Chronicles. Given that interest, I find it significant that all the phraseology I have referred to anticipates language used in, and almost unique to, this synoptic material: what I am currently calling 'The Book of Two Houses' (BTH). We have seen how language from the promises to David and his house is anticipated in the choice of Eli's house as priests. This is also true in what is said about their replacements. The new priestly line will be 'raised up' (אָקִים, 1 Sam. 3:12) by Yahweh. What he says of them, וּבָנִיתִי לוֹ בַּיִת נֶאֱמָן (1 Sam. 2:35), links together בַּיִת אֶבְנֶה־לָּךְ from 2 Sam. 7:27 with וְנֶאְמַן בֵּיתְךָ in 2 Sam. 7:16 – and, even if we prefer the witness in 1 Chron. 17:15 to the original text there,[3] אמן Niphal is part of the language of Davidic promise in 1 Kgs 8:26.

If Eli and his בֵּית אָב and the line that will replace them are all spoken of in language familiar from the royal house of David and Solomon, it is no less true that Shiloh plays the role of Jerusalem. King Ahab may have a הֵיכָל (1 Kgs 21:1), but the Hebrew Bible knows of no other divine 'palace' than the temple in Jerusalem. We can add

(1) that only the הֵיכָל in Jerusalem and the one in Shiloh are said to contain 'the ark of God',

(2) that only these two shrines are associated with the divine כָּבוֹד (1 Sam. 4:21, 22; 1 Kgs 8:11), and

(3) that the verb שרת is used within Samuel-Kings of priestly service only in 1 Sam. 2:11, 18; 3:1 and in 1 Kgs 8:11. It seems very likely, therefore, that Shiloh here is not being described historically: it is a stage set to evoke Solomonic Jerusalem.

It may be worth pausing again briefly over כָּבוֹד. The Book of Two Houses mentions only once each the כָּבוֹד of Solomon (1 Kgs 3:13 || 2 Chron. 1:12) and of Yahweh (1 Kgs 8:11 || 2 Chron. 5:14). If the

---

[3] That we should frequently prefer the Chronicler's wording in such matters is argued in A.G. Auld, 'What if the Chronicler Did Use the Deuteronomistic History?', in: J.C. Exum (ed.), *Virtual History and the Bible*, Leiden 2000, 141-48.

opening chapters of Samuel are intended to anticipate this later story of the Temple of Jerusalem and the Davidic line, we may be able to offer a fresh account of the somewhat puzzling repetition in 1 Sam. 4:21, 22 of גָּלָה כָבוֹד מִיִּשְׂרָאֵל: the explanation of the name אִי־כָבוֹד given to her son by Eli's dying daughter-in-law. She associates the lost glory not only with the taking of the ark, but also with the loss of her father-in-law and husband. Eli and ark, each with their own 'honour' or 'glory', remind us of Solomon and Jerusalem Temple.[4]

As for the still-childless Hannah, we are told repeatedly in the opening chapter (1 Sam. 1:6, 7, 16) of her being 'irritated', of her suffering 'vexation' (כעס), at the hands of Peninnah. Only Hannah so suffers in Samuel: כעס and the related הכעיס are absent from the remainder of the books of Samuel. In two synoptic portions of 2 Kings, King Manasseh is said to vex Yahweh (21:6; 22:17); and in the rest of Kings הכעיס is an important element in the repeated critique of the kings of the north. Is Samuel's mother-to-be deliberately, but deftly, associated here in her irritation with the deity himself? Her response of weeping is also mentioned not once but three times (1 Sam. 1:7, 8, 10). Though less unique within Samuel than her vexation, her weeping too may prefigure a significant detail in the synoptic texts: the one-and-only instance of בכה in BTH. The same prophetess Huldah who draws attention to Yahweh's כעס also notes in Josiah's favour that he has 'wept' before Yahweh (2 Kgs. 22:19). However, the most frequently featured element in the depiction of Hannah is her praying (וַתִּתְפַּלֵּל), which is mentioned as often as five times. In the Book of Two Houses, and also still in Chronicles,[5] only kings are reported as praying – although even a foreigner may do so. In Samuel and Kings, only kings[6] and prophets[7] actually pray – and Hannah, more than any other.[8]

The first mention of her son Samuel, weaned and installed at Shiloh, and 'serving Yahweh' (מְשָׁרֵת אֶת־יְהוָה) uses a word which may refer properly to the intimate attendant or page of a king, or even a quasi-royal figure such as Moses or Elisha. However, as suggested

---

[4] We should also mention that 'Yahweh Sebaoth seated on the cherubim' in 1 Sam. 4:4, as in 2 Sam. 6:2 from which it is immediately drawn, anticipates the cherubim of the Jerusalem temple.

[5] David (1 Chron. 17:25), Solomon (2 Chron. 6:20, 21), Hezekiah (2 Chron. 30:18; 32:20, 24), and Manasseh (2 Chron. 33:13).

[6] David (2 Sam. 7:25), Solomon (1 Kgs 8:28, 29), and Hezekiah (2 Kgs. 19:15, 20; 20:2). Samuel (1 Sam. 7:5; 8:6; 12:19), the man of God from Judah (1 Kgs 13:6), and Elisha (2 Kgs. 4:33; 6:17, 18).

[7] Samuel (1 Sam. 7:5; 8:6; 12:19), the man of God from Judah (1 Kgs 13:6), and Elisha (2 Kgs. 4:33; 6:17, 18).

[8] 1 Sam. 1:10, 12, 16, 27; 2:1.

above, שרת is used most often in the Bible of priestly service to the deity. The theme of Samuel's service is repeated in these opening chapters, with interesting and somewhat puzzling variations:

2:11   מְשָׁרֵת אֶת־יְהוָה אֶת־פְּנֵי עֵלִי הַכֹּהֵן
2:18   מְשָׁרֵת אֶת־פְּנֵי יְהוָה נַעַר חָגוּר אֵפוֹד בָּד
3:1   מְשָׁרֵת אֶת־יְהוָה לִפְנֵי עֵלִי

In whichever way these three formulations relate to each other, and possibly modify each other, it is clear that each presents his 'service' as priestly, whether he is held to be serving Yahweh directly, or only in relation to the service of Eli the priest.

The second of these passages adds the detail that he was 'a lad girt with a linen ephod' (1 Sam. 2:18).[9] The exact phrase חָגוּר אֵפוֹד בָּד is used only once more in the Bible, of David when bringing the ark to Jerusalem in 2 Sam. 6:14. In only one other biblical passages is אֵפוֹד בָּד a secure reading: the parallel 1 Chron. 15:27 does not use חָגוּר, but says instead of David וְעַל־דָּוִיד אֵפוֹד בָּד.[10] I am not concerned to explore which was the earlier form of the note about David in the story of the ark. What interests me more here is that this is the only mention the Chronicler ever makes of an ephod. Given his interests in so many things priestly, and the considerable expansion offered in 1 Chron. 15:27 of the shared tradition, it seems that this detail about David was a piece of tradition which he had to report (at the end of his new text) but could not exploit. Was David wearing something that was properly priestly? And did that embarass the later Chronicler? In that case, young Samuel may have been depicted in normal priestly garb, even if no other priest in the Bible is so described. On the other hand, and just because no other priest in the Bible is so described, Samuel's uniform here may be an early hint of a connection with the later king David.

2 Samuel Called

1 Sam. 3 is a chapter particularly rich, or even dense, in associations with other biblical passages. Even a summary review of Samuel's encounter by Yahweh should pause at the following points:

---

[9] Given other links noted below between the opening chapters of Samuel and Solomon's first vision, it is possible that the use of נַעַר (1 Kgs 3:7) is another such; however, this word is absent from the parallel in 2 Chron. 1, and so most probably was not part of BTH. See also n. 32 below.

[10] While MT notes of the priests at Nob slaughtered by Doeg (1 Sam. 22:18) that אִישׁ נֹשֵׂא אֵפוֹד בָּד, the final בָּד is not well supported in the versions.

(1) Both Eli and Samuel lie down in their 'place' (1 Sam. 3:2, 9). מָקוֹם is used of the 'place' where the divine ark belongs (2 Sam. 6:17; cf 1 Kgs 8:6, 7), the 'place' to which prayer should be directed (1 Kgs 8:29, 30, 35), and of the 'places' where a divine break-through or פֶּרֶץ has occurred (2 Sam. 5:20; 6:8). In these synoptic texts, מָקוֹם appears to denote not so much a 'location' defined by spatial coordinates, as a 'locus' of divine-human encounter.

(2) Samuel was lying 'within the temple of Yahweh where the ark of God was' (1 Sam. 3:3). We have already noted, in our discussion of Shiloh, that the Bible only associates הֵיכָל and אָרוֹן as here in the account of the dedication of Solomon's Temple.

(3) The statement that 'Samuel did not yet know Yahweh' (1 Sam. 3:7) is unremarkable at first sight. Yet, in the synoptic chapters shared by Samuel-Kings and Chronicles, 'knowledge' related to Yahweh is a remarkably rare commodity associated only with David and possibly Solomon. We are told in 2 Sam. 5:12 that David, on his capture of Jerusalem, did 'know' that Yahweh had established him as king over Israel. He notes in his prayer that Yahweh knows him (2 Sam. 7:20), and has done something great letting his servant know it (2 Sam. 7:21). The only other instance of 'know' with David as subject in the synoptic chapters is at the other end of his story (2 Sam. 24:2): his fatal wish to count and know the number of this same Israel. As for Solomon, 1 Kgs 3:7 uses ידע and 2 Chron. 1:10, 11, 12 use דַּעַת in the story of his vision at Gibeon, but not at the same point; and so we cannot be certain that 'knowing' was part of the shared story. Samuel **will be** comparable to David; but is not yet so.

(4) Samuel is taught to respond to Yahweh as his 'servant' (עַבְדֶּךָ – 1 Sam. 3:9, 10); and that expression is particularly densely used in the synoptic chapters which include the prayers of David (2 Sam. 7 || 1 Chron. 17 [x12]) and Solomon (1 Kgs 8:23-50a || 2 Chron. 6:14-39 [x11]) – mostly Solomon's reference is to David or himself in the singular; and even where the plural 'servants' is used it appears that only the wider royal house is in mind. The use of 'servant' is in fact restricted to these two contexts within the synoptic texts with the sole exception of David's plea to Yahweh for forgiveness after his census (2 Sam. 24:10 || 1 Chron. 21:8).

(5) Yahweh makes a declaration (וְהִגַּדְתִּי – 1 Sam. 3:13) to Samuel about Eli, just as to Nathan about David (2 Sam. 7:11). The following statement that Samuel was 'too afraid to declare the sight' (יָרֵא מֵהַגִּיד אֶת־הַמַּרְאָה – 3:15) goes on to link three distinctive words. The first two are used just once each in all of the synoptic chapters: both in

2 Sam. 6-7 – David's 'fearing' Yahweh when he breaks out on Uzzah (2 Sam. 6:9); and Yahweh's 'declaring' that he will build David a house (2 Sam. 7:11). The third is unique within the Former Prophets, and rare elsewhere.[11]

(6) The 'guilt' of Eli's house (עָוֹן – 1 Sam. 3:14) uses a term drawn from the synoptic account of David's census (2 Sam. 24:10 ‖ 1 Chron. 21:8).[12]

(7) Eli's response that Yahweh will do what 'is good in his eyes' (1 Sam. 3:18) uses words of David in a synoptic text (2 Sam. 10:12 ‖ 1 Chron. 19:13).[13]

(8) When the verb גדל is used of Samuel's development (1 Sam. 2:21; 3:19), the only available comparisons in the narrative books of the Bible are 2 Sam. 5:10 of David and 1 Kgs 10:23 of Solomon, with their parallels in 1 Chron. 11:9 and 2 Chron. 9:22. And the second note about Samuel's growth in greatness (1 Sam. 3:19) goes on to note that 'Yahweh was with him' – another manifest anticipation of what is said about David.

(9) 'All Israel', defined as being 'from Dan to Beersheba' (1 Sam. 3:20), will be drawn from the account of David's census in the Book of Two Houses. There, as we noted at (3) above, David wanted to 'know' their number. Here they 'know' that Samuel is 'sure' or 'firm' as prophet of Yahweh, so echoing David knowing that Yahweh had established him as king. And again we have already noted, when discussing 1 Sam. 2:35 above, the Davidic associations of אמן Niphal.

(10) נָבִיא לַיהוָה (1 Sam. 3:20) is what BTH had called Micaiah ben Imlah (1 Kgs 22:7 ‖ 2 Chron. 18:6).

And finally (11) the use of ראה Niphal, of Yahweh 'letting himself be seen' (1 Sam. 3:21), can be parallelled in Samuel and Kings only in the reports of Solomon's two visions (1 Kgs 3:5; 9:2 ‖ 2 Chron. 1:7; 7:12). It is also cognate with the unique מַרְאָה in v.15.

The chapter opens with the final resumption or modification of the statement about Samuel's service of Yahweh, already discussed. Its next statement, about 'word' (דָּבָר) being 'precious' (יָקָר) is without biblical parallel. But two remarks are appropriate. The only other instances of יָקָר in biblical narrative are in synoptic chapters dealing with David (2 Sam. 12:30 ‖ 1 Chron. 20:2), Solomon (1 Kgs 10:2, 10,

---

[11] Only Gen. 46:2; Exod. 38:8; Num. 12:6; Ezek. 1:1; 8:3; 40:2; 43:3; Dan. 10:7, 8, 16.

[12] I exclude an immediate link with בְּהַעֲוֹתוֹ in 2 Sam. 7:14b, which is a Sam. 'plus' not represented in 1 Chron. 17.

[13] David will use the phrase once more: in 2 Sam. 15:26.

11 || 2 Chron. 9:1, 9, 10), and the Temple (1 Kgs 7:9-11 || 2 Chron. 3:6). Then the divine 'word' is itself very rare in synoptic texts, and is restricted to as few as three contexts: the oracle to Nathan (2 Sam. 7:4 || 1 Chron. 17:3), the oracle to Shemaiah (1 Kgs 12:22 || 2 Chron. 11:2), and the story of Micaiah ben Imlah and the two kings (1 Kgs 22:5, 19 || 2 Chron. 18:4, 18). Shemaiah's oracle forbids civil war within the whole people of Israel, while the story of the two kings provides a rare example of cooperation between Judah and [the rest of] Israel.

As to the final element in 3:1, there are two big questions about אֵין חָזוֹן נִפְרָץ: what does נִפְרָץ mean? and how does this statement relate to what has just been said about word being precious? But first the matter-of-fact but significant observations that 'vision' is found elsewhere in the Latter Prophets only in the report of Nathan's vision (2 Sam. 7:17 || 1 Chron. 17:15); and that פרץ is not just used, but actually featured with Yahweh as subject, in two neighbouring synoptic chapters, as well as in 2 Kgs 14:13 which is also part of BTH. 2 Sam. 5:20 explains the name בַּעַל פְּרָצִים, and 2 Sam. 6:8 the name פֶּרֶץ עֻזָּה, in terms of break-through by Yahweh. Our statement at the beginning of 1 Sam. 3 is built from rare elements in the core David story.[14] However, the well-informed reader of Samuel might also do well to consider the relevance of two verses in Proverbs:

25:18   עִיר פְּרוּצָה אֵין חוֹמָה
'a city broken into – no wall'
29:18   בְּאֵין חָזוֹן יִפָּרַע עָם
'with no vision, a people is set loose'

Each uses אֵין. The former uses the Qal passive participle of פרץ, the closest analogue to the unique Niphal of this verb in 1 Sam. 3. The latter associates אֵין with חָזוֹן; and יִפָּרַע is the Bible's only instance of the Niphal theme of the assonant verb פרע. If all of these resonances are relevant,[15] the intention may be to suggest that 'word' is all the more prized where vision has not broken through. Samuel's experience of the deity is certainly reported as wholly auditory and not at all visual.

It was not part of my purpose in preparing this paper to offer further arguments in support of the case I first presented in *Kings without Privilege*, that the material shared by Samuel-Kings on the one side and Chronicles on the other was also their principal source.

---

[14] Robert Polzin notes that חָזוֹן constitutes one of several 'visual allusion[s] to David' (*Samuel and the Deuteronomist*, Bloomington IN 1989, 53).

[15] And otherwise the coincidences seem too many!

I had intended rather to ask you to assume this theory, and consider with me whether it would provide a perspective not just fresh but also useful on the opening chapters of Samuel. And yet some of these word studies have produced striking results which I interpret in two ways. I take them of course to be further evidence of the artistry of the Book of Two Houses. But I think they also testify to the careful attention to its artistry which was paid by the author of 1 Sam. 3 and the material around it.

The next stage must be to extend our comparisons to the wider context.

(12) Solomon's words in 1 Kgs 8:20, וַיָּקֶם יְהוָה אֶת־דְּבָרוֹ, will have supplied the language of Elkanah's wish in 1 Sam. 1:23; and קוּם Hiphil has Yahweh as subject again in the promise to establish a כֹּהֵן נֶאֱמָן in 1 Sam. 2:35.

(13) The unique instance of נְאֻם־יְהוָה in synoptic chapters of the narrative books is spoken by Huldah in 2 Kgs. 22:19. We already noted the unique mention in that verse of Josiah 'weeping'. In the Books of Samuel, נְאֻם is used only in the speech of the 'man of God' (1 Sam. 2:30) near the beginning and to introduce David's 'last words' near the end (2 Sam. 23:1).[16]

(14) After 1 Sam. 2:35, the only instances of 'house' as object of the verb 'build' in the books of Samuel relate to David, and are in the synoptic chapters 2 Sam. 5:11; 7:5, 7, 13, 27.

(15) In his prayer (2 Sam. 7:27), David had acknowledged that Yahweh had 'tipped him off' (גָּלִיתָה אֶת־אֹזֶן עַבְדְּךָ) about the house he would build him. This is now anticipated in Yahweh tipping off Samuel (1 Sam. 9:15) that Saul should be anointed.

And (16) in the Chronicler's version of Nathan's vision, what comes to Nathan at night is not the expected דְּבַר־יְהוָה (as in 2 Sam. 7:4), but דְּבַר־אֱלֹהִים (1 Chron. 17:3); and the latter is exactly what Samuel lets Saul hear the morning following the divine tip-off (1 Sam. 9:27).[17]

The next stage in our discussion must be to recapitulate this information, and mention some of the new questions these observations raise.

(a) Eli was a priest, and a father of active priests; and he is also

---

[16] The second part of the divine threat in 1 Sam. 2:30, וּבֹזַי יֵקָלּוּ ('and who spurn me shall be slighted'), has a further cognate in 2 Kgs. 22:19; however, קְלָלָה there is a Kgs 'plus' not found in 2 Chron. 34:27.

[17] With this significant agreement between 1 Samuel and the Chronicler's wording of synoptic material, we should compare the use of חָזוֹן in 1 Sam. 3:1 and 1 Chron. 17:15 over against חִזָּיוֹן in 2 Sam. 7:17. On the general issue, see n. 3 above.

said to have judged Israel. His rebuke to his sons (1 Sam. 2:22-25), though perhaps sufficiently described as a (late – NB 1 Sam. 3:13) exercise of paternal responsibility, is also consistent with these two roles. However, in the address by the 'man of God', the choice and then replacement of his 'house' are described not in general royal terms, but precisely in language specific to Yahweh's promises to the kingly house of David and Solomon. And his sitting on the כִּסֵּא at beginning and end of his story adds silent emphasis to this. As for his sanctuary at Shiloh, every one of its features mentioned in these chapters is shared with the Jerusalem of David and Solomon. We might add, although significant language links are absent in this case, that the death of Eli's two sons together at the hands of the Philistines (1 Sam. 4) followed immediately by the related death of their father, while not strictly at Philistine hands, anticipates very closely the death of Saul's three sons and then Saul's own death as recorded in the opening scene of BTH, the first synoptic chapter (1 Sam. 31=1 Chron. 10).

(b) Hannah's vexation and her weeping may both be themes drawn from the response to Josiah by the prophetess Huldah, especially since other features of these early chapters of Samuel are also shared with 2 Kgs. 22:14-20. We might also note that Hannah goes on to sing a song (1 Sam. 2:1-10); and that Miriam (Exod. 15:20) and Deborah (Judg. 4:4), the other two biblical women to whom songs are ascribed, are both explicitly termed 'prophetess'.

(c) Samuel starts as priest, or priestly assistant; but his wearing a linen ephod offers an early indication of his alignment with David. His story as a whole is closely connected with the David and Solomon stories in the Book of Two Houses: his growth in greatness, that Yahweh was with him, the role of knowledge in the story, the geographical definition of his people. Most importantly, the report of his encounter in the sanctuary at Shiloh is especially reminiscent of David's dealings with Nathan in Jerusalem as recorded in 2 Sam. 7.

- The divine word, featured at beginning (1), middle (7), and end (21) of 1 Sam. 3, is drawn from 2 Sam. 7:4, and used in only two other parts of the Book of Two Houses.

- חָזוֹן (1 Sam. 3:1) and divine speech are also closely linked in 2 Sam. 7:17; but, when 1 Sam. 3 returns to the theme of 'vision' (15) and the deity being 'seen' (21), it is forms of ראה which are used.[18]

---

[18] And we have already been told that Eli is unable to 'see' (1 Sam. 3:2).

- David appeals to Nathan for help (2 Sam. 7:2), and Samuel runs to Eli when he hears himself called (1 Sam. 3:4-8).

- David asks about the ark (2 Sam. 7:2) and Samuel lies beside it (1 Sam. 3:3).

- Eli, just like Nathan, does not give the correct answer the first time.

- The divine word comes to Nathan 'at night' (2 Sam. 7:4), and Samuel lies where he is after his audition 'till the morning' (1 Sam. 3:15).

- Nathan communicates to David a divine message which includes styling David 'my servant' (2 Sam. 7:5, 8), and in David's following prayer to Yahweh he calls himself 'your servant'. Eli instructs Samuel to respond as 'your servant' to the divine call, and he does so (1 Sam. 3:9, 10).

I have pointed out that much of 1 Sam. 3 is composed of words and themes from chapters common to Samuel-Kings and Chronicles. What is interesting is how this old coinage is reminted; and I give just two examples.

(1) There is visual language in plenty: Eli is unable to see, the visions of Nathan, Solomon, and Micaiah are evoked, and both חָזוֹן and מַרְאָה are explicitly used. But this is not living language for the principal characters in the story. Samuel himself is not reported as seeing anything or anyone.[19] He is called and he hears; Yahweh speaks and Samuel receives his word. The conclusion of the chapter encapsulates the situation: Yahweh does permit his own unveiling – but in his word.

(2) The re-presentation of servanthood of Yahweh is quite as radical. In addition to the synoptic 2 Sam. 7 and 24, just noted above, the books of Samuel use the expression only in 1 Sam. 23:10, 11; 25:39; and 2 Sam. 3:18 – and in each case it refers to David.[20] This makes

---

[19]Polzin (*op. cit.*, 50) makes a different but attractive point, associating מַרְאָה here with the differently pointed מַרְאֵה found in 1 Sam. 16:7; 17:42 – Samuel has to be warned against judging on the basis of mere 'appearances'. Uriel Simon (*Reading Prophetic Narratives*, Bloomington IN 1997, 285, n. 35) appeals to 2 Kgs. 8:10, 13 where he claims that the cognate הִרְאַנִי refers to an 'auditory disclosure'; however, I wonder if he is sufficiently sensitive to the influence on word-choice there of the play on the name חֲזָאֵל, occasionally written חֲזָהאֵל.

[20]In this respect, the rest of Samuel is like Chronicles: the only two non-synoptic occurrences in Chronicles both refer to kings: 2 Chron. 6:42 (David) and 32:16 (Hezekiah).

the portrayal of Samuel, as in some sense anticipating the Davidic 'servant' of Yahweh, quite isolated in the books of Samuel, and all the more striking. He does go on to become Israel's national leader: he and his sons do 'judge' Israel,[21] as Eli had before him. Yet he is not being aligned with David as pre-royal or quasi-royal leader of his people. 1 Sam. 3 brilliantly evokes, in the language it uses, the promises made by Yahweh to the family of David and also each prophetic episode shared by Samuel-Kings and Chronicles.[22] When we reach the end of this chapter, it is made explicit to us that the 'establishment' (נֶאֱמָן) of Samuel is as 'prophet of Yahweh': his servanthood is not royal but prophetic. These two aspects of the narrated redefinition in 1 Sam. 3 are neatly recapitulated in 1 Sam. 9:9 – 'he who is now called a prophet was formerly called a seer' (NB ראה as in 1 Sam. 3:15, 21 and not חזה which 1 Sam. 3:1 inherited from 2 Sam. 7). The narrative in 1 Sam. 9, which introduces us to Saul, is very rich in echoes of the beginning of the book.[23] Equally, the many royal aspects in the presentation of Samuel have immediate implications for Saul and his relations with prophets (1 Sam. 10:5-13): 'Is Saul also among the prophets?'

3 Samuel and Kings

Within the books of Samuel, there is no figure analogous to Samuel. However, there are comparators in the books of Kings, which are much richer in any case in talk of Yahweh's servants. How the title 'servant' is used in Kings is immediately illustrative. Even in non-synoptic portions of that book, royal servanthood remains prominent, with 14 instances additional to those shared by Kings and Chronicles: David [x11][24] and Solomon [x3].[25] But alongside these we find mention of the

---

[21] 1 Sam. 7:15-17 and 8:1-3.

[22] For discussion of these episodes, see A.G. Auld, 'Prophets Shared and Recycled', in: T. Römer (ed.), *The Future of the Deuteronomistic History*, Leuven 2000, 19-28.

[23] We are invited, if not required, to seek out comparisons backwards and forwards by the striking similarity between 1 Sam. 1:1 and 9:1. We find that Samuel is וְכָבֵד (1 Sam. 9:6) unlike Eli who was simply כָּבֵד (4:14); 'all he says actually comes' (1 Sam. 9:6) fulfils 'let none of his words fall to the ground' (3:19); both Yahweh and Samuel 'declare' (נגד Hiphil) in 1 Sam. 3:13, 15, 18, and this verb remains closely associated with Samuel (1 Sam. 8:9; 9:6, 8, 18, 19; 10:16; 15:16), especially in 1 Sam. 9; and we have already noted the links between 1 Sam. 9:15, 27 and 2 Sam. 7 || 1 Chron. 17.

[24] 1 Kgs 3:6; 8:66; 11:13, 32, 34, 36, 38; 14:8; 2 Kgs. 8:19; 19:34; 20:6.

[25] 1 Kgs 3:7, 9; 8:59.

divine word spoken by individual servants, Moses [x3],[26] Ahijah [x2],[27] Elijah [x2],[28] Jonah [x1],[29] and also by the plural 'his/my servants the prophets' [x5].[30] It is the appeal to Yahweh by Elijah in 1 Kgs 18:36 (which brings this sub-total to 14 as well) which most resembles the thrust of 1 Sam. 3: 'let it be known this day that you are God in Israel, and that I am your servant, and that I have done all these things by your word'. 'Known ... your servant ... by your word': each of these three expressions is a vital element of 1 Sam. 3. It is in the first part of this verse uniquely that Elijah is styled 'the prophet', and just a few verses earlier (18:22) he has called himself 'prophet of Yahweh', just like Samuel in 1 Sam. 3:20.

The same point is also achieved by narrative strategies. Still earlier in 1 Kgs 18, the vizier Obadiah (significantly named) is caught between Ahab and Elijah: two figures of similar status – indeed, if anything, Elijah is more effectively monarchical than Ahab. Then Elisha, though never himself styled 'servant of Yahweh', succeeds officially to Elijah's position (2 Kgs. 2), is frequently approached with the deference due to royalty (2 Kgs. 2:16; 5:15, 17, 18; 6:3; 8:13), and takes responsibility for his people at a time when the king of the time has all but vanished into obscurity.[31]

I am full of admiration for Jan Fokkelman's epic demonstration of the poetics of the books of Samuel,[32] including his impatience with traditional compositional history. Reading him on the larger structures and tiny details of the books of Samuel is rather like watching an expert examine a monument of oriental art – such as the *minbar* or pulpit which Nur ad-Din commissioned for the Mosque of al-Aqsa in Jerusalem. Much of the art is concealed by the art; and the patterning is operative at several different levels at the same time. I share Fokkelman's distrust of earlier 'sources' such as an Ark Narrative[33] or a History of David's Rise. But, in this respect, I do note my surprise that his first of his four volumes accedes implicitly to the separation of 2 Sam. 9–20 + 1 Kgs 1–2 as connected material, though divided in

---

[26] 1 Kgs 8:53, 56; 2 Kgs. 21:8.

[27] 1 Kgs 14:18; 15:29.

[28] 2 Kgs. 9:36; 10:10.

[29] 2 Kgs. 14:2.

[30] 2 Kgs. 9:7; 17:13, 23; 21:10; 24:2.

[31] I am indebted here to the Edinburgh doctoral dissertation of W.B. Aucker, *2 Kings 2-9 and Narrative (Dis)Integration*, 2000.

[32] *Narrative Art and Poetry in the Books of Samuel: A Full Interpretation Based on Stylistic and Structural Analyses*, 4 vols, Assen 1981-93.

[33] A distrust also shared in K.A.D. Smelik, *Converting the Past* (OTS, 28), Leiden 1992, 34-58.

the text as it stands by 2 Sam. 21–24.[34] He does recognise in a footnote[35] that the books of Samuel 'are parts of a larger composition, which composition comes to the fall of Jerusalem and the exile'; but one wonders how successfully he integrates this recognition into his account of Samuel. On the other hand, I am becoming increasingly confident that some of the compositional history of Samuel and Kings can be traced, and the detailed artistry detected by Fokkelman even better appreciated.

His account of the A[1–3] B[4–9] X[10–15] B'[16–18] A'[19–4:1] structure of 1 Sam. 3 is a fine example of his craft.[36] But his inattention to the resonances of some of the language in the central long divine speech have him overlook its most radical implications. Yahweh's opening words about ears that will tingle at the hearing of what he is to do (1 Sam. 3:11) have parallels only in 2 Kgs. 21:12 and Jer. 19:3 –

אֲשֶׁר כָּל־שֹׁמְעוֹ תְּצִלֶּינָה שְׁתֵּי אָזְנָיו	הִנֵּה אָנֹכִי עֹשֶׂה דָבָר בְּיִשְׂרָאֵל	1 Sam. 3:11
אֲשֶׁר כָּל־שֹׁמְעָיו תְּצִלְנָה שְׁתֵּי אָזְנָיו	הִנְנִי מֵבִיא רָעָה עַל־יְרוּשָׁלַם וִיהוּדָה	2 Kgs 21:12
אֲשֶׁר כָּל־שֹׁמְעָהּ תִּצַּלְנָה אָזְנָיו	הִנְנִי מֵבִיא רָעָה עַל־הַמָּקוֹם הַזֶּה	Jer. 19:3

Wherever the expression is original, these three passages are elements within a significant triangular linkage. It is precisely Manasseh's wrongs which call down the divine threat in 2 Kgs. 21. His wrongs flouted what had been commanded by 'my servant Moses' (2 Kgs. 21:8), and the terrible threat is communicated 'by his servants the prophets' (21:10). Outside the Bible's narrative books, Samuel is named only in Jer. 15:1 and Ps. 99:6.[37] In both he is mentioned alongside Moses; and in Jer. 15:1-4 the passage will go on to mention Manasseh (15:4).[38] Jeremiah and 2 Kings are the books which mention

---

[34] Of course Fokkelman also recognises that they do not appear out of the blue (*op. cit.*, vol. 4, 1). While he has been prepared to flirt with the idea that the historical David could have written some of the poetry ascribed to him, such as the elegy over Saul and Jonathan, he asserts (*op. cit.*, vol. 4, 108) that the song of Hannah was written for its setting by the author of Samuel.

[35] *op. cit.*, vol. 4, 109, n. 171.

[36] He pays tribute (*op. cit.*, vol. 4, 163, n. 8) to Michael Fishbane's pioneering '1 Samuel 3: Historical Narrative and Narrative Poetics', in: R.R. Gros Louis, James Ackerman (eds), *Literary Interpretations of Biblical Narratives*, vol. 2, 191-203; as also do Polzin (*op. cit.*, 235, n. 37) and Simon (*op. cit.*, 282, n. 14).

[37] It is also true that Jeremiah is the only book of the Latter Prophets to mention Shiloh (7:12, 14; 26:6, 9; 41:5); and that Jeremiah alone of them is styled נַעַר at his call, like Samuel.

[38] The wider context in Jer. 14:1–15:9 is the most extended treatment within Jeremiah of the repeated theme in that book that Jeremiah should not pray for his people. We noted above (nn. 7, 8) the prominence of praying in the portrayal of Samuel and his mother.

'my/his servants the prophets' most (five times each, out of a total of fifteen). Samuel points as far as, and almost certainly beyond, the end of David's line. No less than the future David, Samuel has the privilege of being called 'servant of Yahweh'. But, greater than the future David, he unites the traditions of king and prophet.

Another distinctive, and somewhat more common, clause not only binds the books of Samuel and Kings together:[39] 'So may God do to X and so may he continue ...' Spoken first by Eli (1 Sam. 3:17), it will be uttered in these books only by leaders: Saul (1 Sam. 14:44), Jonathan (1 Sam. 20:13), David (1 Sam. 25:22), Abner (2 Sam. 3:9), David (2 Sam. 3:35), David (2 Sam. 19:14), Solomon (1 Kgs 2:23), and the 'king of Israel' (2 Kgs 6:31). Prophets are not a regular feature of this group of passages; however, it may well be significant that this curse is first spoken to Samuel and last used in a threat against Elisha.

Of course Fokkelman is correct to argue that 1 Sam. 3 intends to restate and radicalise the divine threat already pronounced against Eli by the man of God (1 Sam. 2:27-36): the man of God had said only that a new and sure priestly house would replace Eli's. He is right in the immediate context to contrast the certainty of divine unveiling to Samuel (כִּי־נִגְלָה יְהוָה אֶל־שְׁמוּאֵל – 1 Sam. 3:21) with the question about an unveiling to Eli's בֵּית־אָב in the past (הֲנִגְלֹה נִגְלֵיתִי אֶל־בֵּית אָבִיךָ – 1 Sam. 2:27). The end of chapter 3 does assure us that it is Samuel who will henceforth mediate the divine will. And we have already noted, in the context of both books of Samuel, that the death of Eli and his sons prefigures the end of the house of Saul in favour of a new and different order. However, in the whole context of Samuel and Kings, the message Samuel receives is also pregnant with threat against David's house.[40] And, in case we are unable to hear it in 1 Sam. 3, we may see it in 1 Sam. 4, when we observe Eli fall off his throne – the כִּסֵּא on which Saul never sat, but David did.

---

[39] In fact it is almost unique to Samuel-Kings – the only other instance is in Ruth 1:17.

[40] If the use of כעס to describe Hannah's mistreatment by her husband's other wife is drawn, as suggested above, from the Book of Two Houses, then it constitutes the earliest hint in the books of Samuel-Kings that their author has Manasseh in his sights.

Pancratius Beentjes   *Utrecht – The Netherlands*

Prophets in the Book of Chronicles

1 Some Statistical Data

In the Book of Chronicles the noun נָבִיא ('prophet') is found 29 times in total, with a remarkable concentration of seven occurrences in 2 Chronicles 18.[1] With respect of the verb נבא ('to prophesy') a similar feature emerges.[2] These statistical data might create the impression that 2 Chronicles 18 is the most obvious passage in the Chronicler's book to find out what is his own understanding of prophet and prophecy.[3] That, however, is absolutely not the case, since 2 Chronicles 18 with some small changes is identical to 1 Kings 22.[4] In fact, 2 Chronicles 18 is the only narrative resembling the prophetic 'biographies' of the Deuteronomistic History, in which the prophet himself is the central figure in the story. Whereas in the Book of Kings the narratives on Ahijah, Elijah, Elisha and others commonly included miraculous elements and were concerned with the efficacy of the prophetic pronouncements, in the Book of Chronicles the ministry of the prophets is nowhere described in terms of ecstasy, miracles or political dimensions, such as e.g. the exhortation to rebellion by Ahija of Silo (1 Kgs 11:29-39) or the anointing of Jehu by one of Elisha's disciples (2 Kings 9).[5] The entire complex of the Elijah narratives has been skipped by the Chronicler; instead of it only a letter by Elijah is brought to the fore (2 Chron. 21:12-15). Similar interventions take place with respect of Isaiah and Jeremiah; they no longer are persons who make their appearance in narratives.[6] They more or less coincide with or have

---

[1] 1 Chron. 16:22; 17:1; 29:29; 2 Chron. 9:29; 12:5, 15; 13:22; 15:8; 18:5, 6, 9, 11, 12, 21, 22; 20:20; 21:12; 24:19; 25:15, 16; 26:22; 28:9; 29:25; 32:20, 32; 35:18; 36:12, 16.

[2] 1 Chron. 25:1, 2, 3; 2 Chron. 18:7, 9, 11, 17; 20:37.

[3] In this contribution the word 'Chronicler' refers only to the author of the Books of Chronicles.

[4] R. Micheel, *Die Seher- und Prophetenüberlieferungen in der Chronik* (BET, 18), Frankfurt 1983, 23-9; K. Strübind, *Tradition als Interpretation in der Chronik: König Josaphat als Paradigma chronistischer Hermeneutik und Theologie* (BZAW, 201), Berlin/New York 1991, 155-64.

[5] R.B. Dillard, *2 Chronicles* (WBC 15), Waco 1987, 92-3; J. Kegler, 'Prophetengestalten im Deuteronomistischen Geschichtswerk und in den Chronikbüchern: Ein Beitrag zur Kompositions- und Redaktionsgeschichte der Chronikbücher', *ZAW* 105 (1993), 491.

[6] '... the literary prophets play no part in the Chronicler's narrative', S. Japhet, *The Ideology of the Book of Chronicles and its Place in Biblical Thought* (BEAT,

been reduced to the books bearing their names (2 Chron. 26:22; 32:32; 35:25).[7]

On the other hand, in the Book of Chronicles a total of eighteen prophetic addresses is found, of which no less than fourteen have no parallel in 1-2 Samuel or 1-2 Kings and can therefore be characterized as a creation by the Chronicler himself.[8] At least ten times these prophetic addresses are put into the mouth of persons who nowhere else in the Bible are known as prophet, seer, or man of God.[9] In a number of instances they are expressly presented with the help of a special introductory formula of divine inspiration.[10] It is hardly surprising that it is exactly in these prophetic addresses that fundamental theological notions of 1-2 Chronicles are to be found.

During the last 25 years or so, Biblical scholars have investigated a lot of aspects dealing with the Chronicler's view of prophet and prophecy.[11] In my opinion there is one particular aspect, however,

---

9), Frankfurt a.M. 1989, 181.
[7] Kegler, 'Prophetengestalten', 487 (Table 5).
[8] See 'List 8: Prophetic Speech Material', in: R.K. Duke, *The Persuasive Appeal of the Chronicler: A Rhetorical Analysis* (JSOT.S, 88), Sheffield 1990, 175-6.
[9] Kegler, 'Prophetengestalten', 487 (Table 4).
[10] 1 Chron. 12:19; 2 Chron. 15:1; 20:14; 24:20.
[11] Y. Amit, 'The Role of Prophecy and Prophets in the Theology of the Book of Chronicles', *BetM* 93 (1983), 3-23 [Hebrew]; C. Begg, 'The Classical Prophets in the Chronistic History', *BZ* 32 (1988), 100-7; E. Hernando, 'El Profetismo en los libros de las Crónicas', *ScrVict* 34 (1987), 45-66; Kegler, art. cit. (see n. 7); R. Kuntzmann, 'La fonction prophétique en 1-2 Chroniques: Du ministère de la parole au service de l'institution communautaire', in: F. Diedrich, B. Willmes (eds), *Ich bewirke das Heil und erschaffe das Unheil (Jesaja 45,7): Studien zur Botschaft der Propheten (Fs L. Ruppert)* (FzB, 88), Würzburg 1998, 245-58; R. Mason, 'The Prophets of the Restoration', in: R. Coggins et al. (eds.), *Israel's Prophetic Tradition: Essays in Honor of Peter Ackroyd*, Cambridge 1982, 137-54; Idem, *Preaching the Tradition: Homily and Hermeneutics after the Exile*, Cambridge 1990; R. Micheel, op. cit. (see n. 4); J. Newsome, *The Chronicler's View of Prophecy* (PhD Vanderbilt University), Ann Arbor (UMI), 1973; D. Petersen, *Late Israelite Prophecy: Studies in Deutero-Prophetic Literature and in Chronicles* (SBLMS, 23), Missoula, MT 1977; H. van Rooy, 'Prophet and Society in the Persian Period According to Chronicles', in: T.C. Eskenazi, K.H. Richards (eds), *Second Temple Studies 2: Temple and Community in the Persian Period* (JSOT.S, 175), Sheffield 1994, 163-79; W. Schniedewind, *The Word of God in Transition: From Prophet to Exegete in the Second Temple Period* (JSOT.S, 197), Sheffield 1995; I.L. Seeligman, ' Die Auffassung von der Prophetie in der deuteronomistischen en chronistischen Geschichtsschreibung', in: J.A. Emerton et al. (eds), *Congress Volume: Göttingen 1977* (VT.S, 29), Leiden 1978, 254-79; K. Strübind, op. cit. (see n. 4), esp. 155-64; R. Then, *'Gibt es denn keinen mehr unter den Propheten?' Zum Fortgang der alttestamentlichen Prophetie in frühjüdischer Zeit* (BEAT, 22), Frankfurt a.M. 1990; S. de Vries, 'The Forms of Prophetic Address in Chronicles', *HAR* 10 (1986), 15-36; J.P. Weinberg, 'Die "Ausserkanonischen

which appears to be neglected. Looking at this impressive list of publications one could get the impression that the Chronicler did not make use of what we term ' the Latter Prophets'.

In this contribution therefore, I like to pay some more attention to this specific topic. The first point to be emphasized will be that the Chronicler never uses marked formulae to introduce quotations. Even in cases such as 2 Chron. 36:21-22, where he seems to use introductory formulae (לִמְלֹאות דְּבַר־יְהוָה בְּפִי יִרְמְיָהוּ / לִכְלוֹת דְּבַר־יְהוָה בְּפִי יִרְמְיָהוּ), however, the subsequent wording cannot be coined as a straight quotation, being adopted from one specific text. Here the Chronicler has constructed a mixture of Jer. 25:11-12 and 29:10-14 with Lev. 26:34-35, 43. The most likely place to find out if, and in what context, the Chronicler makes use of classical prophetic texts is to take a closer look at one of the fourteen prophetical speeches which are his own creation.

2   2 Chronicles 15:1-7[12]

The Chronicler used the narrative of 1 Kgs 15:9-24 as the framework for a completely new composition dealing with Asa, king of Judah. Whereas 1 Kgs 15:9-24 includes 16 verses, the Chronicler's narrative on Asa covers no less than 47 verses, so that the majority of it (esp. 2 Chron. 14:2-15:15; 16:7-10) is specific to the Book of Chronicles.[13]

After the victory over the Cushites, which in accordance with the Chronicler's theology has entirely been described as a divine act (2 Chron. 14:11-12), Asa and his men returned to Jerusalem (14:15). Then with the help of the 'possession formula' הָיְתָה עָלָיו רוּחַ אֱלֹהִים, which in the Hebrew Bible is never used with regard to classical prophets, in 15:1 a literary character called Azariah son of Oded is introduced.[14] Schniedewind who offers a fine analysis of the two pos-

---

Prophezeiungen" in den Chronikbüchern', *Acta Antiqua* 26 (1978), 387-404; T. Willi, *Die Chronik als Auslegung* (FRLANT, 106), Göttingen 1972.

[12] R. Dillard, 'The Reign of Asa (2 Chronicles 14-16): An Example of the Chronicler's Theological Method', *JETS* 23 (1980), 207-18; M. Fishbane, *Biblical Interpretation in Ancient Israel*, Oxford 1985, 388-92; Idem, *The Garments of Torah*, Bloomington 1988, 14-6; W. Rudolph, 'Der Aufbau der Asa-Geschichte', *VT* 2 (1952), 367-71; G. Snyman, ' "Tis a Vice to Know Him": Reader's Response-Ability and Responsibility in 2 Chronicles 14-16', *Semeia* 77 (1997), 91-113.

[13] For a detailed synoptic overview, see: A. Bendavid, *Parallels in the Bible*, Jerusalem 1972, 100-2.

[14] The same possession formula is used once more (2 Chron. 20:14) to introduce Jahaziel, a Levite of the line of Asaph, addressing a prophetic speech to 'all Judah, the inhabitants of Jerusalem and King Jehoshaphat'. See: P.C. Beentjes, 'Tradition and Transformation: Aspects of Innerbiblical Interpretation in 2 Chronicles

session formulas being used in the Hebrew Bible,[15] viz. וַתְּהִי / הָיְתָה רוּחַ עַל [...] on the one hand[16] and רוּחַ [...] לָבְשָׁה אֶת on the other,[17] arrives at this conclusion: 'In Chronicles, the possession formulas represent a claim to divine authority. They are used in cases of *ad hoc* prophetic inspiration of non-professional prophets'.[18] The Chronicler, not being hampered by an existing canonical text referring to Azariah, feels free to compose a prophetic address of his own. By creating the literary character of Azariah who with the help of a possession formula speaks with divine authority, the Chronicler puts himself into a position to select and transform canonical prophetic texts for his own purpose. Azariah is used as a vehicle to present 'a mosaic of longer or shorter citations from existing prophetic texts, slightly altered and sophistically interwoven, to serve the new context and form a coherent statement of the Chronicler's view'.[19]

Here in 2 Chronicles we met the first of three occurrences in which it is stated that a *prophet* goes out to meet a king (15:2; 19:2) or an army (28:9) after a victory. The phrase in 2 Chron. 15:2 looks like a modified echo of 2 Chron. 14:9. Therefore a military connotation of the phrase יָצָא לִפְנֵי as used e.g. in Judg. 4:14; 1 Sam. 8:20; 2 Sam. 5:24; Ps 68:8; 1 Chron. 14:15 should not be denied for 2 Chron. 15:2 in advance.[20]

Though it is said that Azariah 'went out to meet Asa' (15:2a), it is not by chance that Azariah's address from the very beginning is in the plural (שְׁמָעוּנִי). His exhortation – being an excellent summary of the Chronicler's theology – is not only meant for Asa's ears, but for 'Asa and all Judah and Benjamin'. It is the basic attitude all people need in their relationship with God.

Azariah's address which opens with a call to attention (שְׁמָעוּנִי, v. 2) and is concluded with a strong exhortation (וְאַתֶּם חִזְקוּ וְאַל־יִרְפּוּ יְדֵיכֶם, v. 7) consists of two blocks. The first one (v. 2b) has been formulated as 'an axiom, which for the Chronicler is the underlying principle of all history'.[21] The second, major part of Azariah's address (vv. 3-6) is a sort of historical review.

20', *Bib* 74 (1993), 258-68, esp. 263-66.

[15] Schniedewind, *The Word of God in Transition*, 66-74.

[16] See Num. 24:2b (Balaam); Judg. 3:10 (Othniel); 11:29 (Jephthah); 1 Sam. 19:20b (the messengers of Saul); 19:23b (Saul).

[17] Judg. 6:34 (Gideon); 1 Chron. 12:19 (Amasai); 2 Chron. 24:20 (Zechariah).

[18] Schniedewind, *The Word of God in Transition*, 74.

[19] S. Japhet, *I & II Chronicles* (OTL), London 1993, 716.

[20] Japhet, *I & II Chronicles*, 717-8. In *DCH*, vol. 4, 259-60, all instances of the phrase יָצָא לִפְנֵי have been listed.

[21] Japhet, *I & II Chronicles*, 718.

3 Azariah's Axiomatical Statement (2 Chron. 15:2)

(1) 'YHWH is with you when you are with him;
(2) if you seek him, he will let himself be found,
(3) but if you forsake him, he will forsake you'.

Needless to say that a strong echo of Deuteronomistic theology, in particular from Deut. 4:29-30 and Jer. 29:13-14, is heard in the opening lines of Azariah's statement.[22] Almost every single element of this poetic[23] and prophetic statement can be considered as repeating and recalling other passages in Chronicles.

The first part of line (1) is found only twice in the Book of Chronicles. The first time, in 1 Chron. 22:18, it is phrased as a rhetorical question (הֲלֹא יְהוָה אֱלֹהֵיכֶם עִמָּכֶם) in David's address to his son Solomon to seek YHWH, in order to set about building his sanctuary.[24]

The second time the phrase יְהוָה עִמָּכֶם shows up is in the prophetic address by Jahaziel to 'all Judah, and the inhabitants of Jerusalem and King Jehoshaphat' (2 Chron. 20:17). It hardly can be an accident that this prophetic address is introduced in 2 Chron. 20:14 by exactly the same possession formula as in 2 Chron. 15:1 and is found in the Book of Chronicles in these two texts only.

The most close parallel to line (2) is to be found in 1 Chron. 28:9, where it – also being phrased conditionally (אִם) – is part of the conclusion in King David's personal address to Solomon. Both addresses hold the key phrase 'to seek YHWH',[25] which is one of the most important theological notions of the Book of Chronicles.[26] ' "Seeking Yahweh" is frequently used to typify commitment to Yahweh and his worship according to legitimate norms'.[27] It hardly can be coin-

---

[22] This is confirmed by the repetition of specific vocabulary, e.g. בצר ל in 2 Chron. 15:4 (cf. Deut. 4:30), קבץ in 2 Chron. 15:9 (cf. Jer. 29:14), and 'to seek YHWH ... with all their heart and soul' in 2 Chron. 15:12.

[23] E.g. the fourfold ending ־כֶם, the twofold opening וְאִם, and the twofold rhyme הוּ ־.

[24] The phrase 'Is not the LORD your God with you?' (1 Chron. 22:18) is immediately followed by another rhetorical question: 'Will he not give you peace on every side?'. The notion of God giving peace on every side is a theological notion governing the overall structure of 2 Chron. 14–15.

[25] Expressed with either דרש (2 Chron. 15:2, 12, 13) or בקש (2 Chron. 15:4, 15).

[26] Without dispute, the verb מעל is another major theological motif in the Book of Chronicles. See e.g.: W. Johnstone, 'Guilt and Atonement: The Theme of 1 and 2 Chronicles', in: J.D. Martin, P.R. Davies (eds), *A Word in Season (Fs W. McKane)* (JSOT.S, 42), Sheffield 1986, 113-38.

[27] B.E. Kelly, *Retribution and Eschatology in Chronicles* (JSOT.S, 211), Sheffield 1996, 46-53 (52); see also: C. Begg, ' "Seeking Yahweh" and the Purpose

cidence, of course, that this important theological notion of 'seeking YHWH' has already been incorporated in the preceding chapter (2 Chron. 14:3, 6). In fact, it is this notion of 'seeking YHWH' together with the phrase 'the Lord had given ... security on every side' (2 Chron. 14:5, 6; 15:15) that creates a kind of an *envelope structure* for the first part of the Chronicler's narrative on King Asa.

Whereas the key notion 'seeking YHWH' of 2 Chron. 15:2 forms part of an *overall* structure to the Asa narrative as a whole, it is the verb מצא Niphal (2 Chron. 15:2, 4, 15) which appears to be the leading principle structuring Azariah's address. The conditionally phrased opening statement of the prophet ('If you seek him, he will let himself be found', v. 2) and its realization in v. 15 ('they had sought the LORD earnestly; he had let himself be found by them') are linked with the help of an appeal to history: 'But when, in their distress, they turned to the LORD the God of Israel and sought him, he let himself be found by them' (v. 4). Before paying further attention to this appeal to history in 2 Chron. 15:3-6, let us quickly dwell on line (3) of Azariah's opening statement: 'But if you forsake him, he will forsake you'. Two times in the Book of Chronicles a similar phrase is uttered by a prophet. In 2 Chron. 12:5 Shemaiah adresses these words to Rehoboam and the leading men of Judah on the occasion of Shisak's attack on Jerusalem; and in 2 Chron. 24:20 the spirit of God takes possession of Zechariah who reproaches the people with their forsakening the LORD. It is, however, again 1 Chron. 28:9 – the conclusion of King David's personal address to Solomon – where we find a conditionally (אם) phrased parallel to line (3) of Azariah's address. This is in line with a characteristic feature of the Book of Chronicles noticed by James Newsome: '... that, under the Chronicler's pen, the Davidic king himself received the divine word and, on several occasions, passed it on to others, thus assuming the prophetic role'.[28]

---

of Chronicles', *LouvSt* 9 (1982), 128-41. The dissertation of G.E. Schaeffer, *The Significance of Seeking God in the Purpose of the Chronicler* (Southern Baptist Theological Seminary, 1972) was not available to me.

[28] J.D. Newsome, 'Toward a New Understanding of the Chronicler and his Purposes', *JBL* 94 (1975), 201-17. However, in his synopsis (pp. 203-4) Newsome does not mention 2 Chron. 8:14, where David is called 'man of God' (איש־האלהים)! '... daß bei unserem Autor die Könige und ihre Reden nicht selten prophetische Züge tragen', Seeligman, ' Die Auffassung von der Prophetie', 271.

4 Azariah's Appeal to History (2 Chron. 15:3-6)

In vv. 3-6 Azariah impresses upon his audience that the principle as brought out in v. 2 is crucial for Israel's welfare. In other words: vv. 3-6 serve as documentary evidence to the axiomatical statement of v. 2. Since v. 3, however, contains no verb, the phrase may just as well refer to the past as to the future.[29] Both the Septuagint and the Vulgate have taken Azariah's words as a prophecy of the future. Though modern scholarship almost unanimously assumes that the pericope refers to the past, more specifically to the time of the Judges, some authors presume that the Chronicler is referring either to the (end of the) exile[30] or to his own days.[31]

The Chronicler, as Azariah's ghostwriter, presents a speech which undeniably is Scripture oriented. There are a lot of references to passages in the Hebrew Bible, especially from the 'Latter Prophets'. An inventory of these instances reveals an intriguing pattern; the Chronicler appears to design his own manner of using authoritative words from tradition:

וְיָמִים רַבִּים ... לְלֹא ... לְלֹא ... לְלֹא	2 Chron. 15:3
יָמִים רַבִּים ... אֵין ... אֵין ... אֵין ... אֵין ... אֵין	Hos. 3:4
אֵין שָׁלוֹם לַיּוֹצֵא וְלַבָּא	2 Chron. 15:5
וְלַיּוֹצֵא וְלַבָּא אֵין־שָׁלוֹם	Zech. 8:10
מְהוּמֹת רַבּוֹת	2 Chron. 15:5
מְהוּמֹת רַבּוֹת	Amos 3:9
וְאַל־יִרְפּוּ יְדֵיכֶם	2 Chron. 15:7
אַל־יִרְפּוּ יָדָיִךְ	Zeph. 3:16
כִּי יֵשׁ שָׂכָר לִפְעֻלַּתְכֶם	2 Chron. 15:7
כִּי יֵשׁ שָׂכָר לִפְעֻלָּתֵךְ	Jer. 31:16[32]

With the exception of the idiomatic expression מְהוּמֹת רַבּוֹת, Azariah's historical review contains not a single *verbal quotation* from the Hebrew Bible. Words from tradition are handled on different levels. In 2 Chron. 15:3 it is mainly the *pattern* that is unmistakably adopted from Hos. 3:4. Hosea's prophecy, however, refers to a situation in

---

[29] An extensive list of various interpretations is given by E.L. Curtis, A.A. Madsen, *A Critical and Exegetical Commentary on the Books of Chronicles* (ICC), Edinburgh 1910, 384.

[30] M. Fishbane, *Biblical Interpretation in Ancient Israel*, 389.

[31] H.G.M. Williamson, *1 and 2 Chronicles* (NCB), Grand Rapids MI 1987, 268; P.R. Ackroyd, *I & II Chronicles, Ezra, Nehemiah* (TBC), London 1973, 138.

[32] Not Jer. 31:6, as indicated by Japhet, *I & II Chronicles*, 721.

the future, whereas the Chronicler's focus is on some event(s) in the past.³³

With respect to 2 Chron. 15:5 / Zech. 8:10 a special comment is appropriate. W. Beuken in his excellent doctoral thesis has circumstantially argued that, in spite of striking similarities, a direct literary dependence on Zech. 8:10 cannot be assumed for 2 Chron. 15:5.³⁴ I want to resist my 'Doktorvater' on this particular point, since in my opinion the Chronicler uses a literary device which I have coined *inverted quotation*.³⁵ Within an existing formulation from tradition (a sentence, a colon, a set phrase, a rare or unique combination of words) an author sometimes reverses the sequence. By such a deviating model he attains a moment of extra attention in the listener or the reader, because they hear or read something else than the traditional words: the reversed order is a sign that there is something special going on.

Since Zech. 8:10 and 2 Chron. 15:5 are the only two instances within the entire Hebrew Bible where the participles יֹצֵא and בָּא have been constructed with a preposition, and, moreover, we have the only occurrence within the Book of Chronicles here where the noun שָׁלוֹם is found in a negative context, a direct link is obvious. And because 2 Chron. 15:3-7 as a whole holds so many resemblances to Biblical texts, the most plausible inference must be that Zech. 8:10 is the parent text.

With respect to the last two couples of texts (2 Chron. 15:7a ‖ Zeph. 3:16; 2 Chron. 15:7b ‖ Jer. 31:16), the Chronicler makes only one small alteration in each of the two prophetic texts, changing the suffix of the second person singular (יְ -) into a plural one (כֶם-). This is done in order to emphasize again that Azariah is not just addressing King Asa, but 'all Judah and Benjamin' (v. 2).

William Schniedewind has convincingly demonstrated that, as far as the Book of Chronicles is concerned, one has to differentiate between speeches by speakers with prophetic titles (אִישׁ הָאֱלֹהִים, חֹזֶה, רֹאֶה, נָבִיא) and speeches by speakers without prophetic titles, but being introduced by 'possession formulas' (' the spirit of God was upon ... ', 'the spirit enveloped ...). Speakers with prophetic titles usually address themselves only to the king, whereas socalled 'inspired mes-

---

³³Possibly the Chonicler has deliberately used the verbs בקש and שוב in 2 Chron. 15:4 as an echo from Hos. 3:5.

³⁴W.A.M. Beuken, *Haggai-Sacharja 1-8: Studien zur Überlieferungsgeschichte der frühnachexilischen Prophetie*, Assen 1967, 162-3.

³⁵P.C. Beentjes, 'Discovering a New Path of Intertextuality: Inverted Quotations and Their Dynamics', in: L.J. de Regt *et al.* (eds), *Literary Structure and Rhetorical Strategies in the Hebrew Bible*, Assen 1996, 31-50.

sengers' generally address themselves to the people.³⁶ After a carefull investigation Schniedewind arrives at the conclusion that persons with prophetic titles 'often give explanations for past or future events, functioning as *interpreters of events*'.³⁷ In the speeches of the 'inspired messengers', the group to which Azariah is reckoned, emphasis is put on another aspect, viz. 'the *inspired interpretation of authoritative texts* which revitalized the word of God anew for the post-exilic community'.³⁸ It is hardly an accident that precisely in the final chapter of the Book of Chronicles a clear-cut distinction has been made between 'messengers' and 'prophets'! (2 Chron. 36:16)

5   Conclusion

The majority of the prophets and inspired messengers we met in the Book of Chronicles have been 'invented' by the Chronicler and should therefore be characterized as 'literary personages' rather than historical persons. Consequently, the speeches delivered by these literary personages are the most appropriate place to look for the Chronicler's own theological convictions and accents.

---

³⁶There are five 'inspired messengers': Amasai (1 Chron. 12:19), Azariah (2 Chron. 15:1), Jahaziel (2 Chron. 20:14), Zechariah (2 Chron. 24:20), and Neco (2 Chron. 35:21). On Jahaziel, see: P.C. Beentjes, 'Tradition and Transformation: Aspects of Innerbiblical Interpretation in 2 Chronicles 20', *Bib* 74 (1993), 258-68.
³⁷Schniedewind, *The Word of God in Transition*, 127 [Italics by me, PCB].
³⁸Schniedewind, *ibid.* [Italics by me, PCB].

Ulrich Berges *Nijmegen – The Netherlands*

Personifications and Prophetic Voices of Zion in Isaiah and Beyond

1 Introduction

The extent of the literature on Zion and Jerusalem is overwhelming. Although it has been well documented in nearly every aspect of archaeology and tradition history, there are only a few studies enquiring about the literary place of Jerusalem/Zion in the Hebrew Bible.[1] Simply: what roles do Jerusalem and Zion play in the literature of biblical Israel? Are both terms simply synonyms that can be used interchangeably, or are there traces of a more distinguished usage of these terms?

Jerusalem is more frequently mentioned in political contexts, esp. in connection with Judah,[2] than Zion.[3] This might also explain why Jerusalem is used more often with regard to the context of judgement.[4] In the Book of Isaiah the political side of Jerusalem is mentioned for the last time in the 'Sennacherib'-chapters (Isa. 36:2, 7, 20; 37:10). In DtIsa the term Zion stands for the restoration of post-exilic Israel.[5]

---

[1] See the older studies of N.W. Porteous, 'Jerusalem-Zion: The Growth of a Symbol', in: A. Kuschke (ed.), *Verbannung und Heimkehr: Beiträge zur Geschichte und Theologie Israels im 6. und 5. Jahrhundert v. Chr.*, Tübingen 1961, 235-52; G. Fohrer, 'Zion-Jerusalem im Alten Testament', in: Idem, *Studien zur alttestamentlichen Theologie und Geschichte (1949-1966)* (BZAW, 115), Berlin 1969, 195-241; more recently, E. Otto, ציון, in: *ThWAT*, Bd. 6, 994-1028; B.C. Ollenburger, *Zion: The City of the Great King: A Theological Symbol of the Jerusalem Cult* (JSOT.S, 41), Sheffield 1987; M.E. Biddle, 'The Figure of Lady Jerusalem: Identification, Deification and Personification of Cities in the Ancient Near East', in: K.L. Younger, *et al.* (eds), *The Biblical Canon in Comparative Perspective* (ScrC, 4), Lewiston 1991, 173-94; J.J. Schmitt, 'The City as Woman in Isaiah 1-39', in: C.C. Broyles, C.A. Evans (eds), *Writing and Reading the Scroll of Isaiah: Studies of an Interpretive Tradition* (VT.S, 70), Leiden 1997, 95-119.

[2] Isa. 1:1; 2:1; 3:1, 8; 5:3; 22:21; 36:7; see with the 'cities of Judah' in Isa. 44:26 and 'the temple' in Isa. 44:28; 'houses of Israel' in Isa. 8:14; with 'Samaria' in Isa. 10:10, 11.

[3] In Isa. 46:13 (|| Israel) and 59:20 (|| Jacob).

[4] See Isa. 5:3; 8:14; 22:10, 21; 28:14.

[5] D. Baltzer, *Ezechiel und Deuterojesaja: Berührungen in der Heilserwartung der beiden großen Exilspropheten* (BZAW, 121), Berlin 1971, 42: 'Der Zionname ist bei Deuterojesaja ausschließlich für die Ereignisse der Gegenwart und dann vor allem der heilvollen Zukunft aufgespart.'

A quick glance through the concordance confirms the impression of a distinctive usage of both terms: while Zion occurs 154 times, Jerusalem is used 669 times.[6] Thus, the frequency of Jerusalem is four times that of Zion. Although Jerusalem is employed in a much wider range than Zion, this term nevertheless is more distinct, i.e. theologically sharper. In the Book of Isaiah Zion and Jerusalem stand parallel to each other 17 times. However, in none of the cases pre-exilic provenience can be surely claimed.[7] The coalescence of Zion-Jerusalem seems to be a sign of a later period, i.e. exilic-postexilic.

It is worthy to take note of the distribution of Zion in the Hebrew Bible too. One third of the 154 times Zion is used, is found in the Book of Isaiah (47 times): (PrIsa: 29 times; DtIsa: 11 times; TrIsa 7 times.), but only 17 times in Jeremiah, and not even once in Ezekiel. This cannot be a coincidence, but must rather be considered as a conscious avoidance of Zion in this book.[8] It is interesting to note that the term 'YHWH Zebaot' likewise lacks in Ezekiel (62 times in Isaiah; 82 times in Jeremiah; 53 times in Zecheriah; 24x Malachi).[9] Why did the priestly circles, which stood behind the Book of Ezekiel, have such a problem to integrate Zion in their vision of a restored post-exilic Israel? Did they fear that 'Zion' would not work well together with their concept of the temple?[10] Were they afraid that Zion would attract foreigners – those invited to Zion in Isaiah and the Psalms – and so pollute the holy city and the temple?

Jerusalem is mentioned 49 times in Isaiah (PrIsa 30 times; DtIsa 10 times; TrIsa 9 times), 107 times in Jeremiah and only 26 times in Ezekiel; conspicuous is the fact that it does not even occur once in Ezek. 40–48.[11] Thus Isaiah qualifies as the only major prophetic book which uses Zion and Jerusalem equally. In the following study

---

[6] See F.I. Andersen, A.D. Forbes, *The Vocabulary of the Old Testament*, Rome 1992.

[7] Isa. 2:3; 4:3, 4; 10:12, 32; 24:23; 30:19; 31:9; 33:20; 37:22, 32; 40:9; 41:27; 52:1, 2; 62:1; 64:9.

[8] Th. Renz, 'The Use of the Zion Tradition in the Book of Ezekiel', in: R.S. Hess, G.J. Wenham (eds), *Zion: City of Our God*, Michigan 1999, 77-103: 'It is noteworthy in any case that the Zion tradition does not seem to provide a basis for restoration' (101).

[9] See M. Rösel, *Adonaj – warum Gott 'Herr' genannt wird* (FAT, 29), Tübingen 2000, 162-3: 'Möglicherweise spiegelt sich hier eine Tendenz wider, die später besonders in Qumran beobachtet werden kann, daß JHWH entweder als 'Herr' (אדני) oder als 'Gott' (אלהים/אל) angesprochen wird'.

[10] U. Berges, 'Gottesgarten und Tempel: Die neue Schöpfung im Jesajabuch', forthcoming in *QD*, Freiburg 2001.

[11] J. Galambush, *Jerusalem in the Book of Ezekiel: The City as Yahweh's Wife* (SBL.DS, 130), Atlanta 1992.

attention is given to the concept of Zion in the Book of Isaiah, with special focus on Zion as literary personage in the plot of the book.[12]

2 Zion in the Book of Isaiah

The foregoing overview has shown that in no other prophetic book Zion stands in such a prominent position as in Isaiah. Reading the book from the beginning to the end shows how Zion develops not only as a literary personage but as one with prophetic traits, resembling more and more the Ebed YHWH. Zion grows into the figure of the female servant who has to be convinced by God and others to accept her prophetic commission and to act according to that task.

2.1 Zion in Isaiah 1–39

The book opens with the title of 'a vision which Isaiah saw about Judah and Jerusalem' (Isa. 1:1; cf. 2:1) It has already been remarked that in a older stratum of the text both designations were used the other way around,[13] but little attention has been given to the fact that Zion is not mentioned at all in the title. This is even more remarkable if one notices that Sir. 48:24 (see also Sir. 48:18) places Zion exactly in the centre of Isaiah's prophetic activity: 'By his dauntless spirit he saw the future, and comforted the mourners in Zion'. Sirach does not mention Jerusalem or Judah in this context but puts full emphasis on Zion. Is it possible that Isa. 1:1; 2:1 do not mention Zion because of the political context of the kings of Judah, suggesting that humans may well have been kings over Judah and Jerusalem but not over Zion?

The following accusation where God summons heaven and earth is directed against his children which he had brought up (Isa. 1:2-3). The logical implication that YHWH is their father (and not Baal: see the word-play in Isa. 1:3 with his master's crib (אֵבוּס בְּעָלָיו), cf. Jer. 2:8) is pointed out in Isa. 63:16; 64:7. The woe-cry in Isa. 1:4, borrowed from the genre of a funeral lament, identifies the whole nation with these evil children. It seems that the *whole* nation is corrupt and sinful, that not one healthy spot is left on the afflicted body of the nation. There is a sudden shift from the plural 'sons/children' to the singular 'head', 'heart' and 'body'. What in modern terms might be defined as a 'national catastrophe' is here presented as a body almost beaten to

---

[12]Differently from earlier studies focusing on 'Zion' as a main theme of the Book of Isaiah, see: U. Berges, 'Sion als thema in het boek Jesaja: Nieuwe exegetische benadering en theologische gevolgen', *TTh* 39 (1999), 118-38; Idem, 'Die Zionstheologie des Buches Jesaja', *EstB* 58 (2000), 167-98.

[13]Isa. 3:1, 8; 5:3; 22:21; but see also Isa. 7:6; 36:7; 37:31, 32.

death, covered with blood and streams. This male picture is – again without previous notice – further developed by female images (Isa. 1:7). Your *country* lies desolate and your *cities* are burned down with fire, foreigners devour your *land* (אֶרֶץ, עִיר, אֲדָמָה are all feminine). Right at the end of this verse stands the *nota objectivi* fem. sing. אֹתָהּ. The desolate 'She' resembles the afflicted 'He' (cf. Lam. 1:13). The description of the wounded person in Isa. 1:5-6 has much in common with that of the suffering servant in Isa. 53: 'beaten' (נכה Hophal: Isa. 1:5; 53:4); 'sickness' (חֳלִי: except Isa. 38:9 only in Isa. 1:5 and 53:4); 'sores' (חבורה: Isa. 1:6; 53:5). Already right from the beginning of the book the reader is prepared to switch from masc. pl. to masc. sg. and to fem. sg. forms which all point to one and the same reality, i.e. to Zion and her country-side. In the midst of the devastated country a female person is left, i.e. בַּת־צִיּוֹן (Isa. 1:8) together with a group of 'we'.[14] In contrast to the beaten body of Israel provoked by the misbehaviour of the evil children there are Zion and a group of 'we'. That is to say: country and city are intimately connected with their inhabitants – for better or worse. Right from the very beginning one encounters the double-play of the suffering 'He' and the suffering 'She', a fact also noteworthy in the case of the alternation of the texts about the Ebed and Zion (Isa. 49–55).

The designation בַּת־צִיּוֹן (cf. Isa. 47:1, בְּתוּלַת בַּת־בָּבֶל) occurs in Isaiah only three times more: Isa. 37:22 'virgin daughter Zion' and Isa. 52:2 'captive daughter Zion' and Isa. 62:11 'daugther Zion'. Without overstating the issue it can be claimed that these four occurrences of בַּת־צִיּוֹן are placed on strategic points of the book: 1. at the very beginning; 2. at the moment of greatest distress because of the assault of the Assyrian army; 3. just before the return of YHWH as king and 4. after her coronation as God's bride. The designation of Zion as 'daughter' – not daughter *of* Zion, but *daughter Zion* – does not refer exclusively to Jerusalem as the capital city of Judah[15] but to the intimate relationship of YHWH with his bride. Here we encounter the West-Semitic idea of the high god of the pantheon as husband of the city. Certainly Zion is not pictured as a goddess[16] but rather as

---

[14] See J.M. Oesch, 'Jes 1,8f und das Problem der "Wir-Reden" im Jesajabuch', *ZKTh* 116 (1994), 440-6.

[15] Thus the well-known thesis of A. Fitzgerald, '*BTWLT* and *BT* as Titles for Capital Cities', *CBQ* 37 (1975), 167-83; differently E.R. Follis, 'The Holy City as Daughter', in: Idem (ed.), *Directions in Biblical Poetry* (JSOT.S, 40), Sheffield 1987, 173-184. The extra-biblical evidence is well documented in: L. Lucci, 'La figlia di Sion sullo sfondo delle culture extra-bibliche', *RivBib* 45 (1997), 258-87.

[16] But see K. Baltzer, 'Stadt-Tyche oder Zion-Jerusalem? Die Auseinandersetzung mit den Göttern der Zeit bei Deuterojesaja', in: J. Hausmann, H.J. Zobel

spouse of YHWH. Because of the destruction of Judah and Jerusalem by the Babylonians 'daughter Zion', YHWH's bride, lies desolate. The destruction of a city was – different from the modern perception – not just a mere fact of destruction but also involved the relationship of herself, her inhabitants and the main deity. In the case of the destruction of Jerusalem בַּת־צִיּוֹן mourns over the apparent loss of her relationship with YHWH. In the persona of 'daughter Zion' the cruel experience of war and destruction is highlighted. This is the case too in Jer. 4:31: 'For I heard a cry as of a woman in labour, anguish as of one bringing forth her first child, the cry of *daughter Zion* gasping for breath, stretching out her hands, "Woe is me! I am fainting before killers".'[17] To speak of a metaphor does not really hit the mark.[18] It is not *as if* Zion mourns but she *is* the one who cries bitterly. In her distress she represents a threefold relationship: a. with YHWH, her husband, b. with the population, her children and c. with her inner self.

The relationship with her children becomes visible in a twofold manner: negatively because her misbehaving children are the reason for her cruel punishment and positively because YHWH has left a small number of survivors (Isa. 1:9). Although many are struck by disaster, there is still hope left because of the remaining few (cf. Isa. 4:3).

In the funeral lament of Isa. 1:21-26 (אֵיכָה, cf. Lam. 1:1; 2:1; 4:1) Zion is depicted as totally perverted: 'How the faithful city (קִרְיָה נֶאֱמָנָה) has become a whore ...' (Isa. 1:21). The behaviour of her population has transformed Zion into the opposite of her destination. Everybody who lives in a metropolis knows how a population can pervert a city and how a mega-polis can pervert her inhabitants. The way out of this vicious circle is paved by 'justice' and 'righteousness' which have to be put into practice (Isa. 1:27). This is exactly what happens in Isa. 59:20-21 through the ones who repent from their transgressions and with whom YHWH establishes his covenant by bestowing his spirit upon them. Without these inspired people there would have been no post-exilic restoration. This is made clear right from the beginning of the book. For beter or worse Jerusalem and its people, Zion and

---

(eds), *Alttestamentlicher Glaube und Biblische Theologie (Fs H.D. Preuß)*, Stuttgart 1992, 114-9.

[17] See also Jer. 6:2, 23; Lam. 2:1, 4, 8, 13, 18.

[18] O.H. Steck, 'Zion als Gelände und Gestalt: Überlegungen zur Wahrnehmung Jerusalems als Stadt und Frau im Alten Testament', in: Idem, *Gottesknecht und Zion: Gesammelte Aufsätze zu Deuterojesaja* (FAT, 4), Tübingen 1992, 126-45: 'Kategorien wie "Personifikation" oder "Bildrede" tun ein übriges, das eigentümliche Phänomen "wegzurationalisieren" ...' (127).

her children are bound to each other.[19] Redemption does not come through an angel of God slaughtering the Assyrian army but through the ethical behaviour of Zion's population.

Once Zion is restored Torah will go forth from her for the nations (2:3). Here for the first time she plays a role regarding the nations: does her motherhood embrace also foreign peoples as it is the case in Ps. 87? The immediate context of specific locations, 'mountain', 'temple', 'Jerusalem' let one think of Zion only as a geographical place. But the expression 'to go forth' (יצא) reminds of the temple-vision in Ezek. 47; there יצא is constantly used to describe the flowing, life assuring waters from the altar of the temple. So Isa. 2:3 could be translated: 'for out of Zion flows forth the Torah' as life giving force at whose water the just send forth their roots and yield fruit in its season (Ps. 1; Jer. 17:6). It seems to be no coincidence that the song of thanksgiving in Isa. 12, at the very end of the first main section of the book, refers likewise to water in relation to Zion and the nations: 'With joy you will draw water from the wells of salvation ... let this be known in all the earth ... sing for joy, inhabitants of Zion' (יוֹשֶׁבֶת צִיּוֹן, Isa. 12:3, 6). This invitation to draw water from the wells of salvation reminds of Ps. 87:7, where pilgrims from all over the world dance and sing: 'All my springs are in you', refering to Zion.[20] It is noteworthy that the *Talmud Sukka* makes notice of the fact that on Sukkot water was drawn from the well of Shiloah and brought to the altar of the temple after a priest had recited Isa. 12:3 at the 'water-gate'. The connection of Sukkot with the gift of Torah is well established, but Isa. 2:2-4 and Isa. 12 do not point to the Torah for Israel given through Moses on mount Sinai but to the Torah for the nations to be given on mount Zion.

The expression 'out of Zion flows forth Torah' (Isa. 2:3) ought to be seen in connection with the mission of the Ebed to bring forth justice to the nations (42:1; cf. Hab. 1:4). Not only in their suffering but also in their commission to the nations Zion and Ebed fulfill an equal task – the difference: the Ebed brings forth justice to the peoples while Zion receives the nations coming to her.

---

[19] See H.-J. Hermisson, 'Die Frau Zion', in: J. van Ruiten, M. Vervenne (eds), *Studies in the Book of Isaiah (Fs W.A.M. Beuken)* (BEThL, 132), Leuven 1997, 19-39: 'Jerusalem, auch die Frau Jerusalem, ist also eine komplexe Größe aus Mauern und Menschen, und nur so nimmt sie ihre Funktion wahr: als Jahwetreue und darum die Rechtsordnung wahrende Stadt – oder sie verfehlt sie in Gestalt der Hure' (22).

[20] E. Zenger, 'Zion as Mother of the Nations in Psalm 87', in: N. Lohfink, E. Zenger, *The God of Israel and the Nations: Studies in Isaiah and the Psalms*, Collegeville 2000, 123-60.

But the only one who is himself the source of Torah is YHWH: 'Listen to me, my people, give heed to me, my nation; for Torah goes out (יצא) from me and my justice – for a light to the peoples I let rest it' (51:4). The two main lines regarding 'Torah for Israel' and 'Torah for the nations' in the Book of Isaiah come together at this point.[21] But there is one major difference: while the nations come in touch with the Torah only through the intermediation of the Ebed and Zion, the just ones of Israel possess God's Torah in their heart. This remains the privilege of the members of God's people.

To resume the findings from the occurences of Zion in the first section of the Book of Isaiah (1:1–2:5): the Book is not only about the fate of a city but about the relationship of YHWH, his wife, i.e. daughter Zion with his and her children. Like the suffering man, symbol of the nation, also Zion, the bride of YHWH, lies desolate as a dead corps. Through the sinful behaviour of her children she is transformed into a whore and only regained righteousness can save her. Hence, Zion stands for a dynamic relationship which on the one hand embraces suffered sinfulness and on the other hand the hope of restoration. Once restored through righteousness she will become the well of salvation, the spring of Torah for the nations.

But before that happens she has to be cleansed form all idle luxury and human pride symbolized by the precious outfit of the 'daughters of Zion' (Isa. 3:16-17).[22] The land which is filled with sinfulness (Isa. 2:6-22) will be cleansed from all of this and shall be '... replaced with an exalted remnant in a purified Jerusalem.'[23] The verb 'to take away' (סור) plays an important role at the beginning of the male (Isa. 3:1b) and female section (Isa. 3:18a) of the cleansing process: YHWH takes 14 items (2x7) away from the male part of the population (Isa. 3:1-3) and from the female part (Isa. 3:18-23) 21 items (3x7).[24] Thus the male and female part of the population were held equally responsible for the impurity of the city, i.e. for the transformation of her mother into a whore. Again we notice an awareness of an equal treatment of the male and female components[25] (cf. Isa. 1:2-9). This is also

---

[21] I. Fischer, *Tora für Israel – Tora für die Völker: Das Konzept des Jesajabuches* (SBS, 164), Stuttgart 1995. Tora for Israel in Isa. 1:10; 5:24; 8:16, 20; 30:9; 42:21, 24; 51:7; Tora for the nations in Isa. 2:3; 24:5; 42:4; 51:4.

[22] Schmitt, 'The City as Woman', 99: 'The city as woman is not far in the speaker's mind when the topic is women in the city'.

[23] M.A. Sweeney, *Isaiah 1-39: With an Introduction to Prophetic Literature* (FOTL, 16), Grand Rapids 1996, 108.

[24] A.H. Bartelt, *The Book around Immanuel: Style and Structure in Isaiah 2-12*, Winona Lake 1996, 220.

[25] See J. Magonet, 'Isaiah 2:1–4:6: Some Poetic Structures and Tactics', *ACEBT*

the case of the conclusion of the 'cleansing section' in Isa. 3:25–4:1: 'your men (מְתַיִךְ) shall fall by the sword and your leading class in battle (גְבוּרָתֵךְ).' What is important is the fact that just at the end of the section Isa. 1:2–4:6 Zion is addressed personally. At the moment where the deadly fate of her children comes into the picture Zion herself is addressed: it is *your* men who are slaughtered (cf. Lam. 2:21). For a short moment the personification of Zion as a female figure is intensified: she is spoken to – we will see later on that she also has a voice to speak. That Zion is addressed here is also confirmed by the mention of 'her gates' (Isa. 3:26) which lament and mourn – a fact comparable to that in Lam. 1:4; 2:8, 18. That the walls, gates, streets or places of Jerusalem are mourning simply means that the city herself laments over her destruction ('synecdoche'): she sits ravaged on the ground like the princess among the provinces in Lam. 1:1. What happens to the inanimate elements of the city and what happens to the population means one and the same thing and has always to do with Zion/Jerusalem herself. This is true for the negative aspects of destruction but also for the positive ones of the restoration. Like abandoned women in the turmoil of war and its aftermath (4:1) lady Zion is searching for help; the fate of her daughters is that of her own (4:4).

It is not by chance that at the end of the first main section of the book (Isa. 12) the motif of Zion stands central, just before the oracles about the nations (Isa. 13–23). The nations are invited to draw water with joy from the wells of salvation, i.e. to accept the life giving Torah flowing forth from Zion. But in order to do so they have to give up their aggression against 'mount Zion'.

The identification of the speakers is especially difficult in this song of thanksgiving which strangely enough begins with 'and you will say': is it the prophet, the visionary from Isa. 1:1; 2:1 who speaks or God himself or somebody else?[26] And who are the 'you' (masc. pl.) in Isa. 12:3-4? The only identification is given right at the end: 'Shout aloud and sing for joy, inhabitants of Zion' (Isa. 12:6a). The term יוֹשֶׁבֶת reminds of Isa. 10:24 (עַמִּי יֹשֵׁב צִיּוֹן) who should not be afraid of the rod of Assyria, and points likewise to Isa. 40:9 (מְבַשֶּׂרֶת צִיּוֹן) who once being consoled (נחם, cf. Isa. 12:1) should not be afraid to proclaim to the cities of Judah: 'Here is your God'. The invitation to burst out in joy points to Isa. 54:1: 'sing, o barren ... burst into song and shout!' This is the final destiny of Zion: to become a place where God's praise

---

3 (1982), 71-85 (especially 82-4).

[26] A.L.H.M. van Wieringen, *The Implied Reader in Isaiah 6-12* (BInt.S, 34), Leiden 1998, 213-241, presents the different possibilities extensively.

is alive; as Isa. 62:7 puts it: 'to make Jerusalem a תְּהִלָּה in the world (cf. Isa. 61:11).

In order to reach that goal there ought to live a community in Jerusalem that fears and praises God. Isa. 12 is presented as a song of thanksgiving of the root of Jesse (Isa. 11:1, 10) which stands as a signal to the nations. As Moses and the Israelites sang a song of deliverance (Exod. 15), so does now the renewed community of Zion quoting Exod. 15:2a (cf. Ps. 118:14). To be precise: Isa. 12 does not present Zion already singing but says what she will sing 'on that day'.

The female figure of Zion as the personification of the suffering community which stands central in DtIsa can be seen too in Isa. 22:1-4 and 21:1-10.[27] The outcry in Isa. 22:4, 'Look away from me, let me weep bitter tears: do not try to comfort me (נחם) for the destruction of my beloved people (בַּת־עַמִּי)', is very close to that in Lam. 2:11, 13; 3:48 and there is no reason why Zion should not be the speaker. The same is true for the vision in Isa. 21:1-10: could it not be Zion who is invited to receive the vision of the destruction and fall of Babel? Differently from Mic. 4:10 or Zech. 2:11 where Zion herself is exiled to Babylon, in Isaiah she does not move. What Zion has heard from the LORD she makes known to 'my threshed one, the son of my threshing floor', i.e. to the suffering community in Jerusalem ('to you', 2. masc. pl.). Zion is not only dressed in prophetic garments but also in those of someone who receives an audition from God.[28]

At the end of Isa. 33 one finds the expression 'Zion, the city of our appointed festivals' (v. 20) which points to a liturgical setting; even more so because of the designation of Jerusalem/Zion as a 'tent', whose stakes will never be pulled up. This picture returns in Isa. 54:2, where Zion is told to enlarge her tent. The liturgical context is confirmed by the close relation of Isa. 33:17-24 with the psalms of the Korahites (esp. Pss. 46; 48) and the stress with lies on the 'we' of the community (Isa. 33:2, 14, 20, 21, 22). The most probable candidate for the feast is Sukkot, regarding the elements of 'tent', 'water'[29] (cf. Isa. 12) and 'God as the one who establishes the law' (Isa. 33:22).

But how can YHWH be proclaimed as saviour by the remnant community (Isa. 33:22) while Zion had been destroyed? At this point of the 'drama', the Book of Isaiah shows a specific interest, different

---

[27] Female personification of Jerusalem occurs also in Isa. 17:10-11; 29:3-6, both in a context of judgement.

[28] B. Gosse, 'Le "moi" prophétique de l'oracle contre Babylone d'Isaïe XXI,1-10', *RB* 93 (1986), 70-84, detects a number of analogies between Isa. 21:1-10 and Isa. 60–62.

[29] See Isa. 33:21; compare with Ps. 46:5; Ezek. 47; Joel 4:18; Zech. 14:8.

from that of Jeremiah or Ezekiel. While those books record explicitly the fall of Judah and Jerusalem the same is not true for Isaiah. Here the exilic disaster forms without doubt too the background for the book, but at no point does one hear about the burning of the city, the killing or the deportation of her inhabitants. This lacuna has to do with the ideological outlook of the Book of Isaiah: Zion cannot fall into the hands of the enemy because YHWH protects her. She is well punished and ravaged but she is never conquered! To strengthen this point the destruction of Edom (Isa. 34), symbol of all hostile forces, preludes the eschatological scenery of Zion (Isa. 35): 'For the LORD has a day of vengeance, a year of vindication by Zion's cause' (Isa. 34:8; cf. 61:2). While Isa. 34 presents the fatal end of the enemy, Isa. 35 depicts the salvation of Zion: 'The ransomed of the LORD shall return, and come to Zion with singing ...' (v. 10). At the point where the exilic fate of Zion should have been placed in Isaiah one finds the attack of Sennacherib against the city of God (Isa. 36–37). And just at the moment of greatest affliction Hezekiah, the example of a pious king, prays to God in the temple (37:14). His prayer culminates in the petition: 'So now, YHWH our God, save us (cf. 33:22) from his hands, so that the kingdoms of the earth may know that you alone are the LORD' (37:20). In reaction to this prayer YHWH answers that Zion despises the futile attempts of Sennacherib to conquer her. At this crucial point of the book one finds a beautiful personification of Zion: 'She despises you, she scorns you – virgin daughter Zion; she tosses her head – behind your back, daughter Jerusalem.' Here in a word of YHWH himself the expression בְּתוּלַת בַּת־צִיּוֹן comes very close to the West-Semitic idea of the capital city as goddesses married to the patron god of that city, i.e. Zion to YHWH.[30] YHWH is bound to Zion by marriage; this is clearly stated in Isa. 50:1 ('bill of divorce'). He is her husband who for a moment had forsaken her (Isa. 54:4-7). In Isa. 62:4-5 YHWH marries the land of Israel and rejoices as her bridegroom.[31]

Not only does 'daughter Zion' shake her head but YHWH gives her important things to say too. She plays the role of a *defensor fidei* who asks scornfully: 'Whom have you mocked and reviled? Against whom have you raised your voice and haughtily lifted your eyes? Against the Holy One of Israel!' (Isa. 37:23). It is in *her* mouth that the 'mono-

---

[30] M.C.A. Korpel, *A Rift in the Clouds: Ugaritic and Hebrew Descriptions of the Divine* (UBL, 8), Münster 1990, 230: 'In view of this evidence one is inclined to regard the frequent use of *btwlh* "young woman" to denote Israel or Jerusalem as a conscious replacement of the Canaanite epithet for goddesses'.

[31] Compare Jer. 2:32; 3:14; Ezek. 23; Hos. 1–3.

logue of arrogance' of Sennacherib (37:24aβ-25) is placed. In the centre of the attack, daughter Zion stands firmly, sure of YHWH and of herself, an example for everybody in similar situations of distress! That she is called בְּתוּלַת בַּת־צִיּוֹן also underlines her queenly qualities: unlike Sidon (Isa. 23:12) and Babel (Isa. 47:1) who are lowered from their queenly status, she is presented as fearless and as a strong warrior. The representation of Anat as female warrior comes to mind;[32] but unlike her, Zion is God's female consort, his bride, giving birth to their offspring.

It is not by chance that in Isa. 37:31-32 Zion is pictured for the last time as 'mountain'.[33] After the defeat of Sennacherib at the foot of the holy mountain the imagery of Zion changes significantly. She is neither the place to which nations move for pilgrimage (Isa. 2:3), nor the place against which the enemy direct their hostile forces (Isa. 10:32), nor the place of refuge (Isa. 37:32), but a personage to whom God orders to speak to the heart (Isa. 40:2). Contrary to the feminine personification of Zion in Isa. 40-66, in Isa. 1-39 she is never depicted as mother of growing or grown children.[34]

2.2 Zion in Isaiah 40-55

The personification of Zion gets intensified in these chapters which have one major goal: the restoration of Zion and of the cities of Judah. The guiding term throughout Isa. 40-52, 'to comfort' (נחם),[35] comes by surprise: why should Zion be comforted, after her enemy had been defeated (Isa. 36-37) and she herself had been presented as a fearless woman? This incoherence shows anew how the Book of Isaiah avoids to depict the exilic disaster which nevertheless stands at the background of these chapters (see Cyrus in 44:28; 45:1). In the same way Isa. 40:1-11 presents an exilic scenery without explicitly stating it. The reader has to fill in this gap with his own knowledge, especially with information from 2 Kgs 24-25 and from the Book of Lamentations.

---

[32] See P.L. Day, 'Anat', in: K. van der Toorn et al. (eds), *Dictionary of Deities and Demons in the Bible*, Leiden 1995, 62-77: 'Her epithet *btlt* indicates that she is (as defined by her culture) a marriageable adolescent female, but it is precisely because she "refuses to grow up" and take her place in the adult, female sphere of marriage and reproductivity that she can remain active in the male spheres of combat and hunting' (65).

[33] See Isa. 2:3; 4:5; 8:18; 10:12, 32; 16:1; 18:7; 24:23; 29:8; 31:4.

[34] Thus J.J. Schmitt, 'The City as Woman in Isaiah 1-39', in: C.C. Broyles, C.A. Evans (eds), *Writing and Reading the Scroll of Isaiah: Studies of an Interpretive Tradition* (VT.S, 70), Leiden 1997, 118.

[35] Isa. 49:13; 51:3, 12, 19; 52:9.

It has been indicated that the exile reactivated the old ancient Near Eastern tradition of city laments[36] in Israel in which the city-goddess mourns over the destruction of her city and over the death and deportation of the inhabitants. This tradition too is important for the interpretation of the Zion-texts in Isa. 40–66. What has been widely accepted as an explanation for the discourses in the Book of Lamentations that '... the grief of Daughter Zion is expressed in a way reminiscent of the weeping goddesses of Mesopotamian city lament',[37] has to be applied likewise to the situation at the beginning of the restoration. YHWH, Zion's bridegroom tries to convince her that he has taken her back and that her protection is assured. She is addressed as city and woman (as daughter, wife, widow, mother, bride). The act of destruction immediately calls for feminine personifications like the ones in Lamentations and in other texts of the Hebrew Bible. The term בַּת־עַמִּי[38] thereby points to the suffering community itself. But in the process of restoration the feminine personifications of Zion too play an important role. The separation of the city and her inhabitants, i.e. of Zion and her children, has not been overcome with the end of the exile.[39] YHWH and Zion have to find each other again. Only once she gets convinced that consolation becomes effective for her (Isa. 40:1-2) she will be able to act as מְבַשֶּׂרֶת for the cities of Judah (Isa. 40:9-11). The 'deficiency of exile' is not to be resolved by YHWH alone but he needs the cooperation of his bride and city. Therefore he sends messengers to comfort his people and to speak to the heart of Jerusalem (Isa. 40:1-2), a situation similar to that of Gen. 50:21, when Joseph consoled his brethren and spoke to their hearts. The expression דִּבֶּר עַל־לֵב does not come from the language of love and tenderness but from that of rational argumentation. God is arguing *against* (עַל) Zion's fear and mistrust. He tries to convince her to give

---

[36] See recently M. Emmendörffer, *Der ferne Gott: Eine Untersuchung der alttestamentlichen Volksklagelieder vor dem Hintergrund der mesopotamischen Litteratur* (FAT, 21), Tübingen 1998.

[37] P.K. McCarter, 'Zion', in: Van der Toorn *et al.* (eds), *Dictionary of Deities and Demons in the Bible*, 1773; see also P. Tull Willey, *Remember the Former Things: The Recollection of Previous Texts in Second Isaiah* (SBL.DS, 161), Atlanta 1997, 107: 'Monotheistic Israelite literature similarly personified the female city itself, but could not make her divine.'

[38] Isa. 22:4; Jer. 4:11; 6:26; 8:11, 19, 21, 22, 23; 9:6; 14:17; Lam. 2:11; 3:48; 4:3, 6, 10.

[39] Contrary to Hermisson, 'Frau Zion', 28, regarding 45:13-15: 'Hier, wo das Exil schon überholt ist, muß über eine Differenz von Stadt und Bewohnern nicht mehr nachgedacht werden; an die Stelle der Differenz tritt wieder die einheitliche, wenn auch in sich gegliederte Größe »Frau Zion« ....'

up her negative attitude and to trust in a new future with him.[40] But which woman would easily trust a husband who must acknowledge that he abandoned her without a bill of divorce (50:1), thus leaving her in a state of 'legal vacuum'. Does YHWH succeed in convincing her to put her trust in him again, after all the negative experiences she had to endure? Does she accept her role of 'herald of good tidings' (40:9-11)? And what is the reaction of her children in the turmoil of this dramatic relationship?[41] The motto בשׂר (Isa. 40:9) connects the prologue with 41:27; 52:7; 60:6 and 61:1. Similarly to the Ebed (Isa. 42; 49), Zion too receives a prophetic task. As Zion and the Ebed play similar roles in their sufferings so they do in the period of restoration. While his task regards the tribes of Israel (49:6) her commission is directed to the cities of Judah. But while the Ebed becomes more and more silent (53:7), Zion constantly grows in confidence until her prophetic appearance in Isa. 61 in favour of the poor and oppressed.[42] By then her commission, which in Isa. 40:9-11 was still diffused, has become clear. But between receiving her task and acting accordingly, Zion travels a long way, during which she is addressed by God and others.

The first text to be mentioned here is Isa. 45:11-13, 14-17. The vv. 11-13 discuss the question why Cyrus, a foreign king, is called to restore the city of YHWH? Does that mean that the davidic prerogatives have been transferred to the Persian empire? YHWH does not allow any questioning of his decisions: He himself did arouse Cyrus so that he would rebuild 'my city' (עִירִי) and release 'my exiles' (גָּלוּתִי) (cf. Isa. 44:28; 45:1). The emphasis lies upon the rebuilding of Jerusalem, certainly including the reconstruction of the temple. The term גָּלוּתִי does not occur any more in Isaiah and the combination of the restoration of the city together with the mentioning of the 'Gola' reminds of the edict of Cyrus in Ezra 1:1-4, 5-11.[43]

---

[40] G. Fischer, 'Die Redewendung דבר על לב im AT: Ein Beitrag zum Verständnis von Jes 40,2', *Bib.* 65 (1984), 244-250: 'so ergäbe sich als Wort-für-Wort-Übersetzung von דבר על לב: gegen das Herz von jemandem anreden. Die Grundbedeutung des Ausdrucks wäre dann "gegen eine vorhandene (negative) Einstellung anreden=umzustimmen versuchen" ' (250).

[41] See K.P. Darr, *Isaiah's Vision and the Family of God*, Louisville 1994.

[42] O.H. Steck, 'Der Gottesknecht als "Bund" und "Licht": Beobachtungen im Zweiten Jesaja', *ZThK* 90 (1993), 117-34 (esp. 127ff.); U. Berges, *Das Buch Jesaja: Komposition und Endgestalt* (HerBSt, 16), Freiburg 1998, 443-55.

[43] R.G. Kratz, *Kyros im Deuterojesaja-Buch: Redaktionsgeschichtliche Untersuchungen zu Entstehung und Theologie von Jes 40-55* (FAT, 1), Tübingen 1991, 106, regarding Isa. 44:28; 45:13: '... chronistische Theologie in vorchronistischer Gestalt.'

In Isa. 45:14 YHWH addresses a feminine person and promises her the wealth and honour of Egypt, Ethiopia and the Sabeans. There is no reason to change the fem. suffixes into masc. ones in order to make them fit 'Israel', 'Cyrus'[44] or the Gola.[45] They do simply point to Zion as the destiny of the wealth of the nations.[46] It is to her that their riches are brought (cf. Isa. 60). The climax of the procession of the nations (Isa. 45:14) is their confession: 'God is with you alone, and there is no other; there is no god besides him'. It is through the contact with Zion that the nations reach the knowledge of God: 'Truly, you are a God who hides himself, O God of Israel, the Saviour' (Isa. 45:15). Once Jerusalem is rebuild and the nations acknowledge YHWH, the restoration will be completed.[47] Both the Ebed and Zion cannot complete their task without taking into account the reaction of the nations.

That Zion represents the final goal of God's salvific action is highlighted in Isa. 46:13, which stands in the centre of Isa. 46–47. These chapters deal with the fall of her enemy, Babylon: 'I will bring near my deliverance, it is not far off, and my salvation will not tarry; I will put salvation in Zion, for Israel my glory'. There is no other way showing תִּפְאָרָה in post-exilic Israel than to bring salvation for Zion. The identity of Israel after the exile is centred on the 'holy city' where one leans on the God of Israel (Isa. 48:1-2); but this has to be done 'in truth and righteousness'.[48] An important theme in the Book of Isaiah is introduced here: membership of Zion is not any more a question of ethnic descent but of ethical conduct. Merely calling themselves after the עִיר הַקֹּדֶשׁ (Isa. 48:2) is not enough!

Once Babylon has fallen (Isa. 47) all attention rests on Zion. Although God has fulfilled the pre-condition for a renewed relationship with her, does she accept her commission to proclaim the good news to the cities of Judah? Reading Isa. 49:14 that seems not (yet) the case: 'YHWH has forsaken me, my LORD has forgotten me'. Like some

---

[44]See K. Baltzer, *Deutero-Jesaja* (KAT, 10/2), Gütersloh 1999, 312.

[45]W.A.M. Beuken, *Jesaja*, deel 2A, Nijkerk 1986, 246: 'Niet Israël of Sion maar de ballingen worden aangesproken'.

[46]M.C.A. Korpel, J.C. de Moor, *The Structure of Classical Hebrew Poetry: Isaiah 40-55* (OTS, 41), Leiden 1998, 263, note 15: 'The suffixes prove that it is Zion who is addressed here, without being introduced at all. This is not uncommon in prophetic literature, see e.g. Jer. 13:20; Mic. 1:14, 16; 2:10.'

[47]See H. Leene, 'Universalism or Nationalism? Isaiah XLV, 9-13 and its Context', *Bijdr.* 35 (1974), 309-34.

[48]Isa. 48:1fin: 'but not in truth or right', seems to be an addition from a later hand; see R.P. Merendino, 'Jes 49,14-26: Jahwes Bekenntnis zu Sion und die neue Heilszeit', *RB* 89 (1982), 500; differently Beuken, *Jesaja*, deel 2A, 281.

of the greatest prophets (Moses, Elijah, Jeremiah) she struggles with God and goes through a deep crisis of faith, a situation similar to that of the גֶּבֶר in Lam. 3. Zion behaves exactly like Rachel in Jer. 31:15: 'Rachel is weeping for her children; she refuses to be comforted (נחם) for her children, because they are no more'. Since God cannot cope with her depressive mood anymore he argues for a change of attitude: 'Keep your voice from weeping, and your eyes from tears; for there is a reward for your work (שָׂכָר לִפְעֻלָּתֵךְ, see Isa. 40:10) ... they shall come back from the land of the enemy; there is hope for your future' (Jer. 31:16-17).[49] In Jeremiah too, as in Deutero-Isaiah, the destiny of the cities of Judah is linked with that of Jerusalem: 'Once more they shall use these words in the land of Judah and in its towns when I restore their fortunes: "YHWH bless you, O abode of righteousness, O holy hill (נְוֵה־צֶדֶק הַר הַקֹּדֶשׁ)" ' (Jer. 31:23). But differently from Jer. 30-31 the struggle of YHWH with Zion in Deutero-Isaiah does not come easily to a (happy-) end. Zion complains that God abandoned her and left her without any legal protection (Isa. 49:14).[50] It is interesting to see that in the response of YHWH (Isa. 49:15) the female image – now as mother – is applied to himself. The personification of Zion as a woman is so strong that God is presented in a female image.[51] This is even against the logic of the argument which would have required God to be presented as a male, i.e. Zion's husband. Isa. 49:14-26 shows how intermingled the concepts of Zion as mother and as city are. While in vv. 14-20 the aspect of the city is predominent (walls, ruins, crampedness) the emphasis in vv. 21-26 lies upon the motherhood of Zion.

In Isa. 49:21 one hears the voice of Zion confused by what happens with and around her. Her former mistrust changes into confusion. It is the repopulation of the destroyed and abandoned city which strikes her with unbelief: 'You will say in your heart: "Who has borne me these?" ' Slowly she begins to open up for the future. YHWH explains to her how this miraculous repopulation will take place: he simply lifts his hand as a signal to the nations so that they will bring back the once deported children. But Zion is not yet convinced and asks:

---

[49]G. Fischer, *Das Trostbüchlein: Text, Komposition und Theologie von Jer 30-31* (SBB, 26), Stuttgart 1993, 277: 'Der um ihre Kinder klagenden Mutter untersagt er nun das weitere Trauern.'

[50]Baltzer, *Deutero-Jesaja*, 406: 'Damit ist die Frau rechtlich gesehen in einem miserablen Status zwischen Ehe und Scheidung.'

[51]This strengthens the proposal of J.J. Schmitt, 'The Motherhood of God and Zion as Mother', *RB* 92 (1985), 557-69, that the female image of Zion has inspired the depiction of God as mother; see also M.I. Gruber, 'The Motherhood of God in Second Isaiah', *RB* 90 (1983), 351-9: 'The LORD is mother of Zion' (356).

'Can the prey be taken from the mighty, or the captives of a tyrant be rescued?' (Isa. 49:24).[52] She objects that it is not an easy thing to free her children from the hands of mighty nations. God's answer is clear: do not worry, I will free them and make your oppressors eat their own flesh (Isa. 49:25-26). At this point the discussion goes on between YHWH and Zion's children.[53] This indicates clearly that at least three parties are involved in the process of post-exilic restoration: God, Zion and her children. God fiercely contests their charges that he divorced their mother and sold them into debt slavery and he wonders why there is such an unbelief regarding his power to save and to rescue (Isa. 50:1-3). Apparently there is none of Zion's children who is willing to go on with YHWH who left them and their mother abandoned. Here the drama of relationship reaches a climax: Is there nobody left who accepts YHWH's offer of comfort and consolation?

At this crucial moment somebody's voice is heard who is totally receptive to the word of God and who is willing to sustain the weary (Isa. 50:4-9). This one keeps on hoping and knows that the crowd of his enemies will disappear (v. 9b). In the editorial comment (vv. 10-11) the unbelieving children of Zion are invited to join the example of the one who did not turn backwards and is now identified as the Servant.[54] From Isa. 54:17 onwards those children of Zion who are willing to obey to the voice of the Ebed are called עֲבָדִים.[55] They are the promised offspring of the Ebed (Isa. 53:10), Zion's children taught by YHWH himself (Isa. 54:13) (למד: see Isa. 8:16; 50:4). The problem of Isa. 50:2, i.e. God's calling without getting any response, has now been partially resolved. There is a group of people following the Ebed that is willing to react positively to YHWH's invitation. Without these

---

[52] Merendino, 'Jes 49,14-26', 341-2: 'Ist es aber nicht einfacher anzunehmen, dass hier Sion selbst direkt redet und ihre Zweifel über die vorher angekündigte Befreiung der Gefangenen und die Wiederherstellung der Stadt äussert?' See K. Baltzer, 'Liberation from Debt Slavery after the Exile in Second Isaiah and Nehemiah', in: P.D. Miller, et al. (eds), *Ancient Israelite Religion (Fs F.M. Cross)*, Philadelphia 1987, 477-84, interpreting the rescuing as one form debt slavery.

[53] R. Abma, *Bonds of Love: Methodic Studies of Prophetic Texts with Marriage Imagery (Isaiah 50:1-3 and 54:1-10, Hosea 1-3, Jeremiah 2-3)* (SSN, 40), Assen 1999, 64: 'Thus while in Isaiah 49:14-26 Zion is addressed concerning her sons, in Isaiah 50:1-3 the sons of Zion are addressed concerning their mother.'

[54] See W.A.M. Beuken, 'Jes 50,10-11: Eine kultische Paränese zur dritten Ebed-prophetie', *ZAW* 85 (1973), 168-182: 'Der Sprecher setzt nicht voraus, daß unter seiner Zuhörerschaft Leute sind, die Gott fürchten und dabei auf den Knecht hören, sondern er fragt, ob es solche Menschen gibt' (171).

[55] J. Blenkinsopp, 'A Jewish Sect of the Persian Period', *CBQ* 52 (1990), 5-20: 'I read this editorial comment as an important link between the prophetic servant of whom it speaks and the 'servants' of the last two chapters of the book' (13).

people, i.e. without the Servants, Zion's commission to act as herald of good tidings to the cities of Judah would have been frustrated. It is the offspring of the Ebed that keeps mother Zion moving towards a restored relationship with YHWH.

Throughout Isa. 49–55 the features of Ebed and Zion, of his and her offspring are merging more and more. This leads to the identification, up to a certain degree, of both figures. The fact that male and female Ebed share many traits in common has already been extensively shown.[56] But whereas the identification of the female Ebed as Zion/Jerusalem is undisputed the opposite holds true for the identification of the male Ebed. If one accepts the view that the Ebed is a corporate personality representing the Gola, i.e. that part of the deportees which is willing to return to Zion and to strive for her restoration,[57] the merging of both features will be easy to understand. Once the returning part of the Gola comes back to Zion, it will try to convince her to trust in YHWH as creator and liberator. Those invited in Isa. 50:10 to hear the voice of the Ebed, are called upon to give up their unbelief and to join the group of the Servants.[58] They are the true children of Zion who can help her to overcome her grief and to accept her vocation.

After the invitation to listen to the voice of the Ebed (Isa. 50:10), the Servant directs himself to the ones that pursue righteousness and seek YHWH (Isa. 51:1); these are regarded as the new members of the 'Ebed-community'. They should look at the rock from which there were hewn, at the quarry from which they were dug; these are all expressions which refer to Zion.[59] At the same time they should re-

---

[56] See L.E. Wilshire, 'The Servant-City: A New Interpretation of the "Servant of the LORD" in the Servant Songs of Deutero-Isaiah', *JBL* 94 (1975), 356-67; J.F.A. Sawyer, 'Daughter of Zion and Servant of the LORD in Isaiah: A Comparison', *JSOT* 44 (1989), 89-107; M.C.A. Korpel, 'The Female Servant of the LORD in Isaiah 54', in: B. Becking, M. Dijkstra (eds), *On Reading Prophetic Texts: Gender Specific and Related Studies in Memory of Fokkelien van Dijk-Hemmes* (BInt.S, 18), Leiden 1996, 153-67; A. Brenner, 'Identifying the Speaker-in-Text and the Reader's Location in Prophetic Texts: The Case of Isaiah 50', in: Idem, C. Fontaine (eds), *A Feminist Companion to Reading the Bible: Approaches, Methods and Strategies*, Sheffield 1997, 136-50.

[57] See Berges, *Jesaja*, 358-68.

[58] Compare F. Matheus, *Singt dem Herrn ein neues Lied: Die Hymnen Deuterojesajas* (SBS, 141), Stuttgart 1990, 131: 'Vielleicht müssen hier die Gottesfürchtigen (50,10) stärker in den Blick genommen werden; in ihnen spiegelt sich möglicherweise eine Gruppe Gottestreuer wider, die nach dem Exil im Lande das "wahre Israel" verkörpern.'

[59] O.H. Steck, 'Zions Tröstung: Beobachtungen und Fragen zu Jesaja 51,1-11', in: Idem, *Gottesknecht und Zion: Gesammelte Aufsätze zu Deuterojesaja* (FAT,

member the 'success story' of Sara and Abraham which were made into a multitude by God's blessing. Two major pre-exilic traditions are thus combined: the one of Zion which stands for stability and the one of the patriarchs which centres on progeny.

The fact that these new members of the Ebed-community represent the inner side of Zion herself, can be inferred from Isa. 51:12: 'I, I am he who comforts you (masc. pl.), why then are you afraid (2. fem. sing.) of a mere mortal who must die, a human being who fades like grass' (cf. Isa. 40:6-8). This enlarged Ebed-group too receives its prophetic commission in Isa. 51:16: 'I have put my words in your mouth ... saying to Zion: "you are my people".'

The growing group of those listening to the voice of the Ebed urges Jerusalem to stand up and to believe that the time of distress has come to an end (51:17-23; 52:1-2). This includes the end of oppression and social injustice: the uncircumcised and the unclean will have no access to the 'holy city' anymore. The 'captive daughter Zion' is called upon to loose the bounds from her neck. The poor people which were sold for nothing (see Amos 2:6) will be redeemed without money (Isa. 52:3) (cf. Neh. 5). As God was able to free the prey from the mighty (Isa. 49:25), i.e. his people out of the hands of foreign powers, so he is able now to ransom the ones 'taken away' (Isa. 52:5) by internal oppressors. The cry of joy in Isa. 52:7 shows how eagerly YHWH was awaited as just king and liberator of the oppressed.

Once YHWH has arrived as king in Zion, she is invited to burst into singing (Isa. 52:9; 54:1) and to enlarge her tent for all her offspring that will settle the desolate cities (Isa. 54:3). The motif of the desolate towns returns in Isa. 61:4, following the prophetic proclamation of the I-figure. Once again we see that the prophetic commission of Zion is especially directed to the cities of Judah: the post-exilic restoration should not be effective only for the capital but also for the countryside.

Reading through Isa. 54-55 it is striking that Zion/Jerusalem[60] is not mentioned anymore even though feminine images are abundantly present. Likewise the figure of the Ebed has disappeared.[61] Does

---

4), Tübingen 1992, 73-91.

[60] 'Zion' in Isa. 49:14; 51:3, 11, 16; 52:1, 2, 7, 8; 'Jerusalem' in Isa. 52:1, 2. The next following 'Zion-cluster' is found in Isa. 60-62: 60:14; 61:3; 62:1, 11.

[61] F. Landy, 'The Construction of the Subject and the Symbolic Order: A Reading of the Last Three Suffering Servant Songs', in: P.R. Davies, D.J.A. Clines (eds), *The New Literary Criticism and the Hebrew Bible* (JSOT.S, 144), Sheffield 1993, 60-71: 'Are the mystically vindicated servant beyond death and the joyful mother Zion, whose children return to her womb, metaphors for each other, or the same?' (71).

this indicate that male and female Ebed did merge succesfully? The smooth transition of the addressed female figure, i.e. Zion, to the appearance of the Servants in Isa. 54:17 points in this direction: 'No weapon that is fashioned against you (2. fem. sing.) shall prosper ... This is the heritage of the Servants ...'. In Isa. 55 Zion finally gets active and all her unbelief and mistrust are left behind. She invites everyone who thirsts to come to the waters, even the ones who do not have money to buy wine and milk (Isa. 55:1-3a). This is the first time that Zion's voice sounds totally positive. These verses are not only '... an invitation to come to the new Jerusalem where Yahweh reigns and to share in its wealth',[62] but one launched by Zion herself.[63] It is in her, after the arrival of her kingly bride, that the poor and thirsty will participate in God's blessings.[64] Zion's invitation is not simply for feeding the poor but for a rich banquet.[65]

With all those who follow the invitation of city-mother Zion, YHWH will make an everlasting covenant (Isa. 55:3b-5) and establish them as a נָגִיד for the nations. While the duty of the male Ebed was among other things directed towards the nations, it is the female Servant to whom they run because 'YHWH your God, the Holy One of Israel has glorified you' (2. fem. sing.) (v. 5). This is the last feminine form pointing to Zion before Isa. 60, a chapter totally centered on the theme of her splendour (פאר) (Isa. 60:7, 9, 13).

2.3 Zion in Isaiah 56–66

Why does it take so long until the expected splendour of Zion is mentioned anew in Isa. 60-62? Something must have gone wrong in the post-exilic program of restoration which led to a delay in the final realization of God's plan for Zion. What went wrong was the cultic and social behaviour of post-exilic Israel which perverted even Zion. This is clearly to be deduced from 57:6-13 presenting a negative blue-print of her.[66] Facing Zion's apostasy YHWH asked if he could be appeased

---

[62] H.C. Spykerboer, 'Isaiah 55:1-5: The Climax of Deutero-Isaiah: An Invitation to Come to the New Jerusalem', in: J. Vermeylen (ed.), *The Book of Isaiah* (BEThL, 81), Leuven 1989, 357-59 (here 358).

[63] J.L. Koole, *Isaiah III: Isaiah 49-55*, Leuven 1998, 400 proposes 'God' as speaker; Beuken, *Jesaja*, deel 2B, Nijkerk 1983, 278, thinks of the 'prophet'.

[64] In Jer. 31:7-14, 23-25 similar images are used but the emphasis there lies upon the physical weak (blind, lame, those with child).

[65] Baltzer, *Deutero-Jesaja*, 592-93: 'So halte ich es für die wahrscheinlichste Lösung, dass in beiden Fällen Zion/Jerusalem zum Kommen aufruft, d.h. die ganze Einheit v.1-3a spricht. Sie, die Repräsentantin der Stadt – nicht die Frau Weisheit und keine Göttin – lädt zum Festmahl ein.'

[66] M.E. Biddle, 'Lady Zion's Alter Egos: Isaiah 47:1-15 and 57:6-13 as Struc-

(nif. נחם). Does the project of comfort and restoration get frustrated even after the establishment of the Ebed-community? Not only in the deep valleys do abominations take place, but even on top of a high and lofty mountain (עַל הַר־גָּבֹהַּ וְנִשָּׂא) on which Zion has set her bed to offer sacrifices (Isa. 57:7). Her task to ascend to a high mountain to proclaim good tidings (Isa. 40:9) has turned into perversion. What kind of things will the nations see when they come to the high mountain (נשא) to receive Torah from Zion (Isa. 2:2-4; 55:1-3)? A whore on her bed! But these perversions cannot stop God's program of restoration: 'whoever takes refuge in me shall possess the land and inherit my holy mountain' (Isa. 57:13b). As it had occured already before (Isa. 51-52) God's promise to Zion is maintained through some of her children. The separation between the just and the offenders does not only divide post-exilic Israel[67] but Zion herself. The concept of Zion is very broad and dynamic: she is a refuge for the just but at the same time she is sustained by them. It is only to the just that YHWH comes as גֹּאֵל (Isa. 59:20), the only place in Isa. 56-59 mentioning Zion by name: 'He will come to Zion as Redeemer, to those in Jacob who turn from transgression'. The saving action of YHWH is directed only to that part of Zion's population which turns away from sinfulness. It is upon them that God bestows his spirit and entrusts his words to them (Isa. 59:21; cf. 51:16). God's spirit rests permanently on them and their offspring (see Isa. 53:10). The sudden shift from the masc. pl. in Isa. 59:20 to the masc. sing. in v. 21 shows that a specific group is meant. God's plan for the restoration of Zion is assured through a prophetic group of people, as it was the case too in Isa. 51:12-16.

Following the bestowal of God's spirit upon this prophetic group Zion is directly addressed: 'Arise, shine; for your light has come ...'. The same sequence of prophetic bestowal followed by imperatives directed to Zion did occur in Isa. 51:16-17; 52:1.

The motif of 'light' forms an *inclusio* between Isa. 60:1-3 and vv. 19-20 while vv. 21-22, 'your people shall all be righteous; they shall possess the land forever ...' lead to the following chapter. The promise that the just will inherit the land for ever (v. 21) points anew to one of the major social issues in post-exilic times (cf. Ezek. 11:15; 33:24). Ps. 37, with its refrain about the possession of the land for the just (vv. 9, 11, 22, 29, 34), illuminates the social situation of Isa. 60:21. It probably also happened in post-exilic Judah what used to happen

---

tural Counterparts', in: R.F. Melugin, M.A. Sweeney (eds), *New Visions of Isaiah* (JSOT.S, 214), Sheffield 1996, 124-39.

[67] K. Koenen, *Heil den Gerechten – Unheil den Sündern! Ein Beitrag zur Theologie der Prophetenbücher* (BZAW, 229), Berlin 1994.

in such situations: influential people easily got their share while the little ones were pushed aside.

This is the kind of social injustice against which the prophetic figure of Isa. 61:1 stands up for. To the poor and the brokenhearted the good news (בשר) of a year of God's favour and a day of vengeance of 'our God' is proclaimed. Once again the sudden shift from 'I' to 'we' shows that it is a group speaking here. It is that group of people with whom YHWH established a covenant and upon whom he bestowed his spirit so that his word would never depart from them (Isa. 59:20-21). By now it is clear that it is nobody else than the group of Servants (Isa. 54:17) that do intervene for the poor and oppressed. In this sense it is Zion herself[68] who finally acts according to her commission as מְבַשֶּׂרֶת (Isa. 40:9). The mourning ones to whom she proclaims liberation will be called 'oaks of justice, planting of YHWH for his splendour' (Isa. 61:3). These ones will take care to rebuild the devastated cities of Judah (Isa. 61:4; see 54:3). Those among the poor who endured a double portion of shame will possess a double portion of property in the foreign countries (Isa. 61:7; ירש as in 60:21).[69] With them YHWH will establish an 'eternal covenant' (Isa. 61:7; cf. 59:21). These 'oaks of justice' planted in Zion will bring forth their shoots (צֶאֱצָאֵיהֶם) in the midst of the nations and they will be known as YHWH's blessed offspring (Isa. 61:9).

Once this has finally come true Zion will greatly rejoice in YHWH. Only then God's plan with her will be fulfilled and she will be clothed in garments of salvation and justice. Having accepted the comfort and having been strenghtened by the Ebed and his offspring, she herself fights prophetically against the conditions of injustice and oppression. On her fertile ground (Isa. 51:3) YHWH himself will cause righteousness and praise to spring up before all nations (Isa. 61:11: צְדָקָה וּתְהִלָּה). That is what the transformation of Zion by God through the intermediation of the Ebed and the Servants is all about: to become the place where justice and praise sprouts before the eyes of the world.

YHWH himself promises that he will not keep silent until this plan is fully realized (Isa. 62:1): those who work in vineyards and fields shall benefit from the products of the land but not foreigners. In order

---

[68] See the discussion in O.H. Steck, 'Zu jüngsten Untersuchungen von Jes 60-62', in: Idem, *Studien zu Tritojesaja* (BZAW, 203), Berlin 1991, 119-39 (esp. 133-35); differently W.A.M. Beuken, 'Servant and Herald of Good Tidings: Isaiah 61 as an Interpretation of Isaiah 40-55', in: J. Vermeylen (ed.), *The Book of Isaiah* (BEThL, 81), Leuven 1989, 411-42.

[69] N. Lohfink, ירש, *ThWAT*, Bd. 3, 985: 'Jedenfalls kommt hier zu der Aussage von 60,21 eine Steigerung hinzu: In der Heilszeit werden die Bewohner Jerusalems außerhalb des eigenen Landes, unter den Völkern, noch einen Zweitbesitz haben.'

that this promise becomes reality the 'reminders' (מַזְכִּרִים)⁷⁰ should not take rest to remind YHWH constantly to establish Jerusalem as praise (תְּהִלָּה) in the midst of the land (earth?) (62:6-7). This praise is offered by those who will benefit from their labour in the fields and who will be allowed to celebrate their joy in the courts of the temple (Isa. 62:9) (cf. Deut. 26). Once that is realized, restoration has reached the end: 'You (2. fem. sing.) will be called "Sought Out", "City Not Forsaken" ' (Isa. 62:12). In Isa. 62:11 it is for the last time in Isaiah that Zion is named and addressed as 'daughter'. She is neither left like a booth in a vineyard (Isa. 1:8), nor like a 'captive' woman (Isa. 52:2), but she is full of praise and justice – populated by a holy people.

3 Zion in Other Prophetic Writings

As it was indicated in the introduction the great majority of references to Zion is to be found in the Book of Isaiah. Although Zion is present in some of the other prophetic writings,⁷¹ in none of these she forms a 'thread'⁷² as she does in the Book of Isaiah. The exception perhaps is the Book of Joel where, however, Zion is never spoken to in a personal way. The references to Zion in a personal context, i.e. directly addressed or herself speaking, are few.⁷³ These verses can be classified in the following way: firstly, there are occurrences that present Zion as a female person lamenting over her suffering, as in Jer. 4:31, 'Woe is me! I am fainting before killers', (cf. Jer. 6:23) or being aggressive towards her enemy: 'May my blood be avenged on the inhabitants of Chaldea' (Jer. 51:35). Secondly, there are texts where Zion is still addressed as suffering because of the exile, but already in view of the nearby liberation: '... Now why do you cry aloud? Is there no king in you ... writhe and groan, o daugther Zion, like a woman in labour; for now you shall go forth from the city and camp in the open country; you shall go to Babylon. There you shall be rescued ...' (Mic. 4:8-13). An interesting idea is the one, which is absent in

---

⁷⁰ J. Blenkinsopp, *A History of Prophecy in Israel*, Philadelphia 1983, 247: 'These *mazkîrîm* ... are therefore charged with the task of intercession and prayer on behalf of the entire community, functions that since the beginning have been associated with the prophetic office.'

⁷¹ Jer. 3:14; 4:6, 31; 6:2, 23; 8:19; 9:18; 14:19; 26:18; 30:17; 31:6, 12; 50:5, 28; 51:10, 24, 35; Joel 2:1, 15, 23; 3:5; 4:16, 17, 21; Amos 1:2; 6:1; Obad. 17, 21; Mic. 1:13; 3:10, 12; 4:2, 7, 8, 10, 11, 13; Zeph. 3:14, 16; Zech. 1:14, 17; 2:11, 14; 8:2, 3; 9:9, 13.

⁷² For the concept of 'threading' in prophetic writings, see the article of T.A. Collins, 'Threading as a Stylistic Feature of Amos', in this volume.

⁷³ Jer . 4:31; 6:23; 51:35; Mic. 4:8, 10, 13; Zeph. 3:14, 16; Zech. 2:11, 14; 9:9, 13; without the explicit mention of Zion: Mic. 7:7-13.

Isaiah, that 'Zion' is transferred to Babylon: 'Woe, Zion escape [not like the NRSV reads: 'Up! escape to Zion ...'], inhabitants of daughter Babylon' (Zech. 2:11; cf. Mic. 4:10). Thirdly, one encounters Zion in a personal context where she is positively addressed, as in Zech. 2:14: 'Sing and rejoice, o daughter Zion! For lo, I will come and dwell in your midst, says the LORD' (cf. Zech. 9:9, 13). It is remarkable that the end of Zephaniah resembles in many aspects the song in Isa. 12 (cf. Isa. 54:1): 'Sing aloud, daughter Zion; shout, Israel! Rejoice and exult with all your heart, daughter Jerusalem. The LORD has taken away (סור) the judgement against you, he turned away your enemy. The king of Israel, YHWH is in your midst, do not be afraid of further disaster' (Zeph. 3:14-15). The second part comes even closer to the role of Zion in Isaiah: '... do not be afraid Zion; do not let your hands grow weak (cf. Isa. 35:3). YHWH, your God is in your midst, a warrior who gives victory' (גִּבּוֹר יוֹשִׁיעַ, Zeph. 3:16-17). While in Isa. 12 the root ישע occurs three times (12:2 [2x], 3) in Zeph. 3:16-20 it does twice (3:17, 19).[74] Interesting enough the very last verses of Zeph. put great emphasis on תְּהִלָּה (cf. Isa. 61:11; 62:7) and שֵׁם, repeated chiastically in Zeph. 3:19c, 20b: 'I will make them [the lame and outcast] a song and a name'. This is to be connected with the שֵׁם for the castrates in Isa. 56:4-5. But what does it mean that YHWH makes the outcasts into a song? It is they who proclaim God's greatness and kingship before the world. This seems to imply a subtle critique of the official cult, similar to the 'Armentheologie' of the Psalter. These few passages show that Zion, depicted in a personal context, is connected to different stages of the exilic and post-exilic period, beginning with deportation and ending with YHWH's renewed presence in her midst.

A similar pattern has been detected in Isaiah, but with important differences. Firstly, only in Isaiah entire speeches of Zion are found: elsewhere either the personal address to Zion or her own reaction is limited to merely a few words. There Zion's personification surely intensifies the plot but without adding new topics. Secondly, with the exception of Isaiah there is no trace of a dramatic relationship between Zion and her population. There she represents merely Israel or the exilic community. The idea that Zion stands in a dramatic relationship with YHWH, her children and even with herself is exclusive to the Book of Isaiah. Where does this main focus on Zion in the Book of Isaiah come from? In order to find some answers to this intriguing question several studies have already been done, but only some points will be referred to here. O.H. Steck tries to find an answer by looking

---

[74] See H.-P. Mathys, *Dichter und Beter: Theologen aus spätalttestamentlicher Zeit* (OBO, 132), Freiburg 1994, 195-6.

at the pre-exilic celebrations in Jerusalem which highlighted YHWH taking possession of Zion as his dwelling place. Traces of these liturgical feasts are to be found in the Psalter which still preserves different speech-acts ('Sprechakte') of the involved parties.[75] Probably there were professional temple-singers who were engaged in dialogue with the community (see Ps. 46:5-7, 9-11; 48:3-8). Here Jerusalem/Zion represented the eternal protection and the unconditioned trustworthiness of YHWH. But the devastation of the capital and the cities of Judah by the Babylonians produced such a psychological and theological shock that after the exile a straightforward return 'to business as usual' was not possible. Not only the belief in the security of Jerusalem suffered a terrible blow but also the perception of YHWH.[76] The dramatic way in which Zion is personified as suffering woman in Lamentations points to the grieving-process in post-exilic Judah. Looking at the destruction of the city, the land and the temple one could nearly sense the cruel punishment of YHWH in a physical way. Once the exile was over and the restoration got off slowly the believers were strenghtened in their hope of a better future fixing their eyes on mother Zion.

Would it not be natural that in the post-exilic liturgies of fasting and lamenting (Zech. 7; Isa. 58) some elements of hope were introduced? Why would somebody fast if there was not a spark of hope left? One does not have to go so far as to suppose that the whole of Deutero-Isaiah was a script for a post-exilic theatrical performance on the slopes of Jerusalem, as Klaus Baltzer does in his recently published commentary. But certain phenomena would find a more satisfying solution than has been proposed so far – for example the sudden shifts of the speaking voices or the variety of addressees found in the prophetic scrolls. What has likewise to be taken into account is the fact that by fixing these 'living elements' into the scrolls they became part of Israel's literature gaining a wider applicability. The personifications of Zion and her prophetic voices which are to be found in the prophetic books – especially in Isaiah – could probably have been some of the elements in the post-exilic liturgies.

With this historical background in mind some other texts embedded in a context of Zion, but without mentioning her by name, come to

---

[75] O.H. Steck, 'Zion als Gelände und Gestalt: Überlegungen zur Wahrnehmung Jerusalems als Stadt und Frau im Alten Testament', in: Idem, *Gottesknecht und Zion: Gesammelte Aufsätze zu Deuterojesaja* (FAT, 4), Tübingen 1992, 126-45 (here 130-1).

[76] Steck, 'Zion als Gelände', 132: '... die Vernichtung der Manifestation Jahwes in der Stadt wird zur Krise der Jahwewahrnehmung selbst.'

the fore, such as Lam. 3 and Mic. 7:7-13. The many parallels between this Micah passage and the Book of Lamentations have already been indicated,[77] esp. the confession of confidence in Mic. 7:7: 'I will wait (אוֹחִילָה) for the God of my salvation ...' and the similar one in Lam. 3:21, 24: 'The LORD is my portion ... therefore I will hope in him' (אוֹחִיל לוֹ). With regard to Lam. 3 I worked out an interpretation of O. Eißfeldt in which I suggested Zion as speaker in this central chapter of Lamentations.[78] Regarding Mic. 7:7-13 the identification of Zion as speaker in vv. 7, 8-10 and as addressee in vv. 11-13 seems even more obvious. Who else than Zion would get involved into a discussion with a female enemy (vv. 8, 10), esp. when taken into consideration the fact that texts like Obad. 9-14 and Isa. 34; 63:1-6 do point to Edom? This too fits the historical setting of these texts since Edom disappeared at the end of the fifth century BCE.[79]

The identification of Zion in Mic. 7:11-13 as addressee is based upon the fem. suffixes in the expression 'your walls'[80] and the many people coming to an unnamed female personage. In the light of the importance of the repopulation of Zion in Isa. 49-55 it seems hard to believe that somebody else than her is meant in these verses.[81]

4 Zion/Jerusalem in the Deutero-Canonical and Apocryphal Books

There is no space to embark upon a full discussion on this topic but some remarks should suffice to show how some elements of the Zion-motif in the prophetic corpus developed later on in the literature of ancient Israel.

In Tobit's prayer (Tob. 13), just before his death, he gives a sum-

---

[77]See H.W. Wolff, *Micha* (BK, 14/4), Neukirchen-Vluyn 1982, 193: malicious joy over her enemy (Mic. 7:8; Lam. 4:21); the derision of the enemies (Mic. 7:8a, 10; Lam. 1:21; 2:15, 16); lament over the darkness (Mic. 7:8b; Lam. 5:17); confession of guilt (Mic. 7:9a; Lam. 1:5, 8, 17; 5:16); hope on God's mercy (Mic. 7:9b; Lam. 3:31-33).

[78]See U. Berges, ' "Ich bin der Mann, der Elend sah" (Klgl 3): Zionstheologie als Weg aus der Krise', *BZ* 44 (2000), 1-20.

[79]A summary of the discussion is found in Berges, *Jesaja*, 216-21.

[80]Contrary to R. Kessler, *Micha* (HThK.AT), Freiburg 1999, 303, who thinks of a metaphor for the protection of Israel as a whole; but why are fem. suffixes then used?

[81]In a paper read at the Joint Meeting Johannes de Moor argued that the female reading would be a later re-interpretation of what was originally a lament of the prophet Micah, cf. J.C. de Moor, 'Micah 7:1-13: The Lament of a Disillusioned Prophet', published in: M.C.A. Korpel, J.M. Oesch (eds), *Delimitation Criticism: A New Tool in Biblical Scholarship* (Pericope, 1), Assen 2000, 149-96.

mary of his life long experience with the God of Israel: it is a God who afflicts and shows mercy (Tob. 13:2). He transfers this personal experience to Israel (v. 5) and to Jerusalem (v. 10b): 'Jerusalem, holy city, he will afflict you for the deeds of your children, and again will have mercy on the children of the righteous'. Once Jerusalem has been named the focus is kept on it until the end of the prayer. It is the personified city that is invited by Tobit to praise God for his goodness (Tob. 13:11) and with a 'Halleluja' by the streets, i.e. a metonymy for the city itself, the prayer closes. Tobit presents Jerusalem as an example of how the afflicted faithful who has been restored by God's mercy will praise the great king. The suffering and the received mercy bind the faithful and the city of God together: 'Happy are those who grieve over all your afflictions; for they will rejoice over you watching all your glory and they will be happy forever' (13:16a). A deeply rooted solidarity with the fate of the city is to be noted here. This is even more important as the Book of Tobit was written most probably in Alexandria in the middle of the 3rd century BCE. Although written in the diaspora it is nevertheless the linkage with Jerusalem which determines the relation with God.[82]

In the last part of the Book of Baruch (4:5–5:9), written not earlier than the 2nd century BCE, one hears Jerusalem speaking to her neighbours. It is the moment when she is bereft of her children which were taken into exile (Bar. 4:9-29). Since she is the one who brought up her children nourished by God (Bar. 4:8) her grief is without measure. It is not Jerusalem who is responsable for the deportation of her children but they themselves who sinned (Bar. 4:12-13). This is an important element in the further development of Jerusalem's speech: because she is innocent she can intercede on behalf of her children.[83] But before she can do so she must embrace her pain fully by taking off the robe of peace and by putting on sackcloth of supplication. What

---

[82] P. Deselaers, *Das Buch Tobit: Studien zu seiner Entstehung, Komposition und Theologie* (OBO, 43), Freiburg 1982, 470: 'Es kommt darauf an, in treuer Verbundenheit Jerusalem anzuhangen. Wer so lebt, ist gesegnet. Fast grell rückt hier die Stellung Jerusalems in das Blickfeld.' See also P. Söllner, *Jerusalem, die hochgebaute Stadt: Eschatologisches und Himmlisches Jerusalem im Frühjudentum und im frühen Christentum* (TANZ, 25), Tübingen 1998, 43-65.

[83] L. Alonso Schökel, 'Jerusalem inocente intercede: Baruc 4,9-29', in: D. Muñoz Leon (ed.), *Salvación en la Palabra: Targum-Derash-Berith: En memoria A. Diez Macho*, Madrid 1986, 39-51 (with English summary): 'The great novelty of Baruch 4 is the introduction of an innocent Jerusalem who acts as intercessor ... As pater familias God is ready to punish unless someone intercedes. Jerusalem undertakes this role of intercessor and fulfills it in the manner of the prophets by praying for the children, advising them, and exhorting them' (51).

pain a mother must feel who has to encourage her children to leave her alone: 'Go, my children, go; for I have been left desolate'. But she does not remain passive: once dressed in the sackcloth of supplication she cries to the Everlasting without ceasing. Just at the moment of greatest pain and sorrow she puts her hope in God for the salvation of her children (Bar. 4:22; see Mic. 7:9; Lam. 3:21, 24).[84] She is absolutely convinced that the one who brought disaster will soon bring salvation (Bar. 4:18, 29). Jerusalem advises her punished children to endure the wrath of God with patience (Bar. 4:25), crying to him for help and to return seeking him with tenfold zeal (Bar. 4:28).[85] In a time when prophets are no longer to be found in Israel (Ps. 74:9; 1 Macc. 14:41), mother Jerusalem acts according to the prophetic tasks of intercession, encouragement and exhortation. From Zion as destructed city and as mother bereft of her children – but not of her hope – the faithful should learn how to hold fast to the God of Israel.

This is beautifully expressed in the Vision of Zion in 4 Ezra 9:26–10:59, written around the year 100 CE, 30 years after the destruction of the Second Temple. Ezra, the visionary, meets a woman in the fields who weeps bitterly; she wears torn clothes and has ashes on her head, the traditional signs of pain and sorrow. When Ezra asks her why she feels so deeply grieved at first she does not want to give an answer at all. But finally she tells him that after 30 years of barrenness she got a son who, once grown up and ready for marriage, died in the nuptial chamber. All neighbours had come to comfort her but the following day she went out of the city to be left alone in her pain (4 Ezra 9:41–10:4). The reader/hearer of this story acquainted with the history of Israel's suffering already senses that this lamenting woman is 'Zion' herself. Only the protagonist, the visionary, does not have a clue about the real identity of the woman and gets very angry with her because of her refusal to accept any kind of consolation: 'You most foolish of women, do you not see our mourning and what has happened to us?' (4 Ezra 10:6). Looking at the destruction of Zion laying in ruins and seeing the multitude of her children dead or deported Ezra denies her the right to mourn about her one and only child. What in her eyes

---

[84] In the Apostrophe to Zion in 11Q05 (11Q Ps^a) Kol. XXII, 1-15, it is exactly this element of hope which is stressed: 'Nicht ist deine Hoffnung verloren, o Zion, und nicht wird deine Erwartung vergessen! Ging je einer (in) Gerechtigkeit unter oder wurde er gerettet durch sein Unrecht?' Transl. by J. Maier, *Die Qumran-Essener: Die Texte vom Toten Meer*, Bd. 1, (UTB, 1862), München 1995, 338.

[85] O.H. Steck, *Das Buch Baruch* (ATD-Apokryphen, 5), Göttingen 1998, 63: 'Jerusalem ist das Vorbild "kanon" gespeister Hoffnung! Angesichts solcher Gewißheit gipfelt der Abschnitt V. 21-26 in der Aufforderung, bis dahin den Zorn Gottes (Jer 36,7b) geduldig zu ertragen (Mi 7,9).'

constitutes the right to mourn, i.e. the bereavement of her only child, is for Ezra of little value regarding the enormous loss of mother Zion (4 Ezra 10:21-23). Thus he exhorts the lamenting woman: 'Therefore shake off your great sadness and lay aside your many sorrows, so that the Mighty One may be merciful to you again, and the Most High may give you rest, a relief from your troubles' (4 Ezra 10:24). At the moment giving this advice, '... the face of the woman suddenly shone exceedingly, and her countenance flashed like lightening, so that I was too frightened to approach her ... Suddenly she uttered a loud and fearful cry, so that the earth shook at the sound. And I looked, and behold, the woman was no longer visible to me, but there was an established city, and a place of huge foundations showed itself.' (4 Ezra 10:25-28). Thus, the suffering and lamenting woman was in fact Zion herself who had tested Ezra's reaction in front of somebody who did not want to be consoled at all. Fixing his eyes on the suffering of Zion he passed the test.[86] At the very end the angel explains to Ezra what has happened: 'This woman whom you saw, whom you now behold as an established city, is Zion'. (4 Ezra 10:44). The woman has disappeared but the new Zion is still there and Ezra is invited to enter her to see the splendour and vastness of the building, as far as it is possible for his eyes to see it (4 Ezra 10:55).

5 Conclusion

After this long journey through the Zion-texts of the prophetic corpus, and especially through the Book of Isaiah, it has becomes clear that Zion does play a very important role in Israel's coping with destruction and distress. Right from the beginning of the book Zion is depicted as city and as woman (Isa. 1:8). In Isa. 37:22-23 the 'virgin daughter Zion' faces the attack and the scorn of the enemy but still remains strong in her trust in YHWH. A totally different picture of Zion is presented in Isa. 40-55: there she refuses first to be comforted and only gradually she accepts the consolation of her kingly bridegroom. In Isa. 49-52 the threefold relationship between YHWH, Zion and her population, i.e. her children, is intensified. The traits of the male and female Ebed are merging more and more and his offspring is identical with that of mother Zion. It is the believing part of her inhabitants, i.e. those listening to the voice of the Ebed (Isa. 50:10),

---

[86] H. Lichtenberger, 'Zion and the Destruction of the Temple in 4 Ezra 9-10', in: B. Ego *et al.* (eds), *Gemeinde ohne Tempel* (WUNT, 118), Tübingen 1999, 239-249: 'Now, in an admirable hermeneutical device the horizons overlap and – what the reader from the beginning had accepted – is being revealed: the woman really is Zion/Jerusalem, though in a transformed form' (245).

on which God's spirit is bestowed (Isa. 59:21), that bring Zion to the acceptance of her prophetic mission in favour of the poor in post-exilic Israel (Isa. 61).

The dramatic relationship between city and inhabitants, i.e. with the mother and her children, also comes to the fore in texts about Zion like Tob. 13 and Bar. 4–5. Here Zion becomes the paradigm of standfast hope on God's mercy and forgiveness; her prophetic mission centres on the admonition to accept the divine probation. Since Zion had endured hardships and punishments but was finally saved (cf. Lam. 3) the individual Jew can see in her the proof of God's mercy.

After the final destruction of the second temple Zion is presented in 4 Ezra as a symbol of sorrow and distress. It is in her pain and sorrow that the suffering individual should integrate his personal hardship. Individual pain should not be kept private but ought to be placed along Zion's sorrow.[87] Only the one who is engaged in Zion's pain and teaches others to do the same, is allowed to enter the eschatologically transformed city and to see her beauty. Comfort and consolation are not any more presented as something to be achieved in this world – not even in the case of Jerusalem – but to be expected for the world to come (see Rev. 21:1-2).

---

[87] W. Harnisch, 'Die Ironie der Offenbarung: Exegetische Erwägungen zur Zionsvision im 4. Buch Esra', *ZAW* 95 (1983), 75-95: 'Die Abkehr vom individuellen Leiden hat dann heilvolles Ergehen zur Folge, wenn sie sich als Einkehr in die kollektive Klage um den Schmerz Zions vollzieht' (88); see Söllner, *Jerusalem*, 271-281 ('Die Transfiguration einer trauernden Frau zum eschatologischen Jerusalem').

Christoph Bultmann *Cambridge – United Kingdom*

A Prophet in Desperation?
The Confessions of Jeremiah*

The confessions or laments of Jeremiah confront their reader at first sight with someone who is in desperation. How else should one speak of a mood which comes to expression in exclamations such as 'Why does the way of the guilty prosper?' (Jer. 12:1), 'Why is my pain unceasing?' (Jer. 15:18), or 'Cursed be the day on which I was born!' (Jer. 20:14)? And since we find these laments in a prophetic book, it seems reasonable to assume that the speaker is a prophet.[1]

1

Problems may already be seen to arise at this point. K.-F. Pohlmann, for example, offers a long argument about the assumed prophetic authorship of these texts only to conclude that neither can they have been part of the public ministry of a prophet, nor can they have been spoken in front of a small circle of friends and followers of Jeremiah, nor can they originally have been private prayers of the prophet.[2] Thus he sees these texts as later additions to the book and rather surprisingly ascribes them to a school of eschatological thought some time in the postexilic period.[3] Whereas Pohlmann's first claim concerning the confessions and a prophet's speech in public seems well justified, there is not enough evidence either to assert or to deny the possibility that Jeremiah may have shared these first-person singular compositions in an oral or a written form with a circle of friends. As regards an understanding of them as personal prayers, the artistic quality and emotional intensity of the texts in question are likely objections

---

*This article forms part of a wider study of the book of Jeremiah which is supported by a research grant from the Alexander von Humboldt Foundation (Bonn) and the Isaac Newton Trust (Cambridge). I would also like to thank my hosts at Fitzwilliam College, Cambridge, Dr Markus Bockmuehl and Dr Graham Davies.

[1] In addition to the commentaries on Jeremiah, the most comprehensive recent study of the confessions is A.R. Diamond, *The Confessions of Jeremiah in Context: Scenes of a Prophetic Drama* (JSOT.S, 45), Sheffield 1987; cf. also T. Polk, *The Prophetic Persona: Jeremiah and the Language of the Self* (JSOT.S, 32), Sheffield 1984, esp. Ch. 5 on Jer. 17:12-18 and 20:7-18.

[2] K.-F. Pohlmann, *Die Ferne Gottes: Studien zum Jeremiabuch* (BZAW, 179), Berlin 1989, 3-25. Diamond, *op. cit.*, 124-5, makes the methodological decision to refer primarily to the literary context for an interpretation of the texts.

[3] Pohlmann, *op. cit.*, passim; for a convenient summary cf. e.g. 60, 108.

against Pohlmann's hypothesis according to which a prayer would only need to serve its function once, namely in the actual process of supplication, but would not normally become part of a collection of literary compositions.[4] A discussion of critical issues like these does not only concern the literary-historical question of authenticity of the laments, but also the problem of an exegete's preconceptions about what it would have been appropriate for a prophet to pronounce.

Prophetic desperation is not always denied to the historical Jeremiah. A number of commentators see no difficulty at all in ascribing the confessions to Jeremiah and in interpreting them at a biographical level.[5] In his classic study of 1917, W. Baumgartner read the confessions as documents which reflected a 'crack' in the prophet's personality.[6] G. von Rad, in what one might call his reply to this study, in 1936 rejected the prevailing interest in a prophet's personal character and sought to transpose the metaphor of a 'crack' onto a more theological level. Thus, he considered the confessions as reflecting a 'rift' in the 'prophetic office' at a stage in the development of prophecy in ancient Israel when a prophet's humanity, his awareness of himself, began to get into conflict with his mission, i.e. with the *munus propheticum* with which he had been endowed.[7] The notion of a prophetic office remains fundamental to H.-J. Hermisson's thoughtful interpretation of the confessions which he studies as a well structured literary cycle.[8] The prophet is seen as the bearer of the divine word, and the central theme of his laments is identified in Jeremiah's quotation of his opponents' mocking question: 'Where is the word of the Lord? Let it come!' in Jer. 17:15.[9] The prophetic, oracular word is, as Hermisson puts it, the objective reality ('das Objektivum') with which the laments

---

[4] Pohlmann, *op. cit.*, 19, 23.

[5] W.L. Holladay, *Jeremiah*, vol. 1 (Hermeneia), Philadelphia 1986, 6-9 and passim; J.R. Lundbom, *Jeremiah 1-20*, (AncB, 21A), New York 1999, 115-17 and passim.

[6] W. Baumgartner, *Die Klagegedichte des Jeremia* (BZAW, 32), Giessen 1917, 77; ET: Idem, *Jeremiah's Poems of Lament* (HTIBS, 7), Sheffield 1988, 87.

[7] G. von Rad, 'Die Konfessionen Jeremias' (first pub. *EvTh* 3 [1936]), in: Idem, *Gesammelte Studien zum Alten Testament*, Bd. 2, ed. by R. Smend (TB, 48), München 1973, 224-35, 233; ET in: J.L. Crenshaw (ed.), *Theodicy in the Old Testament* (IRT, 4), Philadelphia/London 1983, 88-99, 97.

[8] H.-J. Hermisson, 'Jahwes und Jeremias Rechtsstreit: Zum Thema der Konfessionen Jeremias' (first pub. in: *Festschrift A.H.J. Gunneweg*, 1987), in: Idem, *Studien zu Prophetie und Weisheit* (FAT, 23), Tübingen 1998, 5-36; Idem, 'Jeremias dritte Konfession (Jer 15, 10-21)', *ZThK* 96 (1999), 1-21. In contrast to Pohlmann (above n. 2), Hermisson describes the confessions as a literary work of art written by the prophet himself ('Konfession', 16-17).

[9] Hermission, 'Rechtsstreit', 8, 22.

are concerned.[10] Jeremiah is said to be reflecting on the contradiction that on the one hand he has been commissioned to announce words which are designed to bring about disaster, while on the other hand he is being kept waiting to see them fulfilled. He quarrels with God about this, although, paradoxically, his second prophetic function as intercessor for his people is itself a factor which effects the delay of the coming disaster.[11] Thus the prophet looks back to performing his duty and pleads, 'Remember how I stood before you ... to turn away your wrath from them' (Jer. 18:20). Hermisson tries to show that even where the speaker in more or less conventional expressions calls on YHWH to take revenge on his persecutors, what is really meant is an acceleration of the coming doom for the entire nation.[12]

However, in his recent article on Jer. 15, the interpretative emphasis on the speaker's prophetic office and his divine mission to announce national disaster causes more exegetical problems than it helps to solve. When we read in the Masoretic Text[13] of Jer. 15:16 'Your words were found and I ate them, ‖ and your word became to me a joy and the delight of my heart', it is difficult to think of oracles of doom. Hermisson therefore resorts to the alternative suggestion that the speaker here is jubilant about 'the community with God which is granted through the divine word'.[14] While this is in principle a plausible interpretation, it obviously says nothing very specific about prophecy unless one realizes to what extent the prophet is being styled here as a model for the faithful community. A second point in question is Jer. 15:19 where in a divine address the condition is put to the prophet, 'If you utter what is precious, and not what is worthless, you shall serve as my mouth'. Hermisson comments, '... in the service of Yahweh, Jeremiah has to pronounce Yahweh's word. It is evident that in so doing he must not utter anything "worthless" ...' The preceding lament is thus being dismissed as an example of worthless waffle.[15]

---

[10] Hermission, 'Rechtsstreit', 35; Idem, 'Konfession', 18.

[11] Hermission, 'Rechtsstreit', 22-27; Idem, 'Konfession', 1-2.

[12] Hermisson, 'Konfession', 11 (on נקם in 15:15). For a critique of such an interpretation see W. McKane, *Jeremiah* (ICC), vol. 1, Edinburgh 1986, 351. A similar problem arises with regard to the hendiadys חָמָס וָשֹׁד in 20:8, cf. Hermisson, 'Rechtsstreit', 28 n. 61, and McKane, *op. cit.*, 472.

[13] In v. 16aβ, the MT has a *wayyiqtol* form whereas the LXX has the future tense. For the subject דְּבָר (the noun in the singular), the Qere corresponds to the LXX. In v. 16aα, the LXX version possibly goes back to a text which included the roots נאץ (cf. 23:17) and כלה (cf. 5:3), and it continues the thrust of v. 15. A related text-critical problem is in 23:9. See also A.R.P. Diamond, 'Jeremiah's Confessions in the LXX and MT', *VT* 40 (1990), 33-50.

[14] Hermisson, 'Konfession', 13 ('die im Jahwewort gewährte Gottesgemeinschaft').

[15] Hermisson, 'Konfession', 15 (my transl.); cf. Von Rad, *art. cit.*, 226 (ET, 90),

To put it differently, there is no room for such sentiments and such compositions in a prophetic tradition. – Which is of course not what Hermisson really means and, in fact, says.

The prophet in desperation about the delay of fulfilment of his oracles of doom is a figure which will immediately emerge in any interpretation where the exegete starts from a notion of a specific prophetic office. Such a notion can be informed by strongly theological concerns as in the work of Hermisson, or it can be informed by predominantly phenomenological and comparative concerns as, for example, in recent articles by H. Barstad and R.P. Gordon.[16] It also does not make much difference whether the confessions are regarded as authentic or not. Where they are seen as redactional components of the book, as, for example, in well-known essays by E. Gerstenberger and A.H.J. Gunneweg or in R. Carroll's commentary,[17] the figure of the desperate prophet will still be a feature of their interpretation. Thus we find the image of Jeremiah as the exemplary prophet in a line of succession of Yahweh's servants, the prophets, who were oppressed by a disobedient community, or we find Jeremiah as a model for identification for a community of later recipients of the tradition who suffer from oppression at the hand of the wicked and are in despair about this.[18]

---

and Idem, *Theologie des Alten Testaments*, Bd. 2, München ^{4}1965, 87-9; ET: Idem, *Old Testament Theology*, vol. 2, London 1965, 78-9.

[16] H. Barstad, 'No Prophets? Recent Developments in Biblical Prophetic Research and Ancient Near Eastern Prophecy' (first pub. *JSOT* 57 [1993]), in: Ph.R. Davies (ed.), *The Prophets* (The Biblical Seminar, 42), Sheffield 1996, 106-126; R.P. Gordon, 'From Mari to Moses: Prophecy at Mari and in Ancient Israel' in: H.A. McKay, D.J.A. Clines (eds), *Of Prophets' Visions and the Wisdom of Sages: Essays in Honour of R. Norman Whybray* (JSOT.S, 162), Sheffield 1993, 63-79; Idem, 'Where Have All the Prophets Gone? The "Disappearing" Israelite Prophet Against the Background of Ancient Near Eastern Prophecy', *BBR* 5 (1995), 67-86. – However, M. Weippert's scepticism about traditio-historical links between the ancient Near Eastern texts is still worth noting: 'Assyrische Prophetien der Zeit Asarhaddons und Assurbanipals', in: F.M. Fales (ed.), *Assyrian Royal Inscriptions: New Horizons in Literary, Ideological, and Historical Analysis*, Rome 1981, 71-115, esp. 103-4. See also M. Nissinen, 'Die Relevanz der neuassyrischen Prophetie für die alttestamentliche Forschung', in: M.Dietrich, O. Loretz (eds), *Mesopotamica – Ugaritica – Biblica: Festschrift K. Bergerhof* (AOAT, 232), Neukirchen-Vluyn 1993, 215-58.

[17] E. Gerstenberger, 'Jeremiah's Complaints: Observations on Jer 15.10-21', *JBL* 82 (1963), 393-408; A.H.J. Gunneweg, 'Konfession oder Interpretation im Jeremiabuch' (first pub. *ZThK* 67 [1970]), in: Idem, *Sola Scriptura*, Göttingen 1983, 61-82; R.P. Carroll, *Jeremiah* (OTL), London 1986, repr. 1996.

[18] R.P. Carroll, *From Chaos to Covenant: Uses of Prophecy in the Book of Jeremiah*, London 1981, repr. 1996, 107-30, esp. 123, 130; and cf. his commentary on the individual texts.

2

If one asked the question what impact the confessions have on the image of a prophet in Judah in antiquity, the answer so far would be that their significance is very limited indeed. Neither the prophetic function of giving oracles, nor the prophetic function of intercession for his own people need to be derived from these texts. In such a model of interpretation, the confessions invariably have a secondary status compared with the truly prophetic utterances. They may at best seem to make the personality of the prophet more accessible for the readers of the book. This, however, is different if we abandon such concepts for a moment and take up A.G. Auld's suggestion again that in the prophetic books one should recognize the *poet* where the poet speaks and the *prophet* where the redactors depict him as such.[19] I would therefore like to turn to a closer look at Jer. 15 without the notion of a prophetic office in mind.

The confession in Chapter 15 can best be delimited as a unit beginning with v. 15 and ending with v. 19.[20] The main content of this confession can be outlined as an outburst of an angry and melancholy mood which receives a response in the form of a divine oracle.[21] The speaker complains about persecution, about his isolation amongst

---

[19] A.G. Auld, 'Prophets through the Looking Glass: Between Writings and Moses' (first pub. *JSOT* 27 [1983]), in: Ph.R. Davies (see above n. 16), 22-42; the volume contains a number of critical responses to this article which is also included in R.P. Gordon (ed.), *'The Place is Too Small For Us': The Israelite Prophets in Recent Scholarship*, Winona Lake 1995, 289-307. See further A.G. Auld, 'Poetry, Prophecy, Hermeneutic: Recent Studies in Isaiah', *SJTh* 33, 1980, 567-81, and Idem, 'Word of God and Word of Man: Prophets and Canon', in: L. Eslinger, G. Taylor (eds), *Ascribe to the Lord: Biblical and Other Studies in Memory of Peter C. Craigie* (JSOT.S, 67), Sheffield 1988, 237-51. Although Carroll broadly agreed with Auld's views (see, e.g., his articles in the volume edited by Ph.R. Davies), both authors are too closely linked together and too hastily criticized by A. Rofé, *Introduction to the Prophetic Literature* (The Biblical Seminar, 21), Sheffield 1997, 8, n. 3.

[20] The expression אַתָּה יָדַעְתָּ at the beginning of v. 15 should be omitted, and Jer. 15:10-12 should be regarded a separate unit. The concluding line of v. 19 forms an inclusio with the opening lines in vv. 15 and 17. For a discussion of the delimitation of the texts in Ch. 15 see Diamond, *op. cit.*, 52-78, who does not, however, accept a critical differentiation between v. 19 and vv. 20-21. A complex redactionhistorical suggestion is offered by J. Vermeylen, 'Essai de Redaktionsgeschichte des "Confessions de Jérémie"', in: P.-M. Bogaert (ed.), *Le Livre de Jérémie: Le Prophète et son Milieu: Les Oracles et leur Transmission* (BEThL, 54), Leuven 1981, ²1997, 266.

[21] According to Hermisson, 'Rechtsstreit', 10, the introductory formula in v. 19 may be secondary.

cheerful contemporaries, and about his radical disillusionment with God. For this last aspect, he uses the metaphor of a 'spring whose water has failed'.[22] In the response, two conditions are set out for his readmission into the presence of God. 'If you turn back, I will take you back, and you shall stand before me. ‖ If you utter what is precious, and not what is worthless, you shall serve as my mouth.' The confession thus is a poetic composition in which the poet employs different literary forms – the direct address to God as well as the direct speech by God – and connects them to each other at the point where the first part of the poem has reached its climax in a radically negative statement. Through this compositional move, the poet expresses an insight which takes him beyond his assertion of a complete loss of trust in God and – more importantly in the present context – gives his poetic speech a special status.

In what sense then is prophetic authority an issue in these lines? Where the first line speaks of 'standing in God's presence', neither the idea of a divine council as in Jer. 23:18,[23] nor the concept of an intercessory role seem to be implied.[24] Rather, the expression is used in a general sense similar to its occurrence in Jer. 7:10 (cf. Deut. 29:14) where it refers to people who visit the temple. The second line, however, specifically aims at an interpretation of the poet's speaking as having in some way a revelatory character. Where he is designated as 'YHWH's mouth' in case he utters what is 'precious', the speaker is given divine authority for what he himself comes to understand as valuable and valid insights. At this point the literary convention of talking about a prophet as a messenger becomes transparent and, un-

---

[22] McKane's translation. It is sometimes suggested that the word אַכְזָב implies itself a metaphorical element, cf. McKane, *op. cit.*, 355-6. However, the line may be seen as an example of a movement from literal to figurative locution as described by R. Alter, *The Art of Biblical Poetry*, Edinburgh 1990, 3-26, esp. 16-7.

[23] It is far from obvious that the speaker in 23:18 (and 23:22) claims to have himself had access to the divine council when he attacks presumptuous prophets who make such a claim; see, however, the articles by Gordon (above n. 16). The question should also be asked at what stage in the development of the tradition the notion of a סוֹד יהוה became part of it, especially as the presentation of the prophet in Jer. 1 makes no reference to it (despite its borrowing from Isa. 6). For the philological issues involved see McKane, *op. cit.*, 581-2. On Amos 3:7 see A.G. Auld, 'Amos and Apocalyptic: Vision, Prophecy, Revelation', in: D. Garrone, F. Israel (eds), *Storia e tradizioni di Israele: Studi in Onore di J. Alberto Soggin*, Brescia 1991, 1-13; on 1 Kings 22 see H. Weippert, 'Ahab el campeador? Redaktionsgeschichtliche Untersuchungen zu 1Kön 22', *Bib.* 69 (1988), 457-79.

[24] Hermisson, 'Konfession', 9 n. 27, understands the expression עָמַד לִפְנֵי in Jer. 18:20 as referring to a prophetic office of intercession ('Fürbittamt') and in Jer. 15:19 as referring to a prophetic office as a messenger ('Botenamt'). The reference in Jer. 7:10 is not considered.

derlying it, the humanity of the speaker becomes visible. The prophet is someone who is struggling to decide what he can accept and pronounce as an insight which would meet the condition set out in Jer. 15:19. It would make no sense to explain the conditional clause as meaning something like 'If you distinguish between my words which I am sending you to convey to the people and your own, worthless thoughts and complaints ... ' W. McKane is right in his comments on this verse when he emphasizes the prophet's own 'intellectual striving and spiritual growth'.[25] The speaker accepts the responsibility for what he pronounces, and he is aware of asserting a specific truth claim with his 'precious' utterances. In this sense the poet becomes a prophet and the prophet a poet. It is therefore no wonder that the confessions are included in a prophetic tradition which in its origin is altogether a collection of poetic compositions which are *precious words* in the sense envisaged in Jer. 15:19.[26]

The image of a prophet which emerges from v. 19 finds a strong counterpoise in another verse of the same confession in Jer. 15, and objections against putting any interpretative emphasis on a poet's artistic speech in the context of prophecy might be based on that verse. V. 16 (in the Masoretic Text) speaks about words which the speaker 'finds' and 'eats' and 'delights in'. However, the interpretation of this verse by McKane remains unconvincing when he comments, 'There is a joy which even a prophet of doom finds when he stands in the path of duty and says what he must.'[27] The two statements in v. 16 about the divine word cannot possibly refer to oracles of doom which the prophet receives and passes on as a messenger who fulfils his duty. Instead, an entirely new tone of piety is introduced into the confession here and reference is made if not to the torah, then to an even wider body of authoritative scriptures.[28] The statement refers

---

[25] McKane, *op. cit.*, 358. A more general discussion of this issue is offered in Idem, *A Late Harvest: Reflections on the Old Testament*, Edinburgh 1995. It is also worth comparing the characterization of the late 8th century prophets as 'dissident intellectuals' in J. Blenkinsopp, *Sage, Priest, Prophet: Religious and Intellectual Leadership in Ancient Israel*, Louisville 1995, 141-50.

[26] Most prophetic sayings are commonly described as 'poetic' solely on stylistic grounds. Although the formal criterion of 'parallelism' should not be overemphasized, R. Alter, *op. cit.*, esp. Ch. 6, gives an excellent introduction to the issues involved; cf. also J.C. de Moor, W.G.E. Watson, 'General Introduction', in: Idem, idem (eds), *Verse in Ancient Near Eastern Prose* (AOAT, 42), Neukirchen-Vluyn 1993, ix-xviii; W.G.E. Watson, *Traditional Techniques in Classical Hebrew Verse* (JOST.S, 170), Sheffield 1994; Idem, *Classical Hebrew Poetry: A Guide to its Techniques* (JSOT.S, 26), Sheffield, ²1995.

[27] McKane, *op. cit.*, 353.

[28] For a highly speculative historicizing reading cf. Lundbom, *op. cit.*, 743-5. A

to the life-giving power of the divine word and may best be placed half-way between the deuteronomistic reflections on the Manna in the desert and the divine word in Deut. 8:3 on the one side,[29] and the devotion to the torah in Ps. 40:9, for example, on the other.[30] The verse may also echo the relationship between prophecy and the law which lies at the roots of the concept of a succession of 'God's servants, the prophets' who called for obedience to the law as it is found, for example, in Jer. 26:4-5. In Jer. 15, v. 16 should therefore be considered a secondary scribal gloss. Form-critical observations would further support the case for identifying a gloss here[31] as would an analysis of the formulaic use of the expression 'your name is called upon me' in the concluding line. In the book of Jeremiah, the formula otherwise refers to the temple.[32] In applying it to the prophet, a scribe here puts the figure of the torah-oriented prophet in the place of the temple as the central religious institution. With this, he moves further into the direction of the concept which already lies behind Jer. 15:20 (cf. Jer. 1:18-19). The inviolability of the prophet functions as an assertion of the authority and irresistibility of the prophetic word.

3

The confession thus conveys two conflicting and mutually exclusive images of a prophet. The one which presents the prophet as a poet who composes 'precious words' could have a major significance for our understanding of prophecy. What looks like a prophetic functionary's cry of desperation should rather be seen as a poet's cry of liberation. It reflects a process in which the speaker gains the confidence that what he judges from his experience to be a valid religious insight can be pronounced in the name of God. Poetry here is precisely the means

---

more cautious discussion of the use of the root מצא here can be found in Diamond, *op. cit.*, 75-6. There is, however, nothing in v. 16 which would suggest a historical or literary link with 2 Kings 22:8.

[29] On Deut. 8 cf. T. Veijola, ' "Der Mensch lebt nicht vom Brot allein": Zur literarischen Schichtung und theologischen Aussage von Deuteronomium 8', in: G. Braulik (ed.), *Bundesdokument und Gesetz: Studien zum Deuteronomium* (HBS, 4), Freiburg 1995, 143-58.

[30] In this sense, Hermisson's comment, quoted above, seems a possible interpretation.

[31] Whereas v. 15 (four cola) and v. 17 (three cola) show a distinctive formal pattern, the three components of v. 16 – except, perhaps, for the hymnic conclusion – lack a poetic structure.

[32] Jer. 7:10, 11, 14, 30; 32:34; 34:15. In Jer. 25:29, the formula refers to Jerusalem, in Jer. 14:9 to the people (in an invocation of YHWH in the first-person plural); cf. Carroll, *From Chaos to Covenant*, 117; Idem, *Jeremiah*, 330-1; Diamond, *op. cit.*, 237, n. 67.

for giving expression to such insight. If we take a look at some of the other confessions, we can set this process of reflection in parallel with the inner tension of which Jer. 20:7-9, the first of the three poems in Ch. 20, speaks.[33] In Jer. 20:9 the speaker states that it is impossible for him to withhold what in the context of that confession is called the 'word of YHWH'. The poet has moved from the idea that pronouncing what is 'precious' means speaking as 'YHWH's mouth' to the idea that in what he pronounces he is subjected to the force of the divine word. In both these confessions, the same inner necessity to speak up is in view. While the poem in Jer. 20:7-9 would thus corroborate the interpretation of Jer. 15:15-19 which I have suggested, a further poem in Jer. 17:14-18 seems to offer a strong argument against it. In the mocking question 'Where is the word of YHWH? Let it come!' (Jer. 17:15), the speaker's words are solely conceived of in terms of announcement and fulfilment and thus as the speech of a prophet who – arguably in a presumptuous way – serves as a messenger. Yet in the same confession the speaker comes back to the concept of words for which he is himself responsible when he appeals to God and submits his words to God: 'You know what came from my lips; it was before you' (Jer. 17:16). As in the case of Jer. 15:19 it would be difficult to refer this statement to oracles which were communicated to the speaker by God. Furthermore the question of announcement and fulfilment only arises in a quotation, and this may indicate that it was only the speaker's contemporaries who classified his words as oracles. Within the context of a religious culture in which in all probability a class of נְבִיאִים played a prominent role,[34] this is not surprising. However, it is no firm evidence for concluding that the poet himself considered himself to be involved in the performing of the religious office of a נָבִיא.[35] The aspect of prediction may have been a corollary of his poetry, but not its genuine substance.

So far, speaking of the author of the confessions as a poet may have looked like a rather obvious possibility. However, what I have also wanted to argue is that within these texts in their context in a prophetic book an understanding of prophecy is developed which offers a basis for classifying a prophet as a poet. This poet is given a specific authority for poetic compositions in the sense of the 'precious

---

[33]It is sometimes suggested that Jer. 20:7-13 should be considered a literary unit, cf. Diamond, *op. cit.*, 101-13. See, however, McKane, *op. cit.*, 468-9, 476; and Rofé's remarks on the 'three elegies' in Ch. 20, *op. cit.*, 49-52.

[34]The book of Jeremiah refers not only to false נְבִיאִים (Jer. 2:8; 23:9-32; etc.), but also to true ones (Jer. 4:9-10).

[35]See A.G. Auld in: P.R. Davies (above n. 16), 85.

words' of Jer. 15:19. All this is not only a theoretical model in contrast to the one which can be based on Jer. 1.[36] There are a number of texts in the book of Jeremiah which one might, for example, describe as poems on apostasy or as poems on defeat and destruction. Examples for the first category would be Jer. 2:5-13 and Jer. 8:4-7, examples for the second one Jer. 4:5-8 and Jer. 8:21-23. In many cases, the poet does of course employ the form of first-person singular speech in the name of YHWH,[37] as he even does in the confessions themselves (Jer. 15:19; cf. Jer. 12:5 and 15:12). Nevertheless, in a perspective from Chapter 15 this should be seen as a feature of his poetry rather than as a function of his assumed prophetic office.

Finally, the question of authenticity should briefly be addressed even though I do not pretend to have a ready answer to it. Do the confessions go back to an author around 600 BCE and can other poems in the book of Jeremiah be attributed to this same author? One wonders whether, as Baumgartner suggested, all of the characteristic formal and linguistic elements of the laments would have been available for purposes of poetic composition in late 7th century Judah. However, as regards the confession in Chapter 15, one cannot only notice a close correspondence between the metaphor of a 'spring of living waters' in Jer. 2:13 and the metaphor of a '(spring) whose water has failed' in Jer. 15:18. One could also discover the same intellectual attitude behind the discussion of theodicy in Jer. 2:5-9 where the question is asked whether YHWH has done anything wrong (עָוֶל), and the critical reflections in Jer. 15:18 where YHWH is accused of having been false to the speaker (אַכְזָב) or in Jer. 20:7 with its metaphorical use of the verbs פתה and חזק. Parallels can also be noted between the speaker's indignation at his contemporaries in Jer. 15:17 or 20:8 and their moral condemnation in a text like Jer. 8:4-7. Again, one could detect a similar intellectual attitude behind the fundamental questioning of the

---

[36] The close correspondence between Jer. 15:20 and Jer. 1:18-19 may be taken as an indication that at one redactional level the competing significance of both Ch. 1 and Ch. 15 for the presentation of the prophet had been realized. For aspects of a critical analysis of Ch. 1 see S. Herrmann, *Jeremia* (BK, 12/1-2), Neukirchen-Vluyn 1986-90; C. Levin, *Die Verheißung des Neuen Bundes* (FRLANT, 137), Göttingen 1985, 146-56; M. Köckert, 'Zum literargeschichtlichen Ort des Prophetengesetzes Dtn 18 zwischen dem Jeremiabuch und Dtn 13', in: R.-G. Kratz, H. Spieckermann (eds), *Liebe und Gebot: Studien zum Deuteronomium, Festschrift L. Perlitt* (FRLANT, 190), Göttingen 2000, 80-100.

[37] In Jer. 4:5-8, v. 6b may be a secondary addition to a poem which originally spoke of YHWH in the third person only (v. 8); cf. also Jer. 6:26b. In consequence of H. Leene's contribution to this volume, it would follow that Jer. 6:16-21 is an example of a scribal הִנְנִי מֵבִיא רָעָה-type of prophecy (cf. Jer. 11:11; 2 Kings 22:16).

truthfulness of God in Jer. 15:15-19 and the no less fundamental problem in Jer. 8:4-7 of a universal divine order of reality which the birds under the heavens obey but which human beings fail to recognize. There may be a coherent perception of the human relationship with God in the background of the confessions as well as other poems in the collection, and a similar pattern of employing poetic language to express this. To think in terms of a succession of poets and scribes here may be less plausible than to attribute them to the same author (who could of course still be either the historical Jeremiah or a 6th or 5th century Deuteronomist).

The question of authorship does not affect my main argument very strongly. The impact of the confessions on the image of a prophet is that the prophet becomes recognizable as a poet who utters 'precious words'. The confessions do not exhibit a prophet in desperation, but a prophet, be it said, in poetic furore. They have this significance, whether Jeremiah himself not only was a poet but, in the confessions, also reflected on himself as being a poet, or whether he was a poet but was presented as such only by later redactors who added the confessions to the collection of his words. This they may perhaps even have done in order to counterbalance the powerful presentation of the prophet as a speaker of divine oracles in Chapter 1.[38]

Any interpretation of Jeremiah as a prophet will be guided by only a few specific aspects of the complex literary tradition. What I am suggesting is that we should allow the image of the prophet as a poet at least a place beside that of the prophet as a religious specialist for delivering oracles. Further research will be needed if we want to establish which of these images comes closer to a historical figure in ancient Judean culture around 600 BCE. To conclude, I would like to apply to Jeremiah a quotation from an essay by T.S. Eliot on Shakespeare:[39] 'About anyone so great as Shakespeare, it is probable that we can never be right; and if we can never be right, it is better that we should from time to time change our way of being wrong.'

---

[38] One wonders whether in terms of the so-called canonical approach the confessions, in case they should be 'late' additions to the book, would have to be considered an aspect of its canonical shaping, and if so, how this would affect the discussion of a prophet's freedom in B.S. Childs, *Old Testament Theology in a Canonical Context*, London 1985, 123-8. It would of course be possible to acknowledge Jer. 15:16 only as an element of canonical shaping (cf. also Ezek. 2:8–3:3).

[39] T.S. Eliot, 'Shakespeare and the Stoicism of Seneca' (1927), in: Idem, *Selected Essays*, London 1951, repr. 1999, 126.

Terry Collins *Oxford – United Kingdom*

Threading as a Stylistic Feature of Amos

1 Preliminaries

The feature of the language[1] of Amos that I want to focus on here is what might be called its 'inconsequentiality' or disjointedness. A large proportion of Amos is made up of short segments which move abruptly from one topic to another without any warning. The writer seems to have a very short attention span. Is the inconsequentiality of the text of Amos completely haphazard and uncontrolled? Or is there some kind of rhyme and reason to it? Is it the result of a mindless process of agglomeration, or could somebody have actually planned to compose a text in this way?[2]

In order to deal with this feature of the language of the text, I am going to use the idea of 'threading', borrowed from the internet vocabulary of electronic Newsgroups. Gaining access to a Newsgroup involves downloading a hundred or more messages. While concerned with the topic of interest to the group, each message is normally not related to the one immediately before and after it in the sequence of delivery or reception. A given message may not receive a response until several messages later. In effect, you are faced with the task of trying to deal with several different conversations that have been scrambled together. Naturally, the software programmes available for accessing Newsgroups have found a solution to this problem. They can scan through the messages and select those related to the same line or thread of conversation. This feature is widely referred to as 'threading'.

---

[1] The approach to 'stylistics' that underpins this paper is the one which was developed in the 1970's for English literature. It is a stylistics based on linguistic features, and it aims to analyse the style of a text in objective rather than subjective terms. In such an approach, the 'stylistic features' tend to be mainly concerned with phonology, morphology and the lexical aspects of the text, but semantic questions, such as ambiguity, are not excluded. The approach is derived ultimately from the ideas of the Russian formalist critics via the Prague school and the New Criticism movement. Needless to say such an approach to stylistics can only highlight certain aspects of the text, but its main advantage is that it can operate without reference to the biographies and backgrounds of individual authors. That makes it relevant to the general theme of this conference. See for example: R. Chapman, *Linguistics and Literature*, London 1973; A. Cluysenaar, *Introduction to Literary Stylistics*, London 1976.

[2] The disjointedness of most of Amos is thrown into even greater relief when we contrast it with the sustained artistry in certain parts of the text: – e.g. the oracles on the nations in Amos 1:3–2:5 and the prose narrative in Chapter 7.

Threading as a Stylistic Feature of Amos

At first glance, large sections of Amos resemble a batch of Newsgroup messages. The text appears to be a mixed bag of questions and answers which are vaguely related but hopelessly jumbled together. Time and again we find that an idea or image is mentioned and then dropped, only to be taken up again a page or two later. I am suggesting that this patchwork quilt of messages can be seen to be not entirely haphazard, if we adopt a kind of 'threading' technique as we read the text, trying to keep the different strands before our mind's eye and observing how they interact.

2 The Example of the Lion

In Amos 3:4 there is a reference to the lion roaring and the young lion giving voice. 'Does the lion roar, if it has not already taken its prey?' This is one of the riddles beloved of Amos, and is designed to raise questions rather than give answers. One thing is clear: the reference to the prey is rather ominous. Actually, the juxtaposition of the words 'roar' and 'give voice' are part of a thread that was already started back in 1:2. 'The Lord roars from Sion and gives voice from Jerusalem'. In this terse opening statement, the 'roaring' is evidently a threatening noise, but nothing more is said, and we are left to guess at what is meant. I am suggesting that these verbal links between 1:2 and 3:4 lead us to conclude that, in the latter, we are meant to equate the lion with the Lord. Consequently, the reference to the lion in 3:4 is the second element in a thread which starts very tentatively and gradually develops in explicitness and complexity.

We see the thread developed further in Amos 3:8, where the lion's roaring is explicitly equated with the Lord's speaking. 'The lion roars. Who will not fear? The Lord speaks. Who will not prophesy?' In effect, the thread is gradually being drawn out and is revealing itself to be a comment on the nature of prophecy, but the comment is offered to us in a piecemeal, suggestive fashion rather than as a sustained exposition. The start of the thread in the first mention of the Lord 'roaring' in 1:2, is fleeting and imprecise. Its full significance only becomes evident as the thread is developed in later passages.

We should also note how the use of דבר in Amos 3:7 and 8 evokes another thread on the word of the Lord, found in 3:1. 'Listen to this word which the Lord has spoken', leading us right back to the opening lines in 1:1, 'The words of Amos, which he saw concerning Israel'. I mention this here simply to draw attention to the fact that the threads can intertwine.

The lion reappears in Amos 3:12. 'As the shepherd rescues from the mouth of the lion two pair of hooves and a piece of an ear'. Taken by itself, this is a very cryptic statement, but when we read it as part of the thread which we have identified, its meaning becomes clear: there will not be much left of Israel after the Lord has finished with it. Again we see a combination of threads. The thread involving the lion is interwoven with another thread relating to remnants, survivors and escapees.

The interweaving of these threads is taken a step further in Amos 5:19, where the unlucky man flees from the lion and a bear meets him; he comes home and rest against a wall and a snake bites him. The theme of no escape, centred on the root נוס, was in fact initiated back in Amos 2:14 וְאָבַד מָנוֹס מִקָּל. 'There will be no escape for the swift ... even the bravest warrior will only escape naked (on that day)' (Amos 2:16). It is interesting to note that BHS wants to delete the phrase 'on that day' בַּיּוֹם־הַהוּא as an addition. However, we shall see in a moment that this reference to a particular day is itself part of a related thread that will be further developed as the text proceeds. The upshot of all this is that, in the six lines in Amos 5:18-20, we can detect three established threads running side by side: – the lion, no escape, the day of reckoning. To these we can add a fourth thread on the theme of opposites in the form of light and darkness, but for the moment let us continue to follow the thread of the beasts from which there is no escape. Especially the snake.

The theme resurfaces towards the end of Amos in 9:1-4 in a statement which includes the use of the root נוס. There is no escape: in Sheol, in the heavens, or on the top of Carmel. And it continues in 9:3: 'If they hide from me at the bottom of the sea, there I shall command the snake and it will bite them'. This occurrence in Chapter 9 means that we have now followed a complex thread about beasts and the Lord from whom there is no escape, beginning with the opening lines of Amos and continuing through to the closing section. At the very least, the existence of such a thematic threading argues in favour of a unity of composition for these nine chapters (however we define the word 'composition').

3 Destruction of Buildings

Throughout Amos there are references to buildings, particularly to their destruction. Buildings can be destroyed through earthquakes or through the agency of fire inflicted by attacking armies. In either case, of course, from the point of view of Amos, it is really the Lord who does it. The first mention of an 'earthquake' occurs in Amos 1:1, which says that the word of the Lord was revealed to Amos 'two years before the earthquake'. As a means of dating, this information is quite useless, but it is in fact the start of a major thread. The apparently motiveless introduction of the word רַעַשׁ is a hint of things to come, since earthquake imagery is found throughout Amos. The strongest of threads in a text can have the most insignificant of beginnings.

The word רַעַשׁ can also mean 'agitation' or 'uproar', and since polysemy is a noticeable feature of the language of Amos, we must ask ourselves about the full significance of the references to the destruction of buildings. Chapter 1 provides a clue to the answer to this question in the formulaic oracles against the other nations. Alongside the repeated statements that the Lord will send fire against walls, burn strongholds (אַרְמְנוֹת) and shatter gates of various cities, we should note that structural damage is also to be inflicted on societies through the 'cutting off' of the leaders – the rulers, kings, princes and judges – as punishment for the crimes of each city or nation: the פִּשְׁעֵי דַמֶּשֶׂק or the פִּשְׁעֵי עַזָּה etc.

This thread is resumed in Amos 3:14-15. 'On the day when I punish the sins of Israel, the horns of the altar will be cut off and fall to the ground. And I shall smite the summer palace and the winter palace'. We can note a number of relevant points here.

- There is the mention of a specific day of punishment.

- The punishment for the פִּשְׁעֵי־יִשְׂרָאֵל will include the cutting off of the horns of the altar in Bethel. By implication this includes the destruction of the whole sanctuary.

- In addition there will be a smiting of the summer palace and the winter palace. The verb נכה Hiphil 'smite' is significant for this particular thread.

A further hint about the destruction of walls in Israel occurs in Amos 4:3 with the reference to the פְּרָצִים 'breaches', and the thread continues in 5:6 where we find that the Lord himself is threatening to be the fire which will devour the House of Joseph בֵּית יוֹסֵף and Bethel. Again there is some significance in the polysemy of the word בַּיִת, 'house', which can be a building or a structured group of people.

The houses come in for further punishment in Amos 6:11. 'He will smite the great house into fragments and the small house into splinters'. Again we note the use of the word נכה Hiphil. It is not clear who will actually do the smiting, but there is no doubt that it is the Lord who orders it to be done, כִּי־הִנֵּה יְהוָה מְצַוֶּה. The destruction of buildings continues in the series of visions in Chapters 7 and 9. Whatever we make of the wall and the אֲנָךְ in 7:7-8 in the fourth vision, the outcome predicted in Amos 7:9 is the destruction of the high places of Isaac and the sanctuaries of Israel.

The thread on the theme of buildings continues in Amos 9:1, 'Smite the כַּפְתּוֹר and the סִפִּים will shake', usually rendered as: 'Smite the capital and the foundations will shake'. This is the fifth vision report, and it includes a number of elements already noted.

- First, the Lord is standing by an altar, which reminds us of the threat against the altar of Bethel in 3:14.

- Secondly, the command to smite (הַךְ) is an echo of 6:11.

- Thirdly, the effect of the smiting is to cause the building to shake. The verb used is וְיִרְעֲשׁוּ, which takes us back to the earthquake רַעַשׁ of Amos 1:1.

- Finally, the imagery of architectural features suddenly switches to people. There is a play on words centred on the capitals of pillars and the heads of people. 'And smite them on the head, all of them, and what is left I shall kill by the sword'. The word 'head' itself involves a second ambiguity (skulls or leaders), which takes us back to the fate of the leaders in the oracles against the nations. The talk about architectural features in this thread is as much about the damage to societies as it is about the demolition of buildings.

Once again, we have here an example of a thread that begins in the opening lines of Amos and is continued all the way through to Chapter 9, thus underlining the unity of composition of the text despite its apparent disjointed character.

4 An Encounter with the Lord

Some of the references to earthquakes occur in those passages which refer to an appearance of the Lord. Three of these make up a well known group of texts (Amos 4:13; 5:8-9; 9:5-6). They are frequently referred to as doxologies, but they are better viewed as theophanies. They are sometimes considered as intrusions into the text, but even a brief observation will reveal that each of them fits remarkably well into its context. What I wish to point out here is that they are also involved in the phenomenon of threading. In fact we can detect a number of different threads present in them, one of which relates to the dramatic appearance of the Lord and the effect this has on people and on the physical world.

The thread relating to the Lord's appearances began in Amos 1:2, where God's presence is manifested through his voice, and the effects are described in terms of withering vegetation. 'The pastures wither and the top of Carmel dries up'. This idea is then taken up in the extended passage in Chapter 4 which contains a series of reproaches against Israel for its refusal to pay heed to the divine warnings. Each of the reproaches refers to an experience of God's power in the form of a punishment such as disease or blight on the vegetation. This is accompanied by the refrain : 'You did not return to me'. In other words, no meeting took place. The series of reproaches reaches its climax in Amos 4:12 with the prediction of a final encounter with the Lord's power: 'Therefore ... Because I will do this to you, prepare to meet your God, O Israel', הִכּוֹן לִקְרַאת־אֱלֹהֶיךָ יִשְׂרָאֵל where the לִקְרַאת implies a hostile encounter with a foe in battle.

This announcement that the time for warnings is over leads immediately into the first theophany in Amos 4:13, the purpose of which seems to be to underline the awesome power of the one they are going to meet. He is the maker of mountains and creator of the wind, controlling light and darkness. And his name is YHWH God of Hosts. The thread is continued in Amos 5:8, in a similar passage which stresses the cosmic dimension of the Lord's power as the creator of the heavenly constellations who can control the waters of the sea.

Eight verses later, in Amos 5:16-17, there is a prediction of a time of great mourning to come: 'in every vineyard'. The mourning is associated directly with the Lord's presence: 'when (or: because) I pass through your midst', כִּי־אֶעֱבֹר בְּקִרְבְּךָ. These words form the immediate context for the introduction of the phrase, יוֹם יְהוָה 'The Day of the Lord', in Amos 5:18, which is an important element in this thread on encounters with the Lord, and perhaps its climax.

The topic of the violent effects of the Lord's coming to punish evil deeds is taken up again in Amos 8:8. The effects are varied: – 'the earth trembles, its inhabitants mourn and the land will rise and fall like the Nile of Egypt'. The use of אבל is reminiscent of 1:2, and the earthquake description takes us back to the רַעַשׁ of 1:1. The thread concerning an encounter with the Lord is thus intertwined with the thread on earthquakes. Moreover, given what we have observed about threading in Amos, it comes as no surprise to find that the next line refers us to the special Day appointed for God's intervention. The link between these various threads is reiterated one page later in the third theophany in Amos 9:5-6. It uses almost identical words, with the added detail that the earth melts when the Lord touches it. Once again, the thread stretches from Chapter 1 to Chapter 9.

5 The Reversal Motif

In the theophanies we can detect another important thread made up of a variety of semantic elements that come under the general heading of 'reversal'. This is one of the dominant threads in the text of Amos, which shows a certain predilection for turning things upside-down or back-to-front. The first manifestation of this fondness for unexpected twists in logic occurs in Amos 3:2. 'Only you have I known out of all the families of the earth. Therefore I shall punish you ... ' The same feature of the surprise ending is evident in 4:4 with regard to human activity. 'Come to Bethel and sin!' These may be small beginnings, but when we hold onto the thread and follow it through, we find that it is really quite substantial.

The verb הפך is a significant marker for this thread, and we see it in Amos 4:11, which introduces the first theophany and asserts God's power to turn things upside-down. 'I overthrew some of you like the overthrowing of Sodom and Gomorrah.' The reversal idea is continued in the theophany itself, in 4:13, in the phrase עֹשֵׂה שַׁחַר עֵיפָה 'making dawn darkness'. The text is ambiguous.[3] Which is made into which? Is darkness turned into dawn, or is dawn turned into darkness? Turning 'darkness into dawn' would be a normal process, and is in fact a daily occurrence in God's governance of his creation. Turning 'dawn into darkness', on the other hand, would be a violent reversal of the normal expectation. The first notion is comforting and reassuring. The second is threatening and frightening. The Hebrew text of 4:13 by itself leaves us in suspense, with both possibilities open. We will be in a better position to interpret it, when we follow up the thread of which it is a part.

The idea of contrasting opposites is taken up in Amos 5:7, but it is in terms of human rather than divine activity. Humans turn good things into bad. 'You who turn justice into wormwood'. We can immediately note two things about this example. First there is the linguistic marker הַהֹפְכִים which is characteristic of the thread of reversals. Secondly, it is clear from the inclusion of a preposition ל in לְלַעֲנָה that the word order is that of indirect object before direct object. In the light of this latter point, we can look back to the earlier part of the thread in Amos 4:13 and be more confident about reading

---

[3]Word order is not conclusive in Hebrew verse. Neither is the absence of a preposition. The LXX finds a solution by introducing a copula: 'who makes dawn and darkness'. It is followed by the *Bible de Jérusalem* and *The New American Bible*, whereas *The New English Bible* introduces a preposition: 'who darkens the dawn with thick clouds'.

it as 'turning darkness into dawn' in the reassuring sense of God's continuing control over creation. That same message is repeated in Amos 5:8, which is part of the third theophany. 'He turns deep darkness into morning, and he darkens day into night'. There is no ambiguity about what is going on here. God is controlling the regular passage of day into night and night into day.

The theme of contrasting opposites surfaces again in Amos 5:14-15 where the people are urged to seek good and not evil.[4] Soon after that, in the 'Woe' oracle[5] of Amos 5:18-20, we find that the reversal of light and darkness is associated with the Day of the Lord. Human perversity, which turns good into evil, will be matched by an unnatural reversal of night and day. God will reverse things and make darkness rule where there should be light, הוּא־חֹשֶׁךְ וְלֹא־אוֹר. Since 5:18-20 also figured in our discussion of the two previous threads, it is a good example of the way the threads can occur in clusters.

More reversals of good into bad are seen in Amos 6:12. 'You have turned justice into poison, and righteous fruit into wormwood'. This time the thread of reversal is associated with the form of the riddle, which Amos uses elsewhere (3:3-6). In this passage, the riddles are rhetorical questions about the natural world, the right and wrong way of doing things or the logical sequence of cause and effect. They go well with the thread of reversals, and that thread re-emerges very clearly in Amos 8:9. 'I shall remove the sun at noon and darken the earth in the day time'. Once again we are presented with the sight of God reversing his own established way of doing things and turning light into darkness in the middle of the day, when such things are not supposed to happen. It is a reversal of Amos 5:8 above and a reprise of 5:18. The reversals continue in Amos 8:10 but the image changes to the language of rejoicing and mourning. 'I will turn your feasts into mourning and all your songs into laments'.

6 Conclusions

I have looked at four examples of threading in Amos, but there are many other threads.[6] Their existence is an observable feature of the

---

[4]The language of 5:15 is remarkably close to the ideas and language of Deut. 30:15, 'See I set before you this day life and good, death and evil'. Perhaps the inevitability of the bad ending to the story is implied in both, because they both see it retrospectively.

[5]The reversal theme is in fact a regular feature in woe oracles, the prime example being found in Isa. 5:20, 'Woe to those who call evil good and good evil, who put darkness for light and light for darkness, ... bitter for sweet and sweet for bitter'.

[6]The principal ones are those connected with the following topics: – feasting

language of the text. Their behaviour can be analysed without reference to authorial purpose and intentionality, although this latter topic cannot be excluded from discussions about the significance of such a feature in the text. The author of the text may have been operating consciously according to known procedures of composition, or he may simply have been acting instinctively and unconsciously according to what was generally felt to be the right way of composing, that is to say 'of putting a text together'. The threads are certainly not put together in any rigid mechanical way, though perhaps if we observed enough of them in Amos and in other texts,[7] we might be able to deduce some empirical 'rules' about their behaviour.

The limited observations we have made here point us in the direction of the following general conclusions.

1. The threads are developmental in nature. Initially, a thread may be quite slender. Its full significance only becomes evident as it is developed in later passages. Each time a thread comes to the surface it increases in explicitness and complexity.

2. Because of this developmental aspect, we can use the later occurrences of a thread to guide us in our interpretation of the earlier ones. Obscure passages can be more easily clarified, if we can establish that they are part of a thread. If you want to know what an apparently isolated unit means, find the thread it belongs to.

3. Clusters of threads can occur in a single passage. Such clustering is of course more likely to occur as the text progresses. Sections with the thickest cluster of threads are thereby identified as key passages in the text.

4. Some threads begin in the opening lines of ' Amos' and are continued throughout the text. The existence of such sustained threading argues in favour of a unity of composition for the nine chapters.

5. The existence of threading in Amos is also an argument against any temptation to try and improve the text by transposing lines to what we think is a more logical place.

6. The suggestion that a given passage is a later intrusion into Amos

---

and mourning, cultic worship, vegetation, the land, election, exile, rich and poor, the role of the prophet, cities and numbers.

[7] The next step would be to examine threading as a feature of *The Twelve Prophets*. For example, the Lord is likened to a tearing lion in Hos. 5:14, as well as to various other aggressive wild animals including a bear in Hos. 13:7-8. The feature of threading seems to operate in other prophetical books. The references to Cyrus in Isa. 41:2-3; 41:25; 44:28; 45:1-3; 45:13 can be viewed as an example of threading. So can the Servant Songs.

must be discounted, if that passage contains a thread or threads that bind it into the fabric of the whole text. This applies to the three so-called 'doxologies'. It also applies to the concluding section in 9:11-15, which is frequently classed as a late addition.

All of this comes down to one important conclusion. The text of Amos was composed in a way that demands special techniques of reading, techniques which do not come naturally to the modern, rational, logical mind. The threads we have identified continue to operate even when they are not on the surface. The reader is expected to scan back and forth in order to keep the threads in sight and to appreciate their richness. Reading Amos calls for a high level of sustained attention in order to interact with the whole text simultaneously.

Appendix: Illustrative Texts

THE LION

הֲיִשְׁאַג אַרְיֵה . . . הֲיִתֵּן כְּפִיר קוֹלוֹ	3:4
יְהוָה מִצִּיּוֹן יִשְׁאָג וּמִירוּשָׁלִַם יִתֵּן קוֹלוֹ	1:2
אַרְיֵה שָׁאָג מִי לֹא יִירָא יְהוָה דִּבֶּר מִי לֹא יִנָּבֵא	3:8
שִׁמְעוּ אֶת־הַדָּבָר הַזֶּה אֲשֶׁר דִּבֶּר יְהוָה	3:1
כַּאֲשֶׁר יַצִּיל הָרֹעֶה מִפִּי הָאֲרִי	3:12
כַּאֲשֶׁר יָנוּס אִישׁ מִפְּנֵי הָאֲרִי וּפְגָעוֹ הַדֹּב	5:19
וּבָא הַבַּיִת וְסָמַךְ יָדוֹ עַל־הַקִּיר וּנְשָׁכוֹ הַנָּחָשׁ	5:19
לֹא־יָנוּס לָהֶם נָס וְלֹא־יִמָּלֵט לָהֶם פָּלִיט	9:1
מִשָּׁם אֲצַוֶּה אֶת־הַנָּחָשׁ וּנְשָׁכָם	9:3

BUILDINGS

כִּי בְּיוֹם פָּקְדִי פִשְׁעֵי־יִשְׂרָאֵל	3:14
וְנִגְדְּעוּ קַרְנוֹת הַמִּזְבֵּחַ וְנָפְלוּ לָאָרֶץ	3:14
וְהִכֵּיתִי בֵית־הַחֹרֶף עַל־בֵּית הַקָּיִץ	3:15
וְהִכָּה הַבַּיִת הַגָּדוֹל רְסִיסִים וְהַבַּיִת הַקָּטֹן בְּקִעִים	6:11
וְנָשַׁמּוּ בָּמוֹת יִשְׂחָק וּמִקְדְּשֵׁי יִשְׂרָאֵל יֶחֱרָבוּ	7:9
וּבִצְעָם בְּרֹאשׁ כֻּלָּם וְאַחֲרִיתָם בַּחֶרֶב אֶהֱרֹג	9:1

Encountering the Lord

יְהוָה מִצִּיּוֹן יִשְׁאָג וּמִירוּשָׁלִַם יִתֵּן קוֹלוֹ	1:2
וְאָבְלוּ נְאוֹת הָרֹעִים וְיָבֵשׁ רֹאשׁ הַכַּרְמֶל	1:2
הִכּוֹן לִקְרַאת־אֱלֹהֶיךָ יִשְׂרָאֵל	4:12
כִּי־אֶעֱבֹר בְּקִרְבְּךָ	5:17
הַעַל זֹאת לֹא־תִרְגַּז הָאָרֶץ וְאָבַל כָּל־יוֹשֵׁב בָּהּ	8:8
וְעָלְתָה כָאֹר כֻּלָּהּ וְנִגְרְשָׁה וְנִשְׁקָה [וְנִשְׁקְעָה] כִּיאוֹר מִצְרָיִם	8:8
וְהָיָה בַּיּוֹם הַהוּא	8:9
הַנּוֹגֵעַ בָּאָרֶץ וַתָּמוֹג	9:5
וְעָלְתָה כַיְאֹר כֻּלָּהּ וְשָׁקְעָה כִּיאֹר מִצְרָיִם	9:5

The Reversal Motif

הָפַכְתִּי בָכֶם כְּמַהְפֵּכַת אֱלֹהִים אֶת־סְדֹם וְאֶת־עֲמֹרָה	4:11
עֹשֵׂה שַׁחַר עֵיפָה	4:13
הַהֹפְכִים לְלַעֲנָה מִשְׁפָּט	5:7
וְהֹפֵךְ לַבֹּקֶר צַלְמָוֶת וְיוֹם לַיְלָה הֶחְשִׁיךְ	5:8
דִּרְשׁוּ־טוֹב וְאַל־רָע לְמַעַן תִּחְיוּ	5:14
דִּרְשׁוּנִי וִחְיוּ וְאַל־תִּדְרְשׁוּ בֵּית־אֵל	5:4-5
כִּי־הֲפַכְתֶּם לְרֹאשׁ מִשְׁפָּט וּפְרִי צְדָקָה לְלַעֲנָה	6:12
וְהֵבֵאתִי הַשֶּׁמֶשׁ בַּצָּהֳרָיִם וְהַחֲשַׁכְתִּי לָאָרֶץ בְּיוֹם אוֹר	8:9
וְהָפַכְתִּי חַגֵּיכֶם לְאֵבֶל וְכָל־שִׁירֵיכֶם לְקִינָה	8:10

Meindert Dijkstra *Utrecht – The Netherlands*

'I am neither a prophet nor a prophet's pupil'
Amos 7:9-17 as the Presentation of a Prophet like Moses

> *I do not believe that it is possible to produce a problem-free reading strategy of the Bible.*
>
> R.P. Carroll[1]

1 Introduction: About 'Prophets' and Deconstructive Reading Strategy

In the course of the 'Joint Meeting' of 1988, Hugh Williamson stated that there was a widespread measure of agreement among scholars that the account of Amos's visions (Amos 7:1–8:3) – a set of four visionary reports which according to form and content may be divided into two dramatic word visions (7:1-3; 4-6) and two oracle or omen visions (7:7-8; 8:1-3)[2] – was interrupted by the story of the prophet's encounter with Amaziah, the chief priest of the royal sanctuary in Bethel (Amos 7:9-17)[3] during the reign of King Jeroboam II (Tishri 791-751/0 BCE).[4] The differences in genre and perspective are obvious. A set of 'autobiographically' phrased visionary reports are interrupted by a 'biographical' narrative. By contrast with this consensus, there is now considerable diversity of opinion about how and why this texture of texts was composed in this way. In the past ten years, Amos 7 has received quite a lot of attention. In addition to the classic literary-critical and redactional approaches, several new

---

[1] R.P. Carroll, 'Synchronic Deconstructions of Jeremiah: Diachrony to the Rescue?', in: J.C. de Moor (ed.), *Synchronic or Diachronic? A Debate on Method in Old Testament Exegesis* (OTS, 34), Leiden 1995, 39-51, esp. 50.

[2] B.O. Long, 'Reports of Visions Among the Prophets', *JBL* 96 (1976), 353-65.

[3] H.G.M. Williamson, 'The Prophet and the Plumb-Line: A Redaction-Critical Study of Amos vii', in: A.S. van der Woude (ed.), *In Quest of the Past: Studies on Israelite Religion, Literature and Prophetism. Papers Read at the Joint British-Dutch Old Testament Conference, held at Elspeet, 1988* (OTS, 26), Leiden 1990, 101-21, esp. 101; D.J.A. Clines, 'Metacommenting Amos', in: D.J.A. Clines (ed.), *Interested Parties: The Ideology of Writers and Readers of the Hebrew Bible* (JSOT.S, 205), Sheffield 1995, 76-93; R.F. Melugin, 'Amos in Recent Research', *CurResB* 6 (1998), 65-101; I. Willi-Plein, 'Das Zwölfprophetenbuch', *ThR* 64 (1999), 356-61.

[4] M. Dijkstra, 'Chronological Problems of the Eighth Century BC: New Proposal Dating the Samaria Ostraca', in: J.C. de Moor, H.F. van Rooy (eds), *Past, Present, Future: The Deuteronomistic History and the Prophets* (OTS, 44), Leiden 2000, 76-87.

approaches such as reception-history, rhetorical and reader-response criticism, Group/Grid Cultural Anthropological Model analysis and some more synchronic, syntactical and societal approaches were unleashed on this chapter in Amos, and disagreement grew.[5] Broadly speaking, there are two views on the origin of the story in this context. Either, it was especially invented and written for its present setting,[6] presumably by an member of 'die alte Amosschule',[7] or it was an existing narrative that has been preserved in prophetic tradition and was transferred from that 'source' into the Book of Amos in

---

[5] See the older literature quoted in J. Jeremias, *Der Prophet Amos* (ATD, 24), Göttingen 1995, 106, n.5; Williamson, 'The Prophet and the Plumb-Line', 102-4; further Th.W. Overholt, 'Commanding the Prophets: Amos and the Problem of Prophetic Authority', *CBQ* 41 (1979), 517-32, esp. 523-6; G. Pfeifer, 'Die Ausweisung eines lästigen Ausländers Amos 7 10-17', *ZAW* 96 (1984), 112-18; H. Utzschneider, 'Die Amazjaerzählung (Am 7,10-17) zwischen Literatur und Historie', *BN* 41 (1988), 76-101; R.C. Clements, 'Amos and the Politics of Israel' in: D. Garrone, F. Israel (eds), *Storia e tradizione di Israele: Scritti in onore di J. Alberto Soggin*, Brescia 1991, 49-64; L. Eslinger, 'The Education of Amos', *HAR* 11 (1987), 35-57; F.O. Garcia-Treto, 'A Reader-Response Approach to Prophetic Conflict', in: J. Exum, D.J.A. Clines, *The New Literary Criticism and the Hebrew Bible* (JSOT.S, 143), Sheffield 1993, 114-24; E. Blum, 'Jesaja und der דבר des Amos: Unzeitgemäße Überlegungen zu Jes 5,25; 9,7-20; 10,1-4', *DBAT* 28 (1992/3) [1994], 75-95; I. Jaruzelska, 'Amasyah – prêtre de Béthel – functionaire royal (essai socio-économique préliminaire)', *FolOr* 31 (1995), 53-69; Å. Viberg, 'Amos 7:14: A Case of Subtle Irony', *TynB* 47 (1996), 91-114; G. Ramirez, 'The Social Location of the Prophet Amos in the Light of the Group/Grid Cultural Anthropological Model', in: S.B. Reid (ed.), *Prophets and Paradigms: Essays in Honor of Gene M. Tucker* (JSOT.S, 229), Sheffield 1996, 112-24; J. Jeremias, 'Rezeptionsprozesse in der prophetische Überlieferung – am Beispiel der Visionsberichte des Amos', in: R.G. Kratz, Th. Krüger (eds), *Rezeption und Auslegung im Alten Testament und seinem Umfeld: Ein Symposion aus anlaß des 60. Geburtstag vom Odil Hannes Steck* (OBO, 153), Freiburg 1997, 29-44; A. Behrens, ' "Grammatik statt Ekstase!" Das Phänomen des syntaktischen Wiederaufnahme am Beispiel von Am 7,1-8,2', in: A. Wagner (ed.), *Studien zur hebräischen Grammatik* (OBO, 156), Freiburg 1997, 1-9; P.R. Noble, 'Amos and Amaziah in Context: Synchronic and Diachronic Approaches to Amos 7-8', *CBQ* 60 (1998), 423-39; P. Gilbert, 'A New Look at Amos' Prophetic Status (Amos 7:10-17)', EeT(O) 28 (1997), 291-300.

[6] J.D.W. Watts, *Vision and Prophecy in Amos*, Leiden 1958, 27-50, esp. 31-3; Utzschneider, 'Die Amazjaerzählung', 97-8; Jeremias, *Amos*, 107; F.I. Andersen, D.N. Freedman, *Amos* (AncB, 24A), New York, 1989, 763; Noble, 'Amos and Amaziah in Context', 436-39; A. Behrens, 'Grammatik statt Ekstase', 1-9.

[7] H.W. Wolff, *Joel Amos* (BK, 14/2), Neukirchen-Vluyn 1969, 131, 355-54; Wolff thought of a kind of *apophtegmaton* or *memorabile* told by an eye-witness. So he still thought much of its historical value, in contrast to Utzschneider who thought of a date after 722, but still assumed that the story gave a Pre-Deuteronomistic view on prophecy. Only a very few scholars still see Amos himself as the author, e.g. Pfeifer, 'Ausweisung', 118.

the final stage of redaction.⁸ Both literary and redactional approaches agree that the narrative is an insertion, breaking up the original unity of the visions. For the redactional approach it provides the starting point for a reconstruction of the chapter's redaction history, for the literary approach it allows rediscovery of the final design and of the author's intention for such an arrangement.⁹ Synchronic and diachronic approaches, therefore, should not ignore each other lingering over apparent 'cracks' in the text.¹⁰ As I will show, careful literary analysis of the story suggests a prophetic narrative from a source similar to those from which the Deuteronomistic Historian(s) drew his/their material, in order to create a canon of prophets like Moses.

At present, the problem of origin and redaction has become far more complicated with the debate about the nature of Israelite prophecy as compared with ancient Near Eastern prophecy and divination. The question arose whether the early prophets were indeed $nābî'$ or just spokesmen of a new religious elite, and so the nature of prophetic literature was called in question. Some scholars have suggested that we are heading for a paradigm shift as to the understanding of the idea of 'writing prophets'.¹¹ In 1983, A. Greame Auld read

---

⁸In older scholarship, it was suggested to be part of a more complete biography, originally situated elsewhere in the Book of Amos, e.g. K. Budde, 'Zur Geschichte des Buches Amos', in: K. Marti (ed.), *Studien zur semitischen Philologie und Religionsgeschichte: Fs J. Wellhausen* (BZAW, 27), Giessen 1914, 65-77, esp. 66-7; for other suggestions, see C. van Leeuwen, *Amos* (POT), Nijkerk 1985, 278-9; Williamson, 'The Prophet and the Plumb-Line', 102-3. J.H. Hayes, *Amos: His Times and His Preaching*, Nashville 1988, 231, argues that the narrative makes better sense if the episode follows 9:11-12.

⁹Noble, 'Amos and Amaziah in Context', 425.

¹⁰P.R. Noble, 'Synchronic and Diachronic Approaches to Biblical Interpretation', *JLT* 7 (1993), 130-48; J.C. de Moor (ed.), *Synchronic or Diachronic: A Debate on Method in Old Testament Exegesis* (OTS, 34) Leiden 1995.

¹¹F.E. Deist, 'The Prophets: Are We Heading for a Paradigm Switch?', in: V. Fritz et al. (eds), *Prophet und Prophetenbuch: Festschrift für Otto Kaiser zum 65. Geburtstag* (BZAW, 185), Berlin 1989, 1-18; O. Loretz, 'Die Entstehung des Amos-Buches im Licht der Prophetien aus Mari, Assur, Ischali und der Ugarittexte', *UF* 24 (1992), 179-211; for some warnings about the tendencies in prophetic research leading to the eclipse of the prophet, see H. Ringgren, 'Israelite Prophecy: Fact or Fiction?', in: J. Emerton (ed.), *Congress Volume Jerusalem 1986* (SVT, 40), Leiden 1988, 204-10; J.M. Ward, 'The Eclipse of the Prophet in Contemporary Prophetic Studies', *USQR* 42 (1988), 97-104; Th.W. Overholt, 'Prophecy in History: The Social Reality of Intermediation', *JSOT* 48 (1990), 3-29; H. Barstad, 'No Prophets? Recent Developments in Biblical Prophetic Research and Ancient Near Eastern Prophecy', *JSOT* 57 (1993), 39-60; J. Jarick, 'Prophets and Losses: Some Themes in Recent Study of the Prophets', *ET* 107 (1995), 75-6; J.-G. Heintz, 'La "fin" des prophètes bibliques? Nouvelles théories et documents sémitiques anciens', in: J.-G. Heintz (ed.), *Oracles et prophéties dans*

a paper 'Prophets Through the Looking Glass' at a meeting of the British Society for Old Testament Study.[12] In this and other studies, he demonstrated that the men we call the early prophets, e.g. Hosea, Amos, Isaiah and Micah and even Jeremiah and Ezekiel despite all first appearances to the contrary, were afterwards called 'prophets', but were not such in their own estimate. 'Prophets were people they denounced and abhorred'.[13] Also many, if not all, passages in which the phrase 'The Word of the LORD' was used, were editorial insertions to their collected poetic sayings.[14] In the books of the so-called prophets, he detected a radical change in view on prophets and prophecy in Exilic and Post-Exilic times. In these 'prophets', the attitude to the official *nābî*, whether individual or in groups, was mostly hostile, or at best neutral, though the title is readily applied afterwards to the canonical prophets, even former prophets such as Moses, Samuel and Elijah. Now the story of Amos's conflict with Amaziah, in general, and, in particular his seemingly absolute denial 'I am neither a prophet nor a prophet's pupil', strongly underscores Auld's ideas. If someone wanted to refute his major tenet that Amos, Hosea and other early 'prophets' were not such in their own view, he should certainly adduce a plausible explanation of Amos's denial,[15] especially if this

---

l'antiquité: Actes du Colloque de Strasbourg 15-17 juin 1995, Paris 1997, 195-213.

[12] A.G. Auld, 'Prophets through the Looking Glass: Between Writings and Moses', *JSOT* 27 (1983), 3-23, together with the responses of R.P. Carroll and H.G.M. Williamson (*ibid.*, 25-31, 33-39 and another response of Auld, 41-44); repeating his views in A.G. Auld, 'Prophets and Prophecy in Jeremiah and Kings', *ZAW* 96 (1984), 66-82; Idem, *Amos* (OTGu) Sheffield, 1986; Idem, 'Word of God and Word of Man: Prophets and Canon', in: L. Eslinger, G. Taylor (eds), *Ascribe to the Lord: Biblical and Other Studies in Memory of Peter C. Graigie* (JSOT.S, 67) Sheffield 1988, 237-252, esp. 245-8., Idem, 'Prophecy in Books: A Rejoinder', *JSOT* 48 (1990), 31-2; see the discussion in Jarick, 'Prophets and Losses', 75-6; Barstad, 'No Prophets?', 41-2.

[13] Auld, 'Word of God and Word of Man', 245.

[14] Barstad correctly sees this as the weakest part of his argument (Barstad, 'No Prophets?', 42, n.14), but this is not correct because of what Auld says about the messenger formula (he hardly says anything about it), but because he did not prove his point, apart from a few superficial remarks on the use of the phrase in Hosea and Jeremiah. For example, we may refer here to P.K.D Neumann, 'Das Wort, das geschehen ist ... Zum Problem der Wortempfangs Terminologie in Jer. I-XXV', *VT* 23 (1973), 171-217 and S. Hermann, *Jeremia* (BK, 12), Neukirchen-Vluyn 1986, 9-11, for the editorial use of the different types of 'Wortereignisformel' in the final redaction of a prophetic book, leaving aside whether it concerns a Deuteronomistic redactor.

[15] So one finds explanations of his statement as subtle irony, Viberg, 'Amos 7:14: A Case of Subtle Irony', 91-114; as an example of social awareness, G. Ramirez, 'The Social Location of the Prophet Amos', 112-24. Amos's denial was not an indictment of prophets, but a sign of respect for group boundaries: Gilbert, 'A

statement be part of a Deuteronomistically phrased or revised prophetic narrative incorporated in the Book of Amos, for Auld rightly pointed out that the Exilic and Post-Exilic redactors of the Deuteronomistic History had no difficulties in labelling the canonical prophet as a *nābî*.

Auld's view was warmly endorsed by Robert Carroll, who time and again maintained that the spokesmen known as prophets should not be regarded as prophets, but rather as poets, or members of a critical intellectual elite. In his 1986 commentary, he argued that the 'prophet' Jeremiah was more legend than person and the book about him a Deuteronomistic anthology, a creation based on what the authors believed Pre-Exilic prophecy had been like, a vehicle to enable the Post-Exilic communities to cope with their reality. So, the relation between prophet and prophetic book has become seriously problematic, and much scepticism has been expressed about the quest for 'historical prophets' behind the books. Others were more sceptical about Auld's thesis. The prophets opposed by Amos, or Jeremiah were not rejected because they were prophets of the LORD,[16] but because they were bad ones. They may have been hesitant and, like Amos, sometimes reluctant to use the designation *nābî* for themselves,[17] but that does not mean that the institution, or the social reality of religious intermediation was denied, or rejected. In the 8th and 7th Century BCE, the office of the *nābî* implied both in Judah and Israel,[18] as elsewhere in the ancient Near East, a social institution and role for this religious specialist different from the mantic and ritual skills of the priestly classes. Interestingly, the evidence from comparison with ancient Near Eastern prophecy from Mari, Emar, Assur and so on, is adduced either to support a paradigm shift in our point of view

---

New Look at Amos' Prophetic Status', 291-300 (I am not a prophet in Judah, but rather a farmer!).

[16] Both the prophets in 1 Kgs 22 and Hananiah in Jer. 28 are acting as 'prophets of YHWH' and their professionalism and office are taken for granted (also Noadiah in Neh. 6:14). Though they are seen as pseudo-prophets, it does not mean that the profession or institution is rejected, see Williamson, *JSOT* 23 (1983), 33-9.

[17] After all, the idea that the early prophets did not view themselves as professional prophets, or even rejected this title for themselves was not so new, see H.P. Müller, נָבִיא, *ThWAT*, Bd. 5, Berlin 1986, col. 149, A. Jepsen, *Nabi*, München 1934, 214-15; incidentally, there might have been different reasons for Amos's denial, apart from his hostility to the professionals, see literature quoted in n. 15.

[18] Though regional and societal differences in the evaluation and role of the prophetic office may have existed, see R.R. Wilson, *Prophecy and Society in Ancient Israel*, Philadelphia 1980, 1989, 135ff.; 253ff.; R. Albertz, *Religionsgeschichte Israels in alttestamentlicher Zeit*, Bd. 1 (ATD Ergänzungsreihe Band 8/1), Göttingen 1992, 233-44.

on 'writing prophets', or to claim the societal reality of Pre-Exilic prophecy, notwithstanding the Post-Exilic literary adaptation of the prophetic tradition.[19]

Auld's marshalling of statistics on the use of the title 'prophet' in the Former and Latter Prophets, once again drew scholarly attention to certain lines of discontinuity in the religio-cultural memory of Israel in exilic times. Prophets like Amos, Hosea became figures of memory and, as such, preacher, though they were 'canonized' as 'prophets', more precisely, in the Deuteronomistic view, 'YHWH's servants, the prophets'. Even, if this phrase were not coined by the Deuteronomistic Historian, he certainly adopted it to define his meta-narrative tradition of canonical prophets in Exilic and Post-Exilic times. In the light of recent research, this is still a rather moderate remark, for the advocates of a late, if not 'Hellenistic', provenance of the Old Testament have also taken up the Book of Amos as a book of comfort, revised by circles of *Anawim*, i.e. Jewish pious poor, in the 3rd Century BCE.[20] Several rounds of debate show that a 'paradigm shift' in the scholarly understanding of the prophets is not yet generally accepted. However despite a certain rapprochement, Auld, Carroll, Loretz, Levin *et al.* remain more sceptical about the quest for 'historical' persons behind the named prophets, than Barstad, Overholt, Heintz and others. Many scholars still reckon with the 'social reality' of prophets, in particular against the background of prophecy in the ancient Near East,[21] though they admit that no immediate access to their *ipsissima verba* and performance is possible, because they are blurred by later editorial and subsequent theoretical constructs. It remains however, a matter of interpretation how much of historical personality and performance was transformed into literary personage and ideology. The direct relationship between text and history has been thoroughly questioned, if not severed, in Post-Modern philosophy and science of history, so that the days of 'text minus ideology = history' are irrevocably gone.[22] For some the prophetic books re-

---

[19] See Barstad, 'No Prophets?', 50-1; 56-60; in contrast to Loretz, 'Entstehung des Amos-Buches', 205-6.

[20] Chr. Levin, 'Das Amosbuch der Anawim', *ZThK* 94 (1997), 407-436; about this 'Hellenistic' school itself, see B. Becking, 'Is de Hebreeuwse Bijbel een Hellenistisch Boek?', *NTT* 54 (2000), 1-17.

[21] Barstad, 'No Prophets?', 49-51; Heintz, 'La "fin" des prophètes bibliques?', 212-3.

[22] B.E.H.J. Becking, 'No More Grapes from the Vineyard? A Plea for a Historical Approach in the Study of the Old Testament', in: A. Lemaire, M. Sæbø, *Congress Volume Oslo 1998* (VT.S, 80), Leiden 2000, 123-41; M. Dijkstra, 'Geschiedenis van Israël: ontwikkelingen, problemen en perspectieven', in: *The International*

main a 'distant mirror'. If we date the prophet Amos about 760 BCE, we convey a historical truth based on internal and external evidence, including an earthquake and, perhaps, a solar eclipse, but it were the editors who arranged the literary 'evidence' into their ideological framework of meaning. They introduced this 'historical' remark about the earthquake and made it the hidden theme of the entire book, but they were enabled to do so because of the collective memory generated by these traumatic events (Zech. 14:5).[23] So, there is often an intrinsic relationship between historical reality, literary tradition and theological interpretation, between person, performance and personage, fact, event and meaning.

But it is inherent in the creation of texts that the border-lines between the past and the present become blurred by a process of tradition and continuous change of meaning on the road from person to personage, from author to reader. Meaning can never become fixed because neither events, nor texts about events generate a stable absolute meaning between speakers and listeners, authors and readers.[24] 'A text is not, however, a self-enclosed system of signs with a fixed structure (as seen by structuralists). All texts are linked to one another in an open network of signs that are playfully undermining, constructing and deconstructing one another!'[25] Liberating us from the nostalgia for a stable absolute interpretation, deconstruction as a reading strategy can help to overcome the antagonism of reading about the world behind the text, the world in the text, or the world in

---

Bible Commentary (Dutch version, forthcoming).

[23] D. Kelly Ogden, 'The Earthquake Motif in the Book of Amos', in: K.-D. Schunck, M. Augustin (eds), *Goldene Äpfel in silbernen Schalen: Collected Communications of the XIIIth Congress IOSOT Leuven 1989* (BEAT, 20), Frankfurt a.M. 1992, 69-80; J. Jeremias, 'Zwei Jahre vor dem Erdbeben (Am 1,1)', in: P. Mommer, W. Thiel (eds), *Altes Testament – Forschung und Wirkung: Festschrift für Henning Graf Reventlow*, Frankfurt a.M. 1994, 15-31; D.N. Freedman, A. Welch, 'Amos's Earthquake and Israelite Prophecy', in: M.D. Coogan et al. (eds), *Scripture and Other Artifacts: Essays in Honor of Phillip J. King*, Louisville 1994, 188-98.

[24] For the description of deconstructive reading, I owe much to E. Conradie, 'Deconstruction', in: E. Conradie et al., *Fishing for Jonah: Various Approaches to Biblical Interpretation* (Study Guides in Religion and Theology, 1), University of Western Cape 1998, 182-96 and Carroll, 'Synchronic Deconstructions of Jeremiah: Diachrony to the Rescue?' (n. 1), 39-51; Idem, 'Poststructuralistic Approaches: New Historicism and Postmodernism', in: J. Barton (ed.), *The Cambridge Companion to Biblical Interpretation*, Cambridge 1998, 50-66; diachronic or 'historical' reading is often a help overcoming alleged or real synchronic discrepancies in a text. See also M. Dijkstra, 'YHWH as Israel's *gō'ēl*: Second Isaiah's Perspective on Reconciliation and Restitution', *ZAR* 5 (1999), 239.

[25] Conradie et al., *Fishing for Jonah*, 189.

front of the text. In literary deconstruction, the hierarchy of author-text-reader and any rigid distinctions between synchrony and diachrony, archaeology of the text, the text-itself or reader response are undermined. Formerly, literary criticism as a kind of archaeology of the text, dug for historical content, or for the pure literary source in a process of removing all interpretative layers and ideological overtones. Like the archaeology of the spade itself, it was deemed a destructive approach because digging for older layers and intentions implied that the text-itself was irretrievably destroyed. Deconstruction seems to be the Post-Modern alternative to classical literary criticism, because it seeks meaning in an approach of deconstructive understanding in front of, inside or, if needed behind the text. It is inherent to the text if it introduces the reader to the world beyond the text. 'There is nothing outside the text' is one of Derrida's famous maxims. We have no access to reality but through language and if we wish to communicate with the past the text is our only way of communication.[26] It does not mean that 'anything goes', but that any text we read generates critical questions in the mind of the reader, drawing attention to weak points of argument, inadequacies and loose ends in the texture of the text, but also implies a network of other texts (intertexts), themes, cultural realia and so on hidden in the world behind the text.

So, I have taken up once more the quest for the nature and origin of Amos's 'biography' in Amos 7. Not wholly convinced that Amos 7-8 is 'a well integrated, harmonious whole making excellent sense as it stands',[27] I approach it as a piece of literary patch-work or hand-made fabric with some flaws and seams and I aim at some reconstruction or preferred readings from my perspective as informed reader using a number of intertexts, in order to bridge the gap between Amos as a historical prophetic personality and the literary, perhaps even Deuteronomistic character Amos, who denied being a prophet, because like Moses and David he was taken from behind the flock to be adopted in the Jewish canon of YHWH's servants, the prophets.

2 Some (De)constructive Reading on Amos 7:9-17

'There's a crack in everything. / That's how the light gets in', says a poem of Leonard Cohen, quoted by the late R.P. Carroll to illustrate how ruptures in the fabric of a text or seams in the material allow the

---

[26] J.J. Degenaar, 'Deconstruction: The Celebration of Language', in: B.C. Lategan (ed.), *The Reader and Beyond: Theory and Practice in South African Reception Studies*, Pretoria, 1992, 187-211, esp. 201; Conradie et al., *Fishing for Jonah*, 189; Carroll, 'Poststructuralistic approaches', 52-5.

[27] Noble, 'Amos and Amaziah in Context', 439.

light to shine through. It is also one of the favourite means of classic literary criticism to look for such tensions, duplicates, discrepancies, sudden changes and ruptures in style. There is widespread agreement that somewhere in the course of reading the text of Amos 7 itself, our perspective on the prophet has changed from 'autobiographical' to 'biographical', but where and for what reason?[28] It is the kind of sudden change you might expect in a Post-Modern novel, leaving the reader's understanding of the literary world in fragments. However, did the ancient author or redactor also deliberately intend to confuse the reader's perception?

Scholars have given a great deal of thought to this transition and one of the crucial questions is the position of verse 9 between vision and story. The problem with the view that the story was written for its present setting and was even formed from thematic elements taken from its immediate context and from a wider environment of co-texts, is that it fails to explain why the story was not simply cast in the first person and more smoothly integrated into its context.[29] So, somewhere beyond verse 8, a major shift, break, rupture or some such occurred in the text. There is no need to discuss all the alternatives. Either the prophecy of doom in verse 9 is an integral part of the third vision (i.e. verses 7-8), to which Amos 7:10-17 was added in its present setting according to the catchword principle,[30] or it was a redactionally phrased transition bridging the gap between vision-report and story,[31] or it was originally part of the story and the direct cause

---

[28]'Autobiographical' and 'biographical' are just referents to distinguish between an I-text and a He/She-text. It is not my aim to look for biographical intent behind the visionary reports or narrative.

[29]Williamson, 'The Prophet and the Plumb-Line', 102; unless, of course, we grant the author the use of Post-Modern techniques of composition! To answer this question with a counter-question: Why should it be less acceptable to an original author than to a redactor? (Noble, 'Amos and Amaziah in Context', 437), is not satisfactory. We may expect from a redactor a different attitude to his material than the original narrator.

[30]An old tradition as reflected in Massoretic petuḥah, LXX and found in the majority of translations (KJV, RSV, NIV, NBG, SV, WV, LV, NEB, REB, JB) and commentaries (Weiser, Rudolph, Soggin, Van Leeuwen, Van der Woude).

[31]And as such, neither an original part of the vision report or the story. This middle position is found in Wolff, *Amos*, 340, 348 ('Verdeutlichung und Überleitung'); A.J. Bjørndalen, 'Zur Zukunft des Amazja und Israëls nach der Überlieferung Amos 7,10-17', in: R. Albertz *et al.*, *Werden und Wirken des Alten Testaments: Fs für Claus Westermann zum 70. Geburtstag*, Göttingen 1980, 236-51, esp. 237-38, n. 3 ('zum Zweck der Verbindung und Überleitung'); Clements, 'Amos and the Politics', 62-3 ('editorial addition intended to demonstrate the fulfilment of what is said in visions and story'); Jeremias, Amos, 101-2 ('Brückenvers, präzisierende Auslegung').

of Amaziah's indignation and his interference. Ackroyd, Williamson and, in particular, the commentary of Andersen and Freedman put forward a strong case for the last option and I am inclined to agree with them.[32]

There are some arguments that favour an original coherence of verses 9-17 and the independent provenance of the story: (1) the seven occurrences of 'Israel' in 9-17;[33] (2) וַיִּשְׁלַח is probably the continuation and not opening of the story;[34] (3) word repetitions such as בַּחֶרֶב in 9,11 and 17, the word מִקְדָּשׁ in 9 and 13; the rare form יִשְׂחָק in 9 and 16 in unique parallelism with Israel;[35] (4) the mention of Jeroboam by his title 'king of Israel' and Amaziah as 'Priest of Bethel'. Some scholars have used Argument (4) to stress the relative independence of the narrative, suggesting another readership for the story than for the oracle of doom regarding the House of Jeroboam in verse 9.[36] This argument, however, does not really affect the coherence of v. 9 with vv. 10-17, because the difference could be that the message about the House of Jeroboam is directed to the implied and well informed listeners at Bethel (including Amaziah), whereas the narrative framework concerns a broader, perhaps, Judahite, audience. An interesting parallel may be found in Isaiah 7:1-16(17), also a story about the

---

[32] P.R. Ackroyd, 'A Judgment Narrative between Kings and Chronicles? An Approach to Amos 7:9-17', in: G.W. Coats, B.O. Long (eds), *Canon and Authority: Essays in Old Testament Religion and Theology*, Philadelphia, 1977, 71-87 = Idem, *Studies in the Religious Tradition of the Old Testament*, London, 1987, 195-208; Williamson, 'The Prophet and the Plumb-Line', 103; Andersen, Freedman, *Amos*, 634-8.

[33] Andersen, Freedman, *Amos*, 634-8, though this point of seven occurrences of the name Israel in 7:9-16 is not followed up in the exegesis (*ibid.*, 760ff).

[34] If it is the opening of the story, it plunges the listener into the middle of events. This may sometimes happen in narratives (with שלח, e.g. Num. 20:14; Josh. 2:1; 2 Sam. 12:1; 1 Kgs 5:15), but in a narrative introduction inversion will occur more often (e.g. 2 Kgs 11:4; 14:8; 20:12 = Isa. 39:1; 2 Kgs 22:3 = 2 Chron. 34:8; 2 Chron. 28:16; 32:9; 36:10), whereas וַיִּשְׁלַח usually opens an episode after some preliminary remarks or a narrative introduction (e.g. Gen. 20:2; 28:5; 32:4; Num. 16:12; 21:21, 32; 22:5). On narrative beginnings, see W. Gross, 'Syntaktische Erscheiningen am Anfang althebräischer Erzählungen: Hintergrund und Vordergrund', in: J. Emerton (ed.), *Congress Volume Vienna 1980* (VT.S, 32) Leiden 1981, 131ff; W. Schneider, 'Und es begab sich ... Anfänge von Erzählungen in Biblischen Hebräisch', *BN* 70 (1993), 62-87.

[35] Especially, the parallelism is unique because (House of) Isaac does not appear outside the Pentateuch to indicate Israel. It only appears in the cluster Abraham, Isaac and Israel/Jacob (Josh. 24:3-4; 1 Kgs 18:36; 2 Kgs 13:23; 1 Chron. 16:16= Ps. 105:9; 29:18, 2 Chron. 30:6; Jer. 33:26, in Ps. 105:9 and Jer. 33:26, also in this rare spelling), usually in Deuteronomistic phraseology.

[36] E.g. Wolff, *Amos*, 355; Van Leeuwen, *Amos*, 279; Bjørndalen, 'Erwägungen zur Zukunft des Amazja und Israels', 238, n.5.

prophet which as a 'Fremdbericht' was included in the framework of some 'autobiographical' texts (Isa. 6:1-13, 8:1-4).[37] In this narrative framework, King Ahaz and his enemies are introduced with full names and titles,[38] whereas in the divine instruction and the prophet's word he is simply referred to as Ahaz, or House of David (Isa. 7:3, 13). To these text-immanent arguments, let me add some other arguments to characterize the source of the story and its redaction in the present context (section 3 below).

So, it is becoming less easy to regard verse 9 as having once stood in isolation. If Amos 7:9-17 stands out as a once independent story, incorporated in the Book of Amos, the rupture between the visions Amos 7:1-8 and the story becomes even more transparent, for this story misses a clear introduction.[39] Ackroyd indeed assumed that in the process of redaction the original narrative introduction got lost and was replaced by visionary reports, creating a new, immediate context and environment of related texts for the understanding of Amos's conflict in Bethel.[40] For a reconstruction of this narrative opening, one could think of the standard 'Wortereignisformel': וַיְהִי דְבַר־יְהוָה אֶל־PN לֵאמֹר as it is frequently used in the Books of Samuel and Kings (1 Sam. 15:10; 2 Sam. 7:4; 1 Kgs 6:11; 12:22; 13:20; 16:1; 17:2, 8; 18:1 (inversion), 21:17, 28; 2 Kgs 20:4 (inversion) = Isa. 38:4).[41] The problem is, however, that in Samuel-Kings it only appears as a special introductory formula of the prophetic word within the framework of the prophetic legends,[42] not as an introduction to the narrative itself. This is not found before later prophetic Books, e.g. Jer. 36:1;[43] Jon. 1:1; Hag. 1:1; Zech. 1:1; 7:1 (with inversion after date formula). Ackroyd suggested the loss of a 'historical' introduction as it is found in

---

[37] About the problem 'Ich-bericht' or 'Fremdbericht', see H. Wildberger, *Jesaja 1-12* (BK, 10/1), Neukirchen-Vluyn 1972, 269-70.

[38] The second part of Isa. 7:1 was probably taken over and adapted from 1 Kgs 16:5 by the redactor of Isaiah's Book (Wildberger, *Jesaja 1-12*, 273-4).

[39] As noted by Ackroyd, 'A Judgment Narrative', 81-2; Williamson, 'The Prophet and the Plumb-Line, 101-2.

[40] In this respect, he concurred with Wolff, Williamson, Bjørndalen *et al.* looking for an editorial explanation of the story in its present context.

[41] Neumann, 'Das Wort, das geschehen ist', 174-81, who did not include the formula's with narrative inversion; add to his n. 2: 1 Kgs 18:1; 2 Kgs 20:4 = Isa. 38:4; 1 Chron. 22:8 derives from 2 Sam. 7:4; 2 Chron. 9:2 = 1 Kgs 12:22, so in total 12 times in Samuel-Kings.

[42] Also in Jeremiah (Jer. 28:12; 29:30; 32:26; 34:12; 35:12; 36:27; 37:6, 42:7, 43:8) in a function similar to that in Samuel-Kings, see Neumann, 'Das Wort, das geschehen ist', 175-6.

[43] Similarly, but only in Jeremiah הַדָּבָר אֲשֶׁר הָיָה אֶל־יִרְמְיָהוּ מֵאֵת יְהוָה לֵאמֹר (7:1; 11:1; 18:1; 30:1; 35:1; 44:1) + date formula (25:1; 32:1;), or בְּ–infinitive clause, or another temporal clause (21:1; 34:1, 8; 40:1); a blend of this formula and the 'Wortereignisformel' appears in Jer. 36:1, as in Zech. 7:1.

similar stories about silencing the prophet (1 Kgs 13:1ff.; Jer. 26:1ff.;[44] 36:1ff.; 2 Chron. 25:14-16).[45] If one were to speculate about an original introduction, the simplest solution might be to mirror the words of Amos 7:15b as a reference to the opening of the story, 'The LORD said to Amos ... ' with or without a short remark about the occasion or a date formula. In the prophetic narratives, the predecessor of the 'Wortereignisformel' was, perhaps, as in the four visionary reports, the simple introduction to direct speech: PN וַיֹּאמֶר יְהוָה אֶל (e.g. Isa. 7:3; 8:1, 3; Jer. 1:14; 13:6; 24:3; Hos. 1:2; 3:1). A decision in this matter would finally also depend on answering questions about the nature and origin of the literary source of Amos 7:9-17. So, I would suggest as my preferred reading of this text the following introduction:

> <And the LORD said to Amos, Go to Bethel(?) and prophesy
> to my people Israel
> This is what the LORD says, ... [46]>
> 'The high places of Isaac will be destroyed
> and the sanctuaries of Israel will be ruined
> with my sword I will rise against the House of Jeroboam'

The art of deconstructive reading sometimes includes the intuition to fill in the gaps where a rupture in the text is transparent. Detecting a crack, a weak spot in the fabric may open a window on the understanding about the text in front of us. It is, however, not the only hiatus in the story, that requires for some elucidation, for the story continues,

> Then Amaziah the priest of Bethel sent a message to Jeroboam
> king of Israel, 'Amos is raising a conspiracy against you in the
> very heart of Israel. The land cannot bear all his words. For
> this is what Amos is saying,
> "Jeroboam will die by the sword,
> and Israel will surely go into exile
> away from their native land." '

What is the reason for Amaziah to send an intelligence report to the palace, before he expelled the prophet out of Bethel?[47] Is it the

---

[44] Amos 7:10-17 might have a similar function in Amos's Book as the Micah legend in Jer. 26:18-19, see Th. Lescow, 'Das vorexilische Amosbuch: Erwägungen zu seiner Kompositionsgeschichte', *BN* 93 (1998), 23.

[45] Ackroyd, 'A Judgment Narrative between Kings and Chronicles', 81-2.

[46] Not only does the story miss an introduction, but even more the prophecy of doom in verse 9 lacks motivation. An unconditional, or unmotivated oracle of doom is certainly unusual for Amos, but we can only guess at its content. Quoting a prophecy without its original motivation has an interesting parallel in Jer. 26:18, where Mic. 3:12 is quoted, but the long motivation Mic. 3:9-11 is left out.

[47] I do not believe that Amaziah earnestly intended to warn Amos and advised

narrative about a conflict between priest and prophet, a story about religious competence and different charisma, or a conflict between king and prophet? Amaziah is clearly put in the forefront by the narrator,[48] whereas Jeroboam remains in the background. However Amos's prophecy and Amaziah's response clearly focus on the dynasty of Jehu and the national royal sanctuaries.[49] Ackroyd even speculated that the story was a judgment narrative on Jeroboam II, the absence of which he found noteworthy in Kings. The theme seems indeed to be set with the words of Amaziah: קָשַׁר עָלֶיךָ עָמוֹס בְּקֶרֶב בֵּית יִשְׂרָאֵל (v. 10). The message sent to Jeroboam supposes, if not a direct confrontation between king and prophet, at least some kind of action by the king. Two explanations are conceivable: (1) the priest of Bethel sent only a report to the king, but otherwise acted immediately on his own accord as chief official responsible;[50] (2) the priest asked Jeroboam for instructions and acted at the command of the king. There is evidence for either. In 17th century BCE Mari it was apparently the duty of certain royal officials to send King Zimrilim letters reporting on prophetic actions and words.[51] Whether this was part of a primitive network of intelligence is difficult to say, but it is clear that the letters were sometimes endorsed by witnesses and kept for reference. Occasionally, these letters were sent by the high priest or other temple officials.[52] In Jer. 29:24-32, there are fragments of correspondence about Jeremiah's prophetic activity. A certain Shemaiah, the Nehelamite, wrote to Zephaniah, the high priest in Jerusalem, 'The LORD has appointed you priest in place of Jehoiada to be in charge of the house of the LORD; you should put any madman who acts like a prophet into the stocks and neck-irons. So, why have you not reprimanded Jeremiah from Anathoth who poses as a prophet among you?' (Jer. 29:26-27).[53] The letter is instructive about the role of the chief

---

him to flee for the wrath of Jeroboam (Wolff, *Amos*, 358-9). See below on the intertextual link between Amos 7:12 and Num. 24:11.

[48] Bjørndalen, 'Erwägungen zur Zukunft des Amazja und Israels', 240.

[49] The announcement of Exile could be a Deuteronomistic revision of Amos's words. This does not mean that Amos did not announce deportation (also 4:3; 5:5, 27; 6:7), but the formulation here and 2 Kgs 17:23; 25:21 suggests a close relation of Amos 7:9-17 with Deuteronomistic thought, e.g. Wolff, *Amos*, 357 (summary of Amos's message by the narrator put in the mouth of Amaziah); Williamson, 'The Prophets and the Plumb-Line', 120.

[50] e.g. Wolff, *Amos*, 358; Van Leeuwen, *Amos*, 281 (who thought that Jeroboam did not react at all); Jeremias, *Amos*, 107.

[51] J.-M. Durand, *Archives Epistolaires de Mari* (AEM , 1/1 = ARMT, 26/1), Paris 1988, 381-2, e.g. No 196 [A.3719]:8-10.

[52] *Ibid.*, 382.

[53] M. Dijkstra, 'Prophecy by Letter (Jeremiah XXIX 24-32)', *VT* 33 (1983), 319-22.

priest of Bethel, who was vested with the authority to keep a tight hand over prophets in the royal sanctuary. So, his censure was in line with his regular function.[54] However it is hardly conceivable that the narrator told us about the message to Jeroboam only to inform us about Amaziah's charges against the prophet.

As some scholars have seen, this charge of conspiracy is the axial theme of the story and demands the interference of the king himself. Therefore, the story may belong to a set of conspiracy stories in which a prophet is involved, announcing the downfall of the reigning dynasty, here the dynasty of Jehu, who himself came to the throne as the result of a prophetically inspired conspiracy (2 Kgs 9:1-13, 14).[55] Other stories in which a message or messengers are sent, always informed the reader/listener about the reply, or the response of the addressee. More than once, scholars have expressed their astonishment that the message to Jeroboam was not answered, or that Amaziah did not wait for an answer. But the King's answer may be assumed in the story. The technique of Hebrew narrative allows for such implicit understanding of the narrative structure. The next scene in which the priest expels the prophet should be construed as an action required by the king and executed by his royal representative. It is a well known feature in Old Testament narrative (and also Ugaritic narrative texts)[56] that self-evident repetitions, execution of instructions, transfer of messages and the like, were often left out, either for language economy to gain momentum in the story, or to built up suspense. In the story of David and Bathsheba, David sent a letter to Joab by courtesy of Uriah, but we never hear whether it was given to Joab and read. It is simply implied. The story immediately continues with the execution of the written instruction.[57] Both Amos and Amaziah are in the forefront

---

[54] I. Jaruzelska, 'Amasyah – prêtre de Béthel – fonctionaire royal (essai socio-économique préliminaire)', *FolOr* 31 (1995), 53-69; also in Jeremiah 26, it are officials coming from the royal palace, who dismissed the charge of the priests and prophets(!) against Jeremiah. It is, however, not clear whether they were in charge for law and order in the temple.

[55] H. Schmid, 'Nicht Prophet bin ich, noch bin ich Prophetensohn', *Jud.* 23 (1967), 68-74; Ackroyd, 'Judgment Narrative', 78; Williamson, 'The Prophet and the Plumb-Line', 120; Andersen, Freedman, *Amos*, 766.

[56] M. Dijkstra, 'Contributions to the Reconstruction of the Myth of Ba'al', *UF* 15 (1983), 26-28; in these texts repetition of standard portions are sometimes left out and marked by a double line.

[57] Pfeifer, 'Ausweisung', 113; other examples are easy to provide: Gen. 32:1-5, 6-8 (the return of the messengers is reported, not the transfer of the message); Judg. 11:12-13, 14-27, 28; 1 Kgs 21:17-19; 20 (no transfer of the message is narrated, Ahab's reaction follows immediately); Ezek. 3:16-24, 25. (see M. Dijkstra, *Ezechiël* [Tekst en Toelichting], dl. 1, Kampen 1986, 53, the return of the prophet and his binding is not reported).

of the text, but in their verbal exchange they represent YHWH and the king of Israel. The conflict between Amaziah and Amos portrays the conflict between political authority and God. It is the irony of the story that notably the priest of Bethel did not identify himself with the 'affairs of God', but with state interests. That is why he is condemned so severely in Amos's final words, just as Micaiah son of Imlah condemned Zedekiah son of Kenaanah (1 Kgs 22:25) and Jeremiah condemned his fellow prophet Hananiah, representing the party of the exiled king Jejoiachin, because he preached rebellion against the LORD (Jer. 28:16). Even if the king were not present in the flesh, the story is a king-versus-prophet narrative in structure and genre.[58] The story in Amos 7 depicts Amaziah and Amos not in a personal conflict, but in relation to their respective overlords. He did not act on his own behalf but had been commissioned by the king, who he informed painstakingly about Amos's conspiracy. The narrator makes perfectly clear the source of Amaziah's behaviour and words referring to the message sent to Jeroboam and the emphasis on the state-run sanctuary of Bethel. His words may even have been inspired by the return message of the king.[59] In analogy to Amaziah's fief and loyalties, Amos's relation with his overlord YHWH is spelled out, before he turns his message to the priest himself. Both speakers quote their counterpart in letter and in spirit before their respective suzerains (vv. 11, 16), so that one may surmise that it was the aim of the narrator to mirror the verbal exchange between Amaziah and Amos in vv. 12-13 and 14-15 also with reference to their mutual principals.[60]

3   The Literary Whereabouts of a Story Full of Conflict

Amos 7:9-17 is a late Pre-Exilic prophetic legend that was not included in the Books of the Kings for some reason, but certainly belonged to the type of prophetic tradition that was used by the editors of this history. We can only guess at the reason. Some scholars suppose that Amos fell victim of a deliberate Deuteronomistic 'Pro-

---

[58] Similarly, in the story of 1 Kgs 14, the main characters in the forefront are the wife of Jeroboam and Ahijah, the prophet, who are 'messengers' of the king and YHWH; in a way, here the words of Jesus to Pontius Pilate: 'You would have no power over me, if it were not given to you from above. Therefore, the one who handed me over to you is guilty of a greater sin' (John 19:11), may be applied to Amaziah.

[59] Perhaps, not a literal quotation, for the narrator seems to include a great deal of interpretative 'quotation' in the verbal exchanges between priest, king and prophet, except for the word about Israel's deportation (vv. 11, 17).

[60] Jeremias, *Amos*, 107-8; Idem, 'Rezeptionsprozesse', 29-44.

phetenschweigen.'[61] Crüsemann even suggested that the account of Jeroboam's reign (2 Kgs 14:25-27) had once been drafted to negate Amos's announcement of the end of Israel. Even if it be admitted that there exists such an intertextual link between the prophecy of Jonah son of Amittai alluded to in 2 Kgs 14:25-27 and Amos 6:12-14, this does not imply that the editor of Kings was hostile to the work of Amos because he announced something different.[62] The correspondence and contrast between Jonah's and Amos's words may not have been lost on the Deuteronomistic Historian, just as the observation of 'conspiracy' against the House of Jeroboam (Jehu) in Amos 7:10 and against the House of Ahab (Omri) in the Jehu account.[63] On the contrary, he may have been perfectly aware of how, with subtle irony, Amos turned the positive war-oracle of Jonah into an oracle of defeat.[64] If it be assumed that the events of Israel's salvation (2 Kgs 13:22-25, 14:25) occurred early in Jeroboam's reign,[65] Jonah was already a prophetic figure of the past, when Amos arrived at Bethel from Judah. Stressing the present moment 'to this day, he [YHWH] had been unwilling to destroy them and banish them from his presence' (2 Kgs 13:23), the Deuteronomist seems to have admonished the moment that one of YHWH's servants, the prophets started to announce that he would no longer spare his people Israel. After all, the phrase 'from Lebo Hamath to the valley of the Arabah'[66] could be a less used alternative to the standard locution 'from Dan to Beersheba', so that it remains uncertain whether the intertextual link indeed was consciously generated.[67]

---

[61] F. Crüsemann 'Kritik an Amos im deuteronomistischen Geschichtswerk', in: H.W. Wolff et al., *Probleme Biblischer Theologie: Gerhard von Rad zum 70. Geburtstag*, München 1971, 57-63, esp. 62-3.

[62] Crüsemann, 'Kritik an Amos', 58; K. Koch, 'Das Prophetenschweigen des deuteronomistischen Geschichtswerks', in: J. Jeremias, L. Perlitt (eds), *Die Botschaft und die Boten: Festschrift für Hans Walter Wolff zum 70. Geburtstag*, Neukirchen-Vluyn 1981,115-28; C.T. Begg, 'The Non-mention of Amos, Hosea and Micah in the Deuteronomistic History', *BN* 32 (1986),41-53; G.H. Wittenberg, 'Amos and Hosea: A Contribution to the Problem of the "Prophetenschweigen" in the Deuteronomistic History', *OTE* 6 (1993), 295-311.

[63] Williamson, 'The prophet and the Plumb-Line', 120.

[64] As he often did, see G.V. Smith, ' Continuity and Discontinuity in Amos' Use of Tradition', *JETS* 34 (1991) 33-42.

[65] Perhaps even in the period of co-regency with his father Jehoash, see Dijkstra, 'Chronological Problems', 76-87.

[66] 1 Kgs 14:25 'the Sea of the Arabah', so the verbal correspondence is not complete.

[67] About the concept of intertextuality, see J. Kristeva, *Desire in Language: A Semiotic Approach to Literature and Art*, New York 1980; K. Nielsen, 'Intertextuality and the Hebrew Bible', in: A. Lemaire, M. Sæbø (eds), *Congress Volume*

There are, however, also convincing examples of intertextuality between Amos 7:9-17 and the Deuteronomistic historiography. Perhaps, the story of Amos even underwent some Deuteronomistic revision, although it is difficult to trace conclusive evidence. The spectre of Pan-Deuteronomism looms also over the Book of Amos, so that one has to be careful about calling linguistic and ideological elements in Amos Deuteronomistic.[68] Still, one may expect that if a work once emerged in Exilic and Post-Exilic times that we might for convenience call the Deuteronomistic History, the few literati in Post-Monarchic Judah were familiar with its style and ideas. If it were also these few literati who were about to collect prophetic tradition into larger compilations, they may have used it as an intertext, creating some intertextual links.[69] It seems also appropriate to assume that in such a space of cultural memory the story as included in the Book of Amos and the kind of prophetic narratives used and revised by the Deuteronomistic History all breathe a spirit inspired by the same source of origin. This is the place not to discuss *in extenso* this relationship[70] nor to repeat the similarities between this story and other stories such as Isaiah 7 and the various accounts about the role of the prophets in their encounter with the kings as found in the Deuteronomistic History. What should count here is the extent of correspondence between the Deuteronomistic view of prophecy as stated in the programmatic statement about the prophet like Moses (Deut. 18:15-19) and, in particular, his repeated summary statements about YHWH's servants, the prophets, that is his 'canon' of prophets on the one hand (singular 1 Kgs 14:18, 15:29 (Ahiah), 2 Kgs 9:36; 10:10 (Elijah); 14:25 (Jonah); plural 2 Kgs 9:7; 17:13, 23; 21:10, 24:2; Amos 3:7; Jer. 35:15; Ezek. 38:17; Ezra 9:11), and the story about Amos in the context of his Book on the other.

Two other bench-marks need definition here. What should be construed as Deuteronomistic influence in the Book of Amos? And how can we define a prophet as a prophet like Moses? To open with a remark about literary influence, we may assume that redactors of prophetic books writing Hebrew as their mother-tongue were con-

---

Oslo 1998 (VT.S, 80), Leiden 2000, 18-31.

[68] L.S. Schearing, S.L. McKenzie, *Those Elusive Deuteronomists: The Phenomenon of Pan-Deuteronomism* (JSOT.S, 268), Sheffield 1999.

[69] In this cautious judgment, I agree with E. Ben Zwi, 'A Deuteronomistic Redaction in/among ' The Twelve'? A Contribution from the Standpoint of the Books of Micah, Zephaniah and Obadiah', in: *Those Elusive Deuteronomists*, 232-61, esp. 258-61.

[70] The survey of Williamson, 'The Prophet and the Plumb-Line', 113-9, is quite convincing.

versant with existing relevant literature, stylistic funds of forms and discourses that were part of their literary stock in trade and that they applied from their network of intertexts. However, not every occurrence of a phrase or expression from the 'Deuteronomistic corpus' in another context was generated by a conscious effort on the part of the editor/author to use such an expression or cluster of phrases as 'Deuteronomistic', let alone an attempt to create an intertextual link.[71] Recently, much thought and reconsideration have been given to what 'Deuteronomistic' means, or better what has become to be denoted as 'Deuteronomistic' after the establishment of the theory of a Deuteronomistic History by M. Noth.[72] The major distinction between former and recent usage seems to be between a linkage to the process of redaction underlying the Deuteronomistic History[73]

The second bench-mark concerns the profile of a prophet like Moses. Of course, such a profile does not imply any correspondence in the genealogical, or personal sphere or a relation to a particular group (Levites), or religious specialism (prophecy, priesthood). It concerns first and foremost the Deuteronomic view of Moses as an intermediary standing in the presence of YHWH, 'raised up among his own brothers', a prototype of Israelite prophecy, like Amos called from tending the flocks to be a prophet not by profession, but by virtue of his call to be the mouth of YHWH. The criteria for this new type of true prophet are partly found in the archetypal portrayal of Moses as the ancestor of 'YHWH's servants, the prophets', summarized in Deuteronomy 13 and 18, and applied and refined in Deuteronomistic historiography. Amos 7 like Isaiah 7 and other 'biographies', may have been part of a similar process of conveying a 'Mosaic' flavour to prophetic books including markers for the informed (re)readers that the prophetic personality stood in the tradition of Moses.[74]

---

[71] Ben Zwi, 'A Deuteronomistic Redaction in/among "The Twelve"?', 247-8.

[72] A fine summary is found in R. Coggins, 'What Does "Deuteronomistic" mean?', in: *The Elusive Deuteronomists*, 22-35 = J. Davies *et al.* (eds), *Words Remembered, Texts Renewed: Essays in Honour of John F.A. Sawyer* (JSOT.S, 195), Sheffield 1995, 135-48.

[73] A process of redaction that is nowadays rather variegated in itself since the straightforward theory of Noth's single redactor in the 6th Century BCE was replaced by a number of redaction theories, see R. Smend, *Die Entstehung des Alten Testaments* (ThW, 1) Stuttgart [4]1989, 111-24; R.D. Nelson, *The Double Redaction of the Deuteronomistic History* (JSOT.S, 18), Sheffield 1981; Coggins, 'What Does "Deuteronomistic" mean?', 24-6; Williamson, 'Prophet and Plumb-Line', 114-6; P.S.F. van Keulen, *Manasseh through the eyes of the Deuteronomists: The Manasseh account (2 Kings 21:1-18) and the final chapters of the Deuteronomistic History* (OTS, 38), Leiden 1995, 21-40.

[74] On what follows, see also J. Jeremias, 'Die Anfänge der Schriftprofetie', *ZThK* 93 (1996), 481-99.

In the light of these clarifications about 'Deuteronomistic' intertexts for Amos, I would like to present two sets of linkages between the Deuteronomistic Historiography, particularly its prophetic 'hagiography', and Amos 7, namely one at the level of Deuteronomistic literary phraseology and another at the level of ideas about prophecy and a canon of prophets, and if possible, incidences at both levels. A key-sentence or marker for such a correspondence between Moses and Amos is not immediately found in his 'biographical' story, but rather in the programmatic statement of Amos 3:7: 'Surely, the Sovereign LORD does nothing without revealing his plan to his servants the prophets'. There is a great measure of agreement that this statement, which supposes the existence of a canonical prophetic tradition, selected by the standard of later Deuteronomistic theology, was part of a Deuteronomistic redaction of the Book of Amos.[75] It might be used not only as a kind of hermeneutic key for the understanding of Amos 7:9-17 itself, but also for its present position in the framework of vision reports. The insertion of the story about Amos's performance as a prophet (notwithstanding his denial of being one) is an example of the summary statement in Amos 3:7. He is one of YHWH's servants, for whom he has opened his סוד his circle of confidants, allowing them to be witness of confidential deliberations in heaven. It was for Jeremiah the mark of true prophetic calling (Jer. 23:18, 22), not like 'the prophets' seeing or hearing visions from their own minds, but to see and hear the word of God in the council of the LORD. Amos is presented as a true prophet according to Deuteronomistic standards, because the source of his words and performance in Bethel were his visions seen and heard in the heavenly council. It is apparently this combination of vision and prophecy that was decisive for the editors to claim Amos as one of his servants the prophets.[76] Like Moses, he is depicted as an intercessor whom 'the LORD knew face to face' asking for forgiveness (see סלח in Amos 7:2 and Exod. 34:9, Num. 14:19-20 and the opposite in the Deuteronomistic phrase 2 Kgs 24:4, Deut. 29:19).

---

[75] W.H. Schmidt, 'Die deuteronomistische Redaktion des Amosbuches: Zu den theologischen Unterschieden zwischen dem Prophetenwort und seinem Sammler', *ZAW* 77 (1965), 168-93; Wolff, *Amos*, 137-8; B. Gosse, 'Le recueil d'oracles contre les nations du livre d'Amos et l'histoire deutéronomique', *VT* 38 (1988), 22-24; Williamson, 'The Prophet and the Plumb-Line', 113-5; M. Dijkstra, 'Gelijkenissen in Amos', *NedThT* 48 (1994), 178-90, esp. 184, n.39; Coggins, 'What Does "Deuteronomistic" Mean?', 31.

[76] A similar combination of visionary reports and prophetic performance serving as a bench-mark for true prophecy is found in the story of Micaiah son of Imlah (1 Kgs 22). Presumably, the second vision (1 Kgs 22:19-23) was added by the editors to underscore his authority.

Further, the prophetic legend about Amos resembles in letter and spirit not only similar accounts in the Book of Kings, in which the end of the dynasty and Israel is announced (e.g. 1 Kgs 14:7-11; 16:1-4; 21:20-24; 2 Kgs 9:7-10;⁷⁷ 17:21-23), but *vice versa* the summary prophetic statements in 2 Kgs 9:7, 36; 17:13, 23; 21:10-15; 24:2 also referred to him, once he was identified by the editors as one of YHWH's servants, the prophets. The word spoken against Jeroboam in person as it was quoted in Amaziah's report adducing evidence for Amos's 'conspiracy' (vv. 10-11), is perhaps still Pre-Deuteronomistic, but scholars have suggested that the word about the 'House of Jeroboam' in verse 9 may be construed as a variation on Amos's judgment, updated in the light of 2 Kgs 10:30; 15:12; Hos 1:4 or, in any case, as a reversed dynastic prophecy, may have inspired similar announcements against Jeroboam I and other kings (especially 1 Kgs 14:10; 16:3).⁷⁸ It may be stretching the evidence too far to suggest that the editors indeed thought of Jeroboam I, the royal representative of all that went wrong in the Northern Kingdom. In the light of this evidence, the link between the announcement of the Israelite Exile in the mouth of Amaziah and Amos (vv. 11, 17) on the one hand and in the homilies of the Deuteronomistic History on the other, is more than coincidental. The sentence וְיִשְׂרָאֵל גָּלֹה יִגְלֶה מֵעַל אַדְמָתוֹ which remarkably, if not unexpectedly is taken up by the prophet himself, is exactly the same phrase found in 2 Kgs 17:23; 25:21, where it is expressed in the context of the summary prophetic statements about Israel's and Judah's decline and downfall.⁷⁹ The idea of deportation was certainly not absent in the original words of Amos (Amos 5:27, 6:7), but in the

---

⁷⁷This, like the story of Amos, is marked by the term 'conspiracy'.

⁷⁸It is ascribed by the Göttingen-school to the DtrP revision of DtrH. See W. Dietrich, *Prophetie und Geschichte: Eine redaktionsgeschichtliche Untersuchung zum Deuteronomistischen Geschichtswerk* (FRLANT, 108), Göttingen 1972, 9-11; Williamson, 'The Prophet and the Plumb-Line', 114-5.

⁷⁹If B. Becking, 'From Apostasy to Destruction: A Josianic View on the Fall of Samaria', in: M. Vervenne, J. Lust (eds), *Deuteronomy and Deuteronomic Literature: Fs C.H.W. Brekelmans* (BEThL, 133), Leuven 1997, 279-97, be accepted that 2 Kgs 17:21-23 is not a later addition to the homily 17:7-20, but a Josianic text prior to the final redaction of the Book of Kings, this implies that the idea of a 'canon' of prophets can be traced to late Pre-Exilic times. The homily 2 Kgs 17:2-20 is an Exilic text assessing both Israelite and Judahite conduct, Noth, *Überlieferungsgeschichtliche Studien*, 85; B. Becking, 'From Exodus to Exile: 2 Kgs 17,7-20 in the Context of its Co-text', in: G. Galil, M. Weinfeld, *Studies in Historical Geography and Biblical Historiography presented to Zecharia Kallai* (SVT, 81), Leiden 2000, 215-31, esp. 228. Also Dietrich, *Prophetie und Geschichte*, 41-6, ascribed 2 Kgs 17:13 to a later redaction (DtrN) than 2 Kgs 17:23; 21:10-15; 24:2 (DtrP). The use of the phrase in different redactional layers needs a further clarification which cannot be pursued here.

context of this story it was deliberately couched and emphasized in a Deuteronomistic phrase to claim once more that Amos was one of YHWH's servants the prophets (Amos 3:7; 1 Kgs 17:23).[80]

But there is more than such rather general links in phraseology and tenets of the Deuteronomist. In the judgment over Manasseh by YHWH's servants, the prophets (2 Kgs 21:10-15), the LORD says: 'I will stretch over Jerusalem the measuring line used against Samaria and the plumb-line used against the House of Ahab. I will wipe out Jerusalem ...' (2 Kgs 21:13-14). It has been suggested that the Deuteronomist was inspired not only by the imagery found in Isa. 28:17, but also by his interpretation of Amos as the אֲנָךְ 'a tin plummet', placed in the midst of his people Israel. Williamson, for instance, suggested that the emphatic three-fold repetition of the first person singular pronoun אָנֹכִי in Amos's statement in verse 14 was a deliberate interpretation of and word-play on the אֲנָךְ of the third vision.[81] Thus in the view of the editor, the plumb-line represented the prophet and

---

[80] Gosse, 'Recueil d'oracles contre les nations', 39; Williamson, 'The Prophet and the Plumb-Line', 120. Gosse suggests a similar intertextual relationship for the deportation of the Arameans to Qir (*ibid.*, 39; 2 Kgs 16:8-9 and Amos 1:5, 9:7 contain 'un parallélisme voulu par les rédacteurs des livres des Rois').

[81] Williamson, 'The Prophet and the Plumb-Line',117; following a suggestion of F. Praetorius, 'Bemerkungen zu Amos', *ZAW* 35 (1915), 12-25, esp. 14; R.B. Coote, *Amos among the Prophets: Composition and Theology*, Philadelphia 1966, 92-3; this suggestion would be even more convincing if the three-fold repetition of the pronoun 'I' reflected original three-fold אֲנָךְ (cf. app BHS); ever since, there is a rather broad consensus that a word-play between the first person singular pronoun and the word אֲנָךְ is intended, whatever its exact meaning; K. Baltzer, 'Bild und Wort: Erwägungen zu der Vision Amos in Am 7,7-9', in: W. Gross *et al.* (eds), *Methode und Grammatik: Wolfgang Richter zum 65.Geburtstag*, St. Ottilien 1991, 11-16, referring to a similar word-play in the Ishtar-hymn K 41; notwithstanding new interpretations of this *hapax* by W.Beyerlin, *Bleilot, Brecheisen oder was sonst? Revision einer Amos Vision* (OBO, 81), Freiburg 1988; Chr. Uehlinger, 'Der Herr auf der Zinnmauer: Zur dritten Amos-Vision (Am 7:7-8)', *BN* 48 (1989), 89-104; M. Weigl, 'Eine "unendliche Geschichte": אֲנָךְ (Am 7,7-8),' *Bib* 76 (1995), 343-87; A. Cooper, 'The Meaning of Amos's Third Vision (Amos 7:7-9)', in: M. Cogan *et al.* (eds), *Tehillah le-Moshe: Biblical and Judaic Studies in Honor of Moshe Greenberg*, Winona Lake IN, 1997, 13-22; J.K. Hoffmeier, 'Once Again the "Plumb Line" Vision of Amos 7:7-9: An Interpretive Clue from Egypt?', in: M. Lubetski *et al.* (eds), *Boundaries of the Ancient Near Eastern World: A Tribute to Cyrus H. Gordon* (JSOT.S, 273), 304-19; like Williamson I decline here to speculate on the suggestion that also the original vision intended such a word-play between the word for tin and the northern pronunciation of the pronoun spelled אנך announcing God's presence in Israel's coming judgment (on a possible word-play with dialectical variants in the fourth vision, see Williamson, *ibid.*, 117-8, n.69; A. Wolters, 'Wordplay and Dialect in Amos 8:1-2', *JETS* 31 (1988) 407-10). If so, the editor changed this perspective focusing the text on the prophet as his authoritative representative.

his word became God's measuring line and plummet to be used to test the strength of Samaria's city-wall.

Not every adduced example may be immediately clear and convincing for the association of Amos 7:9-17 with Deuteronomistic thought, but the accumulation of inferred and explicit intertexts for this story is certainly remarkable and requires explanation. These links certainly exist between Amos 7 and similar prophetic narratives in the Book of Kings, used and revised by the Deuteronomistic editors. Moreover, I found also intertexts for Amos 7 elsewhere in the Old Testament. Let me mention here only two examples: the link between Amos's expulsion and the dismissal of Balaam by Balak, King of Moab,

(Amos 7:12) חֹזֶה לֵךְ בְּרַח־לְךָ אֶל־אֶרֶץ יְהוּדָה

(Num.24:11) וְעַתָּה בְּרַח־לְךָ אֶל־מְקוֹמֶךָ

It proves, in my opinion, beyond doubt that Amaziah was not giving a friendly advice to the prophet to withdraw himself, but a command to leave at once, or even less politely, to get lost! The narrator or the editor of the story may have been influenced by the older prophetic legend of Balaam, who was also called as a foreigner to prophesy against Israel, but in Deuteronomic fashion God turned the requested curse into a blessing (Deut. 23:5). As an obedient and humble servant of the LORD, Balaam also finally said to king Balak: 'Must I not speak what the LORD puts in my mouth?' (Num. 23:12, 26; 24:13, see also Deut. 18:18). So, Amos's fate turned out to be similar to that of Balaam, also adopted in the canon of prophets in spite of himself. But the nature of their call and mission was quite different. Balaam is depicted as a professional קֹסֵם 'diviner' who became a נָבִיא against his will. Amos was a נֹקֵד who was called to prophesy against Israel after the LORD took him from tending the flock (יִקָּחֵנִי יְהוָה מֵאַחֲרֵי הַצֹּאן וַיֹּאמֶר אֵלַי יְהוָה לֵךְ הִנָּבֵא אֶל־עַמִּי יִשְׂרָאֵל, Amos 7:15).

The parallel with the call of David elected to be a נָגִיד in the dynastic prophecy of Nathan is remarkable, 'I took you from the meadow, tending the flock to be ruler over my people Israel' (אֲנִי לְקַחְתִּיךָ מִן־הַנָּוֶה מֵאַחַר הַצֹּאן לִהְיוֹת נָגִיד עַל־עַמִּי {עַל־}יִשְׂרָאֵל, 2 Sam. 7:8). The number of collocations is here hardly coincidental, for the same kind of formulation is not found anywhere else.[82] It is significant that the author, who had this ancient prophecy of Nathan in mind,[83] did not formulate

---

[82] Compare, for instance, Ps. 78:70-71, which is more at variance with 2 Sam. 7:8 than Amos 7:15, though it was certainly inspired by the Nathan prophecy; see Van Leeuwen, *Amos*, 286.

[83] The Deuteronomistic revision of 2 Samuel 7:8-17 is still disputed. T. Veijola, *Die ewige Dynastie: David und die Erstehung seiner Dynastie nach der deuteronomistischen Darstellung* (AASF, 193), Helsinki 1975, ascribed 2 Sam. 7:8b, 11b,

לִהְיוֹת נָבִיא עַל־עַמִּי יִשְׂרָאֵל, something that had become impossible after Amos's denial of being a prophet. Clearly, the editors wanted Amos to be one of YHWH's servants, the prophets, even if it be historical that he denied being one. In this subtle way, they were able to emphasize their standards and ideas of what a true peripheral non-professional prophet should be, a person called and qualified to prophesy. Not a נָבִיא such as the professional נָבִיא but one of the 'canonical' prophets standing in the sequence of the former and latter prophets, servants of the LORD, like David and Moses.

4 Story and History in Amos 7:9-17

What is personal in this 'biographical' legend of Amos 7 and where does he become a prophetic personality like Moses? In the light of my narrative (de)construction of the story and the exploration of its immediate context and remote intertexts, there is hardly any reason to doubt the authenticity of the personal word against Jeroboam II (v. 11), Amaziah's interference and Amos's denial of being a professional נָבִיא. The announcement, as quoted by Amaziah from Amos's mouth, was never fulfilled as far as we know. It may be assumed that the historically accurate reference to the House of Jeroboam in v. 9 (see 2 Kgs 15:10) by contrast with v. 11 was intended to update Amos's announcements against the House of Jehu/Jeroboam in the light of the downfall of this dynasty and the eclipse of the Israelite state.[84] Another authentic element is the correspondence between court and temple. Also Amaziah's suggestion that Amos was a Judahite חֹזֵה הַמֶּלֶךְ (2 Sam. 24:11 = 1 Chron. 21:9; 2 Sam. 25:5; 29:29; 2 Chron. 29:25; 35:15) might reveal knowledge about such an office in Judah at the court of Jerusalem.[85]

There were no doubt, prophets and 'prophets' in the Old Testament. It is my contention that the story of Amos 7:9-17 was intentionally inserted into the framework of visionary reports in order to present Amos as a new type of prophetic personage, a prophet like Moses.[86] Not a prophet by profession but, like Moses, a prophet by virtue of his special calling. This presentation placed the story in the

---

13, 16 to DtrG, but see recently H.J. Stoebe, *Das Zweite Buch Samuelis* (KAT, 8/2), Gütersloh 1994, 48, 209-10, 223-4, about the unity and antiquity of 1 Samuel 7 and, already, Noth, *Überlieferungsgeschichtliche Studien*, 99.

[84] Williamson, 'The Prophet and the Plumb-Line', 120; see, however, Andersen, Freedman, *Amos*, 767.

[85] M. Dijkstra, 'The Royal Seer in Judah in Ancient Near Eastern Perspective', *JNWSL* (forthcoming).

[86] Jeremias, 'Die Anfänge der Schriftprofetie', 481-99.

chronological sequence of visions at the autumnal festival in Bethel.[87] Reducing the prophet to silence was in the view of the editors the end and climax of a two-year period of Amos's activity as prophet, apparently a period that was also marked by a severe earthquake according the introduction to the book (Amos 1:1).[88] The editors of the Book of Amos linked his utterances about earthquake and eclipse of the sun (Amos 8:8, 9-10; 9:5) to the vision of the destruction of the temple in Bethel. This connection need not be authentic. What matters is that for the later editors and perhaps already for the circle of Amos's confidants in Judah such ominous events as the great earthquake in the days of Uzzia (Zech. 14:5) and the eclipse (15 June 763 BCE) confirmed Amos's message and his performance as a true prophet. As such, he became part of the prophetic tradition which made a prophetic personage out of the historical Amos, who, just like the Book of Amos itself, was included into the Deuteronomistic 'canon' of the former and latter prophets. Though he was not mentioned initially by name in the Books of the Kings, several unmistakable intertextual links between his 'biography' and Deuteronomistic hagiography of all YHWH's servants the prophets drew the attention of the informed (re)reader to his personality as a prophet in the tradition of Moses.

---

[87] A.P.B. Breytenbach, 'Die herfsfees en die koningsrite by Bet-el as interteks van Amos 7:10-8:14 en Hosea 9:1-9', *HTS* 53 (1997), 513-28.

[88] Freedman, Welch, 'Amos's Earthquake', 188-98; see also literature quoted in n. 23.

Terry Fenton   *Haifa – Israel*

Israelite Prophecy
Characteristics of the First Protest Movement

The broadening of our knowledge of ancient and modern societies over the last century has highlighted the affinity of Israelite prophecy with earlier phenomena. It might indeed appear that notions concerning the uniqueness of the prophetic phenomenon in Israel and its central role in the creation of the specifically Israelite religion have been jeopardized by the new knowledge. It will be argued, however, that this is not the case.

The instinct of late nineteenth century researchers[1] and subsequent views of the early twentieth century and beyond, which saw in the prophetic movement *the* unique constituent of developed Israelite religion, were, I would claim, basically correct. Two divergences from those views, however, may be proposed. Firstly, the 'new'[2] prophetic movement in Israel was not created *ex nihilo* but was a development of and a reaction to, previous prophetic activity throughout the ancient world including the Land of Canaan/Israel. Approaches to such a position are fairly common in recent study but it has not, I think, been stated and argued with sufficient clarity and force. Secondly, those parts of the 'new' prophetic message which were thought, in subsequent[3] research, to be founded upon 'traditional' law or morality, or 'wisdom' ('folk wisdom' or 'court wisdom') belong, equally, to ancient Near Eastern, rather than specifically Israelite, tradition. The parts of the Hebrew Scriptures which purport to present an account of the sequence of religious notions and practice from Abraham to the Babylonian Exile are held to be largely the outcome of the new prophetic movement itself. They are not the product of 'Israelite thought' between the entry into the Land of Canaan, if such an entry there were, and the Babylonian Exile (if such an Exile there were).[4]

---

[1] I am indebted to the critical analysis of W. McKane, *A Late Harvest*, Edinburgh, 1995, 65-113, for a better understanding of this important phase of Old Testament research.

[2] I refer to what has been known as 'classical prophecy' or the 'writing prophets', terms which, I believe, no longer commend themselves to contemporary scholarship, for a variety of reasons. In any case, not all the features of the 'new' prophecy which I propose are found in all of that material (e.g. the Book of Ezekiel) and I would hold that some preceded it (e.g. in the person of Elijah).

[3] Though mentioned in principle, at least, for 'Torah' by Wellhausen, see ref. in n.1, 84-5.

[4] My phrasing here (and the bracket) is in deference to current debate. In fact

Perhaps one may talk of what began, in a sense, as 'coterie literature', the records and writings of a limited group or of limited movements which were eventually accepted as 'national' literature but do not reflect the typical world-picture of Israelite or Judean society during the period of the monarchy. Seen in this light, those whom we regard as the 'prophets of Israel', were a minority group struggling against the main stream of ancient Near Eastern prophecy, which constituted the prophetic norm in pre-exilic Israel and Judah. In this struggle many of the characteristics of the traditional 'prophetic-type' were retained.

A survey of what is known of shamanism, usually regarded as the most primitive example of the 'prophetic phenomenon', of the various prophetic types attested in the culture of Mari of the second millenium, of the pre-Islamic *kāhin*, of the *ahl-as-sir*, 'the family of the secret', amongst the modern Rwala bedouin of Northern Arabia, of the Pythia at Delphi, even of the present-day medium, reveals much which recalls the activities and behaviour of those termed 'prophet', 'man of god', 'seer', 'man of the spirit', and so on, in the Bible.[5] Consideration of the data indicates that their function is essentially that of the mediator and their characteristic behaviour, ecstatic.[6]

The time has long past when, owing to a misunderstanding of the Greek term *prophetes*, the function of the prophet was held to be foretelling. Recently there has been a tendency to regard the meaning as 'public speaker', 'declaimer' and so forth, but it would seem that the true sense is 'mediator', that is, one who speaks for, on behalf of the god, or, indeed, on behalf of the recipient of the divine message. Apollo is the prophet of Zeus, the Pythia, the prophetess of Apollo, and she herself has prophets who interpret her words, for they are unintelligible to the laity. We speak here of the terms *prophetes* and *prophetis* though other terms, such as *promantis*, are also used. However this may be, it would appear that the term *prophetes* came to denote the basic function of the mediator who conveys the message of the spirits, or of the gods, or of a specific god, to an individual or to a community.

I believe both in the entry (which, however, I would agree, was a much longer and more complicated process than Scripture or even 'wave-theory' historians would allow) and in the Exile (though its full scope and significance are subject to discussion and, hopefully, evidence yet to be disinterred).

[5]Comments and references on *homines religiosi* and their Biblical designations in T.L. Fenton, 'Deuteronomistic Advocacy of the *nābî*': 1 Samuel ix 9 and Questions of Israelite Prophecy', *VT* 47 (1997), 30-1 and also 41-2.

[6]For this and the following discussion cf. Fenton, *art. cit.*, 31-6 and addenda 40-1, with further detail and references.

At this point we need to address the question of ecstasy, for the term *prophetes* might seem to have denoted originally the functionary who interpreted the unintelligible words of the ecstatic – the first recipient of the message from the other world, the raving *mantis*. To what extent the Pythia was an ecstatic is disputed. The statements to the effect that her words were delivered in a state of trance which rendered them incomprehensible are held to be late and not to reflect the reality. If so they are influenced by other cases of prophetic ecstasy and this seems to me to shift the question historically or geographically rather than to face up to the existence of ecstatic prophecy throughout antiquity, including 'Classical' antiquity. Plato explains the terms within the framework of the Pythia's delirium and despite recent doubts as to his reliability, his explanation seems to me fully consistent with the comparative data.[7]

In the case of the shaman the descriptions of observers are clear enough. Often he is not in control of his speech when delivering the message of the spirits. It cannot be understood by the community and is relayed to those present by experts who are able to interpret the outlandish sounds uttered in trance. Now here the case of Moses' speech defect is highly significant. The man chosen to convey the will of the deity to his people has a stammer! Accordingly, Aaron must be his spokesman. Yet it is from Moses that Aaron receives the message. Thus in words attributed to the deity, Aaron will speak to the people for Moses, he will be Moses' 'mouth' and Moses will be his 'god', Exod. 4:16. As if to make the point quite clear it is repeated at Exod. 7:1, 'See I have made you god to Pharaoh and Aaron your brother will be your *nābî'* '.[8] As in the case of the shaman Moses is the ecstatic and requires an 'intermediary' or 'interpreter' and that notion is conveyed by the word *nābî'*. It is precisely the function of the Pythia's *prophetes* and here we probably have the reason for the use of that word to translate *nābî'*. As we have argued, *nābî'* means 'speaker', 'spokesman' (not 'called' or 'summoned')[9] and reflects the primary function of the 'intermediary', 'mediator', between spirit or deity and mankind.

Now it would seem to me that the Biblical account of Moses' mission deliberately plays down the ecstatic quality of prophetic be-

---

[7] Fenton, *art. cit.*, 40.

[8] The repetition, however, is really at 4:16. Since earlier sources would not, presumably, be exercised with such a matter, our understanding of the passage would appear to support its attribution (on other grounds) to a post-P redactor, a suggestion first made (so far as I know) by H. Holzinger, *Exodus* (KHC, 2), Tübingen 1900, 9 and 16.

[9] Fenton, *art. cit.*, 34-5, 42.

haviour. The incomprehensible babble of the man of god becomes a speech defect, a stammer. As in fifth century Athens[10] so the developing Yahwistic religion was embarrassed by the phenomenon of the ecstatic servant of the deity. Modern scholars of the Classics and some O.T. researchers might appear to share this embarrassment. The explanation of prophetic ecstasy, however, surely lies close at hand. Communication with spirits or deity requires a being different from his fellow-men. The mediator must be abnormal. Abnormal human behaviour is perceived in terms of madness. The prophet must be mad: 'foolish is the prophet, mad the man of the spirit'. Three times in the Hebrew Scriptures, as often noted, the prophet is designated as 'mad': in the line just quoted from Hos. 9:7 (apparently a sentiment attributed to the populace, rebellious Ephraim), in the letter of complaint against Jeremiah (29:26), 'every madman and prophesier', and in the account of the 'young prophet' who anoints Jehu king (2 Kgs 9:11), 'why came that madman unto you'?

It would appear that the necessary madness of prophets is an immediate cause for the ambivalent attitude to them in many societies. So it is, for example, with various shamanistic societies, apparently in fifth century Athens and, according to amusing reports, with the *ahl-as-sir*.[11] As in the Biblical literature the message of the mediator and his services are sought after, but he is often mistrusted.

It is sometimes remarked that the 'madness' of the prophets is not very prominent in the Old Testament. Their behaviour is sometimes strange, provocative and so forth, but not frenzied: it is the prophets of Baal whose behaviour is depicted as frenzied in 1 Kgs 18 and their antics are clearly regarded with scorn by the writer. The attribution of frenzy to the Baal prophet as distinct from the Yahweh prophet is interesting: but what are we to say of Elijah's 'marathon' ahead of Ahab's chariot in the downpour from Mt. Carmel to Jezreel with 'the hand of Yahweh upon him'? There are, indeed, passages enough which attribute some form of ecstasy to the true prophets of Yahweh. Studies of the psychology of ecstasy and attempts to define the men-

---

[10] See e.g. the Cassandra passage in the Agamemnon of Aeschylus, 1072-1330 with the comments of the chorus, of which 1099 seems to echo popular sentiment. More general doubts about prophets and prophecy may be reflected in the speeches of Oedipus and the chorus throughout the Teiresias scene of Sophocles' Oedipus Rex, where however – perhaps significantly – the mantis does not display ecstatic behaviour.

[11] Though respected on the whole, even feared, they are sometimes scorned and abused – especially novices and those who have not yet won the trust of the clans. 'Fools', 'witless', 'feeble-minded', are amongst the epithets bestowed upon them: A. Musil, *The Manner and Customs of the Rwala Bedouins*, New York 1928, 400.

tal states reflected in extra-Biblical and Biblical accounts of prophetic behaviour are interesting in themselves but they do not seem capable yet of describing in any depth the mechanisms and processes involved (what is actually happening in the 'mind' of the prophet and how this affects his physical behaviour). It seems to me, however, that, so far as the Biblical phenomena are concerned, important points are missed when positions are taken with regard to the type or degree of ecstatic behaviour in the case of this or that prophet. Firstly, the triple attribution of madness to prophets noted above clearly reflects attitudes to and perceptions of prophetic activity in Israelite society – and these are typical of many or more or perhaps all early societies. The prophet is *expected* to behave abnormally. Thus, even if Isaiah or Jeremiah acquired their understanding, their 'message', in a state of cold sobriety or calm imperturbability they would have, willy-nilly, to feign at least a degree of eccentricity in order to inspire any confidence in their audience. It might be going about half(?)-naked in public or with a yoke around one's neck, but it had to be some form of divergent behaviour. Secondly, changes were afoot in the ancient world, as mentioned, and the acceptability of prophetic madness was, in some circles at least, diminishing. Ironically, the new prophets of Israel may have been more sophisticated, in this regard, than most of their target-community. Taking a longer view one might suggest that in this part of the world a declining sympathy with ecstatic behaviour presaged the demise of prophecy itself. At any rate, Amos and Jeremiah do not appear to have felt that their relatively genteel behaviour would diminish yet further the little effect their words were having.

In sum, the 'new' prophets of Israel and Judah have distanced themselves from the old prophetic frenzy and the process nears its culmination with the reconceptualization of Moses' ecstasy as mooted above.

With respect to the form of the new prophetic message we perceive, I think, a noteworthy development. The abnormality of the prophet in ancient societies, so far as his words are concerned, does not always express itself in unintelligible babbling. Sometimes a form of verse is employed and the association of prophetic and poetic inspiration is a theme which has taken on various aspects from antiquity until the romantic movement of the nineteenth century. The word *vates*, poet and soothsayer, is often quoted in this context, together with cognate or parallel terms in other tongues. In the mists of antiquity some prophetic groups must have communicated their messages in genuine poetic compositions. So far as I am aware, however, neither the hexameters of the Pythia (or rather of her *prophetes* – here we have both unintelligibility and verse-transmission) nor the rhymed prose of the *kāhin* are regarded with much enthusiasm from a literary point of view. Hebrew prophecy, on the other hand, exhibits true poetic skill and attains, in some of its best preserved passages, an outstanding quality of inspired composition, as recognized by Hebraists concerned with literary matters (hence the claim that the prophets were in fact poets and not prophets at all). I do not know whether the combination of prophetic message and poetic inspiration is unique, but it is, at least, first attested in the ancient Near East in the new Hebrew prophecy.[12]

What calls forth the bard within the prophet, what passion evokes the poetic creation? The demand for social justice and a negative view of sacrifice would not seem, *prima facie*, to be topics productive of such literary composition. Yet the creative force of the prophetic inspiration is never stronger than when addressing such matters. Perhaps the two most famous show-pieces here are Isa. 1 and Amos 5:21-24 though I would suggest that Ps. 50 is a particularly interesting case of the negation by a cultic prophet of a 'covenant renewal ceremony', or the like, with its accompanying sacrifices. Here the cultic prophet, or one who assumes his role, criticizes with great irony, and poetic virtuosity, the basics of the ritual which he initially invokes. Criticism of the cult is one of the most significant and notorious features of the new prophetic thinking. It does not seem to me that this criticism is conditional or relative. According to the common, but not universal view, the prophets held that sacrifice was a positive form of worship but only when offered by the righteous and morally pure. Such a position would, I think, have been incomprehensible to ancient man, to *homo necans*, and that includes the Israelite who practised the cult 'on every high hill and under every leafy tree'. Sacrifice was the service man rendered to the deity from well before the dawn of history. Indeed, the ubiquitous view of the literature of ancient Babylonia is that he was created specifically for this purpose. Apart from this all societies recognized some code of human behaviour – without which no society could exist. The two obligations were, however, unconnected and independent. To claim that the fulfilment of the one

---

[12] Of course I do not deny that such texts as the dynastic oracles from Mari and the Balaam text from Deir 'Allah do have some poetic coloration. Or that the Neo-Assyrian prophecies of the seventh century BCE may be 'half prose, half poetry', as S. Parpola, *Assyrian Prophecies* (SAA, 9), 1997, LXVII, terms it. But this hardly bears comparison with the sustained poetic form of prophetic literature in ancient Israel.

was valid only if the second were honoured is to posit dependence between mutually exclusive spheres.

However, the sacrificial cult *did* have a function which is relevant to this issue and leads to a further consideration. Whatever the origin of sacrifice its function was to win the favour and support of the deity and that included reconciliation or absolution when that deity was conceived to have been offended by a human fault – of any nature and whether intentional or inadvertent ('expiatory' sacrifices). For the addressees of the new prophecy the notion that the action conceived to absolve sin is effective only if performed by the sinless would have been more than somewhat confusing.

It is clear, in the passages mentioned and others, that the disdain for the entire cultic apparatus is total. The illogicality of sacrifice and the belittling of the deity which it implies are prominent in all of these texts, especially in Ps. 50. The message is that sacrifice does *not* win divine favour and does not procure the remission of sin.[13] Justice on the other hand is an absolute requirement of the deity. Accordingly abrogation of the moral obligation has inevitable consequences. Nevertheless, man being *homo necans* these opposers of sacrifice understood that they could not put paid to it in an instant: they did not propose the immediate cessation of all sacrificial ritual. Probably they hoped their diatribes would bear fruit in due course – and they appear so to have done.

Whether absolute or relative the criticism of the cult is revolutionary: for the first time in its millennia-long existence the sacrificial system is under radical scrutiny. Here again there is a noteworthy change from traditional perceptions. It is also highly significant that the prophetic-type, the mediator, seems to have been connected with the cult in one way or another from the earliest times.[14]

---

[13] This is not the place for one more discussion of all the texts relating to the question of absolute or relative criticism of the cult, although a far more detailed and holistic analysis is, I believe, a desideratum (despite the fact that some *frustula* will probably remain – such as the stumbling-block Isa 1:13b). Meanwhile my opinion is based on the general factors adumbrated. Here, too, I would mention that the few ancient Near Eastern texts thought relevant to this matter seem to me too laconic and ambivalent to be helpful (even the Egyptian text concerning the wise serpent who, apparently, finds sacrifice risible). The same may be said of Prov. 15:8; 21:3, 27, which, in any case, are 'Yahwistic' proverbs and probably influenced by our prophetic texts.

[14] One cannot, within the framework of this paper, attempt to argue the strength of the evidence for 'cultic prophecy' in Israel, but I often wonder why, in this discussion, more stress is not laid on Jer. 35:4, the simplest explanation of which would seem to be that there was a permanent and long-established 'prophetic chamber' adjacent to the 'Ministers' chamber' within the Temple precincts. If this

As for the theme of social justice itself and morality in general, however conceived, this is a familiar topic in ancient Near Eastern literature – in law, in wisdom literature and in narrative.[15] It is, in particular, the duty of rulers to enforce justice and righteousness. So far as the basic concepts are concerned neither the Hebrew Scriptures in general nor the prophets in particular are innovatory.[16] The novelty lies in the zeal of the new prophecy for these values, a zeal which inspires the production of passionate, powerful poetry, profuse in pathos and the potential to move men's minds – a zeal too, which puts the person of the prophet at great risk for it involves an offensive directed against the central authority of the state.

It is probably in this criticism of the rulership and the apparatus of government that the new prophetic activity reaches its apogee. Neglect of social justice, religious apostasy and a consequent incompetence in 'foreign policy' are arraigned. But the prophets do not seek to overturn the regime or to replace the monarchy.[17] Their aim is to 'restore' justice, loyalty to the national deity and an informed and sensible handling of the dangerous forces at work on the international scene. If I am not mistaken, this is the first record we have of criticism directed against a monarchy or central government (over a period of centuries and by a succession of men sharing broadly the same views) without the intent to oust the current ruler or change the form of government. It sought to correct, not to replace.

Now unless all this is the fantastic invention of some post-exilic circle 'reconstructing' the events of the past in the interests of its current concerns (on which see below) there arises the question of

---

is correct there were 'institutionalized' cult prophets at the Jerusalem Temple.

[15] Hence the divergence from nineteenth century scholars mentioned in my opening remarks.

[16] Evidence for these concerns, with particular attention to the weaker elements of society, widows and orphans, for example, extends from the reform of Urukagina of Lagash (about 2355 BCE, probably the first truly interesting document on record) through the Mesopotamian law codes to the Hebrew Scriptures and occurs also in Ugaritic narrative poetry. The striking example is at the end of the Epic of King Krt where that king's would-be successor criticizes his inability to 'feed the orphan before you or the widow behind you'.

[17] With regard to the replacement of the Omride dynasty by Jehu, it has been thought that the redactional activity of prophetic historiographers or Deuteronomistic editing may be responsible for the notion that the revolt was inspired by Elisha representing the loyal YHWH-worshipping anti-Tyrian section of the population (cf. e.g. J. Gray, *I & II Kings*, London ³1977, 537). As hinted above (n. 2) we accept the historicity of Elijah's 'Yahweh-alone' movement but doubt its involvement in Jehu's coup, especially in view of Hosea's condemnation. At any rate, replacement of the monarchy does not seem to be on the agenda of the developed new prophecy.

an appropriate historical assessment of such a phenomenon. In these terms the new prophecy of Israel and Judah should be seen, I would suggest, as essentially a 'protest movement' – possibly the first of its kind, or at any rate, the first we know of. This characterization, and the term 'protest movement' are not far, if I may so observe, from J. Blenkinsopp's analysis and his designation 'dissident intellectuals'.[18] These words, however, smack of the language of opprobium deployed by the propaganda departments of certain totalitarian regimes of recent memory. 'Protest movement', I think, would appeal more, in principle at least, to liberal humanists and here the emphasis is more on moral outlook than pseudo-dialectic differences, though to be fair, many 'dissident intellectuals' were trying to make a moral point and, further, Professor Blenkinsopp describes very clearly what he intends by the term. It will be clear that I concur with much of his treatment, though I make bold to differ on some points, and that I am heartened by his use of the words 'new' and 'protest' in several places.

With regard to our claim of priority for the new prophecy in its criticisms of the rulership a word should be said on the 'intuitive prophecy' which has been revealed in letters to the king at ancient Mari of the eighteenth century. There does seem to be a certain robust freedom of expression, compared with our general record of address to the monarch throughout the ancient Near East, on the part of the Mari prophets. There are, for example, demands, allegedly at the command of this or that deity, for offerings of sacrifices, for grants of land for temple-building, that projects be terminated, that regular reports on the activities of the king's enemies be presented, and these demands are often accompanied by threats of punishment in the event of non-compliance. We even find the sentence 'when a wronged man or woman cries out to you, stand and let his/her case be judged.' The latter, however, seems to me no solemn rebuke by a wrathful accuser but the sort of routine message that gods might be expected to have relayed to rulers, as Hammurabi is summoned by the gods to establish justice and so forth in the prologue to his Code. As for the 'divine' demands, one senses here the employment of artful stratagems in the interests of local institutions, attempts to extract favours for the benefit of temple personnel or other parties on the authority of the god. Now it is possible that Zimri-Lim of Mari did not have the same standing and control of his kingdom as we associate with the famous monarchs of Assyria and Babylon with whose regimes we are familiar from a considerable number of royal ('dis-

---

[18] *Sage Priest Prophet*, Louisville 1995, Chapter 3 (The Prophet), esp. 144-5.

play' or other) inscriptions – whether that control was really exercised by the monarchs themselves or through their powerful central governments. It is possible that Zimri-Lim was subject to pressures from various groups to which he was obliged to make concessions and that the interests of those groups were expressed wholly or partially through prophetic activity claiming divine authority. Either of the two suggestions offered, or a combination of both, might explain the apparent boldness of a number of the prophetic messages found in the royal correspondence of Mari. On the whole, however, one has the impression that the personnel involved – the prophets themselves and the officials through whom their words are transmitted – are to a large extent under the royal control. At any rate there is no sign of militant opposition to the central authority. However, the 'freedom of expression' referred to bears the seeds of possible development. We do not belittle the possibility of some connection across the millennium between the Mari prophecy and the roots of the new prophecy of our discussion, especially in the light of particular features of Mari society and language found in early Israel.[19] The conclusion to this 'excursus' should be, in our opinion, that the Mari phenomenon discussed is at a far remove from the new prophetic protest movement.

Our last point on this matter is that since protest movements have a future orientation there is here a further break with the past: social protest implies an optimistic hope for the betterment of man's condition and a will to achieve it. Whether the eschatological visions of Isa. 2 and 11 belong to this period will be disputed, but the germ of such ideas lies, in fact, in the mentality of protest itself.

To sum up the elements of the pattern argued so far: in the basic matter of the distinguishing mark of the intermediary between deity and man, ecstasy, the new prophecy is firmly attached to its ancient matrix but tends to modify the 'madness' to the degree that public expectation will permit; in the related matter of the abnormal speech of the mediator, incoherent stuttering or some form of verse or quasi-verse delivery are transformed by a poetic inspiration of great power, charged by a passionate humanity; the age-old institution of sacrifice,

---

[19] For a useful brief survey of the salient material see A. Malamat, 'Prophecy at Mari', with references, in: R.P. Gordon (ed.), *The Place Is Too Small for Us: The Israelite Prophets in Recent Scholarship* (SBibSt, 5), Winona Lake, 1995, 50-68, despite the fact that this is an extract from the Schweich Lectures of 1984 and interesting new data have since emerged – including the attestation of the word *nābî'*. For the features common to Mari and Israelite society in general, see the Schweich Lectures themselves, A. Malamat, *Mari and the Early Israelite Experience*, Oxford 1989, as well as Idem, *Mari and the Bible* (SHCANE, 12), Leiden 1998, esp. Chapter 2: Prophecy (pp. 59-162).

with which the prophetic mediator was long associated in divinatory and other cultic roles, is condemned as worthless and an insult to the deity; ethical behaviour, a commonplace requirement of any society, but honoured as much in the breach as in the observance, becomes the paramount demand of the godhead and is enjoined with unprecedented zeal, especially upon its traditional custodians, the nation's rulers; they indeed, are castigated for dereliction of duty precisely in this sphere by personnel practising a function formerly under the strict control of those rulers themselves; finally the new prophecy confronts the passivity of the ancient world-view of the human condition with a melioristic outlook.

According to this discussion then, the new prophecy of Israel, in respect of the various characteristics we have noted, is the product of metamorphosis. The new prophets transform the role of the ancient Near Eastern prophet, modifying or reacting against his traditional function and behaviour.

We have spoken throughout of prophets, but of the 'new' prophets many, if not all (we assume there were more than our records show) would have rejected the term – $n\bar{a}\underline{b}\hat{\imath}$'. As I have argued,[20] this was the most common term for the mediator between the deity and mankind in ancient Israel from its beginnings and throughout the Biblical period. Amos and the 'writing' or 'recorded' prophets claimed, explicitly or implicitly to be fulfilling this function. The term, then, would have been appropriate to them. Its rejection by some of the new prophets, as has sometimes been suggested, may have been due to the fact that most $n^e\underline{b}\hat{\imath}$'îm belonged to a professional body and exercised their skills within the cult under the control of the regime which afforded them their livelihood and upon which they were dependent. Amos and, no doubt, others were not professionals but men who obeyed the call of their conscience to perform a function which appeared to the community to be that of the $n\bar{a}\underline{b}\hat{\imath}$' – despite its alarming departure from the conventional mode. In other cases the protesters may have been trained as professional $n^e\underline{b}\hat{\imath}$'îm but have revolted against the institution from within (the author of Ps. 50?). When then, is a $n\bar{a}\underline{b}\hat{\imath}$' not a $n\bar{a}\underline{b}\hat{\imath}$'? Whether the new type of prophet desired to be so designated or not, this was the term accorded him by the community: hence the confusion in the scriptures and for us. The confusion is prominent, of course, in the notorious passage Amos 7:14-16 (not a $n\bar{a}\underline{b}\hat{\imath}$' but ordered by YHWH הִנָּבֵא) and in Jeremiah, where, in poetic passages the poet clearly distances himself from the

---

[20] Fenton, art. cit., 32(bottom)-3.

$n^e\underline{b}î'îm$ whereas in the prose sections he is designated $n\bar{a}\underline{b}î'$ by the deity and bears the title throughout his functioning life.[21]

If our perception of the rise of the new prophetic protest movement from its ancient Near Eastern matrix is justified, is it possible to discern factors which might have promoted the transformation? Undoubtedly the cardinal factor on the political scene in the western area of the Fertile Crescent from the ninth century on was the increasing power and seemingly inexorable expansion of the Assyrian Empire (its sudden eclipse and 'replacement' by Babylon came late in the development of the new prophecy and did not affect the 'balance of power' from the Judean point of view). From the time of Amos to that of Jeremiah it would appear that prophets, and no doubt others, perceived the threat and the nature of the events which were about to overtake the small kingdoms between the areas of Assyrian control and Egypt. The new prophecy regarded the approaching doom as retribution and Scripture attributes this to revelation. If, however, one shares the unease of many who find difficulty with wide-ranging historical implications of such a complex of ideas and plead for a reading 'without theology', it might be suggested that the growing threat brought about an intensification of the new prophetic view of the social and religious disorder within the nation which was then diagnosed as the source of the impending catastrophe. Such thinking is consonant with the profound passion for justice and the concern with religious apostasy (as it was perceived) which have been noted, but to analyse the international situation in these terms implies also a shift in the perception of deity. It must be assumed that the movement which was to culminate in the recognizable monotheism of Second Isaiah and the Deuteronomists was well under way before the Exile, whether we think of Morton Smith's monolatry ('YHWH alone'), associated particularly with the prophet Elijah, or, which seems to me more likely, an already more refined concept. The universalization of the national deity is a suitable framework for a concept of sin and retribution in the form of conquest by a foreign power.

Which of these concepts, if any, was primary in shaping the new prophetic protest movement? The acute perception of an increased

---

[21]For further points concerning this question cf. Fenton, *art. cit.*, section IV, 36-38 top. The view stated there and in the present paper provides, I would claim, a reasonable explanation for the history of the use of the word $n\bar{a}\underline{b}î'$ in the composition of the Hebrew Scriptures as expounded by A. Graeme Auld in his diligent statistical analyses in 'Prophets and Prophecy in Jeremiah and Kings', *ZAW* 96 (1984), 66-82, and in his celebrated 'Prophets through the Looking Glass', *JSOT* 27 (1983), 3-23.

tempo in the development of political forces in the area? The unprecedented concern with social justice, ethical behaviour and compassion? The radical shift in the concept of deity? Clearly the mutual influence of these factors intensified the process by which a movement of great potency and of lasting significance was created.

The process we have envisaged and the movement it produced involved living persons, not fictional characters. From that process emerged a group of personalities some of whose words and actions were recorded and transmitted, it is believed, as originally spoken, written or enacted, but often through an interpretive prism with adaptations or additions. The attempt to distinguish between the layers of transmission has been and remains an obvious and fascinating task. Convincing results have been achieved and tools for further progress are increasingly refined. The personalities who inaugurated this literary activity have distinct styles of composition and present different treatments of ideological issues. Their words and activities are often recorded within historical contexts and in locations appropriate to them. That these personalities, their backgrounds, their poetry (the acknowledged quality of which we have emphasized), the interpretations of their words, the adaptations and expansions (the entire 'rolling corpus'), the differing styles, treatments, historical contexts and locations should constitute a literary genre invented in an age removed in time and spirit from its subject, might seem unlikely.[22] If such a corpus were indeed the product of such an age it would surely be the most bizarre literary genre ever created. The motivation for such a creation would require a most unusual and complex *Sitz in Leben*. No such setting, nor the way in which it might have generated such a corpus, have, to my knowledge, been proposed.

---

[22] For previous objections to the effacement of the prophetic persona, cf. H.M. Barstad, 'No Prophets? Recent Developments in Biblical Prophetic Research and Ancient Near Eastern Prophecy', *JSOT* 57 (1993), 47-61; R.P. Gordon, 'Where Have All the Prophets Gone? The "Disappearing" Israelite Prophet against the Background of Ancient Near Eastern Prophecy', *BBR* 5 (1995), 67-86, both with further references.

Alastair Hunter   *Glasgow – United Kingdom*

Jonah from the Whale
Exodus Motifs in Jonah 2

1   Introduction

For a number of years Michael Goulder has, with characteristic singleness of mind, pursued the goal of a liturgical explanation of the Psalter in terms of the historical traditions preserved in Tanach. Despite mixed revues on the one hand and the sheer magnitude of the task on the other, he has now produced four volumes[1] of what will presumably be in the end a complete discussion of the psalms. His ability to combine the broader vision with a highly technical analysis of the Hebrew of each individual psalm sets standards for the ongoing discussion which few are equipped to meet. The 'psalm' in Jon. 2 presents an interesting parallel. It is not my purpose to seek any *liturgical* explanation for Jon. 2, but I am aware of a similarity of both method and intention, in that I hope to show that close reading can lead to new insights regarding the oneness of hymn and narrative. In particular, where Goulder's work tends towards understanding psalms as liturgical compositions designed to celebrate and enhance the *legenda* of existing festivals, I am intrigued by the possibility of a reversal of that process.

I take as a further point of departure Watts' study of the phenomenon of hymnic material inserted into Hebrew narrative. There are connections, insofar as Watts' discussion is of explicit examples of what is *implicit* in Goulder's, and differences, in that Watts sees his material as strictly speaking part of the narrative:

> The major literary conclusion ... is that, in the Hebrew Bible, the use of psalms in narrative contexts is a literary device used to achieve compositional (narrative) goals.[2]

---

[1] M.D. Goulder, *The Psalms of the Sons of Korah* (JSOT.S, 20), Sheffield 1982; Idem, *The Prayers of David* (JSOT.S, 102), Sheffield 1990; Idem, *The Psalms of Asaph and the Pentateuch* (JSOT.S, 233), Sheffield 1996; Idem, *The Psalms of the Return* (JSOT.S, 258), Sheffield 1998. These deal, respectively, with Pss. 42–49, 84–86, 87–89; Pss. 51–72; Pss. 50, 73–83; Pss. 107–150.

[2] J.W. Watts, *Psalm and Story: Inset Hymns in Hebrew Narrative* (JSOT.S, 139), Sheffield 1992, 186. See also Idem, ' "This Song:" Conspicuous Poetry in Hebrew Prose', in: J.C. de Moor, W.G.E. Watson (eds), *Verse in Ancient Near Eastern Prose* (AOAT, 42), Neukirchen-Vluyn 1993, 345-58.

I suppose few scholars of the Hebrew Bible are now quite so ready to fillet texts as we once were. There is no longer the same nonchalant attribution of apparent misfits to editorial activity, and only with reluctance are problematic texts explained away rather than explained. Though some commentaries still show signs of the source critic's love of the scissors in respect of famous cruces like Jon. 2 and Job 28,[3] there is a new mood around (in part brought about by often maligned literary theory) encouraging a more integrative and synchronic approach. I propose, therefore, as the second stimulus to my paper, the desirability of preserving in our readings the integrity of that which the ancients saw fit to present as a single composition.

I do not wish, however, to leave aside entirely the still *interesting* questions which lie behind two centuries of critical debate. Simple curiosity prompts us to ask how? and when? – and even sometimes why? – and though our answers to such questions must remain for the most part speculative, the process of looking for answers is instructive, and some of the resulting speculations are fruitful in their own right, stimulating further research. I therefore want to acknowledge as a third strand to my paper: the promptings of natural curiosity. I will give in to the temptation to ask the historical critical questions, albeit with no illusions about the chances of success in answering them.

2 Prophetic Character

The question 'literary or historical character' has a different emphasis in the case of Jonah, not least because there is a broad agreement that he is a literary invention, a fictional device at the service of the unknown author's possibly satirical intent. While the prophet of the same name briefly referred to in 2 Kings 14:25 may have inspired the choice of name, there is no sign that even the minimal information given there is applied to the narrative of our book.[4] Thus we may safely assume that 'Jonah' is an authorial invention. But while that

---

[3]See T.M. Bolin, *Freedom beyond Forgiveness: The Book of Jonah Re-Examined* (JSOT.S, 236), Sheffield 1997, 98-101, for a survey of attitudes to the psalm. It is notable that arguments against its integrity are fewer in recent years. Elihu, however, still fares very badly in the literary stakes, in that the consensus (see, for example, J.L. Crenshaw, 'Book of Job', in: D.N. Freedman, *The Anchor Bible Dictionary*, Vol. 3, New York 1992, 861) remains with those who regard his speeches as secondary and intrusive.

[4]H.W. Wolff, *Obadiah and Jonah*, Minneapolis 1986, discusses the Kings passage in several places (pp. 75, 77, 98, 102) but never establishes any connection beyond the name itself. Similarly J.M. Sasson, *Jonah* (AncB, 24B), New York 1990, 86, 116, 181. He does 'attempt one substantive link, through the phrase '*kidbar* YHWH' (p. 227), but that is hardly impressive.

assumption solves many narrative puzzles,[5] it generates in respect of Ch. 2 a surprising problem: why is the 'fit' between psalm and narrative seemingly so poor? Inserted 'psalms' such as the 'confessions' of Jeremiah are often understood in terms of the use by an editor of material chosen from existing types to epitomise the words of an already given character,[6] and while the fit may not be perfect[7] it is usually plausible. In Jonah, however, the psalm is awkward in terms both of content and of narrative improbability. The standard answer to both of these problems is an appeal to satire, and this is to some extent appropriate. The contrast between the abjectly unprincipled Jonah of the narrative and the hypocritical fraud of the psalm can be seen to form part of the parodic effect of the composition. But it is still worth exploring why *this* psalm, why *those* particular themes? In the remainder of this paper I will examine in detail the intertextual milieu of Jon. 2 and offer some tentative conclusions as a consequence. The most significant will be to reposition the psalm as the heart of the book, with the result that Jonah the character will emerge not as a work of imagination *inspiring* a poetic pastiche but as a fiction *necessitated by* a theological drama whose purpose is to shed a different light on a set of older theological traditions.

3 Intertextual Connections

The extent to which Jonah as a whole reworks material from elsewhere in scripture has often been noted. Thus Magonet[8] provides a detailed account of relevant references for the whole of Jonah, and Sasson[9] lists parallels to the language of the psalm (Jon. 2:3b-10) which he describes as 'illustrative passages'.[10] While much of the psalm appears at first to be typical of the broad generality of such writing, I want

---

[5]We are freed, for example, from the tiresome need to explain (or explain away) historical or geographical errors. One of the most egregious of such explanations is to be found in the NIV translation of Jon. 3:3 (מַהֲלַךְ שְׁלֹשֶׁת יָמִים) where Nineveh is described as being 'three days' journey in breadth' (RSV). This is improbable to say the least, and NIV imaginatively (but with scant regard for the Hebrew) renders it 'a visit required three days'!

[6]Though consider in this respect Robert P. Carroll's scepticism regarding the historicity of 'Jeremiah' in *Jeremiah* (OTL), London 1986, 55-64.

[7]Thus, for example, the proleptic references to the king in Hannah's song (1 Sam. 2:10) or to the peoples of Canaan in Exod. 15:14-15.

[8]J. Magonet, *Form and Meaning: Studies in Literary Techniques in the Book of Jonah* (BET, 2), Bern 1976.

[9]Sasson, *op. cit.*, 166-215, *passim*.

[10]Bolin, *op. cit.*, 106-17, provides a helpful survey of the links between Jon. 2 and the Psalter. What is interesting is that intertextuality in respect of *other* parts of the Hebrew Bible is rather rarely considered.

to argue for a core of rather more specific words and phrases which can form the basis of a somewhat tighter approach to intertextuality. Beginning with the following list of key words (drawn from the whole of chapter two),

אפף בלע גל הֵיכָל הָג/דגה יַבָּשָׁה יוֹנָה מנה מְצוּלָה מִשְׁבָּר סבב סוּף עטף קיא שְׁאוֹל שׁוע שַׁחַת תְּהוֹם

a review of their occurrence elsewhere in the Hebrew Bible indicates several passages which would repay further examination,[11] at least on the basis of the number of these expressions found in close contiguity. They are: Gen. 8:1-12; Exod. 15:1b-13; Neh. 9:9-11; Num. 16:30-34; Isa. 38; Pss. 18 (= 2 Sam. 22); 55; 69:2-4, 14-16; 107:23-32. One of the first things to note about this group is that three of them (Exod. 15; 2 Sam. 22; Isa. 38) are discussed by Watts, along with Jon. 2. Further, as we shall see, the verses from Nehemiah are heavily indebted to Exod. 15, suggesting a similar bracketing to that of Ps. 18 with 2 Sam. 22.[12] It turns out that Num. 16:30-34 finds its way into the list because of the theme of the earth/Sheol swallowing the damned Korahites – a significantly different motif – while Gen. 8 relates to the drying up (יבשׁ) of the land after the flood and the use of the dove (יוֹנָה). While there are superficial links with Jonah, the absence of the term יַבָּשָׁה reduces the pertinence of this passage; I shall therefore ignore it for my present purposes.

Of the passages which remain, I want to leave Ps. 18 and Isa. 38 to one side, mainly because they range metaphorically more widely than Jon. 2, but also because their entirely non-ironic connection with specific individuals (David and Hezekiah) gives them a quite different resonance. In the next section I will consider Pss. 69 and 107, Exod. 15 and Neh. 9; this will lead to the elaboration of a hypothesis concerning the use of exodus motifs by the author of Jonah. Finally I will consider Ps. 55, concerning which I would like to propose a sort of mirror-development to that of Jonah.

---

[11] The significance of the fish is elusive. The feminine form (and only that form) turns up in Gen. 1:26, 28 – though it is the masculine form in Ps. 8:9. The fish which die in the Nile at Moses' command are feminine: perhaps they take their revenge in Jonah.

[12] It is not the same, of course. Nehemiah does not directly *quote* Exod. 15 – but the links are nonetheless very close.

4 Key Passages

4.1 Psalm 69:2-3, 14-19

The main reason for the inclusion of Psalm 69:2-3, 14-19 is the occurrence of מְצוּלָה (twice) and בלע in vv. 3 and 16. Undoubtedly these are both relatively rare words, and their use in this psalm is echoed in Jonah (bearing in mind that it is the *fish* which swallows Jonah). There is a general metaphorical relationship between Ps. 69 and Jonah, but arguably no literary dependence. This perhaps most clearly seen in the vocabulary used in the psalm to describe how the waters sweep over the psalmist (וְשִׁבֹּלֶת שְׁטָפָתְנִי Ps. 69:3, cf. v. 16) and the use of בְּאֵר for 'pit' in v. 16 where Jon. 2 uses שְׁאוֹל and שַׁחַת. I conclude, therefore, that although the *tone* of these verses from Ps. 69 has similarities to Jonah, there is nothing to suggest anything beyond a general similarity of figurative language.

4.2 Psalm 107:23-32

Unlike Ps. 69, we find here both a significant lexical content and an interesting narrative connection with the events of Jonah Ch. 1. The key expressions shared with Jon. 2 are בלע, גַּל, מְצוּלָה, תְּהוֹם and with Jon. 1, שׁתק, סְעָרָה, מְלָאכָה – a somewhat denser frequency than in the case of Ps. 69. The 'story' is of course not specific, being one of a series of examples which the psalmist presents in support of his/her celebration of YHWH's חֶסֶד – a term which is itself important in the rhetoric of Jonah (2:9, 4:2)[13] – but the close narrative connection with Jon. 1 (including the 'sacrifices of thanksgiving' (זִבְחֵי תוֹדָה) of v. 22 – compare Jon. 1:16; 2:10) does bear closer examination. It would be foolish to make confident claims for dependence of Jonah on Ps. 107, but it would be equally irresponsible to ignore what is a very strong set of parallels. Sasson hints at this by quoting Ps. 107:23-30 at the beginning of his discussion of Jon. 1:7-12,[14] but neither he nor other commentators take it any further. In view of other substantive links with the Psalter, I will return to this passage in formulating my

---

[13] I have not included this in my list of diagnostic expressions because it is a very common word in the Hebrew Bible. However it does figure in Phyllis Trible's discussion of Exod. 34:6 (*God and the Rhetoric of Sexuality*, Philadelphia 1978, 1-30), and its prominence in Ps. 107 might suggest that its occurrence in both Jonah and Ps. 107 could be given greater weight. Note the presence of this theme also in Neh. 9:17.

[14] Sasson, *op. cit.*, 107. It is strange how little discussion there has been of this subject. I can only find a few references even to the interesting verbal parallels.

broader conclusions about the literary development of the book of Jonah.

4.3 Exodus 15:1b-13

I have already remarked that this passage has very close links with Neh. 9:9-11; I will therefore treat the latter when we come to it more as an adjunct to the Song of the Sea than as a separate item. What makes Exod. 15 particularly interesting for the purposes of our immediate study is the presence of a few quite remarkable lexical items in common with Jon. 2. In order to spell out their significance I shall treat them in some detail.

1 יַבָּשָׁה (יַבֶּשֶׁת)

There are just sixteen occurrences of these related terms of which the less common יַבֶּשֶׁת only occurs twice. Specifically, the relevant passages are:

Gen. 1:9, 10	Exod. 4:9 (twice)	**Exod. 14:16, 22, 29; 15:19**
Josh. 4:22	Isa. 44:3	**Jon. 1:9, 15; 2:11**
Pss. 66:6; 95:5	**Neh. 9:11**	

Half are in the three passages we have already listed (indicated in bold type). Gen. 1:9, 10 is, of course, within the Priestly creation account, and its substantive links with the language of Exod. 14-15 are patent. Ps. 66:6 is a direct reference to the exodus, and Ps. 95:5 to the creation; Josh. 4:22 is in the context of a tradition (the crossing of the Jordan) which is evidently modelled on the exodus. Given that the only exception to this pattern is Isa. 44:3, we may conclude that the use of this term in Jonah is a strong and perhaps intentional signal that the exodus/creation theme is present.

2 יַם(־סוּף)

The proper name יַם־סוּף occurs in the following places (those indicated in bold type are direct references to the exodus tradition):

Exod. 10;19; 13:18; 15:4, 22; 23:31	Num. 14:25; 21:4; 33: 10, 11	Deut. 1:40; 2:1; **11:4**
Joshua 2.10; 4:23; 24:6	Judg. 11:16	1 Kgs 9:26
Jer. 49:21	**Ps. 106:7, 9, 22; 136: 13, 15**	Neh. 9:9

The noun[15] סוּף, meaning 'reed', is recorded in Exod. 2:3, 5, Isa. 19:6 and Jon. 2:6. Both Exodus and Isaiah explicitly refer to the reeds growing in and around the Nile, and there can be little doubt that this is the meaning the word would convey for readers of Jonah familiar with the traditions.

3 מְצוּלָה

This expression is not so clearly specific to the exodus material. Apart from Jon. 2:4, its distribution is as follows (**bold** type indicates direct reference to the exodus tradition, *italics* indicates its use in relation to the cosmic fear of death in the depths, associated with the sea or the 'pit'):

Exod. 15:5	Mic. 7:19	Zech. 1:8; **10:11**
Ps. *68:23*; *69:3, 16*; *88:7*; 107:24	**Neh. 9:11**	Job 41:23

Zech. 1:8 is a linguistic crux for which emendations have often been proposed, and may, I think, safely be discounted. Mic. 7:19 is rather interesting in that it occurs in a brief concluding passage[16] which also takes up the theme of the mercy of God from Exod. 34:6 (see above, n. 13), and which reads like a brief historical summary. It does not seem far-fetched to associate this instance also with the exodus tradition. Those psalms which use the depths as a metaphor for death are, I would argue, in touch with a clear dimension of the exodus myth which is plainly employed in Jon. 2. Thus the only instances of

---

[15]Lisowsky also lists the root סוּף with the meaning 'to come to an end', and associates with it two derived nouns (סוֹף, סוּפָה) meaning respectively 'end/rear guard' and 'storm-wind'. Whether this root has anything to do with the name of the sea and the expression for 'reeds' is a moot point. For some interesting comments on this point, and on 'meaningful' geography more generally, see N. Wyatt, 'Sea and Desert: Symbolic Geography in West Semitic Religious Thought' in *UF* 19 (1987), 375-89.

[16]For convenience, I reproduce the relevant passage here (Mic. 7:18-20):

'Who is a God like thee, pardoning iniquity
    and passing over transgression for the remnant of his inheritance?
He does not retain his anger for ever
    because he delights in steadfast love.
He will again have compassion upon us,
    he will tread our iniquities under foot.
Thou wilt cast all our sins into the depths of the sea.
Thou wilt show faithfulness to Jacob
    and steadfast love to Abraham
as thou hast sworn to our fathers from the days of old.'

מְצוּלָה which fall outside this single complex are Ps. 107:24 and Job 41:23. We have considered the former already, and noted how that psalm might relate to Jonah; the specific usage both here and in Job, however, seems to be as a non-mythic or metaphoric synonym for the sea. These two apart, we have once more a highly significant term whose presence in Jonah is likely to have prompted echoes of exodus.

4 תְּהוֹם

Gen. *1:2*; 7:11; 8:2; 49:25	**Exod. 15:5, 8**	Deut. 8:7; 33:13
Isa. 51:10; 63:13	Ezek. <u>26:19</u>; 31:4, 15	Amos 7:4 *Hab. 3:10*
Pss. *33:7*; 36:7; 42:8; <u>71:20</u>; <u>77:17</u>; 78:15; *104:6*; **106:9**; <u>107:26</u>; *135:6*; *148:7*	Job 28:14; *38:16, 30*; 41:24	Prov. *3:20; 8:24, 27, 28*

To clarify the argument, I have rendered in bold type those passages (the instance in Jonah is not listed here) which make explicit reference to the exodus traditions, in *italics* those which associate the term with the creation, and by <u>underlining</u> those in which the תְּהוֹם is a violent threat to the safety of the individual or the nation. We have already observed a connection between the motifs of creation and exodus, and between the exodus water experience and the experience of despair in the face of death. Thus these three aspects of תְּהוֹם which belong together in our survey account for twenty-three of the total of thirty-three occurrences. While the proportion is not quite as conclusive as for the first three terms, this still represents a remarkable consistency, and strengthens the probability that the reader will recognise what Jonah points to.

5 (בִּלְבַב יַמִּים, בְּלֵב יַמִּים, בְּלַב־יָם)

These variants of the same basic phrase are found, in addition to Jon. 2:4, only in

Exod. 15:8	Ezek. 27:4, 25, 26, 27; 28:2	Prov. 23:34; 30:19

This is a curious phrase. Its meaning in the Ezekiel and Proverbs passages is in relation to seafaring and to its attendant risk of shipwreck, which makes its use in Jonah obviously relevant. But it occurs not in the near-shipwreck passage of Jonah, but in the psalm which, as we have already noted, has striking connections with the exodus myth. That the author of Jonah places this striking phrase in Ch. 2 and not in Ch. 1, together with its unique occurrence in Exodus, cannot but reinforce the already strong bonds between Jon. 2 and Exod. 15.

These few studies are by no means the whole story, for we could note also the presence of further key terms from Jon. 2 which, while lacking the rather tightly-circumscribed occurrence pattern we have analysed in the above cases, are none-the-less significant. Thus, for example, Pharaoh's army, like Jonah, *goes down* (ירד) into the sea (Exod. 15:5; Jon. 2:7); the poem celebrates YHWH's *salvation* (יְשׁוּעָה) from peril (Exod. 15:2; Jon. 2:10); and we learn (Exod. 15:13; Jon. 2:5, 8, 9) that the return to the realm of God's *holiness* (קֹדֶשׁ) is as a result of God's *steadfast love* (חֶסֶד). In short, there is a very strong case for the thesis that at the heart of Jonah lies a commentary – albeit a very off-beat one – on the cherished exodus myth which lies at the heart of Israel's belief in itself as a people specially covenanted to God.

4.4 Nehemiah 9:9-11

Mention should be made of this passage, which forms part of a narrative historical recital similar in content to Pss. 78 and 105. Goulder[17] makes use of Nehemiah in his interpretation of the Psalms of Ascents, though he largely ignores Ch. 9. Broadly speaking he relates Ezra and Nehemiah to Book Five of the Psalter – a chronological association which fits well with the probability of a post-exilic date for Jonah[18] and the possibility of some intertextual influence between Ps. 107 and Jonah.

The key words which Neh. 9:9-11 shares with Jonah are יַבָּשָׁה, יָם-(סוּף) and מְצוּלָה (חֶסֶד is used in v. 17, in the context of the familiar refrain from Exod. 34:6) – fewer in number than those shared between Exodus and Jonah. In addition, there are several explicit references to Exodus – some predictable, like Egypt and Pharaoh, others which are more likely to indicate direct influence (בקע and רדף and the rare phrase כְּמוֹ־אָבֶן, whose only other occurrence is in Job 41:16 where it is used quite differently). Given that none of the latter group are found in Jonah, while the former are all in Exodus, we may conclude that Nehemiah is probably familiar with the Exodus material – and that references common to Nehemiah and Jonah result from Jonah's familiarity with the Exodus material. There is probably little point at this stage in looking any further into the Nehemiah passage.

---

[17] M.D. Goulder, 'The Song of Ascents and Nehemiah', *JSOT* 75 (1997), 43-58.
[18] For discussions of the date of composition of Jonah see Bolin, *op. cit.*, 33-40, and Sasson, *op. cit.*, 20-8.

5 A Hypothesis – Prolegomenon

Watts[19] includes Jon. 2 in his review of 'inset hymns in Hebrew narrative'. Much of what he says is excellent, and he demonstrates, in my view conclusively, that the debate about the 'fit' between the psalm and the rest of the book should be regarded as over. Both linguistically and in terms of theme and characterisation, there is no need to search for secondary authors and 'dumb redactors'.[20] Watts does not in principle reject the appropriateness of diachronic questions, but he preserves a neutral stance in the case of Jonah, on the grounds that there is insufficient evidence to draw any useful conclusions about the relative priority of psalm and/or narrative. Ignoring his caution, I propose (no doubt unwisely) to engage with that particular question on the basis that some useful insights can emerge from the process of thought entailed.

Attempts to explain the origins of Jonah (the book)[21] often refer to the cryptic reference to the prophet of that name in 2 Kgs 14:23-27 – assuming in addition a 'lost' corpus of Jonah material from while the surviving book was selected – and may in addition note the close correspondence with certain aspects of the Elijah pericope in 1 Kgs 17–19, 2 Kgs 2–9. Sometimes the shipwreck scene in Ezek. 27 is adduced, while on a wider front folk-tale origins have been proposed, the most plausible being the myth of Perseus and Andromeda.

> The felicitous choice of Joppa as Jonah's point of embarkation has been rich fodder for commentators since that city has been the location of the Perseus-Andromeda legend from at least the 4th century BCE. In this story Andromeda, offered to a sea-monster, is chained to a rock overlooking the sea to await her fate. Perseus arrives, does battle with the creature (during which he enters inside of it) and prevails.[22]

---

[19] Watts, *op. cit.*, 132-44.

[20] I refer here to Thomas Bolin's interesting, if not quite conclusive, dismissal of the assumptions commonly used to recognise redaction (*op. cit.*, 44): 'Redactors ... are imprecise in their work, a Godsend for biblical scholars who otherwise would be unable to detect editorial activity. The work of these later scribes is implicitly characterized by a lack of attention to the vocabulary and narrative logic of the original authors. Such distinctions are unprovable.' While this comment has much merit, we can still legitimately detect redaction where a later author has decided to make the best of two apparently incompatible traditions which he/she nevertheless deems to be of equal value. Thus, for example, the sophisticated join in Gen. 2:4 between the creation accounts.

[21] Bolin, *op. cit.*, 36, n. 85; 40-2; 73-5; 91-3, provides useful summaries of the various proposals.

Each of these theories assumes that the task is to explain the origins of the *narrative* portions of Jonah. Even if the psalm is held to be integral,[23] it is tacitly placed in a secondary position – an invention or pastiche created to supplement the story or to give it ironic depth. In the modern period only two very early scholars (Müller and Nachtigal[24]) seem to have given priority to the psalm, suggesting that it was composed in the 8th century BCE, with the narrative added in the exile. Though I have not seen their work, any such gross chronological separation of the genres in Jonah would seem in the light of modern research to be highly improbable. Nevertheless there may be something yet to be said *in principle* for their ordering of the compositional process, and it is to that possibility I want to now.

The first point to make is that, contrary to some of the more dismissive treatments of Jon. 2:3-10, the poem is far from mere pastiche: it has clear narrative structure, uses powerful imagery and highly specialised language, and is replete with striking theological motifs. In itself it represents an individual psalm of thanksgiving[25] in which an opening résumé (v. 3) is followed by a detailed account of salvation (vv. 4-8) leading in turn to an affirmation and exaltation of God (vv. 9-10). The language is, needless to say, metaphoric, drawn from a reservoir of familiar images. Embedded in the brief legend of the fish (just as Jonah himself was interred in the creature) it becomes both literal (Jonah is indeed under threat from water) and ironic (the life-threatening event which is the immediate cause of the psalm's utterance is at the same time the life-*saving* wonder which enables Jonah to pronounce this psalm of reminiscent thanksgiving). We might take this encircling image one stage further: the story begins (Jon. 1:15) with Jonah in the sea which surrounds the fish which will surround Jonah when he celebrates his metaphoric redemption from an earlier water ordeal.[26] However, I want to postpone such literary

---

[22] Bolin, *op. cit.*, 77.

[23] Bolin, *op. cit.*, 98-101, summarises the arguments for and against the integrity of the psalm within Jonah as a whole. See also the tables of verbs found in more than one chapter in Magonet, *op. cit.*, 14. No fewer than twelve verbs from Ch. 2 are used in other chapters.

[24] Referred to in Bolin, *op. cit.*, 42, 98.

[25] See, for example, J. Day, *Psalms* (OTGu), Sheffield 1990, 46. In the present case the introduction (i) is not an 'intention to thank YHWH' but a brief statement of the reason for giving thanks.

[26] Thus P.K. McCarter, 'The River Ordeal in Israelite Literature', *HThR* 66 (1973), 403-12. He proposed that there is evidence for the language of a river ordeal in the Hebrew Bible similar to that familiar from Mesopotamian materials. Jon. 2 and Pss. 18 and 69 are the three examples he singles out. I cannot find any evidence that this idea has been taken further.

flights (not to mention Jonah's flight) for the moment and return to the significance of the psalm.

Those who defend the integrity of Jonah point to both structural and (in a more limited degree) linguistic features which bind the psalm to the rest. Insofar as these are plausible, they are neutral as to priority; that is, they do not in themselves answer the question 'which came first'. However, they do add to the need to provide an explanation which takes account of the overall integrity of the work. It seems to me that accounts of the psalm which rely primarily on pastiche or cut-and-paste fail to deal with this simple point. The text of Jon. 2:3-10 is neither an idle copy nor a lazy crib; it was placed where it is with deliberation, it did not fall accidentally into a gap in some scribe's attention.

There is a third, more general point to be made. It has often been claimed that the primary narrative forms are poetic – that people most naturally tell their tales in ballad form and preserve their traditions lyrically rather than in prose. As literacy develops and scribes emerge (with their penchant for gathering and summarising and categorising) so do more prosaic forms develop, first as a convenient means of collecting traditions in a less expansive form, but subsequently as a separate artistic medium: the sophisticated prose composition.[27] The Hebrew Bible affords some possible glimpses of the first part of this process, most notably in Exod. 15 (compare Exod. 14) and Judg. 5 (compare Judg. 4), and of sophisticated prose composition (parts, if not all of the Joseph material – especially Gen. 37, 39-41 – and such novellae as Ruth and the first chapters of Daniel). I suggest that we might with profit consider the possibility of a version of this process at work in the production of Jonah.

6 A Hypothesis – Substance

Psalms tell stories. Not often, but sometimes – and they do so most effectively. Ps. 132, for example, is a highly effective dramatic re-enactment of the quest for the Ark. Ps. 73 takes us through a dark night of the soul, and Ps. 82 presents a divine court-room scene which leads inexorably to judgement and death. Ps. 55 (to which I shall return in a coda) is a vivid song of betrayal and recovery of trust. I have indicated in the previous section that Jon. 2:3-10 should be seen as a representative of this class of dramatic narrative poems.

---

[27] Closer to home, European ballad traditions have inspired subtle prose compositions. A recent novel by Andrew Greig, *When They Lay Bare* uses a Scottish border ballad as the inspiration for a fascinating and many-layered novel.

It is not, therefore, a mere *adjunct* to the prose context; nor is it the straightforward poetic alternative to a prose version. We cannot therefore understand it in terms of the development from oral to literary forms of transmission. This is in any case what we might expect, given the strong probability of a post-exilic composition date. What we have, rather, is a sophisticated poetic drama set in a prose context with which it has highly ambiguous and subtle relationships. Both the poem and the prose narrative reveal an author whose knowledge of a familiar body of Hebrew scripture is extensive and impressive,[28] and who employs that knowledge in a highly imaginative way.[29] It is on the basis of these facts that my thesis is founded.

Commentators have regularly identified significant parallels elsewhere in the Hebrew Bible for the themes in the narrative chapters of Jonah, though it is important to emphasise that none is a simple imitation. Thus Ch. 1 can be linked to the shipwreck scenes in Ps. 107 and Ezek. 27; both Jon. 1 and Jon. 4 use key motifs from the account of Elijah in the wilderness (1 Kgs 19); Jonah's explanation for his flight (Jon. 4:2); is given in terms of the familiar 'mercy of YHWH' theme in Exod. 34:6 etc; and Magonet shows that Jon. 3 can be meaningfully related both to the Sodom and Gomorrah traditions and to the wickedness of the pre-flood generation.[30] When we turn to Jon. 2, however, the principal connections are made in relation to liturgical phrases rather than narrative motifs. What I want to propose is that the poem is equally definitively influenced by what might be called *epic* motifs – specifically the river ordeal and the exodus escape through the sea.

I believe that McCarter[31] has made a very strong case for the existence of the river ordeal in Hebrew literature, and for its presence being particularly strong in Pss. 18 and 69 and in Jon. 2. My own discussion above has established an equally strong case for Jonah's explicit reference to the themes of the 'Red Sea'. Thus we find combined (uniquely?[32]) in Jonah two themes in such a way as to render personal and individual the national experience of the exodus.

---

[28]Most of the commentaries note this. See especially Magonet, *op. cit.*, 65-84, who is, however, somewhat dismissive of possible links with Ezek. 27 and Ps. 107.

[29]The many literary studies of Jonah which have appeared in recent years constitute eloquent testimony to this claim.

[30]Magonet, *op. cit.*, 65, notes significant verbal usages which link the threat that Nineveh will be overthrown with Sodom and Gomorrah, and the wickedness and violence of the city with Gen. 6:5, 11, 13.

[31]McCarter, *art. cit.*

[32]I have not been able to find any other clear examples of the combination of these themes.

A third component can be added to this potent association of ideas: namely, that of the life and death journey *down* to Egypt and the redemptive return *up* to Canaan. Wyatt[33] refers to the possibility of a punning interpretation of the sea of exodus as יַם־סוּף, 'the sea of extinction' and comments on the prevalence, especially in the Joseph material in Genesis, of the combination ירד and עלה. This implies a metaphoric parallel between Egypt and Sheol which explains the continuing horror of the thought of exile to Egypt in the biblical tradition – a horror, interestingly, which is *not* expressed in relation to the exile in Babylon. There are five places other than Jon. 2 where these two verbs are combined in relation to Sheol: Gen. 44:31, 1 Sam. 2:6, Isa. 14:14-15, Ps. 30:4 and Job 7:9. Apart from the first, which belongs to the Genesis material referred to immediately above, none of these passages makes any reference to Egypt, and none at all hints at the exodus. This amounts, in effect, to a unique threefold conflation of ideas and motifs in Jon. 2 which constitutes a drama of the utmost originality and of high theological significance. Moreover, when we recall that there are echoes also of the creation myths (the special term for 'dry land' and the implication that God's 'appointing' of the fish is an act of creation) we begin to see that here we have encapsulated much that lies at the heart of Israel's covenant mythology.

It is in the light of these findings that I venture to suggest a shift in perspective towards the dramatic poem in Jonah as the instigator of the wider prose drama. I cannot claim to have *proved* that this is even probable in terms of the actual process which produced the book. But I submit that I have established that it is both *possible* and *fitting*, not least in that it gives proper place to what is evidently the high point of the book. How might this work out if we develop it further? In particular, how does the prose narrative *follow from* the poetic drama? In part, the answer to this might lie in a revisiting of earlier studies arguing for the integrity of the book as a whole, to see if my shifting of the perspective introduces new possibilities. But as a start, it is interesting that the two journeys made by Jonah are in the opposite directions implied by the mythology of the exodus. His flight is westwards, to wherever Tarshish may lie, in defiance of God – just as the journey to Egypt is seen as an effective departure from God's realm – and that flight is *downwards*: down to Joppa, down into the ship, and down into the waters. Having been *brought up* out of the waters, his second journey is eastwards, to Mesopotamia whence, in truth, much that came to form Judaism emerged (Ezra and Nehemiah,

---

[33] N. Wyatt, 'Sea and Desert: Symbolic Geography in West Semitic Religious Thought', *UF* 19 (1987), 375-6.

Hillel and Akivah, the Babylonian Talmud). We do not find the verb ירד again, though עלה reappears in the growth of the plant which God 'appointed' to provide shade for Jonah.[34]

The ordeal theme which is found in the poem is also dramatised in the narrative – in the form of ordeal by water in chapter one, and ordeal by heat or fire in chapter four. The motif of creation is explicitly found in Jonah's self-identification (1:9): 'I am a Hebrew; and I fear the Lord, the God of heaven, who made the sea and the dry land', and more indirectly in the repetition of the significant word יַבָּשָׁה in 1:13, and the use of the piel of the verb מנה in respect of the fish, the plant, the worm and the wind (only in Jonah is this verb used of living things). Finally, the mercy of God is revealed in narrative terms through the rescue of the sailors (Jon. 1:15f.) and the forgiveness of Nineveh (Jon. 3:10), and explicitly when Jonah sets out the grounds of his grievance in 4:2.

Any account of Jonah is expected to give some explanation of the stark difference in *tone* between the poem and the narrative. The first choice for most moderns (and I include myself) has been a resort to parody, satire and various forms of humour, and these no doubt conform closely to the contemporary western *Zeitgeist*. Who, for example, can fail to appreciate the bathos of the concluding words of the concluding verse, 'and also much cattle'? Indeed, the incongruity of this ending is so obvious that the pious translators of the NIV, ever alert in the defence of the propriety of God's scripture, have quietly[35] switched the Hebrew around to produce:

> Nineveh has more than a hundred and twenty thousand people who cannot tell their right hand from their left, and many cattle as well. Should I not be concerned about that great city? (Jon. 4:11)

It is, however, of interest to remember that 'man and beast' is, even in English, a normal ordering; moreover, every time the threatened destruction of the firstborn is mentioned in Exodus, the 'beasts' come at the end.[36] Could it be that the incongruity is entirely in the eye of the modern beholder? And if so, might the whole tale be less grotesque from an ancient perspective? The venerable exodus myth itself is, in this respect no less, and no more, incongruous than Jonah, and is indeed equally replete with bizarre natural effects controlled by God.

---

[34]It may be significant that the occasion of God's call to Jonah and its consequences is the fact that Nineveh's 'wickedness has come up before [God]'.

[35]That is, without benefit of footnote – see also their mistranslation of Jon. 3:3.

[36]Thus Exod. 9:25; 11:5, 7; 12:12, 29; 13:2, 15. Compare also the famous passage in Qoh. 3:19, 21 comparing the fate of humankind and the beasts.

What I seem to have arrive at, curiously, is the probability that in its context Jonah was indeed something like an allegory (even, perhaps, a mini-*Bildungsroman*) designed to lead the reader, if not the central character, to some realisation of the practical meaning of the exodus experience. In older tradition the exodus was an ordeal of the birth of the nation; in Jonah it becomes an ordeal associated with the coming to maturity of Israel not as a privileged people in its Judaean ghetto, but as a means to the enlightenment of all nations. A drama, in short, characterising the fulfilment of the vision of both Isa. 2 and Mic. 4.

There is, however, a sting in the tale/tail. The author leaves it open as to the condition of Jonah/Israel at the end. God's final question is left hanging – we do not know whether Jonah got the point – and it is left hanging for every subsequent reader. To each of us it poses the unanswerable question: how far will you allow the mercy of God to go? Are there limits to your חֶסֶד, even if God is unbounded in love? Do even the beasts of the field deserve our love? A suitably 21st century note on which to end.

7 Coda: Psalm 55

One tantalising possibility is that the dove in Ps. 55 can be seen as the basis of an alternative 'Jonah' tale. The psalmist longs (v. 7) to have wings like a dove ('Jonah'), to fly away and to rest (Jonah flees from YHWH and sleeps in the boat). The psalmist seeks a shelter (v. 9) – i.e., a place for a fugitive to hide – where he will be safe from the tempest. Likewise the fugitive Jonah seeks shelter, and is endangered by the same tempest. The next section (vv. 10-12) describes the wickedness rampant in the city (cf. Nineveh); and immediately afterwards we have a passage (vv. 13-15) where the psalmist complains that he could bear the insults of an enemy – but it is his close companion who has deserted him. We remember how Jonah accuses God of betraying him. In two places (vv. 16, 24) we read of the fate of the wicked who will go down to the pit; and Jonah himself speaks of that dreadful experience. And of course, when the psalmist calls to God (vv. 17-20) he is heard and saved. The following is a synopsis of possible parallels:[37]

---

[37] There is, in addition to these more obvious similarities, a nice play on the terms דָּבָר and מִדְבָּר in that, while the Psalmist hides in the desert (בַּמִּדְבָּר), Ps. 55:8; Jonah flees from God's word (Jon. 1:1-3), returns to hear and obey the word (Jon. 3:1-3), and speaks his mind to God (Jon. 4:2); and the Ninevites respond to God's word (Jon. 3:6).

Ps. 55	Jonah	
7	O that I had wings like a dove!	1:3
	I would fly away and be at rest	1:5b
9	I would hurry to find a shelter for myself	1:5b
	From the raging wind and tempest	1:4
10-12	Confuse, O Lord, confound their speech;	1:1-2
	for I see violence and strife in the city.	
	Day and night they go round on its walls,	
	and iniquity and trouble are within it;	
	ruin is in its midst;	
	oppression and fraud do not depart from its marketplace	
13-15	It is not enemies who taunt me – I could bear that; –	4:1-3
	It is not adversaries who deal insolently with me –	
	I could hide from them.	
	But it is you, my equal,	
	my companion, my familiar friend	
	with whom I kept pleasant company;	
	we walked in the house of God with the throng.	2:5
16, 24	Let death come upon them;	2:3, 7
	let them go down alive to Sheol;	
	for evil is in their homes and in their hearts.	
	But you, O God, will cast them down	
	into the lowest pit.	
17-20	But I call upon God,	2:3a
	and the Lord will save me.	
	Evening and morning and at noon	
	I utter my complaint and moan,	
	and he will hear my voice.	
	He will redeem me unharmed	2:3, 10; 3:10
	from the battle that I wage,	
	for many are arrayed against me.	
	God who is enthroned from of old,	
	will hear and will humble them –	
	because they do not change,	
	and do not fear God.	

William Johnstone   *Aberdeen – United Kingdom*

The Portrayal of Moses as Deuteronomic Archetypal Prophet in Exodus and its Revisal

This paper seeks to plot a couple of points on the profile of the declining acceptability of prophecy in the exilic and post-exilic periods.

In order to position the argument of this paper, first a necessarily brief and impressionistic sketch of the general profile of the decline of the acceptability of prophecy, in the normative tradition of the Hebrew Bible at any rate, in the exilic and post-exilic periods is offered. In DtrH,[1] prophecy is presented as an inherently ambiguous phenomenon, potentially acceptable, potentially open to misuse: e.g., in 1 Sam. 10:1-16, the sign of Saul raving among the prophets is given by the seer Samuel; whatever the interpretation of that passage, it is clear that perception through heightened awareness may involve paranormal manifestations that can, however, be counterfeited by mechanical means. For the exilic age, prophecy is, indeed, part of the problem: it is contributory to the exile itself (e.g., Lam. 4:12-13: '...foe and enemy enter the gates of Jerusalem, for the sins of her prophets and the transgressions of her priests who shed the blood of the righteous in her midst'). Dispute between mutually exclusive claimants to prophecy is dramatically presented in Jer. 23:9-40; 27–28 and continued to rage in the *golah* (e.g., Jer. 29). In the post-exilic period, Zech. 13:2-6[2] shows that, while prophecy as a phenomenon may not – could not?[3] – have come to an end, its acceptability in normative circles certainly did cease. Part of the reason for that decline was, perhaps, its redundancy in face of the growth of scripture,[4]

---

[1] What may be meant by 'DtrH' is discussed, among other matters, in the symposium, L.S. Schearing, S.L. McKenzie (eds), *Those Elusive Deuteronomists: The Phenomenon of Pan-Deuteronomism* (JSOT.S, 268), Sheffield 1999, to which some reference will be made below.

[2] However that passage is interpreted. For a consideration of the possible party rivalries reflected in this text, see R. Rhea, 'Attack on Prophecy, Zechariah 13,1-6', *ZAW* 107 (1995), 288-93. See also E.M. Myers, 'The Crisis of Mid-Fifth Century BCE: Second Zechariah and the "End" of Prophecy', in D.P. Wright *et al.* (eds), *Pomegranates and Golden Bells* (Fs J. Milgrom), Winona Lake 1995, esp. 720-3.

[3] I am thinking here of the classic presentation of the psychology of prophecy as a constant in religious experience in J. Lindblom, *Prophecy in Ancient Israel*, Oxford 1962, 1-46. For a more recent discussion, see, e.g., W.M. Schniedewind's survey of 'Post-exilic Prophecy' in, 'Prophets and Prophecy in the Books of Chronicles', in M.P. Graham *et al.* (eds), *The Chronicler as Historian* (JSOT.S, 238), Sheffield 1997, esp. 205-10.

[4] E.g., B.D. Sommer, 'Did Prophecy Cease? Evaluating a Reevaluation', *JBL*

or its perceived failure in the delivery of its expectations.[5] The Chronicler in the fourth century shares, perhaps originates, the view of prophecy later found in Josephus (*Apion*, I.38-42), that it represents an unbroken succession of written normative interpretation, ending, as Josephus indicates, with Ezra.[6] Though the Chronicler also records an unfailing succession of prophetic voices interposing whenever the king of the House of David makes a wrong decision, that is for him always in accordance with the canons of Torah; prophecy also becomes for him the celebration of the already known acts of God through the song of the Levitical choir in the liturgy of the Temple (1 Chron. 25:1). Prophecy is thus regulated by absorption into the tradition of approved routine religious practice and affirmation, as defined by Torah.[7]

It is hardly surprising, then, that the *locus classicus* for the discussion of criteria for the discernment of true prophecy from false is already to be found in Deuteronomic exilic texts, Deut. 13:2-6 and 18:14-22.[8] It is widely recognised that these criteria are developed in Deuteronomistically edited Jeremiah.[9] It is the contention of this pa-

---

115 (1996), 31-47: 'one may legitimately speak of a decline of prophecy or a transformation from prophecy to exegesis during the Second Temple period' (47). See also his: *A Prophet Reads Scripture: Allusion in Isaiah 40-66* (Contraversions: Jews and Other Differences), Stanford 1999.

[5] R.P. Carroll, *When Prophecy Failed: Reactions and Responses to Failure in the Old Testament Prophetic Traditions*, London 1979.

[6] 'From the death of Moses till the reign of Artaxerxes...the prophets...wrote down what was done in their times'; cf. R. Meyer, 'Bemerkungen zum literargeschichtlichen Hintergrund der Kanontheorie des Josephus', in: O. Betz *et al.* (eds), *Josephus-Studien*, Göttingen 1974, 285-99.

[7] That compressed statement is expounded in my *1 & 2 Chronicles* (JSOT.S, 253, 254), Sheffield 1997. P.B. Dirksen, 'Prophecy and Temple Music: 1 Chron 25:1-7', *Henoch* 19 (1997), 259-65, disputes this interpretation (but his argument involves regarding 1 Chron. 23:2–26:32 as from a hand different from that of the Chronicler [and 1 Chron. 27 as still later], a view I should resist).

[8] The coherence of these passages is affirmed by C. Schäfer-Lichtenberger, *Josua und Salomo: Eine Studie zu Autorität und Legitimität des Nachfolgers im Alten Testament* (VT.S, 58), Leiden 1995, esp. 102. On the topic of true and false prophecy see J. Jeremias, ' "Wahre" und "falsche" Prophetie in AT: Entwicklungslinien eines Grundsatzkonfliktes', *ThBeitr* 28 (1997), 343-9.

[9] See now H.J. Hermisson, 'Kriterien "wahrer" und "falscher" Prophet im AT: Zur Auslegung von Jer 23,16-22 und Jer 28,8-9', *ZThK* 92 (1995), 121-39 (though related mainly to the specifics of the reception of the book of Jeremiah, he correctly sees that continuity with Moses and his Torah is now the standard of prophecy, 134-7). The breakthrough in perception in this case was achieved, in my view, by W. Thiel, *Die deuteronomistische Redaktion von Jeremia 1-25* (WMANT, 41), Neukirchen-Vluyn 1973; Idem, *Die deuteronomistische Redaktion von Jeremia 26–45* (WMANT, 52), Neukirchen-Vluyn 1981, who first opened my eyes to the fact

per that these Deuteronomic criteria are elaborated, however, not just in subsequent Dtr-edited books of the HB but also in the preceding Tetrateuch. In Exodus (and, indeed, Numbers) there is recoverable a version which matches the reminiscence, and, in certain cases including this one, the legislation, in Deuteronomy; this D-version of Exodus/Numbers undergoes further modification at the hands of the P-editor.[10] This D-version and its revision in the P-edition thus provide, it is contended, two points on the profile of the decline of prophecy in the exilic and post-exilic periods: the idealisation of prophecy in the persona of Moses, its fictionalised archetypal figure, provides in the D-version of Exodus/Numbers the criteria for the evaluation of prophecy; these criteria become in the P-version an instrument for the control of prophecy which leads to its assimilation into normative religious observance and ultimately to its cessation.

The criteria for the discernment of true prophecy in the legislation in Deut. 13:2-6 and 18:14-22 must first, then, be looked at. One might pick out from these chapters two different, if complementary, criteria. But it soon becomes apparent that the second criterion is subordinate to the first and that both may be subsumed under yet a third. In Deut. 13 the chief criterion is conformity with the Torah,[11] as focussed in the Decalogue and the Shema.[12] In Deut. 18 the chief

---

that, over against the complexity of S. Mowinckel's account of the growth of the book of Jeremiah, it is unnecessary to proliferate redactors. In the Bible, reinterpreters of underlying texts, besides adding their own material (independently or from whatever source), are their own editors and 'redactors'. This perception lies at the basis of my reapplication of the Chronicles analogy in Pentateuchal study. See the elaborated statement in W. Johnstone, *Chronicles and Exodus: An Analogy and its Application* (JSOT.S, 275), Sheffield 1998. W.H. Schmidt offers a diachronic study of the interplay between Jeremiah (esp. chs. 1, 27, 28) and Deut. 18:9-22 in 'Das Prophetengesetz Dtn 18,9-22 im Kontext erzählender Literatur', in: M. Vervenne, J. Lust (eds), *Deuteronomy and Deuteronomic Literature* (Fs C. Brekelmans) (BEThL, 133), Leuven 1997, 55-69.

[10] This may not be altogether a truism in the light of such a remark as that of R.J. Coggins, ' Prophecy – True and False', in: H.A. McKay, D.J.A. Clines (eds), *Of Prophets' Visions and the Wisdom of Sages* (Fs R.N. Whybray) (JSOT.S, 162), Sheffield 1993, 87: '...in Genesis–Numbers there is no section giving any systematic attention to the role of prophets'.

[11] V.5: 'You shall follow the LORD your God ... it is his commandments that you shall keep; his voice you shall obey ...'; for 'Torah' as appropriate summary term for Deuteronomy, see, e.g., Deut. 1:5; 4:8, 44. The whole section follows the absolute postscript to the previous section: 'As for the whole word which I am commanding you, it is what you will observe in order to practise; you shall neither add to it, nor shall you subtract from it' (Deut. 13:1).

[12] In vv. 3 and 6 the teaching of the false prophet, 'Let us follow אֱלֹהִים אֲחֵרִים ... וְנַעַבְדֵם, echoes the first prohibition of the Decalogue in Deut. 5:7, 9aβ, even down to the anomalous hophal with direct object; v.6, 'the LORD your God who

criterion is eventuation: 'How shall we recognise the word which the LORD has not spoken? – The word that does not eventuate' (18:21-22). The latter criterion, eventuation/non-eventuation, seems at first sight particularly unhelpful for decisions about the truth or falsity of prophecy that need to be made in the heat of the moment. But should the biblical writers really be so underestimated? If it is assumed that this criterion is expounded in the Deuteronomistically edited account of the confrontation between Jeremiah and Hananiah in Jer. 27–28,[13] then it becomes clear that it concerns prophecy of שָׁלוֹם.[14] (I shall argue below that mutuality of interpretation, as evidenced in this case, is an important principle in understanding the relationship between Deuteronomy and Dtr-edited passages.) The word of the true prophet is expected to be one of doom; non-eschatological salvation prophecy is by definition false. Something so obviously impracticable as the test of eventuation can only be a bit of playfulness, a joke, of the kind found in mAb. 2:15, 'Repent one day before your death'. Like repentance, prophecy of doom is always in season; carefree hopefulness is always wrong. In fact, as Deut. 13:3 makes clear, even if a prophecy does eventuate but fails the first criterion, conformity with the Torah, it is false.

But these two criteria in Deut. 13 and 18 for the discernment of true prophecy are subsumed under a still more fundamental criterion: conformity with the role of Moses in both form and content. This comparison is explicit in Deut. 18:15: 'A prophet from your midst, from among your siblings, like me, the LORD your God will raise up' (cf. Deut. 18:18). It is within the context of that comparison with Moses, in particular with his role as mediator at Horeb, 'בְּיוֹם הַקָּהָל', that the criterion of Torah, specifically the Decalogue, is explicitly set (Deut. 18:16-17, a reminiscence within the legislation). It is the argument of this paper, then, that the exposition of the fundamental Deutero-

---

brought you out of the land of Egypt ... out of the abode of slaves', quotes the first 'word' of the Decalogue; v.4 echoes the Shema, Deut. 6:5. The integrality of the Decalogue to the covenant pericope in the D-version of Exod. 19–24 will be defended below.

[13] The punch-line about speaking apostasy (דִּבֶּר סָרָה) against the LORD in Jer. 28:16; 29:32 echoes Deut. 13:6; 18:20. The proposal to delete the phrase in Jer. 28:16 (as in BHK/S) is, therefore, to be resisted. This is yet another example of mutuality of interpretation.

[14] See, especially, Jer. 28:6-9: prophecy concerning great lands and kingdoms has consistently hitherto been of war, disaster, and pestilence; therefore a prophecy of שָׁלוֹם is only to be believed when it has eventuated, i.e., never, this side of the restoration. Schmidt, 'Das Prophetengesetz', 65, differentiates the law of Deut. 18:21-22, as applying the criterion of eventuation to prophecy in general, from the narrative of Jer. 28:8-9, as applying it only to prophecy of שָׁלוֹם.

nomic criterion of true prophecy – conformity with the role of Moses in both form and content – is to be sought in Deuteronomistically edited passages, principally the narratives in Exodus (and Numbers) which match both the reminiscences in the narrative framework of Deut. 1–11 and the legislation on the criteria for the recognition of the true prophet in Deut. 13:2-6 and 18:14-22.[15] These criteria set unattainable standards in both form and content for subsequent prophets by contrast with the incomparable Moses; they thus represent a relativisation of the prophet by subordination to Torah. The revision of this portrayal in the final P-edition heightens these criteria still further to the point of the assimilation of prophecy within the authorised practice of the systems of religion and, thence, to its redundancy.[16] The two levels within Exodus, the D-version and the P-edition, thus provide evidence for two points on the profile of the decline of the acceptability of prophecy in the exilic and post-exilic periods; indeed, they are likely to have functioned precisely as instruments of that decline.

Only two features of the portrayal of Moses as archetypal prophet can be selected for study in this context:[17] Moses as mediator; and

---

[15] Material correspondences between the legislation in Deut. 13 and 18 and the narrative in Exodus provide a *prima facie* case. E.g., the prophet as 'a dreamer of dreams' (Deut. 13:2, 4, 6; dreams are repeatedly rejected in Jer. [23:25, 28; 27:9; 29:8]; divination of any kind is excluded, Deut. 18:14) is implicitly contrasted with Moses as the one to whom 'the LORD spoke face to face as a man speaks to his neighbour' (Exod. 34:11; cf. Deut. 34:10); the ability of the prophet to 'give sign and portent' (Deut. 13:2) is eclipsed by Moses's unsurpassable capacity in this role (Exod. 3:12; 4:21); ' hearkening unto' (Deut. 13:4) is a 'Leitmotif' in Exodus (but not always with the same preposition, e.g., 3:18; 4:1); 'testing' (Deut. 13:4) and the ' fear' of God (Deut. 13:5) are the point of the self-manifestation of God at the Mountain (Exod. 20:20; the reaction of the people in this passage is cross-referred to in Deut. 18:16).

[16] The argument of this paper thus runs in parallel with the argument in my 'The Revision of Festivals in Exodus 1–24 in the Persian Period and the Preservation of Jewish Identity in the Diaspora' in the Proceedings of the first meeting of the European Association for Biblical Studies, R. Albertz, B. Becking, (eds), *Yahwism after the Exile*, Assen, forthcoming 2001.

[17] Within a short paper it is impossible to deal with other equally significant characteristic features of Moses as prophet *par excellence*. Moses as warrior, for instance, is a necessary part of his role as leader of exodus and wilderness wandering: the armed encounters with Sihon of Heshbon and Og of Bashan figure in the D-reminiscence; in Exod. 13:18 Israel escapes from Egypt חֲמֻשִׁים, in battle formation; Israel prevails over Amalek thanks to the upraised arms of Moses (Exod. 17:8-16, in my view a P-displaced and expanded section). It is only in the equally fictive presentation of Samuel's victory over the Philistines that we find such a role among the later prophets (1 Sam. 7:7-14).

In this regard, the narrative of Dathan and Abiram in Num. 16 provides an

Moses as intercessor. These two features lead us to two different passages in Exodus (chs. 19–20 on the one hand, and ch. 32 on the other). These two passages also give opportunity to illustrate characteristic editorial techniques: in the D-version, the process of mutual interpretation between the narrative counterpart in Exodus and the reminiscence (and legislation) in Deuteronomy (such as has already been noted above between Deut. 18 and Dtr-Jer. in the interpretation of the criterion of eventuation); in the P-edition, the technique of transposition of materials in the underlying D-version.

Just before turning to these two features of Moses as prophet *par excellence* as criterion of true prophecy, a brief illustration of these editorial techniques is in order. I have been arguing since the mid-1980's that the book of Exodus (the same holds, I believe, for Numbers) has passed through two major literary stages: a D-version that can be reconstructed from the reminiscences and legislation of Deuteronomy; and a P-edition which has produced the final form of the book as it now stands.[18] One of the clearest examples of these editorial techniques is provided, I think, by the parallel between Exod. 34:1-4, 27-29

---

instructive example of editorial procedures. The editorial processes through which the text has passed mirror the fate of the phenomenon of prophecy. In the light of Deut. 11:6 the story of the Reubenites, Dathan and Abiram, was known to the D-version of Numbers. The details of cause and occasion are lacking, but are probably referred to in Deut. 9:23. The event is twice referred to in Numbers, chaps. 16 and 26:9-11, the latter presupposes the elaborated version of the former. The basic core of Num. 16 concerns a military issue: the refusal of these Reubenites to obey Moses' command as military commander 'to go up' (v.12; cf. the refusal to obey Moses' exhortation to mount the assault on the southern hill-country from Kadesh, alluded to in Deut. 1:21, 26; 9:23, where the verb עלה is used). This material continues to the end of v.15 and is resumed in vv.25, 27b-34.

The remainder represents reuse by P of a substratum of D-material (vv. 1-4), which has been edited and then extended by the addition of vv. 5-11, 16-23, 35. Bolted onto the Dathan and Abiram story is the entirely different narrative of the trial of strength between Aaron and the family of Qorah among the Levites on the matter of rights to the priesthood. The progression in the editorial activity is thus instructive: Moses, the peerless military leader, is sidelined in favour of a dispute which confirms hierarchy within the Levites. Prophecy has been overtaken by priesthood. At all events, this narrative has undergone characteristic transformation in the hands of the P-editor, which has introduced a remarkable incoherence into the text. It is this incoherence that makes me sceptical about the claim, 'the sum is more than the parts', for the ' final form' of the text such as is made by C. Houtman, *Exodus* (HCOT), vol. 3, Leuven 2000, 606 (though with qualifications in mild criticism of Childs's 'superb, new literary composition', to which I should add, 'would one really think of bestowing such an accolade on Chronicles?'). It is the dynamics of the interrelationship between the two partly inconsistent layers of the work that account for its essential vitality.

[18]See, e.g., my work referred to in n. 9.

The Portrayal of Moses

and Deut. 10:1-5 (MT/NRSV; Deut. 10:1-5 will be relevant to part of the discussion of the second feature of Moses as prophet *par excellence* below):

Exod. 34:1 וַיֹּאמֶר יְהוָה אֶל־מֹשֶׁה
The LORD said to Moses,
פְּסָל־לְךָ שְׁנֵי־לֻחֹת אֲבָנִים כָּרִאשֹׁנִים
'Cut two tables of stone like the former ones,

וְכָתַבְתִּי עַל־הַלֻּחֹת אֶת־הַדְּבָרִים אֲשֶׁר הָיוּ
עַל־הַלֻּחֹת הָרִאשֹׁנִים אֲשֶׁר שִׁבַּרְתָּ׃
and I will write on the tablets the words that were on the former tablets, which you broke.

2 Be ready in the morning, and come up in the morning to Mount Sinai and present yourself there to me, on top of the mountain. 3 No one shall come up with you, and do not let anyone be seen throughout all the mountain; and do not let flocks or herds graze in front of the mountain'.

וַיִּפְסֹל שְׁנֵי־לֻחֹת אֲבָנִים כָּרִאשֹׁנִים 4
וַיַּשְׁכֵּם מֹשֶׁה בַבֹּקֶר
4 So Moses cut two tablets of stone like the former ones; and he rose early in the morning

וַיַּעַל אֶל־הַר סִינַי
כַּאֲשֶׁר צִוָּה יְהוָה אֹתוֹ
וַיִּקַּח בְּיָדוֹ שְׁנֵי לֻחֹת אֲבָנִים׃
and went up Mount Sinai, as the LORD had commanded him, and took in his hand the two tablets of stone.

34:28 וַיְהִי־שָׁם עִם־יְהוָה אַרְבָּעִים יוֹם וְאַרְבָּעִים
לַיְלָה לֶחֶם לֹא אָכַל וּמַיִם לֹא שָׁתָה
He was there with the LORD forty days and forty nights; he neither ate bread nor drank water.

וַיִּכְתֹּב עַל־הַלֻּחֹת אֵת דִּבְרֵי הַבְּרִית
עֲשֶׂרֶת הַדְּבָרִים׃

Deut. 10:1 בָּעֵת הַהִוא אָמַר יְהוָה אֵלַי
At that time the LORD said to me,
פְּסָל־לְךָ שְׁנֵי־לוּחֹת אֲבָנִים כָּרִאשֹׁנִים
'Carve out two tablets of stone like the former ones,
וַעֲלֵה אֵלַי הָהָרָה וְעָשִׂיתָ לְּךָ אֲרוֹן עֵץ׃
and come up to me on the mountain, and make an ark of wood.

2 וְאֶכְתֹּב עַל־הַלֻּחֹת אֶת־הַדְּבָרִים אֲשֶׁר הָיוּ
עַל־הַלֻּחֹת הָרִאשֹׁנִים אֲשֶׁר שִׁבַּרְתָּ
I will write on the tablets the words that were on the former tablets, which you smashed.
וְשַׂמְתָּם בָּאָרוֹן׃ 3 וָאַעַשׂ אֲרוֹן עֲצֵי שִׁטִּים
and you shall put them in the ark'. 3 So I made an ark of acacia wood,

וָאֶפְסֹל שְׁנֵי־לֻחֹת אֲבָנִים כָּרִאשֹׁנִים
cut two tablets of stone like the former ones,

וָאַעַל הָהָרָה

וּשְׁנֵי הַלֻּחֹת בְּיָדִי׃
and went up the mountain with the two tablets in my hand.

וַיִּכְתֹּב עַל־הַלֻּחֹת כַּמִּכְתָּב הָרִאשׁוֹן
אֵת עֲשֶׂרֶת הַדְּבָרִים ...

And he wrote on the tablets the words of the covenant, the ten commandments.

Then he wrote on the tablets the same words as before, the ten commandments ...

וַיִּתְּנֵם יְהוָה אֵלָי:
and the LORD gave them to me.

29 וַיְהִי בְּרֶדֶת מֹשֶׁה מֵהַר סִינַי וּשְׁנֵי לֻחֹת הָעֵדֻת בְּיַד־מֹשֶׁה בְּרִדְתּוֹ מִן־הָהָר

5 וָאֵפֶן וָאֵרֵד מִן־הָהָר

Moses came down from Mount Sinai. As he came down from the mountain with the two tablets of the covenant in his hand ...

So I turned and came down from the mountain ...

The parallels are clear; the coincidence of language and sequence leads me to suggest that they were cast in the same D-mould. In Exod. 34:28b the muddle that has bedevilled much of the discussion over the pronominal subject in the verb, 'and he wrote', and what 'he' wrote, is clarified by Deut. 10:4: it was God who wrote and what he wrote was the Decalogue. This mutual interpretation has fundamental significance for the interpretation of the intervening verses, Exod. 34:5-26. It makes the search for an alternative Decalogue in these verses unnecessary: rather, what is to be found in these verses is, first (vv.5-16), an elaboration of the covenant loyalty expressed in the opening of the Decalogue, focussed here on the challenge to that covenant loyalty posed by intermarriage with the Canaanites; second (vv.17-26), a largely verbatim repetition of the conclusion of the legislation of the Book of the Covenant (Exod. 23:10-19). This elaboration in Exod. 34:5-26 beyond material in Deuteronomy can be called 'Deuteronomistic'; yet it provides what passages in Deuteronomy presuppose, that the covenant endures in precisely the terms on which it was originally concluded (as, I shall argue in moment, Deut. 4:14; 5:31 explicitly state).[19]

The editorial procedure of P is also illustrated by the parallel between Exod. 34:1-4 and Deut. 10:1-3. It is the intervention of P that explains both omissions and additions to the present Exodus text. The ark material, which in the light of Deut. 10:1-5 was originally present in the D-version of Exod. 34:2-3, has been removed by P because of P's revisionist views on the ark which is now specified in Exod. 25:10-22 and constructed in Exod. 37:1-9. In place of the ark, P's preoccupations with graded holiness and hierarchy are introduced.

---

[19]The similarities to, and differences from, the influential approach of E. Blum may be noted. Blum (*Studien zur Komposition des Pentateuch* [BZAW, 189], Berlin 1990, 181) notes the 'Wechselbezüge' ('reciprocal relations') between Deuteronomy and his KD. But he interprets these diachronically in a complex history of redaction. I interpret these mutual cross-references synchronically.

It is appropriate that this revisionist P-layer be called an *edition*: it knew the earlier D-version and entered into radical engagement with it, rather as the Chronicler engaged with Samuel and Kings.[20] Exodus 34 thus rather clearly exposes the editorial history of Exodus: a basic D-version recoverable from Deuteronomy; a Dtr elaboration of that D-version which is, nonetheless, presupposed by D; a polemical re-editing of that D/Dtr version by P.

We return, then, to two features of the portrayal of Moses as archetypal prophet in the D-version and their revisal in the P-edition.

1. Moses as mediator of the terms of the covenant: a mutual reading of Exodus 19–20 and the reminiscence of Deut. 4:9–5:31 and legislation of Deut. 13:2-6; 18:14-22.

Moses's role as mediator is explicitly referred to in Deut. 18:16-17, a reminiscence, embedded in the legislation, of what happened at the moment of the revelation of the Decalogue on the day of the congregation at Horeb: the people requested that they be no longer subjected directly to the experience of revelation and that Moses should be their mediator. Deut. 4:9–5:33 in the narrative framework of Deuteronomy contains the fuller reminiscence; Exod. 19:2b–20:21 the matching narrative. These are notoriously controversial passages, not least on the question of how much the people themselves heard directly of the revelation of the Decalogue.[21] My view is now that Moses's mediatorial role is absolutised consistently throughout: he is portrayed as mediator of the Decalogue in its entirely, as well as of the Book of the Covenant.[22] This is what is said explicitly in Deut. 5:5: despite

---

[20] The importance of recognising P as an *edition* can be illustrated from the Decalogue in Exod. 20:1-17. I agree that the Decalogue there is in P-edited form: the reason for keeping the sabbath relates to the P-account of creation in Gen. 1:1–2:4a. But the other variations from the D-form of the Decalogue in Deut. 5:6-21 are minimal. That is to say, what is presently in Exod. 20 is the D-form of the Decalogue which has been quite lightly edited in the P-edition. I shall reaffirm below my view that this D-form of the Decalogue, recoverable from Deut. 5, was already integral to the D-version of Exod. 19–20.

[21] The range of possibilities is neatly caught, at least in part, by M. Strassfeld, *The Jewish Holidays: A Guide and Commentary*, New York 1985, 81: according to tradition 'only the Ten Commandments, not the whole Torah, was heard at Sinai. Or, according to another tradition, only the first two commandments. Or perhaps, according to a third tradition, only the first word, *anoki* – "I am". Or perhaps just the first letter of the first word, the *aleph* – the mystery of the sound of a silent letter'. As I indicate in the text, I think that none of these interpretations is quite right: Israel heard sound but no content.

[22] I was initially sufficiently impressed by the arguments that the Decalogue was communicated directly to the people (see E.W. Nicholson, 'The Decalogue

the abbreviated statement of the 'face to face' encounter with the people in the preceding verse, it is clear that Moses 'stands between' Israel and the Lord in order to declare his word to them.²³ This is not necessarily in contradiction to the reminiscence in Deut. 4:9-13. Parts of that account appear to suggest that Moses's role was confined to acting as marshal, and that there was direct communication of the Decalogue to the people (especially Deut. 4:10aδ). But other parts of that reminiscence suggest otherwise: הַדְּבָרִים were what the people *saw* (v.9aβ); what they *heard* was not הַדְּבָרִים but קוֹל דְּבָרִים, 'the *sound* of words/happenings' (v.12b; not even קוֹל הַדְּבָרִים!). This presentation of events seems to me to be entirely consistent with the matching narrative in Exod. 19:9, 16–20:21 (in which I identify 19:18, 20-25 as P, as the use of 'Sinai', for example, indicates). The Exodus narrative makes it clear that the people could not have heard any intelligible speech. The theophany is accompanied by the roar of a massive thunderstorm, which is complemented by the ear-shattering din of the ram's horn announcing the theophany of the LORD. It is an overwhelming experience of undifferentiable sound, the impact of which is to drive the people in terror from the mountain. The syntax of the narrative underlines the point. Exod. 20:18 resumes the narrative from 19:19. But this does not mean that the Decalogue in Exod. 20:1-17 is a secondary insertion. The participle at the beginning of Exod. 20:18 begins with a circumstantial clause (וְכָל־הָעָם רֹאִים) in which the participle expresses action contemporaneous with the durative action expressed through the finite verbs in the two circumstantial clauses of 19:19b (מֹשֶׁה יְדַבֵּר וְהָאֱלֹהִים יַעֲנֶנּוּ בְקוֹל). 20:1 is the principal clause which introduces the main verb. Hence the translation: 'While the sound of the ram's-horn was rising in a crescendo extremely loudly, and Moses was speaking and God was answering him with [this stupendous] noise, God spoke all these words ... But while all the people were witnessing the thunderbolts and lightning flashes and the blare of the ram's horn ... they recoiled and stood at a distance and said to Moses, "You speak with us ... but let not God speak with us, lest we die." '²⁴ This interpretation is confirmed by the preview in Exod. 19:9:

---

as Direct Address by God', *VT* 27 (1977), 422-33) as to adopt that view in my *Exodus* (OTG), Sheffield, 1990, 106. That view will be modified in the revised edition (forthcoming 2001).

²³Despite the forceful words of the commentators, e.g., A.D.H. Mayes, *Deuteronomy* (NCB), London 1979, 'the whole verse is incompatible not only with v. 4 but also with v. 22'.

²⁴There is a similar construction in 2 Chron. 5-7 (though from a quite different writer), where 7:1-2 resumes 5:14 to mark the simultaneity of the priests' action with Solomon's prayer which is meantime taking place in ch. 6.

'... that the people may hear while I speak with you ...'. In view of this portrayal, it is hardly sufficient to term Moses even 'archetypal

> It may be apposite at this point to indicate the radical differences of my interpretation from others currently being offered, particularly that of J. Van Seters; a recent statement is to be found in his article, 'Is there Evidence of a Dtr Redaction in the Sinai Pericope (Exodus 19-24, 32-34)?', in: L.S. Schearing, S.L. McKenzie (eds), *Those Elusive Deuteronomists*, 160-70. For Van Seters, Exod. 20:1-17, being the P-version of the Decalogue, must be a late insertion. 'The unit [19:20-24 (sic); 20:1-17] is clearly an addition between 19.19 and 20.18 and belongs together with the rest of the P material in 24.15b-18a' (166). The underlying version of Exodus which he detects, he thus argues, is distinct from, and even in some respects incompatible with, Deuteronomy, and he identifies it as 'exilic J'. This 'exilic J' thus went straight from Exod. 19:19 to 20:18 and made the 'Covenant Code', 20:22-23:33, the sole basis of the covenant. This J version is thus totally distinct from D, for whom the Decalogue was the sole basis of the covenant at Horeb (cf. J. Van Seters, *The Life of Moses: The Yahwist as Historian in Exodus-Numbers* [CEBT, 10], Kampen 1995, 279).
>
> This account seems to me to be very fragile. If Van Seters regards P not as an independent source but as a later editor, as he does, in my view, correctly, then there is no reason for regarding the relatively restricted variations in the P-version of the Decalogue as other than a new edition of what was already present in the text (as Deuteronomy's reminiscence suggests it was); Von Seters' argument ignores the harsh connection between 19:25 and 20:1 which can hardly have belonged in origin to the same source, 'P'.
>
> The other alleged incompatibilities which Van Seters lists between D and his 'exilic J' seem to me to be no more compelling. See the further statement of his view in his chapter, 'The Pentateuch', in: S.L. McKenzie, M.P. Graham (eds), *The Hebrew Bible Today: An Introduction to the Critical Issues*, Louisville 1998, esp. 35-8 (also 47-8 for the relative dating of lawcodes). E.g., 'there is no plague tradition reflected in Deuteronomy, and statements in D exclude that possibility' (35; but what do the מוֹפְתִים, Deut. 4:34, etc., refer to?); 'the climax of the exodus ... the event at the sea ... is not in D' (35; but see Deut. 11:4). The alleged difference between D and 'exilic-J' about the basis of the covenant is repeated: 'In contrast to D, which has two covenants – the corporate law that is part of the national covenant in Deuteronomy 12-26 and the code for individual conduct given at Horeb, which consists of only the Ten Commandments – in J there is only the one covenant at Sinai. J does not have a separate Ten Commandments (those of Exod. 20:1-17 belong to P)' (36, cf. 48). As I have indicated above, I disagree with almost every word of that statement.
>
> I disagree, too, with his relative dating of the lawcodes and the purpose which they were designed to discharge: 'The Covenant Code [i.e., Exod. 20:22-23:33] ... is formulated to regulate life in the Jewish community of the Babylonian exile' (47). On the contrary, as the earliest of the codes (indicated as such by the Deuteronomic framework with which it is now supplied), it represents part of the D-writer's gathering of lore of all kinds from the pre-exilic age in order to present his epic of ideal national origins; this then becomes the basis of his eschatological projection of the return from exile, at the heart of which the revised code in Deut. 12-26 shall stand.
>
> On other matters, however, I do agree with Van Seters, e.g., in his criticism of E. Zenger and E. Otto's view that the Sinai pericope began life as a theophany

prophet', as in the title of this paper: his is the uniquely privileged experience, normative both in form and in content, which no other mediator of the word of the LORD can match. The relativising and subordinating of any successor is absolute.

Deut. 5:5, is thus, I believe, entirely consistent with Deut. 4 in the light of the Exodus narrative of which it is a reminiscence.[25] The elevation of the mediatorial role of Moses to an absolute is in line with the general insistence throughout Deuteronomy on the sole mediatorship of Moses and his multiple roles in addressing the people: he is the revealer, to whose revelation nothing more or less is to be added or subtracted (4:2); the lawgiver (6:1-3), who even assumes the *persona* of the LORD (11:13-14: 'my commandments ... I will give rain, etc.'), the proclaimer (5:1; 29:1), the preacher, offering the choice of blessing or curse (11:26), the exhorter (4:1), the warner (4:26), the teacher (4:5). The verbs associated with Moses throughout Deuteronomy (apart from ch. 34) are consistently those of saying, speaking, calling, commanding, explaining, blessing, or writing; even when he 'goes', it is in order to speak (31:1).[26] As covenant-maker, he is supreme exponent of the explanatory power of the D-concept 'covenant', with its mechanistic theology that again reduces the scope of prophecy to the merely ancillary.

All the more notable is, then, the revisal of the P-insertion, Exod. 19:20-25. This passage elevates Aaron to equal status with Moses on Sinai (v. 24aβ). The Aaron now associated with Moses is no longer the subordinate spokesman on behalf of Moses to the people as in the D-version of Exod. 4:14-16; he is explicitly נָבִיא (Exod. 7:1[P]; more properly, נְבִיאֶךָ: Aaron is still only prophet in so far as he is spokesman for the normative Mosaic tradition). But this נָבִיא is in the P-edition at the same time Aaron the founding-father of the priesthood. The

---

narrative, later edited as a revelation of law (Van Seters, 'Is there Evidence ...', 165-9). His objection, that theophany as a commonplace of ancient near eastern religious traditions is related rather to Zion and thus not to be recovered by the analysis of *this* text, has to be amplified with the observation that the Exodus narrative exploits a much larger reservoir of religious practice. It did not grow from the elaboration of a nucleus, such as a theophany tradition (I should part company on this point also with T.B. Dozeman, *God on the Mountain: A Study of Redaction, Theology and Canon in Exodus 19-24* [SBL.MS, 37], Atlanta 1989); rather, it is a selection of the whole range of religious practice of the monarchical period (that is why in my *Exodus* [OTG] the study of six religious institutions, as providing part of the lore which the D-version exploits in its account, precedes [ch. 2] the consideration of literary questions [ch. 3]).

[25] Even if it were a later addition, it would simply attest the development of the understanding of Moses's status as sole mediator.

[26] If the text is sound; cf. BHS *in loc.*

prophet, already irretrievably subordinated to Moses the sole exponent of revelation of law and covenant in the D-version, is now in the rehabilitation of Aaron in the P-edition assimilated to the priestly function, and so institutionalised and finally made redundant. This process of assimilation is confirmed in the P-edition of the Song at the Sea, Exod. 15:20-21: there Miriam, identified significantly as sister of Aaron, is presented as נְבִיאָה (the only other occurrence of the root in Exod.),[27] hymning the mighty acts of God in the exodus after the manner of the 'prophecy' in the liturgy of the cult in 1 Chron. 25:1.

2. Moses as intercessor: Exod. 32:11-14 and P's technique of transposition of reused D-materials.

For the prophetic role of the intercessor we might compare, in particular, Jer. (especially Jer. 15:1 for the combination of Moses and Samuel; cf. Jer. 7:16, and frequently).[28] The reminiscence in Deut. 9:7–10:11 again clarifies the underlying D-version in Exodus, in my view. In my reading of Deut. 9:7–10:11, Moses spends two periods of forty days and forty nights on the mountain.[29] It is only on the second of these that Moses acts as intercessor, successfully first for Aaron, then for the people. The sequence of ensuing events in Deuteronomy is logical: at the intercession of Moses, the prophet *par excellence*, the gracious mercy of God enables the remaking of the covenant on its original terms (cf. Moses's successful intercession even at Taberah, the occasion of the first rebellion after Horeb, Num. 11:2-3 [D-version]); the Decalogue is reinscribed on stone tablets in token thereof; Moses constructs an ark for the tablets, by implication a tent for the ark, and ordains the Levites as bearers of the ark. The whole company then sets off from Horeb to the Promised Land via Kadesh. I believe that a text matching that clear and logical sequence of events

---

[27] Otherwise in the Pentateuch, besides these passsages in Exodus and Deut. 13:2, 4, 6; 18:15, 18, 20, 22, only in Gen. 20:7; Num.11:25-27, 29; Deut. 34:10.

[28] Though the verb typically used is הִתְפַּלֵּל, not חִלָּה פָּנִים, as in Exod. 32:11 (though that expression is used in Jer. 26:19). It is a role of Samuel that Saul usurps in 1 Sam. 13:12; cf. 1 Kgs. 13:6; 2 Kgs. 13:4. There is a brief sketch of intercession in the HB prophets in R.P. Gordon, 'Where have all the Prophets Gone? The "Disappearing" Israelite Prophet Against the Background of Ancient Near Eastern Prophecy', *BBR* 5 (1995), 83.

[29] Houtman, *Exodus* (HCOT), vol. 3, 607, claims that Deut. 9:7–10:11 implies that Moses was on the mountain for three periods of forty days, citing Deut. 9:9, 18, 25; 10:10. But 9:25 is the resumption of 9:18 (so too J. Blenkinsopp, 'Deuteronomic Contribution to the Narrative in Genesis-Numbers: A Test Case', in: L.S. Schearing, S.L. McKenzie (eds), *Those Elusive Deuteronomists*, 113, n. 68) and 10:10 indicates by its 'as on the first days' that only two periods of forty days are envisaged.

can be recovered in Exodus and Numbers.[30] The break-up of that D-version is caused (as in Exod. 34:1-4) by the interposition of P, with his radically different view of events: the primacy of Law at Sinai (the covenant was made long ago with the Patriarchs, Exod. 6:2-5); the demands of holiness the Law imposes, with the concomitant institution of the sanctuary with its rites and personnel. The chronology of departure from the Mountain after two periods of forty days is greatly lengthened: the departure now takes place on the 20th of the second month of the second year (Num. 10:11). The huge blocks of material, Exod. 25:1–31:17; 34:29–Num.10:28 are, accordingly, inserted. In the process the underlying D-narrative has been splintered and redistributed; 'spatchcocked' (as of a specimen on a dissection board) seems an appropriately drastic term.

In particular, P has radically adjusted the narrative of Moses's intercession in Exod. 32:11-14, 30-35. It now takes place during the first forty-day period on the mountain (not the second, as in Deut. 9:18, 25–10:11). This leaves room for the complete reformulation of the second period, so that the Levites now become appointed as agents of punishment. This is not pure P-material but represents the transposition of part of the material on Massah and Meribah which P has brought forward from its original position between Num. 11 verses

---

[30]This has been elaborated in my *Chronicles and Exodus*, 276:

- Exod. 32:11-14 Moses' intercession on the second occasion of 'forty days and forty nights', which P has transposed into the first period of 'forty days and forty nights' and replaced with the extant 32:30-35;

- Exod. 34:1, 4* the hewing of the second set of tablets, with the Ark material restored from Deut. 10:1aγ, b, 2b, 3aα and P-material removed;

- Exod. 34:5-9a the gracious response of God to Moses' intercession, supplemented with Exod. 33:13b-16;

- Exod. 34:10-28 the terms of the Covenant in Decalogue and Book of the Covenant reaffirmed;

- Exod. 33:1-6 the command to depart from the Mountain;

- Exod. 34:29a reformulated in terms of Deut. 10:5a, 'And Moses turned and descended from the Mountain and put the tablets in the Ark';

- Exod. 33:7-11 the habitual practice of pitching the Tent of Meeting for the Ark;

- an equivalent to Deut. 10:8abα: 'The LORD set aside the tribe of Levi to carry the Ark of the Covenant of the LORD, to stand before the Lord to serve him and to pronounce blessing in his name';

- Exod. 18:1-12, the coming of Jethro, would continue the narrative, linking directly with Num. 10:29.

3 and 4, as Deut. 9:22; 33:8 makes clear (P has already transposed part of the Massah/Meribah material into Exod. 17:2, 4-7).[31] The Levites are now ready to serve in the Tabernacle (P) which will be constructed before the departure from the Mountain. There they will function as practitioners of prospective and retrospective atonement (cf. their fearsome role portrayed in Chronicles as teachers, monitors, temple police, and itinerant judges; the need for intercession is heavily qualified by the mechanisms of religion now in place).[32] The role of Joshua as successor to Moses (Deut. 34:9) disappears with the integration of the Tent of Meeting (Exod. 33:7-11) into the Tabernacle (Exod. 25:1-31:17; 35-40; for the integration see 39:32). In Deuteronomy, the D-version of Exodus, and DtrH, Joshua is the successor of Moses *par excellence* in accordance with the criteria of prophecy in Deut. 13 and 18. In the P-edition, such a prophetic role is redundant; Joshua is replaced in importance by Aaron and the Levites.[33]

The changing attitude to the phenomenon of prophecy in the two layers of Exodus is thus conveniently personalised: it is focussed in the relative status of the three siblings, Moses, Aaron, and Miriam; Joshua; and the Levites. In the D-version, the word of the LORD is primary; Moses is the direct recipient and sole mediator of it and

---

[31] Johnstone, *Chronicles and Exodus*, 255-7.

[32] *Ibid.*, chaps. 4-6.

[33] Once again, it is perhaps apposite to set my interpretation over against others presently on offer. Blenkinsopp, *art. cit.*, follows the method of comparing the reminiscences in Deuteronomy with the Exodus narrative (the failure to do so is, in my opinion, the weakness of E. Blum's discussion, as I have argued in *Chronicles and Exodus*, 18-34). I welcome his confirmation of the D-character of material in Exodus and his view of the redundancy of Van Seters' 'exilic J'. But he attributes the differences in sequence in the D material in Exodus as due to Dtr modification, not to P.

I welcome also B. Renaud's independent work, *L'alliance un mystère de miséricorde: Une lecture de Exode 32-34* (LD, 169), Paris 1998, esp. 9-89, 297-8, insofar as it, too, follows the procedure of comparing the texts of reminiscence in Deuteronomy with material in Exodus. He abandons the Documentary Hypothesis and concentrates on the D and P materials. His account of the two latter, however, diverges significantly from mine. He regards the material in common to Exod. 32-34 and Deut. 9:8 (on his definition) -10.11 as 'pre-' or 'proto-Deuteronomic'. This has been 'complemented' differently in Exodus and Deuteronomy by the D/Dtr school. It is that school which has in Exod. 32:11-14 reformulated Moses' prayer, originally placed on the plain at the base of the mountain (cf. Deut. 9:26-29), and added 32:26-29 as one of the 'fragments d'origines diverses' from an unknown source (88). Rp has inserted the Dtr version into the already existing Pg with a few adjustments. This account not only misreads, in my view, Deut. 9:26-29 within the context of Deut. 9:7-10:11; it also attributes to the wrong hand (Dtr rather than P) the adjustment of the D-text, as well as unnecessarily distinguishing between Pg and Rp.

remains subject to it. In this regard Joshua is his successor, the נַעַר constantly present in the Tent of Meeting (Exod. 33:11). That word is codified in Decalogue and Book of the Covenant. Aaron is the mouthpiece of Moses, spokesman in that sense: when bereft of the guidance of Moses, he constructs the golden calf, the emblematic sin which was the downfall of northern and southern kingdoms; he is representative of the culpable priesthood who bear their share of responsibility for the exile (cf. Lam. 4:13). The Levites, bearers of the Ark, emerge as Moses's agents of retribution only at Massah and Meribah, the second incident of rebellion (Deut. 9:22) on the eleven days' journey after the departure from Horeb on the way to Kadesh. In the D-version, the prophet is already doubly relativised: in comparison to Moses; and in subordination to Torah. In the P-edition of Exodus, the prophet is relativised to the point of redundancy. Aaron is thoroughly rehabilitated: possessed of a miracle-working staff on a par with Moses (Exod. 7:9), he is the head of the house of Levi who minister in the Tabernacle which has assimilated the Tent of Meeting of Moses and Joshua. Joshua is left without function. It is thus ironical that control of the prophet by the high priest, the failure in performing which is the complaint by Jeremiah's opponent, Shemaiah the Nehelamite (Jer. 29:26), is the fate that ultimately awaits prophecy in the normative tradition.

The primary version and the secondary edition of the books of the 'tetrateuch', understood as Genesis, Exodus, Numbers and Deuteronomy, edited in the exilic and post-exilic periods, thus reflect the decline and disappearance of the phenomenon of prophecy, at least officially. It is probable that the production of these two editions is attributable to the same hierocratic forces[34] that account for the demise of prophecy; they functioned precisely as instruments of that demise.

---

[34] Whatever the reservations one may have about its overall argument, the currency of the term should be acknowledged as arising from the influential work of P.D. Hanson, *The Dawn of Apocalyptic: The Historical and Sociological Roots of Jewish Apocalyptic*, Philadelphia 1975.

Hendrik Leene *Amsterdam – The Netherlands*

Blowing the Same Shofar
An Intertextual Comparison of Representations of the Prophetic Role in Jeremiah and Ezekiel

1 Introduction

In recent scholarly research the affinities between the books of Jeremiah and Ezekiel and their literary dependence have been a much debated subject.[1] It has been the prevailing opinion that the priority in this dependence belongs to Jeremiah.[2] In connection with the general theme of this conference, I will discuss some cognate passages concerning the prophetic roles of Jeremiah and Ezekiel themselves in connection with the roles of the treacherous prophets condemned in their books. This limitation of the extensive material offers the following comparable passages:

Jer. 6:9-15   Ezek. 13:1-16   Peace, when there is no Peace
(cf. 8:10-13)

Jer. 6:16-21   Ezek. 33:1-9   The Prophets as Watchmen
                (cf. 3:16-21)

Jer. 18:18-23   Ezek. 7:23-27   The Word/Vision shall [or shall not]
                                 Perish from the Prophet

This paper pursues a threefold purpose. First, it will reflect on the methodology of intertextual comparison in the light of each of these examples.[3] Studies in this field have too often been guided by pre-

---

[1] For an extensive bibliography, see: D. Vieweger, *Die literarischen Beziehungen zwischen den Büchern Jeremia und Ezechiel* (BEAT, 26), Frankfurt a/M 1993, 171-97.

[2] The most important models of explanation are: 1. Influence via personal recollection and oral tradition (Jeremiah's preaching → the man Ezekiel) or direct literary dependence between the books ('Jeremiah' → 'Ezekiel'); 2. Common environment; 3. All kinds of combinations of 1 and 2, e.g., J.W. Miller, *Das Verhältnis Jeremias und Hesekiels sprachlich und theologisch untersucht*, Assen 1955; Vieweger, *op. cit.*; 4. Common deuteronomistic redaction, e.g., S. Herrmann, *Die prophetischen Heilserwartungen im Alten Testament* (BWANT, 85), Stuttgart 1965; W. Thiel, *Die deuteronomistischen Redaktion von Jeremiah 1-25* (WMANT, 41), Neukirchen 1973.

[3] The concept of intertextuality as a universal literary theory goes back to the work of Julia Kristeva, who followed ideas of the Russian literary critic Mikhail Bakhtin (J. Kristeva, *Semeiotikè: Recherches pour une sémanalyse*, Paris 1969).

conceived ideas and subjective impressions. In recent years, however, the computerised text of the Hebrew scriptures has made it possible to strive for a larger degree of precision and objectivity in the establishment of similarities and differences between texts.[4] Without tiring the audience with the technical details of searching after lexical sets in combination with syntactical clause patterns, I should add here, that some experience in this field is part of my procedure and argumentation. I have made use of the program QUEST, which has been developed in my faculty by my colleague Prof. Eep Talstra.[5] The second aim is, of course, to reach an answer as convincing as possible in the matter of literary priority as far as these three textual examples are concerned. And finally I will indicate how, in my opinion, this answer might bear upon our vision of Jeremiah and Ezekiel as historical persons and as literary characters.[6]

In discussions on the application of this concept in recent Old Testament research the distinction between receptional and productional intertextuality plays a major role, see, e.g.: A. Laato, *History and Ideology in the Old Testament Prophetic Literature: A Semiotic Approach to the Reconstruction of the Proclamation of the Historical Prophets*, Stockholm 1996, 322-35; E. van Wolde, 'Texts in Dialogue with Texts: Intertextuality in the Ruth and Tamar Narratives', *BInt* 5 (1997), 1-28, esp. 4-7. I do not see why the diachronic aspect should be excluded from the concept, as it has been argued by B.D. Sommer, 'Exegesis, Allusion and Intertextuality in the Hebrew Bible: A Response to Lyle Eslinger', *VT* 46 (1996), 479-89, esp. 487: 'the study of intertextuality is synchronic, the analysis of allusion diachronic or even historicist'. A nice example of a careful diachronic application in the research of prophetic literature, for instance, is offered by J.D. Nogalski, 'Intertextuality in the Twelve', in: J.W. Watts, P.R. House (eds), *Forming Prophetic Literature: Essays on Isaiah and the Twelve in Honour of J.D.W. Watts* (JSOT.S, 235), Sheffield 1996, 102-24. – In the present contribution 'intertextual' is used as a purely descriptive term for the interrelationship between two or more texts, mainly on clause level. Although my special interest concerns questions of literary dependence, the term 'intertextual' as such does not yet anticipate any possible interpretation of the phenomenon described.

[4] According to Sommer, *art. cit.*, the tracing of allusions in a text 'constitutes an art, not a science' (486). I feel rather inclined to reverse this statement, precisely on the basis of the many objective criteria mentioned by Sommer himself.

[5] J.A. Groves, H.J. Bosman, J.H. Harmsen, E. Talstra, *Quest: Electronic Concordance Application for the Hebrew Bible*, Haarlem 1992.

[6] For the use of the concept of intertextuality in connection with the book of Jeremiah, see: R.P. Carroll, 'Intertextuality and the Book of Jeremiah: Animadversions on Text and Theory', in: J.C. Exum, D.J.A. Clines (eds), *The New Literary Criticism and the Hebrew Bible* (JSOT.S, 143), Sheffield 1993, 55-78: 'Any examination of the books making up the Prophetic collection (Isaiah-Jeremiah-Ezekiel-the Twelve) will discover a whole intertextual world where each individual book will be found to contain a considerable amount of material common to other books [...]'(60). See alo R.P. Carroll, 'Jeremiah, Intertextuality and Ideologiekritik', *JNWSL* 22 (1996), 15-34. Although Laato, *op. cit.*, 319, may be right

2 Peace, when there is no Peace (Jer. 6:9-15 and Ezek. 13:1-16)

2.1

While the book of Jeremiah contains many warnings against misleading prophecy, the book of Ezekiel virtually confines itself in this respect to only one address against the prophets and prophetesses of Israel, chapter 13. That is all there is, as far as Ezekiel is concerned, apart from a few indications in the preceding and following chapter, Ezek. 12:21-25 and 14:1-11, and a short allusion to Ezek. 13 in 22:28. For that reason it is most practical to take Ezek. 13 as our starting point for a stock-taking of intertextual affinities regarding the subject. A translation of Ezek. 13:1-16 will follow below. In this first part of the chapter – the second part concerns female prophets – the reader is again and again reminded of passages from Jeremiah by single words or phrases or even by complete clauses. This is provisionally indicated by references in the margin of the translation.

Ezekiel 13:1-16
1 And the word of YHWH came to me |
  saying |
2 Son of man |
  prophesy against the prophets of Israel |
  who prophesy |
  and say to them |
  who prophesy[a] out of <u>their own hearts</u>[a] | [a] Jer. 14:14; 23:16, 26
  hear the word of YHWH |
3 Thus says the Lord YHWH |
  woe to the fool prophets |
  who follow their own spirit |
  while they have not seen |
4 Like foxes among ruins your prophets |
  o Israel |
  have been |
5 You have not gone up into the breaches |
  and built up a wall for the house of Israel |
  that it might stand in battle in the day of YHWH |
6 They have <u>seen</u>[b] vanity and false <u>divination</u>[b] | [b] Jer. 14:14
  <u>who say</u>[d] | [d] analogous sequence of clauses
  <u>a saying of YHWH</u>[d] | Jer. 6:14=8:11
  and YHWH <u>has not sent them</u>[cd] | [c] analogous clause Jer. 14:14, 15;
  and they have expected | 23:21, 32; 27:15; 28:15; 29:9, 31;
  that he would fulfill the word | 43:2; cf. 28:9

---

in his judgement that Carroll accepts Barthes' intertextual approach (which is in agreement with Kristeva's definition of the text as 'a mosaic of quotations') without much criticism, Carroll's insights are no less interesting as a modification to the usual redaction critical approaches to the book of Jeremiah.

7	Have you not seen a <u>vision</u>ᵉ of vanity |	
	and spoken false <u>divination</u>ᵉ |	ᵉ Jer. 14:14
	*whenever <u>saying</u>*ᵍ |	ᵍ *analogous sequence of*
	*a saying of YHWH*ᵍ |	*clauses Jer. 6:14=8:11*
	*and I, <u>I have not spoken</u>*ᶠᵍ |	ᶠ *analogous clause Jer.*
8	Therefore |	*14:14; 23:21; Ezek. 22:28*
	thus says the Lord YHWH |	
	because you have spoken vanity |	
	and have seen lies |	
	*therefore behold I am against you*ʰ |	ʰ *analogous sequence of*
	*is the saying of the Lord YHWH*ʰ |	*clauses Jer. 23:30, 31, 32*
9	And my hand will be <u>against the prophets</u>ⁱ |	ⁱ Jer. 32:30, 31, 32
	who <u>see</u>ʲ vanity |	
	and <u>divine</u>ʲ lies |	ʲ Jer. 14:14
	they shall not be in the circle of my people |	
	and not be listed in the register of the house of Israel |	
	and not enter the land of Israel |	
	and you will know |	
	that I am the Lord YHWH |	
10	*Because yea because they have misled my people*ᵏ |	ᵏ *analogous clause Jer.*
	*<u>saying</u>*ᵐ |	*23:13, 32 (Mic. 3:5)*
	*<u>peace</u>*ˡᵐ |	ˡ Jer. 14:13; 23:17; 28:9
	*<u>and there is no peace</u>*ᵐ |	ᵐ *analogous sequence of*
	and (because) that (people) builds a wall |	*clauses Jer. 6:14=8:11*
	and behold they are daubing it with plaster |	
11	Say to those who daub with plaster |	
	that it will fall |	
	there is a deluge of rain |	
	and (as far as) you (are concerned) |	
	hailstones will fall |	
	and a stormy wind will break out |	
12	And behold |	
	the wall has fallen |	
	will it not be said to you |	
	where is the daubing |	
	with which you daubed it |	
13	Therefore |	
	thus says the Lord YHWH |	
	I will make a <u>stormy</u>ⁿ wind break out in my <u>wrath</u>ⁿ |	ⁿ Jer. 23:19
	and there shall be a deluge of rain in my anger |	
	and hailstones in wrath to destroy |	
14	And I will break down the wall |	
	that you have daubed with plaster |	
	and I will bring it down to the ground |	
	and its foundation will be laid bare |	
	and she will fall |	
	and you will perish in the midst of her |	
	and you will know |	
	that I am YHWH |	
15	And I will spend my wrath upon the wall and upon those |	
	who daubed it with plaster |	
	and I will say to you |	
	there is no wall |	
	and there are not those |	
	who daubed it |	
16	The prophets of Israel |	
	who prophesied to Jerusalem |	
	*and who saw for her a vision of <u>peace</u>*ᵒᵖ |	ᵒ Jer. 14:13; 23:17; 28:9
	*<u>and there is no peace</u>*ᵖ |	ᵖ *analogous sequence of*
	is the saying of the Lord YHWH |	*clauses Jer. 6:14=8:11*

2.2

What can we infer from these similarities in the matter of literary dependency? In order to be able to answer this question, one should make a careful distinction between common vocabulary outside or within analogous clauses, and subsequently between analogies of different degrees.

Underlinings in the above translation mark all the phrases and word fields that Jeremiah and Ezekiel share with regard to the theme 'false prophecy' (isolated words have been disregarded). Of course, these phrases and word fields as such do not indicate literary dependence in an acceptable sense of that term. Literary dependence is best understood to mean evident borrowing from one text into the other. I would rather avoid speaking about *probable* literary dependence as much as possible: the evidence is part of the definition. The definition does not cover every form of influence via texts. Common vocabulary indicates shared language and it may be assumed that, in many cases, an author became familiar with that language by reading or copying texts written by someone else. This is not, however, what is normally called literary dependence. Literary dependence goes beyond this and concerns the specific relationship between two literary texts. It requires at least that common words in related texts are embedded in similar clause patterns. An accepted term for a similar clause in different texts is an analogy.[7] In the above translation, deliberately following the clause division of the Hebrew, the analogous clauses are marked by italics. These analogies, which are partly based upon the underlined words and partly upon the position of these words within the syntactical patterns, are crucial when it comes to the question of dependence.[8] Even if not every analogy is indicative of literary dependence, the reverse is always true: (evident) literary dependence

---

[7] For an extensive methodological discussion, see: A.L.H.M. van Wieringen, *Analogies in Isaiah* (Applicatio, 10), vol. A, Amsterdam 1993, 1-29; cf. H. Leene, 'Psalm 98 and Deutero-Isaiah: Linguistic Analogies and Literary Affinity', in: R.-F. Poswick (ed.), *Actes du Quatrième Colloque International Bible et Informatique*, Paris 1995, 313-40. It is an advantage of the term 'analogous clause' or 'analogy' (casually used by M. Fishbane, *Biblical Interpretation in Ancient Israel*, Oxford 1985, 219) that it does not anticipate any explanation of the similarity (implied in terms like formular language, literary influence, borrowing, allusion, quotation, or inner biblical exegesis).

[8] About the role of vocabulary as well as of syntax in establishing literary dependence, see also: H.W.M. van Grol, 'Exegesis of the Exile – Exegesis of Scripture? Ezra 6:6-9', in: J.C. de Moor (ed.), *Intertextuality in Ugarit and Israel* (OTS, 40), Leiden 1998, 31-61, esp. 40-2.

cannot exist without analogies. They are a necessary, albeit not sufficient condition for establishing quotations, allusions and other forms of literary borrowing. Let us start with some examples of their insufficiency:

Ezek. 13:6	ויהוה לא שלחם	
Jer. 28:15	לא שלחך יהוה	
Jer. 43:2	לא שלחך יהוה אלהינו	
Jer. 14:15	ואני לא שלחתים	
Jer. 29:31	ואני לא שלחתיו	
Jer. 27:15	כי לא שלחתים	
Jer. 14:14	לא שלחתים	
Jer. 23:32	לא שלחתים	
Jer. 29:9	לא שלחתים	
Jer. 23:21	לא שלחתי את הנבאים	
Ezek. 13:7	ואני לא דברתי	
Ezek. 22:28	ויהוה לא דבר	
Jer. 14:14	ו לא דברתי אלהים	
Jer. 23:21	לא דברתי אלהים	

Some analogous clauses automatically appear as soon as people speak about the same subject. It simply belongs to the definition of a false prophet that YHWH did not send him or did not speak to him. At best it might be observed that in Jer. 14:13-16 these two analogies occur together and, moreover, in combination with a considerable number of other words from Ezek. 13:1-16: שלום, 'peace', חזון, 'vision', קסם, 'divination', and לבם 'their (own) heart'. For a really evident literary borrowing, however, this is not yet enough in itself.

A dubious example is also the similarity between Jer. 23:30ff. and Ezek. 13:8f. (see the translation): the combination הנני with אל or על for 'I am against so-and-so' appears 6 times in Jeremiah and 14 times in Ezekiel and does not concern false prophets elsewhere.[9] These analogies seem to be too weak and too general to prove literary dependence and might be merely based upon common linguistic usage. There are, however, more promising instances. The following analogy, for example, is much stronger and more exclusive:

Ezek. 13:10	את עמי	הטעו
Jer. 23:13	את עמי את ישראל	ויתעו
Jer. 23:32	את עמי	ויתעו
Mic. 3:5	את עמי	המתעים

---

[9] Other places in the Old Testament are: Nah. 2:14 (transl. 13); 3:5.

According to HAL, תעה is a root variant of טעה, 'to err about'.[10] In collocation with 'my people', the verb in the Hif., 'cause to err, mislead', is also found in Isa. 3:12 (not in connection with prophets, but see Isa. 9:14f.) and in Jer. 50:6. The participial clause in Mic. 3:5 gives the impression of a derivation, for it seems to refer to what is already known about these prophets from another source. The suffix of the first person in עמי, which is syntactically incongruous with the rest of the sentence, might even suggest a quotation.[11] Does it concern a quotation from Ezek. 13? In any case, the reader is reminded of Ezek. 13:5, 10 by the opposition of שלום and מלחמה in Mic. 3:5. The analogy between Ezek. 13:10 and the two clauses in Jer. 23 might indicate literary borrowing as well, although it still remains difficult to decide whether priority lies with 'Jeremiah' or 'Ezekiel' (or even to exclude the possibility of formular language beyond a doubt).

2.3

Such a decision, however, does seem possible to me on the basis of those texts in Jeremiah and Ezekiel that summarise the prophetic message in the word 'peace'. Here the similarity extends itself over three successive analogous clauses, so that it can hardly be doubted that this is a case of genuine literary dependence, either direct or indirect, either in this direction or in the other:

Ezek. 13:10	ואין שלום	שלום	לאמר
Jer. 6:14	ואין שלום	שלום שלום	לאמר
Jer. 8:11	ואין שלום	שלום שלום	לאמר
Jer. 4:10	ונגעה חרב עד הנפש	שלום יהיה לכם	לאמר
Ezek. 13:6	ויהוה לא שלחם	נאם יהוה	האמרים
Ezek. 13:7	ואני לא דברתי	נאם יהוה	ואמרים
Ezek. 22:28	ויהוה לא דבר	כה אמר אדני יהוה	אמרים
Ezek. 13:16	ואין שלום	והחזים לה חזון שלם	
Jer. 8:15	ואין טוב	קוה לשלום	
Jer. 14:19	ואין טוב	קוה לשלום	
Ezek. 7:25	ואין	ובקשו שלום	
Ezek. 28:9	ואתה אדם ולא אל	אלהים אני | לפני הרגך	האמר תאמר

---

[10] For other examples of 'Aramaic' replacements of ת by ט, see: J.F.A. Sawyer, Art. תעה, in: *THAT* 2, 1055-57, sub 1.

[11] According to many commentators (e.g., A.S. van der Woude, *Micha* [Pred OT], Nijkerk 1976, 108; H.W. Wolff, *Micha* [BK, 14/1], Neukirchen 1982, 61) the suffix may refer to the prophet, cf. Mic. 1:9; 2:8f.; 3:3; but even so, the formal analogy remains striking. Signs of editorial activity have been observed in Mic. 3:5, at least in the messenger's formula (Wolff). The spirit as the source of prophetic inspiration in Mic. 3:8 is also reminiscent of Ezekiel (Ezek. 11:5, 24; 37:1).

The occurrences have been ordered, more or less, according to their decreasing resemblance to the text mentioned first, Ezek. 13:10. All kinds of variants of this statement are found both in Ezekiel and in Jeremiah.[12] The similarity that is most important in view of the question of priority is the pattern 'they say A and it is not-A'. In Ezekiel, this pattern also occurs in several other places than Ezek. 13:10 and with other lexical contents. It is not only found elsewhere in the same passage (Ezek. 13:6, 7) or in a later reference to the same theme (Ezek. 22:28), but it also turns up in a totally different connection (Ezek. 28:9, 'Will you still say "I am a god" ... though you are ... no god'). In Jeremiah, on the other hand, we only meet this rhetorical pattern in the wording known from Ezek. 13:10, namely in Jer. 6:14 = 8:11.

In other words, in Jeremiah the pattern is exclusively linked to this single lexical interpretation.[13] This means that from a syntactical and rhetorical point of view the statement is more deeply rooted in the language of Ezekiel than it is in the language of Jeremiah. Rhetoric that deviates from the usual rhetoric of a speaker or writer characterises a quotation. If a quotation extends its influence over other parts of its new context, it is by its content rather than by its formal pattern, because speakers and writers are usually unaware of syntax.[14]

While the relative originality of Ezechiel's statement is already strongly suggested by this linguistic argument in itself, it seems to receive additional support from the literary structure of Ezek. 13:1-16. To put it negatively, this structure does not give the slightest impression that v. 10 has been cited or borrowed from another text.

---

[12] In connection with false prophecy, the word שלום also occurs in Jer. 4:10; 14:13; 23:17; 28:9; to be sure, the book of Jeremiah not always associates the clause 'there is no peace' with this theme: 12:12, אין שלום לכל בשר; cf. 30:5, פחד ואין שלום. Outside these two books, we find the combination אין שלום in Isa. 48:12; 57:21; Zech. 8:10; Ps. 38:4; 2 Chron. 15:5.

[13] The nearest variation of the pattern in Jeremiah is Jer. 4:10, '[YHWH] saying "Peace will be with you", and the sword has reached the soul'.

[14] Does this mean that all occurrences of שלום referring to false prophecy in Jeremiah should be derived from Ezek. 13? This seems to be more plausible for Jer. 4:10; 14:13 (see above) and 23:17 than it is for Jer. 28:9. The word in itself might simply belong to the common language of the subject.

1		*And the word of YHWH came to me saying:*
2		*Son of man prophesy ... :*
		Hear the word of YHWH
3-5		*Thus says the Lord YHWH: ...*
	A	Woe word to the fool prophets who did not build a wall around the people in view of the imminent war
6-7	B	Illusion and lies: they have said 'saying of YHWH' while YHWH had not spoken
8-9		*Therefore, thus says the Lord YHWH:*
	C	Because ... illusion and lies therefore ... exclusion from the circle of the people
		and you will know that I am the Lord YHWH
10-12	D	Because ... they have said 'peace' while there is no peace, the daubers will be held responsible once the wall has fallen
13-14		*Therefore, thus says the Lord YHWH: ...*
	E	YHWH will make a storm break out, the wall will collapse and the prophets will perish among its ruins
		and you will know that I am YHWH
15-16	F	YHWH's anger will only end when he has put an end to the wall and its daubers, i.e. the prophets who see a vision of peace while there is no peace

As to its main structure, the oracle is composed of six elements, two of them (A and B) in the diagnostic and four (C, D, E and F) in the prognostic part.[15] The motifs of the protecting wall and the illusory saying of YHWH, which were only loosely connected in A-B, flow together in C-D where they lead to the statement under discussion, '... peace, while there is no peace'. The formal reference to prophecy is replaced at this point by a more substantial reference, 'peace', apparently because the motif of the divine saying has been interwoven with the wall motif. In this connection, the word שלום in the segments D and F contrasts with the word מלחמה in segment A, the war from which the prophetic wall had not been able to keep the people safe.

It might, therefore, be said that the statement 'peace, while there is no peace' naturally follows from the progress of the passage itself. It is born of the combination of a more substantial reproach in vv.

---

[15] The main caesura in Ezek. 13:1-16 has often been laid between vv. 9 and 10 in order to stress the double 'Erweiswort' structure (cf. W. Zimmerli, *Ezechiel* [BK, 13/1-2], Neukirchen-Vluyn 1969, 285-88; R.M. Fuhs, *Ezechiel 1-24* [NEB], Würzburg 1984, 71; R.M. Hals, *Ezekiel* [FOTL], Grand Rapids 1989, 85). A 'bottom-up' analysis of the clause hierarchy, however, seems to locate the main caesuras after v. 7 and v. 11, where they would match the division into $s^e t\hat{u}m\hat{o}t$. The division I propose is largely similar to that of W.H. Brownlee, *Ezekiel* (WBC), 1986, 187, who speaks of a 'carefully designed composition', without denying its editorial character.

3b-5 (no wall against the war) and a more formal reproach in vv. 6-7 ('saying of YHWH' while YHWH has not spoken).

The closing function of segment F is underlined by the fact that it not only takes up words from D and E ('wall', 'daubing' and 'plaster' on the one hand, 'peace' on the other) but also repeats literary elements from A (prophets of Israel!) and B (vision). Whatever these prophets have been blamed for earlier in the passage can be summarised for the present in this single climactic statement that they saw a vision of peace while there was no peace.

If one compares Jer. 6:9-15, the corresponding sentence appears to be less deeply integrated into the entire structure of that passage.[16] Moreover, there is a remarkable shift of *meaning* between Ezek. 13:10 and Jer. 6:14 = 8:11, one which can be more easily understood if Jeremiah's statement depends on Ezekiel's statement rather than the other way round. This shift of meaning even causes a certain tension between the formal pattern 'they say A and it is not A' on the one hand and the new semantic filling-in of A on the other. Ezek. 13:10 still stressed the fact that the prophetic anouncement did not match reality. The word שלום, as we have seen, corresponded in the context of Ezek. 13 with the image of the plastered wall that could not protect against the מלחמה (v. 5). The parallel between אין שלום 'there is no peace' and אין הקיר 'there is no wall' (v. 15) is another illustration of this correspondence. In Jeremiah, on the other hand, the double שלום שלום sounds more soothing, it means: arguing away the seriousness of the wound in retrospect, trying to heal this wound by speaking magical language. In this connection, Jeremiah seems to ascribe the utterance not only to the prophets but also to the priests, thus less exclusively linking it to prophetic anouncements.

Other occurrences of the double שלום שלום in the Old Testament are: Isa. 26:3; 57:19 (with ל and in collocation with רפא and בצע!); and 1 Chron. 12:19.[17] As it appears from 1 Chron. 12:19 (transl. 18; cf. ל) the doubling may indicate a blessing. In Isa. 57:19 שלום שלום is called 'the fruit of the lips', which means the fulfillment of the blessing words people speak to each other, 'I create the fruit of the lips: peace peace to the far and to the near, says YHWH, and I will heal him'.

This collocation of 'peace' and 'healing' is as interesting as the doubling of the word 'peace' in itself. It always refers to the recovery

---

[16] W.L. Holladay, *Jeremiah I* (Hermeneia), Philadelphia 1986, 211, sees a stylistic connection between שלום שלום in v. 14 and the root repetitions in vv. 9, 13 and 15, but these are no simple repetitions in MT and are syntactically incomparable.

[17] LXX has taken up the doubling into Ezek. 13:10: Εἰρήνη εἰρήνη, as a sign of its intertextual reading.

after the crisis of the exile (cf. Isa. 53:5; Jer. 33:6).[18] The collocation of שבר 'wound' en רפא 'to heal' is always linked to the national crisis as well: Isa. 30:26; Jer. 6:14 = 8:11; Ps. 60:4; Lam. 2:13. The prophets and priests in Jer. 6:14 = 8:11 apparently presuppose a legitimate promise of recovery, although they anticipate it too easily in their magical incantations. From an illusory announcement in Ezekiel the clause has become a premature blessing, hardly fitting into the original rhetorical pattern 'they say A and it is not-A'.[19] Was Isa. 57 already running through the author's mind when he wrote Jer. 6:14? That bold suggestion might be difficult to prove indeed. But the conclusion that this author was not the person who invented the basic pattern of the sentence would seem inevitable to me.

2.4

A complication is, of course, that Ezek. 13 and Jer. 6 each must have had their own genesis.[20] Jer. 6 might depend on an earlier stage of the present text of Ezek. 13, or an earlier stage of the present text of Jer. 6 might depend on Ezek. 13, etcetera. Some of these theoretical possibilities are represented in the following graphics. Each of them would do justice to the above observations.

---

[18] Cf. S. Talmon, 'The signification of שלום and its Semantic Field in the Hebrew Bible', in: C.A. Evans, S. Talmon (eds), *The Quest for Context and Meaning: Studies in Biblical Intertextuality in Honor of J.A. Sanders*, Leiden 1997, 75-115, esp. 91.

[19] With καὶ ποῦ ἐστιν εἰρήνη, 'but whence peace?', LXX seems to have adapted the rhetoric of the third clause to the second.

[20] The diachronic analysis of Ezek. 13:1-16 has mainly been dominated by discussions about the frequent changes in the direction of speech (second and third person) and the pureness of the generic form ('Erweiswort'). Whereas older commentators assumed a combination of two parallel oracles (e.g., G. Fohrer, *Ezechiel* [HAT, 1/13], Tübingen 1955, 68-73), Zimmerli, *op. cit.*, 285-8, holds that two texts vv. 3, 5, 7a, 8-9 and vv. 10, 13, 14 must have been combined and expanded during the editorial process. See also J.W. Wevers, *Ezekiel* (CB), London 1969, 105; Fuhs, *op. cit.*, 71. In this reconstruction, the sentence 'saying peace' etc. in v. 10 belongs to the original text. – With some minor variations, Jer. 6:12-15 also occurs in Jer. 8:10-12 where it has been omitted by LXX. R.P. Carroll, *Jeremiah* (OTL), London 1986, 198, reckons that these verses are independent of both their present contexts, but most commentators treat them as part of Jer 6:9-15, marked out as a $s^e t\hat{u}m\bar{a}h$ in L. Although it has been noted that the expression 'rest of Israel' in v. 9 might presuppose the exile, the Jeremian origin of the passage as a whole has hardly been questioned by the commentators.

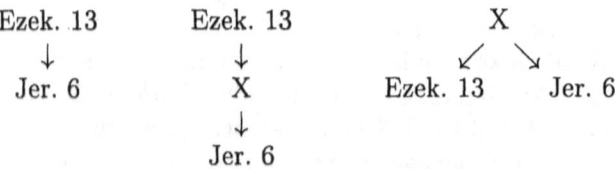

As far as the question of priority is concerned, however, it would make no difference. If Ezek. 13 itself, in its present form, does not offer us the stemmatological point of suspension in the supposed relationship of dependence, this point must have been much closer to Ezek. 13 than it was to Jer. 6 in any case.[21] The language of the analogous clauses I discussed is the language of Ezekiel's circle. This is the essential element in my argument. It is illustrated by the graphic below, in which the squares represent the texts themselves *or* their earlier stages or variants.

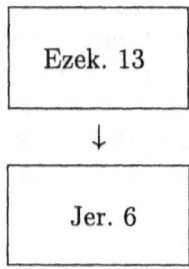

Apart from that, it still seems a plausible assumption (in line with Zimmerli's theory of 'Fortschreibung') that the book of Ezekiel came into existence in a relatively isolated circle and that only in a progressive stage of its growth it started to influence other circles of prophetic tradition.

2.5

Let me summarise some methodological considerations and formulate some provisional conclusions regarding my first example. Ezek. 13:1-16 brings to mind the book of Jeremiah, or in other words, many places in Jeremiah remind us of Ezek. 13:1-16. The corresponding phrases and lexical sets as such do not indicate literary dependence. The common subject of false prophecy alone might even explain some of the analogous clauses. Other analogies, however, are so strong that they do suggest literary dependence. The statement 'they say "Peace" while there is no peace' rhetorically fits into the language of Ezekiel.

---

[21] On stemmatology, see: P. van Reenen, M. van Mulken (eds), *Studies in Stemmatology*, Amsterdam 1996.

The doubling of the word 'peace' in Jeremiah's version causes a shift of meaning which strengthens the impression of its secondary character compared to the original rhetorical pattern. This conclusion might even invite us to reconsider some of the affinities discussed earlier: If the priority in *these* clauses belongs to Ezekiel or his circle indeed, who else is more likely to have created the preceding clause saying that they 'misled my people' as well? And is it not a plausible implication that Ezek. 13 has also influenced the 'deuteronomistic' Jer. 14:13-16, after all?[22]

These provisional results deviate from the usual opinion, as it is formulated by Zimmerli in his commentary on Ezek. 13: 'Da der Einfluß Jeremias auf Ez auch sonst nicht zu verkennen ist (Miller), so wird auch hier Ez von Jeremia her bestimmt sein. Die Vermutung wird sich in der Einzeldurchsicht bestätigen'.[23] A linguistic approach of the question of dependence, however, is lacking in this 'Einzeldurchsicht'. Zimmerli's judgement seems to be mainly based upon the general (but debatable) concept that, in cases of literary affinity, long arguments of Ezekiel must derive from short statements of Jeremiah.[24]

3 The Prophets as Watchmen (Jer. 6:16-21 and Ezek. 33:1-9)

3.1

The next step is an analysis of the affinities concerning a more positive image of the prophet, that of the watchman. There is no need to repeat all the earlier methodological considerations. In this case I approach the problem from a different angle and, for a change, choose the relevant passage from Jeremiah as my starting-point. The translation of Jer. 6:16-21 offers provisional references to the book of Ezekiel in the margin.[25]

---

[22] The style of Jer. 14:13-16 is deuteronomistic according to several commentators. As a section of the composition Jer. 14:1–15:4(9), the passage offers no other clue as to its date of origin.

[23] Zimmerli, *op. cit.*, 288. See also H.G. May, 'The Book of Ezekiel', in: *The Interpreter's Bible*, vol. 6, New York, Nashville 1956, 130: 'Ezekiel may be quoting'; D. Vieweger, *Die literarischen Beziehungen zwischen den Büchern Jeremia und Ezechiel* (BEAT, 26), Frankfurt a/M 1993, 31.

[24] Compare the general judgement of R.L. Schultz, *The Search for Quotation: Verbal Parallels in the Prophets* (JSOT.S, 180), Sheffield 1999, 58: 'The direction of borrowing usually was determined on the a priori basis of the prevailing scholarly consensus regarding literary chronology rather than as a result of a passage-by-passage comparison'.

[25] In v. 18, the Hebrew text causes problems. The collocation of גוים and עדה does not occur elsewhere in the Old Testament, nor does the clause את אשר בם.

Jeremiah 6:16-21
16 Thus says YHWH |
    stand by the ways<u>a</u> |
    and look |
    and ask for the ancient paths |
    (look) where the good <u>way</u>^a is | ^a Ezek. 33:8
    and go in it |
    and find rest for your souls |
    but they said |
    we won't go |
17 *And I have set <u>watchmen</u> over you*^b | ^b *analogous clause Ezek. 33:2, 7*
    give heed to the sound of the shofar^c | ^c *analogous clause Ezek. 33:4, 5*
    but they said |
    we won't give heed |
18 Therefore |
    hear |
    nations |
    and recognise |
    congregation |
    what is in them |
19 Hear |
    earth |
    behold I am bringing evil upon this people^d | ^d *analogous clause Ezek. 33:2 etc.*
    the fruit of their plots |
    because they have not given heed to my words |
    nor to my law |
    and they rejected it |
20 Why frankincense for me |
    that comes from Sheba |
    and the good cane from a distant land |
    your burnt offerings are not acceptable |
    and your sacrifices are not pleasing to me |
21 Therefore |
    thus says YHWH |
    behold I will give to this people stumbling blocks |
    and they will stumble over them fathers and sons together |
    a neighbour and his friend will perish |

3.2

The analogous clauses have again been marked by the use of italics in the translation. For the sake of completeness, the underlinings in Jer. 6:16 indicate that the passage also shares the word דרך with Ezek. 33. The analogies to Ezek. 33 are both based upon the syntactical patterns of the clauses and upon part of their vocabulary. It concerns the following clauses:

The only other occurrence of the imp. שמעו addressed to the גוים is Jer. 31:10. The combination ידע את אשר, however, is very common: Gen. 9:24; 30:29; Exod. 33:12; Num. 16:5; 22:6; Deut. 8:2; 29:15; 1 Sam. 10:8; 16:3; 28:2, 9; 2 Sam. 11:20; 1 Kgs 2:5, 9; 20:22; 2 Kgs 8:12; Isa. 5:5; Dan. 8:19. Therefore the most plausible meaning of the Hebrew text is: 'acknowledge, congregation, what is in them'. The suffix of בם in the relative clause can only refer to those who did not give heed in v. 17. The imp. of ידע is not unusual in Jeremiah as a call for acknowledgement: 2:19, 23; 3:13; 15:15; 31:34. In the present text it is the nations that are summoned as witnesses against the people of YHWH.

Jer. 6:17	והקמתי עליכם צפים
Ezek. 33:2	ונתנו אתו להם לצפה
Ezek. 33:7	צפה נתתיך לבית ישראל
Jer. 6:17	הקשיבו לקול שופר
Ezek. 33:4	ושמע השמע את קול השופר
Ezek. 33:5	את קול השופר שמע
Jer. 6:19	הנה אנכי מביא רעה אל העם הזה
Ezek. 33:2	כי אביא עליה חרב

Two analogies are formed by 'to set (give) watchmen (a watchman) over' (verbal form in the first person in Jer. 6:17 and Ezek. 33:7) and 'to give heed to (hear) the sound of the shofar'.[26] These analogies mutually strengthen each other because they collocate and link the same texts. As a matter of fact, nowhere else in the Old Testament the 'watchman' and the 'shofar' are so closely linked as they are in these two cases of their *metaphorical* use. In both pericopes, the 'watchman' is an image of the prophet and the 'shofar' refers to the prophetic word.

In the same context YHWH 'causes to come evil (the sword)', although this analogy is not that striking in itself because of the frequency of the expression;[27] and finally both passages make mention of the 'way' or 'ways' in a moral sense.

3.3

One could ask whether the frequent occurrences of the image of the prophet as a watchman in the Old Testament should keep us from linking these two passages of Jeremiah and Ezekiel too closely.[28] In Hos. 9:8 this image also seems to involve drawing attention to imminent danger,[29] as it does in Ezekiel; and the shofar in Hos. 8:1 might

---

[26] Occurrences of קול [ה]שופר with שמע are: Josh. 6:5, 20; 2 Sam. 15:10; 1 Kgs 1:41; Jer. 4:19, 21; 42:14; Ezek. 33:4, 5; Neh. 4:14; 1 Chron. 15:28; with הקשיב: Jer. 6:17; other occurrences of קול [ה]שופר are: Exod. 19:16, 19; 20:18; 2 Sam. 6:15; Amos 2:2; Ps. 47:6; 98:6; Job 39:24. The combination נתן ... צפה or הקים ... צפה, 'to give/set a watchman', is not found outside Jer. 6:17; Ezek. 3:17 and 33:2, 7.

[27] In Jeremiah, הביא רעה על/אל is found in: 6:19; 11:11, 23; 19:3, 15; 23:12; 32:42; 35:17; 36:31; 42:17; 44:2; 45:5; 49:37; 51:64; cf. 17:18; 39:16.

[28] Vieweger, *op. cit.*, 127, holds that literary dependence (Smend 1880, Burrows 1925, Fohrer 1955: Jeremiah → Ezekiel) is improbable in view of the extension of the metaphor. Regarding the latter, see: G. Steins, Art. צפה, in: *ThWAT*, Bd. 6, 1087-93, sub III.3.

[29] Although Hos. 9:8 belongs to the most difficult verses of the book, it is plausible to read צפה as a cstr. and to relate 'Ephraim's watchman' to the prophet; cf. H.W. Wolff, *Micha* (BK, 14/1), Neukirchen 1982, 193; F.I. Andersen, D.N. Freed-

be explained in this connection. In turn, these places remind us of a well-known word from Amos 3:6f., 'Is the shofar blown in the city, and the people are not afraid? Does evil befall the city, unless YHWH had done it? Surely the Lord YHWH does nothing without revealing his plan to his servants the prophets'. In Jer. 4:5, 19, 21, the shofar signals imminent danger as well, but in that chapter the prophet is among those who should hear the signal, not the person who should give the signal himself. In Ezek. 3:16-21, the passage in which Ezekiel is installed as a watchman for the very first time, the imminent danger and the shofar are still lacking and the *tertium comparationis* between the prophet and a watchman is confined to their warning role. Ezek. 3:16-21 is mostly seen as a secondary passage compared to Ezek. 33:1-9.[30] In Hab. 2:1, the prophet takes his stand on the watch tower in order to receive a revelation, 'I will ... look forth to see what he will say to me', and the same concept seems to be on the background of Isa. 21:1-10. These places remind us of the cultic use of choosing a special vantage-point for visionary experiences, like Balaam in Num. 23:14; 24:1f.; see for this possible cultic background also Ps. 5:4; Mic. 7:7. In Mic. 7:4, the 'day of your watchmen' is the day of punishment announced by the prophets (cf. Hos. 9:7f.).

Meanwhile, this variety means that these concepts cannot simply be lumped together. The image of the prophet as a watchman could apparently be worked out in entirely different directions: reception of revelations (cultic), timely signalling danger (military), warning to help oneself to safety, and even (along these lines) the exhortation to other moral behaviour. Note that in the last case the intended reality has already deeply interfered with the image side of the metaphor. This element of moral exhortation is only found in Ezek. 33 (cf. Ezek. 3) and Jer. 6. Only in these places the shofar has become a *chiffre* for the prophetic call to conversion.

This unique element in the thematic similarity, added to the analogous clauses mentioned before (which have no counterparts in the other prophetic books), suggests a special relationship between the two passages. It confronts us with the familiar dilemma: 'Ezekiel' has spun out a single image to a complete allegory, or 'Jeremiah' has summarised and generalised what he was able to remember of the story of Ezekiel's installation as a watchman. A careful comparison of the two passages led me to the second alternative, almost to my own amazement. Let us follow the argument in the two passages once again.

---

man, *Hosea* (AncB), New York 1980, 515; G.I. Davies, *Hosea* (NCBC), Grand Rapids 1992, 222.

[30] Cf. Zimmerli, *op. cit.*, 88.

3.4

After the introduction, Ezek. 33:1-9 can be divided into two sections, a section in which the story about a watchman is told (vv. 2-6) and a section in which the watchman's story is applied to Ezekiel (vv. 7-9). At this stage it appears that the image side of the comparison was geared to the application from the outset: although the story spoke about a watchman of a people threatened by YHWH, YHWH nevertheless held the watchman responsible. If the watchman neglects his duty, he is to blame, irrespective of the own guilt of those who were not prepared to accept his warning anyway. The same holds true for Ezekiel in his role as a prophet (v. 7). If he does not warn the people in time, he will be held responsible for his negligence (v. 8). If he does warn them, he will go free (v. 9). These two alternatives chiastically link up with the alternatives of the story in the first part of the the passage.

At first sight Jer. 6:16-21 gives a less homogeneous impression and by many commentators is considered to have grown in phases.[31] Yet this pericope also displays a deliberate composition. Synchronically, I detect this chiastic structure there:

16	Accusation of not *going* in the good way
17	Accusation of not *giving heed* to the sound of the shofar
18-20	Therefore: evil (mainly linked to v. 17)
21	Therefore: stumbling (mainly linked to v. 16)

A comparison, however, reveals a striking difference in the sequence of action. In Ezekiel: coming evil / performance of the watchman / disobedience of the people. In Jeremiah: performance of watchmen / disobedience of the people / coming evil. Whereas in Ezek. 33 the signal quite logically follows the imminence of the disaster, this disaster is only presented as a consequence of neglecting the signal in Jer. 6.[32] More than that, the reader of Jer. 6 is supposed to understand that watchmen point out the old paths – something that watchmen do not tend to do in real life and which at least requires Ezek. 33 as an explanation. In other words, the metaphor of the prophet as an exhorting watchman has already been lexicalised in Jer. 6. The sequence

---

[31] Vv. 18-19 or 18-20 have usually been seen as a deuteronomistic addition, cf. W. Thiel, *Die deuteronomistischen Redaktion von Jeremiah 1-25* (WMANT, 41), Neukirchen 1973, 99ff.; J. Schreiner, *Jeremia 1-25,14* (NEB), Würzburg 1985, 53.

[32] In this respect, there is a large difference between the shofar in Jer 6:17 and the shofar in Jer. 4:5, 19, 21 and 6:1, where it is really a matter of signalling advancing danger.

of v. 16 and v. 17 even seems to hint at the sequence $tōrāh\text{-}n^eb\hat{\imath}'\hat{\imath}m$: the prophets as watchmen have become those who call back to the ways of the law.[33]

3.5

Summing up: striking analogies between Jer. 6 and Ezek. 33 warrant the assumption of literary dependence. This case of dependence again presents us with the question of priority, a plausible question since these passages are linked by more than only a vague thematic affinity or a mere lexical resemblance. My analysis has led me to the following answer to this question: Ezek. 33 takes us closer to the stemmatological point of suspension than Jer. 6 does.

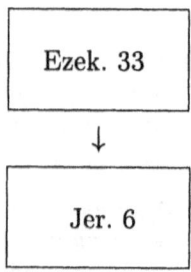

4 The Word/Vision shall [or shall not] Perish from the Prophet (Jer. 18:18-23 and Ezek. 7:23-27)

4.1

For my third and last example I have written out *both* relevant passages in translation. Of all the texts under discussion, these two are perhaps the most moving and as to the passage from Jeremiah, it is also the first one that introduces the prophet in person. Compared to the preceding examples, this one seems to offer the strongest linguistic argument in the problem of priority.

---

[33]This view of the direction of dependence makes it improbable that in Jer. 6:17 'the term [watchmen] may simply be a metaphor for those who warn' (Carroll, *Jeremiah*, 200). 'Watchmen' is rather another word for prophets. – The argument that Ezek. 33:1-9 is prior to Ezek. 3:16-21 (cf. note 30) is also valid for Jer. 6:16-21: both Ezek. 3 and Jer. 6 need Ezek. 33 in order to be understandable.

Jeremiah 18:18-23

18 And they said |
    come |
    and let us make plots against Jeremiah |
    for the <u>torah</u> shall not perish from the priest^a | ^a *analogous sequence of clauses*
    <u>and</u> <u>counsel</u> <u>from</u> the wise^a | Ezek. 7:26
    and the word <u>from the prophet</u>^a |
    come |
    and let us smite him with the tongue |
    and let us not heed any of his words |
19 Give heed |
    YHWH |
    to me |
    and hear to the voice of my opponents |
20 Is evil a recompense for good |
    for they have dug a pit for my soul |
    remember |
    how I stood before thee |
    to speak good for them |
    to turn away thy wrath from them |
21 Therefore |
    deliver their children to famine |
    give them over to the power of the sword |
    and let their wives become childless and widowed |
    and may their men be slain by death |
    their youths become victims of the sword in battle |
22 May a cry be heard from <u>their houses</u>^b | ^b [Jer. 5:27; 6:12] Ezek. 7:24
    when thou <u>bringest</u> the maraude suddenly upon them^c | ^c *analogous clause Ezek. 7:24 etc.*
    for they have dug a pit |
    to take me |
    and they laid snares for my feet |
23 But thou |
    YHWH |
    knowest all their plotting to slay me |
    do not forgive their iniquities |
    do not blot out their sins from thy sight |
    and let them be stumbling before thee |
    deal with them in the time of thine anger |

Ezekiel 7:23-27

23 Make a chain |
    for the land is full of bloody crimes |
    and the city is full of violence |
24 *And I will <u>bring</u> the worst of the nations*^a | ^a *analogous clause Jer. 18:22 etc.*
    and they will take possession of <u>their houses</u>^b | ^b Jer. 18:22
    and I will put an end to the proud of the powerfull |
    and their sanctuaries will be profaned |
25 Anguish has come |
    and they seek peace |
    and there is none |
26 Disaster comes upon disaster |
    and rumour follows rumour |
    and they seek a vision <u>from the prophet</u>^c |
    and the torah will <u>perish from the priest</u>^c |
    <u>and</u> <u>counsel</u> <u>from</u> the elders^c | ^c *analogous sequence of clauses*
27 The king will mourn | Jer. 18:18
    and the prince will be wrapped in despair |
    and the hands of the people of the land will be paralysed by terror |
    according to their ways I will do to them |
    and according to their own rules I will judge them |
    and they will know |
    that I am YHWH |

4.2

The analogies between the two passages are the following:[34]

Jer. 18:18	כי לא תאבד תורה מכהן	
Ezek. 7:26	ותורה תאבד מכהן	
Jer. 18:18	ועצה מחכם	
Ezek. 7:26	ועצה מזקנים	
Jer. 18:18	ודבר מנביא	
Ezek. 7:26	ובקשו חזון מנביא	
Jer. 18:22	כי תביא עליהם גדוד פתאם	
Ezek. 7:24	והבאתי רעי גוים	

Although the analogy between Jer. 18:22 and Ezek. 7:24 may attract some attention by the occurrence of בתיהם 'their houses' in its immediate context, it is not strong enough to warrant definite conclusions. The frequent expression 'bringing evil over' was already found in Jer. 6:19 and Ezek. 33:2 (see above). At best one might say that the two passages match each other in their moving depiction of the coming disaster, one which will even enter into the houses. In Ezekiel בתיהם only occurs in this place, in Jeremiah it is found in 5:27; 6:12; 18:22. The evil called down by Jeremiah upon his opponents (18:21ff.) is the evil that will render them completely powerless in Ezekiel.

The three pairs of analogies mentioned first concern two series of clauses in different sequences (1-2-3 and 2-3-1). The similarities can only be caused by literary dependence. The difference that is crucial in view of the question of priority is the use of the negative in Jer. 18:18. Other occurrences of אבד מן 'perish from, lose' are Deut. 22:3, 'any lost thing of your brother's, which he loses'; Jer. 25:35, 'A refuge will be lost to the shepherds, a way to escape to the lords of the flock'; with the same subject in Ps. 142:5 and Job 11:20; Jer. 49:7, 'Has counsel perished from the prudent, has their wisdom vanished?'; and Amos 2:14, 'Flight shall perish from the swift'. There is no other place in the Old Testament, however, where אבד מן occurs with לא and it is this negative in Jer. 18:18 that decides about its secondary character compared to Ezek. 7:26. A positive statement like the one in Ezek. 7:26 is presupposed by the negative statement in Jer. 18:18. The reader of this verse should realise that Jeremiah's opponents thereby reject the vision of their own helplessness. This even goes further

---

[34] The analogy of Jer. 18:21 והגרם על ידי חרב to Ezek. 35:5 (cf. Ps. 63:11) seems not to be based upon a special literary relationship between these texts but must be due to common language. See also Vieweger, *op. cit.*, 109.

than mere borrowing: as readers we are expected to become aware of the *allusion*. An allusion is a case of literary borrowing that should be recognised. Visions of helplessness and powerlessness over against YHWH's day of judgment should hover in the background of Jer. 18:18, thanks to the 'simultaneous activation of two texts'.[35]

The sequence Ezekiel → Jeremiah also offers an easy explanation for the other differences between the analogous clauses. In Ezekiel, the series starts with: 'and they seek a vision from the prophet', following on 'they seek peace' in the preceding context. It concerns a central motif from Ezek. 13, discussed earlier. The analogous clause in Jeremiah has been replaced to the end of the triad in view of the immediate continuation: 'and the word [shall not perish] from the prophet, come and let us smite him with the tongue'. The replacement of Ezekiel's 'vision' by Jeremiah's 'word' also fits into the entire verbal atmosphere of the scene. The opposition between Jeremiah and the authorities is 'an opposition of word and teaching'.[36] In this context it would also seem understandable, that Ezekiel's elders had to stand aside for the wise, in accordance with Jer. 49:7.[37]

4.3

Vieweger adduces the plural זקנים, 'elders', in Ezek. 7:26 as an argument for the priority of Jeremiah: in this stylistic lapse, Ezekiel clearly

---

[35] A basic publication concerning allusion remains Z. Ben-Porat, 'The Poetics of Literary Allusion', *A Journal for Descriptive Poetics and Theory of Literature* 1 (1976), 105-128. One of her illuminating examples (113) is a clause from the English cinematic version of Rostand's *Cyrano de Bergerac*, 'This is the nose that launched a thousand battles', as an allusion to a clause from Marlowe's *Dr. Faustus*, referring to the beautiful face of Helen of Troy and the Greek navy it commanded, 'Is this the face that launched a thousand ships?' Ben-Porat defines literary allusion as 'a device for the simultaneous activation of two texts' (9). In recent time allusion and quotation are mostly taken together in the sole concept quotation, whereby subsequently the need may be felt to distinguish between, for instance, formal quotation and allusive quotation; cf. A.L.H.M. van Wieringen, *Analogies in Isaiah* (Applicatio, 10), vol. A, Amsterdam 1993, 3. Concerning the recognisability of a quotation, see also R.L. Schultz, *The Search for Quotation: Verbal Parallels in the Prophets* (JSOT.S, 180), Sheffield 1999, 227: 'a knowledge of the *quoted* context is essential in order to properly understand the *quoting* context'.

[36] Carroll, *Jeremiah*, 378.

[37] An additional consideration, supposing that the author based himself directly upon Ezek. 7 indeed, might have been that he wanted to keep the elders aside for a more neutral role, cf. Jer. 19:1. The only other collocation of 'elders', 'priests' and 'prophets' in the Old Testament is found in Jer. 29:1; the combination of 'priest', 'wise' and 'prophet' in Jer. 18:18 is unique.

deviates from his Jeremian 'Vorlage'.[38] The schema sing.-sing.-plur., however, is also followed by the next triad: 'king', 'prince', 'hands of the people'. A plural at the end of a series of nouns in the singular is a quite normal stylistic phenomenon.

A good theoretical possibility, of course, remains that both passages depend on a source X that is unknown to us. In that case, however, this source X can only have been a statement concerning the *powerlessness* of priest, wise and prophet.[39] Whereas Ezekiel's version would have been in keeping with the tenor of such a statement, Jeremiah's opponents rejected it. In other words, this alternative would not detract from my conclusion that Ezek. 7:26 takes us closer to the stemmatological point of suspension than Jer. 18:18. For a global picture of the relationship of dependence between the two scribal circles, it would make no essential difference.

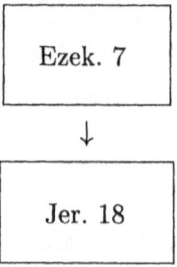

4.4

To sum up: the analogy between the three clauses in Jer. 18:18 and Ezek. 7:26 is, either directly or indirectly, based upon literary dependence. Priority in this relationship belongs to Ezekiel. Apart from all other considerations, one linguistic argument seems to be decisive, namely the negative in Jer. 18:18. Although the analogy between Jer. 18:22 and Ezek. 7:24 is less strong, it supports the affinity between the two passages as a whole: the time of anger that Jeremiah invokes upon his opponents is the day of YHWH as announced in Ezek. 7.

5 Conclusions

If we size up the three examples in retrospect, they yield a coherent picture. The misleading prophet, if I may put it that way, is focused in a later stage of his performance in the book of Jeremiah than he is in

---

[38] Vieweger, *op. cit.*, 107, n. 533, following Hertzberg and Zimmerli.
[39] Cf. B. Duhm, *Das Buch Jeremia* (KHC), Tübingen 1901, 157; Thiel, *op. cit.*, 217f.

Ezekiel. For both of these books it holds true that YHWH did not send him and did not speak to him. In Ezekiel, however, this misleading prophet is mainly the person who does not see the coming disaster in advance, in Jeremiah he is also the person whose magical words should reverse the disaster once it has come. This difference can only reveal, I think, a later reader's position. It is the reader who should be exhorted in this way to accept YHWH's historical judgement as it has taken place, because this sense of reality is the only real condition for any hopeful future. The misleading prophet in Jeremiah, therefore, is not only powerless, but he is also the person who denies his own powerlessness after the event and who is not prepared to see how 'the word' has already 'perished from him' through YHWH's judgement.

This leads me to my viewpoint on the relative distance between these texts and historical reality that differs from the most common opinion. According to Walther Zimmerli, for instance, this distance is largest in Ezekiel. In his commentary on Ezek. 13 he states: 'Der heiße Atem einer persönlich-unmittelbaren Auseinandersetzung, der in Jer 28f. gegenüber namentlich genannten Propheten zu verspüren ist, aber auch in Jer 23, wo keine Namen fallen, nicht verborgen bleiben kann, weht in Ez 13 1-16 nicht in gleicher Weise. Hier wird im zusammenfassenden Urteil der Distanz zur Prophetie Israels geredet'.[40] It might be asked, however, whether stories like those of Hananiah in Jer. 28 or Jeremiah's letter to the exiles in Jer. 29 should be read as historical reports indeed and not as rather late theological reflections on history. Without pursuing this question further, I may recall this statement from Robert Carroll's stimulating commentary: 'The peculiarities of [Jer.] 28 should warn the exegete against treating it as anything other than a disjunctive story in the tradition'.[41] Is the historical distance in Ezek. 13, the chapter that, among other things, even touches the practical problem of ownership of these prophets in the future land of Israel (cf. v. 9), really that large? In this connection it surprises me that Zimmerli did not involve the prophecy against the *female* prophets (Ezek. 13:17-23) in his judgement, although such a lifelike portrait of divinatory practices would seem to be virtually unique in the Old Testament.[42]

---

[40] Zimmerli, *op. cit.*, 289.

[41] Carroll, *Jeremiah*, 543. Also compare Carroll, 'Intertextuality', 72, about the distance implied by an intertextual approach to the text of Jeremiah 'between the "historical Jeremiah" and the written words we now read'.

[42] Cf. M.C.A. Korpel, 'Avian Spirits in Ugarit and in Ezekiel 13', in: N. Wyatt et al. (eds), *Ugarit, Religion and Culture: Essays presented in Honor of J.C.L. Gibson* (UBL, 12), Münster 1996, 99-113; N.R. Bowen, 'The Daughters of Your People: Female Prophets in Ez. 13:17-23', *JBL* 118 (1999), 417-33.

With regard to the positive image of the prophet as a watchman, Ezekiel's priority seems as obvious and revealing. Whereas Ezekiel is still appointed in a rather unique position (even in the introductory story of Ezek. 33 a single watchman standing on a single vantage-point is enough to overlook the entire threatened country!), the book of Jeremiah already refers to watchmen in the plural. The term encloses all legitimate prophets, at least uniting Ezekiel and Jeremiah themselves in one aspect: *the two of them blow the same shofar.* There is, for this author or editor of Jer. 6, no essential difference between the message of Jeremiah and that of Ezekiel and it is only logical, therefore, that he could also ascribe some other prophetic statements of Ezekiel to Jeremiah. Meanwhile one thing should be clear: it is Jeremiah who has been elevated by these statements to the ranks of Ezekiel, and not the reverse.

It is impossible, of course, to work out this view in full detail. There are a lot of other analogies between Jeremiah and Ezekiel still to be studied. The hardware of the linguistic facts should be more important in this field than the software of our preconceived historical ideas. Earlier syntactical and rhetorical examinations of the proverb of the unripe fruit and of the promises of inner renewal in Jeremiah and Ezekiel already confronted me with the question whether the book of Ezekiel might not have been the oldest large prophetic book, originated in its outlines before the end of the sixth century BCE and exerting a considerable influence in the circles that cherished the traditions of Isaiah and Jeremiah during the Persian era.[43] If I have not yet been able to *answer* this intriguing question today, perhaps the present contribution has at least shown that the *question* is a fruitful one and that, among other things, in answering it lies the reconsideration of the role of the prophet as a watchman in Jeremiah and Ezekiel. If, for the time being and in view of the few passages we were able to discuss today, someone would ask me the question: who is the historical person and who is the literary personage, my answer would be: Ezekiel and Jeremiah, and not the other way round.[44]

---

[43]Cf. H. Leene, 'Unripe fruit and dull teeth (Jer 31,29; Ez 18,2)', in: *Narrative and Comment (Fs W. Schneider)*, Amsterdam 1995, 82-98; Idem, 'Ezekiel and Jeremiah: Promises of inner Renewal in Diachronic Perspective', in: J.C. de Moor, H.F. van Rooy (eds), *Past, Present, Future: The Deuteronomic History and the Prophets* (OTS, 44), Leiden 2000, 150-75.

[44]I dedicate this paper to my students Annelies Claessens, Alinda Damsma, Rosalie Kuyvenhoven and Reinoud Oosting in appreciation of their helpful suggestions during our seminar on the texts discussed.

Andrew Mein *Cambridge – United Kingdom*

Ezekiel as a Priest in Exile

1 The Paradox of a Priest in Exile

The opening verses of the book of Ezekiel present the reader with an intriguing paradox. On the one hand, it is very clear that its central character is one of a group of Jewish exiles in Babylonia. The prophet's vision appeared 'as I was among the exiles by the river Chebar' (Ezek. 1:1), and in Ezek. 1:3 the place is described as 'in the land of the Chaldeans'. On the other hand, when he is named in the same verse it is as 'Ezekiel the son of Buzi, the priest'.[1] For Ezekiel to be a priest in exile puts him in a rather awkward position, since he is removed from the Jerusalem temple which provided the priestly class with its reason for existence. That Ezekiel is both priest and prophet is a commonplace of modern scholarship, but is it in fact legitimate to describe Ezekiel as a priest at all?

Amongst ancient writers it appears that Josephus was aware of the problem. Daniel R. Schwartz has demonstrated that it was possible for Greek and Latin writers on Judaism to distinguish priestly families in the diaspora from genuine, Jerusalem-based priests. Thus, according to Josephus, Ezekiel left Jerusalem as a child and is therefore merely a 'priest by descent', unable to perform a real sacerdotal function.[2] Rather more recently Margaret S. Odell, examining Ezekiel's initiation into a prophetic role, has reached a similarly negative conclusion about Ezekiel's priestly status. Indeed for her the whole of Chapters 1-5 can be seen as 'an account of a prolonged initiation in which Ezekiel relinquishes certain elements of his identity as a priest to take on the role of prophet'.[3] During this initiation Ezekiel under-

---

[1] While it is syntactically possible for either father or son to be the priest, it is more likely that הַכֹּהֵן refers to Ezekiel himself. Indeed it may be an unnecessary distinction to make since priesthood was hereditary in ancient Israel. See W. Zimmerli, *Ezekiel 1: A Commentary on the Book of the Prophet Ezekiel, Chapters 1-24* (Hermeneia), Philadelphia 1979, 111.

[2] D.R. Schwartz, 'Priesthood and Priestly Descent: Josephus *Antiquities* 10.80', *JThS* 32 (1981), 129-35; Josephus Ant. 10.80, 98, 106.

[3] M.S. Odell, 'You Are What You Eat: Ezekiel and the Scroll', *JBL* 117 (1998), 229. The general topic of priesthood in Ezekiel has received a sudden flurry of interest. It was the focus of the SBL's 'Theological Perspectives on the Book of Ezekiel' Seminar at the November 2000 SBL meeting in Nashville. Three papers read there have since been published in *SBL Seminar Papers 2000* (Atlanta 2000): F. Fechter, 'Priesthood in the Exile According to the Book of

goes a series of experiences that symbolize and confirm his change in status.[4] For example, whereas priestly consumption of the sin offering absolves the guilt of the people, the scroll that Ezekiel eats represents only judgement and destruction (Ezek. 2:8–3:2). The symbolic act of lying on his side to 'bear the iniquity' of Israel and Judah (Ezek. 4:4-6) does not remove guilt, but underlines its inevitable punishment. Indeed when he eats mixed rations rather than the pure offering that would be his due (Ezek. 4:9-15), or shaves his head (Ezek. 5:1) we see him forced 'to engage in explicitly anti-priestly behaviour'.[5] As we might suspect, his absence from the temple and sacrificial system is at the root of the problem. Odell argues that since priestly purity functions within the sacrificial system to absolve the corporate guilt of Israel, away from the temple a priest's purity has little value: 'Unable to offer sacrifices that would harness his purity to the greater good of the community, Ezekiel has become a vestigial member of the body politic.'[6] Over the course of his initiation Ezekiel does not entirely give up his priestly persona, but it is only by virtue of his newly-acquired prophetic status that he has anything substantial to offer the exiles.

It is true that Ezekiel is first and foremost a prophet, and if an active priestly ministry alongside this depends on participation in the sacrificial worship of the Jerusalem temple, then Ezekiel cannot be considered to have a priestly role, whatever his genealogical qualifications. However, the matter is not so simple. In what follows I seek to address this problem by considering three related questions. First, does the understanding of priesthood that the book of Ezekiel promotes leave room for any priestly role in exile? Second, how does the book's portrayal of the prophet relate to its understanding of the priestly task? Third, what might we learn from this portrayal about the community of exiles and the impact it might have had on them?

At least initially, it will be necessary to consider the prophet more as a literary figure than a historical individual. While it is certainly

---

Ezekiel' (673-99); C. Patton, 'Priest, Prophet and Exile: Ezekiel as a Literary Construct' (700-727); M.A. Sweeney, 'Ezekiel: Zadokite Priest and Visionary Prophet of the Exile' (728-51). These and a further paper by I.M. Duguid (' "What did You Do During the Exile, Daddy?": Ezekiel's Contribution to the History of the Old Testament Priesthood') can also be found on the internet at http://www.smsu.edu/relst/ezekiel/papers2000.html. Unfortunately they became available to me too late to incorporate into the substance of this paper, which was written for the SOTS/OTW meeting earlier in the same year.

[4]Odell, *art. cit.*, 238-48.
[5]Odell, *art. cit.*, 247.
[6]Odell, *art. cit.*, 240.

possible, even probable, that a prophet called Ezekiel was active in at least some of the ways the book recounts, it provides little information of the sort that would help a biographer.[7] The prophet is hidden behind the role he performs as mediator between YHWH and Israel. Ezekiel emerges not so much as a historical person as the carrier and embodiment of a particular theological perspective, yet it is likely that through his work and actions he represents attitudes and theological commitments to be found among at least some exiles. Thus, despite the rather limited access to the 'historical Ezekiel' that the book provides, its portrayal of the prophet may give us some insights into the concerns of the Jewish community in Babylonia.[8]

2 Priesthood in Ezekiel

The first question to address, then, is whether the understanding of priesthood in Ezekiel would allow for the prophet to continue some kind of priestly ministry in exile. It is not my intention here to add to the considerable volume of literature on what might be learnt from Ezekiel about the history of Israel's priesthood or the relationship between priests, Levites, Zadokites and Aaronites.[9] More significant

---

[7] We learn little more than that he came from a priestly family (Ezek. 1:1), was married to a woman who died during the final siege of Jerusalem in 587 BCE (Ezek. 24:15-18), that he was consulted at home by the leaders of his community (Ezek. 8:1; cf.14:1; 20:1), and that according to the dates throughout the book he was active as a prophet between at least 593 and 571 BCE.

[8] Despite numerous attempts over the past century to disturb the consensus, the majority of commentators remain confident that something approximating the present form of the book was produced during the exilic period. For an account of modern Ezekiel scholarship see e.g. B. Lang, *Ezechiel: Der Prophet und das Buch* (EdF, 153) Darmstadt 1981, 1-17; H. McKeating, Ezekiel (OTGu), Sheffield 1993, 30-61; K.P. Darr 'Ezekiel Among the Critics', *CurResB* 2 (1994), 9-24.

[9] Recent surveys of priesthood in the Hebrew Bible include J. Blenkinsopp, *Sage, Prophet, Priest: Intellectual Leadership in Ancient Israel* (Library of Ancient Israel), Louisville, KY 1995, 66-114; L.L. Grabbe, *Priests, Prophets, Diviners, Sages: A Socio-Historical Study of Religious Specialists in Ancient Israel*, Valley Forge, PA 1995, 41-65; R.D. Nelson, *Raising Up a Faithful Priest: Community and Priesthood in Biblical Theology*, Louisville, KY 1993.

For discussion of how and indeed whether Ezekiel might help reconstruct the history of the priesthood see e.g. R. Abba, 'Priests and Levites in Ezekiel', *VT* 28 (1978) 1-9; S.L. Cook, 'Innerbiblical Interpretation in Ezekiel 44 and the History of Israel's Priesthood', *JBL* 114 (1995) 193-208; I.M. Duguid, *Ezekiel and the Leaders of Israel* (VT.S, 56), Leiden 1994, 58-90; R.K. Duke, 'Punishment or Restoration? Another Look at the Levites of Ezekiel 44.6-16', *JSOT* 40 (1988) 61-81; J.D. Levenson, *Theology of the Program of Restoration of Ezekiel 40-48* (HSM, 10), Atlanta 1976, 129-58; J.G. McConville, 'Priests and Levites in Ezekiel: A Crux in the Interpretation of Israel's History', *TynB* 34 (1983) 3-32.

in our view is the role or function of the priesthood within religion and society. Certainly, the most complete picture of priestly ministry that Ezekiel draws (in Chapters 40–48) shows priests actively engaged in the sacrificial worship of a restored temple.[10] Their principal responsibility is to enter the sanctuary to serve God, making the appropriate offerings to ensure the continued purity of sanctuary and community. In exile Ezekiel's access to this world is strictly visionary: he neither performs sacrifices nor makes atonement for the people. However, the broader evidence of the book (together with the rest of the Hebrew Bible) would suggest that priests are not to be understood simply as ritual performers within the sanctuary, but might undertake a number of different roles within the framework that the cult provides. Within Ezek. 40–48 itself the priests are not limited to a sacrificial role but are shown as both teachers of ritual law (Ezek. 44:23) and ministers of justice in society (Ezek. 44:24).[11]

Also worth examining are two of Ezekiel's earlier oracles of judgement in which there is rather more emphasis on the priests' teaching role. The oracle of doom for Jerusalem in Ezekiel 7 ends with an image of society's leadership in disarray. First in the list are Judah's religious leaders:

> Disaster comes upon disaster, rumour follows rumour; they shall keep seeking a vision from the prophet; instruction shall perish from the priest, and counsel from the elders (Ezek. 7:26).

Here it is תּוֹרָה, 'instruction', that is the mark of the priest: the advice that he is able to give the community. That this was a significant part of the public perception of the priestly task is underlined by the fact that a variant of Ezek. 7:26b is found in Jer. 18:18b, which is almost an inversion of Ezekiel's phraseology: 'instruction shall not perish from the priest, nor counsel from the wise, nor the word from the prophet.' The presence of such similar vocabulary would suggest that we are dealing with a proverbial form of some sort, in which the religious authorities are defined by the kind of advice they give.[12]

The scope of priestly instruction for Ezekiel is defined rather more closely in the condemnation of Jerusalem's priests in Chapter 22:

---

[10] See especially Ezek. 42:13-14; 43:18-27; 44:9-28; 46:2-9, 11-15, 19-21.

[11] Cf. D.I. Block, *The Book of Ezekiel: Chapters 1-24* (NICOT), Grand Rapids, MI 1997, 642-3.

[12] For a comparison between the two texts, see the article of Leene in the present volume. See also Deut. 33:10; Mic. 3:11; R. de Vaux, *Ancient Israel: Its Life and Institutions*, London 1961, 353-5; Nelson, *Raising Up a Faithful Priest*, 42-4.

> Her priests have done violence to my law and have profaned
> my holy things; they have made no distinction between the
> holy and the common, neither have they taught the difference
> between the unclean and the clean, and they have disregarded
> my sabbaths, so that I am profaned among them (Ezek. 22:26).

The whole of Ezek. 22:25-29 looks like a re-working of Zeph. 3:3-4, which briefly states charges against officials, judges, prophets, and priests, in particular accusing the priests of profaning what is sacred and violating תּוֹרָה.[13] Ezekiel's expansion, referring specifically to their failure to maintain and teach ritual distinctions, recalls the injunction in Lev. 10:10-11:

> You are to distinguish between the holy and the common, and
> between the unclean and the clean; and you are to teach the
> people of Israel all the statutes that the LORD has spoken to
> them through Moses.[14]

It is clear that for Ezekiel not simply the priests' role as ritual performers is at issue, but also their failure to make distinctions between ritual categories, and to teach those distinctions to the community. Jacob Milgrom, commenting on both the Leviticus and Ezekiel passages, writes that 'the making of distinctions ($l^e habdîl$) is the essence of the priestly function'.[15] This certainly appears true of Ezekiel. For the book's authors the priests' role as ritual specialists went beyond the practice of sacrifice: they were also theorists and teachers, who defined and regulated the rules of religious observance for the community. If there is an area of priestly responsibilty that might survive in exile, this is it.

---

[13] See M. Fishbane, *Biblical Interpretation in Ancient Israel*, Oxford 1985, 461-3; Block, *Ezekiel: Chapters 1-24*, 724-7.

[14] It is also repeated as part of the instructions for priests in Ezek. 44:23: 'They shall teach my people the difference between the holy and the common, and show them how to distinguish between the unclean and the clean'. Such activity is very much in line with the classic example of priestly תּוֹרָה, found in Hag. 2:10-14, where priestly decisions about holiness and purity provide the subject matter of the oracle. See e.g. D.L. Petersen, *Haggai and Zechariah 1-8* (OTL), Philadelphia 1984, 72-6.

[15] J. Milgrom, *Leviticus 1-16* (AncB, 3), New York 1991, 615. This accords well with the approach of Nelson, *Raising Up a Faithful Priest*, 20, who places the whole of his extensive discussion of priesthood within the context of what he calls 'Israel's culture map', and in particular the paired opposites of clean and unclean, holy and common: to Nelson 'priests were "boundary setters" in the sense that they defined and separated these categories and taught these distinctions to the people'.

3 Ezekiel as Priest?

If the book of Ezekiel does stress the priests' responsibility to give instruction in matters ritual, how far does such an image make itself felt in its portrayal of the prophet? The original context for this language and set of responsibilities is unquestionably the cultic life of Jerusalem temple. If, as an exile, Ezekiel has given up his priestly role, we might reasonably expect purity, holiness, and even the teaching of תּוֹרָה to recede from his vision and analysis of events: new categories would need to be found appropriate to changed circumstances. But, as is apparent from even a cursory reading of the text, the language of ritual continues to dominate Ezekiel's understanding of Israel's past sins, present judgement, and future hope. I should like to suggest three distinct, if overlapping, aspects of this ritual focus, all of which contribute to the image of Ezekiel as priest: the first is the practice of purity, the second the metaphorical or symbolic use of ritual, and the third the vision of ritual.

The first appearance of purity in the book of Ezekiel has a surprisingly practical aspect. We find it in the sign-action of Ezek. 4:9-17, whose overt message is one of scarcity of food and impending doom and exile for Jerusalem, symbolised by the 'siege rations' baked on dung that Ezekiel is compelled to eat.[16] However, embedded within the prophetic drama is a very revealing interchange between Ezekiel and YHWH.[17] First the siege rations are seen to refer to the uncleanness of life in exile: 'Thus shall the people of Israel eat their bread, unclean, among the nations to which I will drive them' (Ezek. 4:13). This mention of uncleanness provokes a startled response from the prophet, who refuses to eat cakes baked on human dung, exclaiming: 'Ah, lord God, behold! I have never defiled myself: from my youth up till now I have never eaten what died of itself or was torn by beasts,

---

[16] See e.g. Zimmerli, *Ezekiel 1*, 168-9; L.C. Allen, *Ezekiel 1-19* (WBC), Waco, TX 1990, 69.

[17] See especially the recent discussion in M. Dijkstra, 'The Valley of Dry Bones: Coping with the Reality of Exile in the Book of Ezekiel' in: B. Becking, M.C.A. Korpel (eds), *The Crisis of Israelite Religion: Transformation of Religious Tradition in Exilic and Post-Exilic Times* (OTS, 42), Leiden 1999, 127-32. A number of recent commentators, including even the normally conservative Greenberg, consider this passage a secondary insertion: M. Greenberg, *Ezekiel 1-20* (AncB, 22), New York 1983, 125-6. Dijkstra relates this and other redactional elements to Pohlmann's *golaorientierte Redaktion*, but seems rather more confident than Pohlmann that reflect the experience of the early exilic community. Cf. K.-F. Pohlmann, *Ezechielstudien: Zur Redaktionsgeschichte des Buches und zur Frage nach den altesten Texten* (BZAW, 202) Berlin 1992; Idem, *Der Prophet Hesekiel/Ezechiel Kapitel 1-19* (ATD, 22/1) Göttingen, 1996.

nor has foul flesh come into my mouth' (Ezek. 4:14).[18] YHWH relents to the extent that he is allowed to cook with cow's dung, and since he complains no further, we may assume that Ezekiel is satisfied with this (Ezek. 4:15). Meindert Dijkstra has recently argued that in this episode we see an early example of halakhic interpretation, which 'deals with the problems of preparing and eating clean and unclean food in exile'.[19] Dung of any kind was not a normal fuel in Palestine, but was an essential for life in Babylonia, and the compromise of cooking with cow's dung represents an accommodation of purity legislation to exilic conditions. This is an attractive interpretation of the passage at hand, and if it is correct, we should note not only that there is thus accommodation in purity regulations to exilic conditions, but also that the distinction between clean and unclean remains of considerable importance to those who recorded the story about Ezekiel. The prophetic message of doom contains within it a certain amount of priestly instruction, and this provides a degree of hope for the exiles: not everything is lost if the ritual categories can be maintained. Within this sign action, then, Ezekiel is one who teaches ritual distinctions, and we may see the prophet acting both as teacher and model for the exiled community.

The second example is both more characteristic and more diffuse than this initial, rather practical treatment of the problem. It is the symbolic use of ritual language which is ubiquitous in Ezekiel's prophecies of judgement and salvation throughout the book.[20] Here the prophet's concerns are portrayed not so much through action as through the authoritative voice which explains and interprets, using ritual categories to provide its single most powerful explanatory framework for understanding Israel's past, present and future. The

---

[18] Odell, 'Ezekiel and the Scroll', 239, notes the strength of Ezekiel's objection, commenting that 'his objection to eating food cooked over dung is his only expression of personal will or desire in the whole book'.

[19] Dijkstra, 'The Valley of Dry Bones', 126.

[20] Numerous studies have demonstrated Ezekiel's dependence on priestly tradition: see e.g. W. Zimmerli, 'Die Eigenart der prophetischen Rede des Ezechiel: ein Beitrag zum Problem an Hand von Ezech. xiv 1-11', *ZAW* 66 (1954), 1-26; H.G. Reventlow, *Wächter über Israel: Ezechiel und seine Tradition* (BZAW, 82), Berlin 1962; K.W. Carley, *Ezekiel Among the Prophets: A Study of Ezekiel's Place in Prophetic Tradition* (SBT, 31), London 1975. However, dependence on tradition is not the same as performance of a priestly role, as Gerhard von Rad, *Old Testament Theology*, vol. 2, London 1965, 224-5, makes clear when he makes the two following statements within two pages of one another: 'the world of ideas in which he lives, the standards which he applies, and the categories according to which he sees Israel's existence ordered before Jahweh, are expressly those of a priest', and 'Ezekiel had, of course, no priestly function'.

most significant feature is the use of language drawn from the cult to describe the actions of the people, and the state into which they have put themselves. This language is present in Ezekiel to a degree unparalleled outside the priestly legislation, and it is fair to say that the book is saturated with defilement and profanity [21]

Of many possible examples probably the most concentrated is the oracle in Ezek. 36:16-38, where we find a number of key cultic metaphors. It begins by detailing the state of affairs that brought about the exile:

> Son of man, when the house of Israel dwelt in their own land, they *defiled* (טמא) it by their ways and their doings; their conduct before me was like the *uncleanness of a menstruating woman* (טֻמְאַת הַנִּדָּה). So I poured out my wrath upon them for the blood which they had shed in the land, for the idols with which they had *defiled* (טמא) it (Ezek. 36:17-18).

The current state of the people in exile is one that profanes YHWH's name:

> When they came to the nations, wherever they came, they *profaned* (חלל) my holy name, in that men said of them 'These are the people of the LORD, and yet they had to go out of his land' (Ezek. 36:20).

It appears that in exile the people not only profane YHWH's name but also remain themselves in a state of uncleanness. Indeed it refers to the state of the people of Judah, who have defiled themselves by their actions. For example, in the oracle of restoration in Ezek. 20:32-44, the people will look back at what caused their exile and recognize their mistakes: 'And there you shall remember your ways and all the doings with which you have polluted yourselves (Ezek. 20:43).'[22] Defilement in exile is also implied by those references to the people's

---

[21] The two most significant terms are טמא and חלל. The root טמא, which signifies concepts connected with impurity, uncleanness, defilement and pollution, occurs 44 times in Ezekiel of approximately 280 occurrences in the Hebrew Bible (compare this with 182 in P, 6 in Isaiah, and 5 in Jeremiah). Ezekiel contains 31 of 79 biblical occurrences of the verb חלל 'to profane' (19 in P, 1 in Isaiah, 2 in Jeremiah), and also includes 4 of the 7 occurrences of the adjective חל. It is noteworthy that the considerable majority of this cultic language occurs *outside* the legislation of Ezek. 40–48. I have elsewhere made a fuller study of Ezekiel's reapplication of ritual language to the ethical sphere: see A. Mein, *Ezekiel and the Ethics of Exile* (OTM), Oxford 2001, 137-76.

[22] This notion of a defiled people or city is Ezekiel's most common use of the root טמא (see also Ezek. 22:15; 24:13; 36:25, 29; cf. 20:7, 18, 30, 31; 22:3, 4; 23:7, 30; 37:23), and is used by Ezekiel as an image for their rejection by God.

cleansing as part of their restoration. Thus in Ezek. 36:25 we read: 'I will sprinkle *clean* water upon you, and *you shall be clean* from all your *uncleannesses*, and from all your idols I will *cleanse* you.'[23] Paramount here, as in all Ezekiel's oracles of restoration, is the idea that YHWH himself will be responsible for cleansing and restoring the people. They do not achieve it for themselves by ritual or any other means.[24] These few examples could be multiplied, and suggest that ritual language is very much at the heart of Ezekiel's message for the exiles. The prophet speaks with a priestly voice that uses the categories of holy and profane, clean and unclean, as central symbols for understanding his people's experience.

My third example of Ezekiel's priestly aspect is perhaps the most obvious, and continues the future orientation we saw at the end of Chapter 36. The vision of Ezekiel 40–48 demonstrates the shape of the restored temple and provides detailed regulations for its cultic service. Our prophet is presented as holding a key role in communicating this vision to the wider community, as he is told by the mysterious man in linen to 'declare all that you see to the house of Israel' (Ezek. 40:4; cf. 43:10). Again the prophet's voice becomes the voice of instruction, and the on ritual within this 'תּוֹרָה of the temple' is intense: indeed the duty of Israel is conceived almost wholly in ritual terms. Within the vision itself, the concern for pure categories to be seen in Ezek. 22:26 is reiterated in one of the principal tasks given to the priests in Ezek. 44:23: 'They shall teach my people the difference between the holy and the common, and show them how to distinguish between the clean and the unclean.' The purpose of this is to ensure that what is unclean or common does not cross over into the realm of the holy, which must remain a fit dwelling place for YHWH. That this is indeed the prophet's concern is confirmed by YHWH's own words as he enters the new temple: 'The house of Israel shall no more defile my holy name' (Ezek. 43:7). YHWH's perpetual presence in the sanctuary depends upon its purity, and so Ezekiel offers his audience the vision of a perfectly ordered temple. The sacrificial system, described in detail in Chapters 43–46, has as its primary purpose the maintenance of this perfect order by the removal of impurity from the sanctuary. Kalinda Rose Stevenson has noted that within Ezekiel's design there are *two* most holy locations: the Holy of Holies and the altar, one the

---

[23] Cf. also Ezek. 36:33; 37:23.
[24] Greenberg comments on the relationship between the language of 36:25 and that of the Day of Atonement ritual in Leviticus 16, noting especially that the plural form טמאות appears only in Ezek. 36:25, 29 and Lev. 16:16, 19: M. Greenberg, *Ezekiel 21-37* (AncB, 22A), New York 1997, 730.

symbolic dwelling place of YHWH, the other the place of purgation. Significantly, it is not the Holy of Holies which is the exact centrepiece of the temple complex, but the altar:

> This focus on the Altar expresses the understanding that societal and cosmic well-being needs more than the presence of YHWH. There is also need for a means of cleansing the society and cosmos from the effects of impurity. This is the function of the Altar and the concentric center of the Holy Place, the Portion, and the land. Israel in exile is suffering the results of impurity which drove YHWH into exile. The solution is to cleanse the impurity of society and cosmos by means of the Altar.[25]

Importantly, this determination to prevent the transfer of impurity to the sanctuary is matched by Ezekiel's concern to protect the boundaries of the new community.[26] A 'fortress mentality' is given physical shape in the dimensions of the temple revealed to the prophet. The building complex is conceived in the form of a walled city (Ezek. 40:2), and one aspect of this is that the walls and gates of the temple are substantial defensive fortifications like those of a city. Stevenson points out that only here in the Hebrew Bible (Ezek. 40:5; 42:20) is the word חוֹמָה used to denote temple walls rather than city walls.[27] Ezekiel gives it a ritual role in terms remarkably similar to that given to the priests: 'to distinguish (לְהַבְדִּיל) between the holy and the common' (Ezek. 42:20).[28] Equally a feature of Ezekiel's temple which distinguishes it significantly from the descriptions of both Solomon's temple and the wilderness tabernacle is the size and prominence of its gates. Such gates are nowhere else associated with temple structures, but only cities, and again, their purpose is to defend the holy by controlling access to it. They are the 'first line of defense against

---

[25] K.R. Stevenson, *The Vision of Transformation: The Territorial Rhetoric of Ezekiel 40–48* (SBLDS, 154) Atlanta 1996, 40-1.

[26] As Nelson, *Raising Up a Faithful Priest*, 113, puts it: 'The new temple pattern safeguards more strongly than ever the boundaries of Israel's fundamental culture map'.

[27] Stevenson, *Vision of Transformation*, 44.

[28] Zimmerli draws attention to the connection with 22:26, and comments: 'As the verbal link with 22:26 shows, the office of the priest is visible in it, The measurements of the building are meant to speak. ... The divine ordinance, according to which the sacred should not be polluted, nor inadvertently mixed or confused with the profane because it belongs to God and because God does not wish to be confused with the world, becomes visible in the architectural layout': W. Zimmerli, *Ezekiel 2: A Commentary on the Book of the Prophet Ezekiel Chapters 25-48* (Hermeneia), Philadelphia 1983, 404.

unauthorized access,'²⁹ protecting the temple and the community it serves. Unlike the clearly post-exilic Ezra–Nehemiah, Ezekiel 40–48 is not much concerned with mixed marriages, but it does legislate to prevent foreigners from entering the temple precincts. Ezek. 44:6-8 describes the past sin of admitting foreigners, 'uncircumcised in heart and flesh' into the sanctuary and thereby profaning it. Ezek. 44:9 provides the solution: no foreigners will henceforth be permitted to enter. The Levites will be given responsibility for this; they will act as temple guards, overseeing the gates (Ezek. 44:10-14). In similar vein Katheryn Pfisterer Darr points out that even the more mythical themes we find towards the end of the Temple Vision are far from universalistic in application: a 'wall around paradise' limits the benefits of the renewed land to YHWH's community.³⁰ Thus, the prophet's vision suggests that ritual categories will not only remain fundamental to Israel's future relationship with YHWH, but also substantially define membership of the community.

Even after a brief survey of the relevant material we can see that a concern to employ and teach ritual categories – the essence of priestly instruction – is basic to the portrayal of Ezekiel in the book. In the light of this, what are we to make of Ezekiel's priestly role? Two points suggest themselves. On the one hand, the vision of a fully operational cult in the new city and temple remains a vision: the new sacrificial system is only ot be put into operation after the restoration has been accomplished by YHWH's power and grace. It is clear that for as long as the exile persists, Ezekiel can have no role in sacrifice and atonement, just as Odell suggested should be the case. On the other hand, through action, oracle, and vision he ensures that the categories of clean and unclean, holy and profane, remain fundamental to the interpretation of Israel's experience. Even if, for the most part, they have been transferred from the practical realm to the realm of vision or metaphor, Ezekiel is continuing to perform his priestly task 'to teach my people the difference between the holy and the common, and show them how to distinguish between the unclean and the clean'.

4 The Impact of Ezekiel's Priesthood

What, then, is the impact of this portrayal, and what can we learn from it about the concerns of the book's readers in exile? The one

---

²⁹Stevenson, *Vision of Transformation*, 45: cf. Nelson, *Raising Up a Faithful Priest*, 114.

³⁰K.P. Darr, 'The Wall Around Paradise: Ezekielian Ideas About the Future', *VT* 37 (1987), 271-9: even in the wonderful vision of Chapter 47 no transformation takes place beyond the perimeter of Israel's territory.

thing that emerges most strongly is the extreme tenacity of ritual categories within the Jewish community. Of course, a great deal has been written both about the increased importance given to ritual and purity (most notably in matters of diet, sabbath, and circumcision) in the exile and afterwards. It has been seen as a highly significant feature of the exiles' response to the situation in which they found themselves, and indeed the development of Judaism itself. Nevertheless, on the face of it, it seems surprising that the ritual system so intimately bound up with the operation of the Jerusalem temple should persist not only at such a geographical distance but even after its destruction.

One important attempt to explain the phenomenon in social terms is that of Daniel L. Smith, who has built upon the early work of the British anthropologist Mary Douglas.[31] According to Douglas, where we find a high degree of anxiety about purity and pollution we also find considerable pressure to maintain group boundaries, and indeed anxiety about group boundaries.[32] Smith has extended Douglas's work to the Babylonian exile, comparing the exiled Judaeans with a number of more recent groups of forced migrants, and arguing that 'ritual in minority, dominated contexts may play an important functional role in the preservation and symbolic resistance of the group in question'.[33] Smith concentrates on P, pointing out its emphasis on ritual categories and association of holiness with separation (especially the separation of Israel from foreigners). He concludes that

---

[31] D.L. Smith, *The Religion of the Landless: The Social Context of the Babylonian Exile*, Bloomington, IN 1989. See especially M. Douglas, *Purity and Danger: An Analysis of Concepts of Pollution and Taboo*, London 1966; Idem, *Natural Symbols: Explorations in Cosmology* (2nd edn.), London 1973.

[32] In Douglas's *Natural Symbols*, 59-64, the prime example of such a community is the London 'Bog Irish' of the mid-twentieth century – traditionalist Catholic immigrants who persist in ritual abstinence from meat on Fridays. For these poor Irish in exile, the ritual may have lost much of its original significance as an act of personal mortification (as their more progressive clergy point out), but it has taken on a new significance in providing continuity between the old world and the new: 'No empty symbol, it means allegiance to a humble home in Ireland and to a glorious tradition in Rome. These allegiances are something to be proud of in the humiliations of the unskilled labourer's lot'. Such a picture is highly suggestive of the situation of the Jews in Babylon, and Douglas herself draws the analogy between the Bog Irish Friday abstinence from meat and the Jewish avoidance of pork.

[33] Smith, *Landless*, 84. He has applied Douglas's insights to groups of forced migrants in the modern world who, like the Babylonian Exiles, were moved largely through the exercise of state power. In particular, Smith notes the increased use of ritual as a form of symbolic resistance among the Zionist Bantu churches of South Africa; the Japanese interned in camps by the U.S. government during the Second World War; and groups of African slaves in the American South (80-4).

the exilic redactors of the priestly legislation served their community by providing them with cultic regulations, which could be used as identity markers in the minority context of exile. In this process we might say that the social value of ritual is enough to overcome the cognitive dissonance caused by the loss of the Jerusalem temple.

Smith largely ignores Ezekiel, drawing substantial attention only to Chapter 8, of which he writes: 'The entire chapter of Ezek. 8, which deals with the defilement of the Temple during the exile, is another example, reflecting the horror of impurity among the exiles themselves and their cultic concerns.'[34] However, it is clear that in Smith's terms the degree of ritualization we find throughout the book would be an appropriate response to the crisis of exile, reflecting the tight social boundaries necessary to maintain communal identity. This is perhaps most obvious in Ezek. 40–48, where the elaborate ritual system works together with an express concern to protect the boundaries of YHWH's new community. However, it is also present elsewhere in the book: in practical concerns for purity in exile and above all the metaphorical use of cultic language.

In this context it is noteworthy that such a turn to ritual in the absence of a temple is not unique in the history of Judaism. It is significant that after both 587 BCE and 70 CE we see an increase in the value placed on ritual. Jacob Neusner makes the following comments about the beginnings of rabbinic Judaism in the aftermath of 70 CE:

> When ideas of purity are removed from the physical temple itself they continue to testify to the importance of the temple, for they serve to define communities which compare themselves to the Jerusalem temple, claiming to constitute a surrogate or to replace it. Or they provide metaphors for social virtues or vices which attain transcendent importance because they can be referred back to the cult. The temple in retrospect, therefore, would turn out to be the one point in Israelite life upon which the lines of structure, both cosmic and social, converge. Therefore social values are going in some measure to depend for both vividness and moral authority upon their capacity to find a place within the temple symbolism.[35]

This might equally well be a description of the situation within the book of Ezekiel and one of Mary Douglas's comments about secular rituals is apt: 'Ritual focuses attention by framing: it enlivens the

---

[34] Smith, *Landless*, 145.
[35] J. Neusner, *The Idea of Purity in Ancient Judaism* (SJLA, 1), Leiden 1973, 28-9.

memory and links the present with the relevant past. In all this it aids perception. Or rather it changes perception because it changes the selective principles.'[36] In some respects Ezekiel's priestly instruction acts the same way: by constant reference to ideas of purity and cult, the temple remains as a frame through which members of the community can express and symbolize their experience.

It is important to remember that the relationship between ritual codes and social relationships is a two-way one. A high degree of ritual behaviour does not merely arise out of the experience of a closely-knit group, but is also instrumental in creating the conditions which allow that group its continued distinctiveness, and indeed its existence. Bruce Lincoln likens its role to that of myth: 'Like myth, ritual is best understood as an authoritative mode of symbolic discourse and a powerful instrument for the evocation of those sentiments out of which society is constructed.'[37] As such, ritualization can act as a powerfully creative force in shaping or even creating new group identities. Therefore in Ezekiel, as in P, we may indeed see what Smith calls 'a creative, Priestly mechanism of social survival and maintenance'.[38] If anything, Ezekiel goes further than P by virtue of the fact that the book's central character is himself a priest in exile. In making the most of what is left of his priestly role, the prophet offers a model for resistance, and a buttress against the disintegration of the community.

5   Conclusion

We began with a paradox: to describe Ezekiel as both priest and exile appears contradictory. Exile has put Ezekiel's priesthood in doubt, since without the context of the Jerusalem temple and its complex sacrificial system, the role of 'ritual specialist' appears to be superfluous. Ezekiel's 'priesthood' must surely be a matter of mere genealogy, or at best traditional influence. However, the book's portrayal of the prophet confounds our expectations. Unable to participate in sacrificial ritual or to make atonement for the people he nevertheless takes on what remains to him of his priestly role. The opportunity to teach, and in particular to impress on his hearers the importance of ritual distinctions is still open to him. The practical concern of Ezek. 4:13-15 suggests that ritually appropriate behaviour is still possible, even in an unclean land. The dominance of metaphors drawn from the cult

---

[36] Douglas, *Purity and Danger*, 65.

[37] B. Lincoln, *Discourse and the Construction of Society: Comparative Studies of Myth, Ritual, and Classification*, New York 1989, 53.

[38] Smith, *Landless*, 149.

implies that ritual distinctions are still relevant and important for the community. The vision of a new order supported and enclosed by ritual categories is one which offers both hope for the future and a structure for making sense of the world.

There remains a paradox in Ezekiel being a priest in exile, but it is not quite the one we began with: it is the paradox that even in the absence of the temple and sacrificial system, he still actively promotes the concepts and categories which belong to them. And in this second paradox lies the compelling power of the portrait. It is tempting to see the maintenance of identity as something both simple and conservative, the attempt to hold on to familiar patterns of thought and life. If the world we see revealed through Ezekiel represents the attitudes of even a minority of exiles, then we are witnessing some profound changes in the nature and self-understanding of the community in Babylonia. The real, historically grounded temple is less important than the symbolic power it provides to categorize and explain the experience of the group. Both the experience of domination and the loss of the Jerusalem temple mean that ritual cannot express what it did for the pre-exilic cult (nor indeed what it might mean for a rebuilt second temple). The rituals that provide meaning and continuity no longer belong to the actual worshipping life of the Jerusalem temple, but neither do they have their principal meaning in a nostalgic remembrance of past glory. Rather, the temple that provides their meaning and context is the temple of Ezekiel's vision and imagination. And as the temple is transformed, so too is Ezekiel's priesthood: the performance of his responsibility to teach תּוֹרָה shows him in no 'vestigial' role, but rather one that is powerfully creative - a priestly ministry appropriate to the new context of life in the Diaspora.

Lénart de Regt   *Amsterdam – The Netherlands*

Person Shift in Prophetic Texts
Its Function and its Rendering in Ancient and Modern Translations

1 Introduction

Prophetic texts sometimes refer to God with third person forms, and sometimes with first person forms. In a book like Hosea, such shifts in grammatical person are hardly announced by introductory formulas. The prophet's voice can unsuspectingly mingle with the Lord's. And the people of Israel are alternately referred to in third person and in second person forms which address Israel anew. So the same referent can be referred to with more than one grammatical person.

Change of grammatical person while still referring to the same participant is a text-structuring device: in a context of, say, third person references, the brief changes to second person address forms mark the beginning (or end) of a new paragraph.[1] Change of grammatical person in reference to the same participant is a genre convention and a structuring device in prophecy as well as in poetry. It is not only part of parallelism, as, e.g., in Isa. 42:20 (יִשְׁמָע ... תִּשְׁמֹר '*you* do not observe ... *he* does not hear')[2] and 1:29. In the poem of Prov. 23:29-35, for example, the second stanza begins in v. 31 with a change from interrogatives in third person to direct admonition in second person ('Do not look at wine').[3]

There are some interesting differences here between the 𝔐 and the 𝔊 in prophetic texts. The 𝔊 and, to a lesser extent, other an-

---

[1] Compare M.C.A. Korpel, 'Introduction to the Series Pericope', in: M.C.A. Korpel, J.M. Oesch (eds), *Delimitation Criticism: A New Tool in Biblical Scholarship* (Pericope, 1), Assen 2000, 46: 'Consequently a change of theme, often formally recognizable by a change of subject, may be regarded as an indication that a new paragraph or canticle has started.'

[2] The 𝔊 and 𝔓 apply homogenisation here by translating second person only. The following editions of ancient versions have been used: J. Ziegler (ed.), *Septuaginta Vetus Testamentum Graecum Auctoritate Societatis Litterarum Gottingensis editum*, 13-16/1, Göttingen 1939-57; M.J. Mulder (ed.), *The Old Testament in Syriac according to the Peshitta Version*, vol. 3.3: Ezekiel, Leiden 1985; R. Weber, R. Gryson (eds), *Biblia Sacra iuxta vulgatam versionem*, Stuttgart ⁴1994.

[3] 'To keep the audience interested, the poet breaks his steady sequence of lamedh-initial lines [in third person] and changes to direct admonition (... 31a)' (W.G.E. Watson, *Classical Hebrew Poetry: A Guide to its Techniques* (JSOT.S, 26), Sheffield 1984, 26).

cient versions sometimes show a tendency to homogenise/harmonise grammatical person in a passage. That is to say, in those versions the number of changes from one grammatical person to another tends to be reduced. From a modern translational point of view, this can be a convincing way of meeting the needs and patterns of receptor languages that lack person shift (or in which person shift may exist, but only marginally, or with a different function).

Below a specimen is given of an analysis of Hosea along these lines.[4] In addition, I would like to show to which extent person shift is important in other prophetic books as well, and how ancient versions have handled it there. The question is, (when) should translators follow their example? At least in many receptor languages, the problem may be that reducing the number of person shifts in comparison with the Hebrew text might lead to a loss of impact, even though the translation would be easier to understand.

2 Shift of Person in Hosea and its Homogenisation in Translations

One good reason for choosing Hosea was that this book contains very few introductory prophetic formulas.[5] Instead, the hearer/reader has to determine every time whether it is God or the prophet who is speaking by interpreting the references of grammatical person in the text. The text reflects a situation of oral communication.

2.1 Hosea 2:4-25

This section, which stands in between the narrative framework of chapters 1 and 3, illustrates the structuring role of second person address forms. נְאֻם־יְהוָה 'word of the Lord' (vv. 15, 18, 23) indicates that the Lord's words are quoted by the prophet.

2:4-7	v. 4a	The Lord (first person) addresses Israel in second person.
	vv. 4b-7	The Lord (first person) refers to Israel in third person.

---

[4] With a few alterations, it is taken from L.J. de Regt, 'A Genre Feature in Biblical Prophecy and the Translator: Person Shift in Hosea', in: J.C. de Moor, H. van Rooy (eds), *Past, Present, Future: The Deuteronomistic History and the Prophets* (OTS, 44), Leiden 2000, 230-50 (233-35, 248).

[5] The messenger speech form, based on the appearance of the messenger formula, is lacking in Hosea, Joel, Habakkuk, and Zechariah (M.A. Sweeney, *Isaiah 1-39, with an Introduction to the Prophetic Literature* (FOTL, 16), Grand Rapids, MI 1996, 23).

2:8-17	v. 8a	The Lord (first person) addresses Israel in second person.
	vv. 8b-17	The Lord (first person) refers to Israel in third person.
2:18-22	v. 18	The Lord (first person) addresses Israel in second person.
	vv. 19-20	The Lord (first person) refers to Israel in third person.
	vv. 21-22	The Lord (first person) addresses Israel in second person.
2:23-25		The Lord (first person) refers to Israel in third person.
	v. 25b	In embedded direct speech, the Lord addresses Israel in second person.

In v. 4a, רִיבוּ בְאִמְּכֶם רִיבוּ 'Rebuke your mother, rebuke' contains imperatives and a second person suffix, which address the Israelites, after which Israel is consistently referred to in third person in vv. 4-7, e.g., '*her* children', 'their *mother*'. The distinction between the children and the mother has been related to a distinction between the individual Israelites and the nation of Israel,[6] between the people and the land.[7] However, it is at least plausible that the distinction corresponds with different generations of Israelites; Israel's personification is transgenerational (cf. Zeph. 3:18 below).

V. 8 clearly begins a new paragraph with two particles and a second person reference to Israel. This is immediately followed by third person references in vv. 8b-17. So, although the 'Urteilsverkündigungen' (לָכֵן 'therefore ...') in vv. 11 and 16 as well as in v. 8 follow the preceding 'Urteilsbegründungen',[8] it is only in v. 8 that this occurs with a shift of person. It is here that the whole passage of 2:4-25 is summarised (vv. 8-9).

> Therefore, lo, I will hedge up *your* way with thorns;
> and I will raise a wall against her, so that she cannot find her paths.
> She will pursue her lovers ...
> Then she will say: 'I will go and return to my first husband ...'
>
> (Hos. 2:8-9)

---

[6]W.R. Harper, *A Critical and Exegetical Commentary on Amos and Hosea* (ICC), Edinburgh 1979, 226.

[7]H.W. Wolff, *Dodekapropheton 1: Hosea* (BK, 14/1), Neukirchen-Vluyn 1976, 40.

[8]Wolff, *Dodekapropheton 1: Hosea*, 37.

In line with this, Breytenbach looks at 2:4-15 as a lawsuit in which the direction of speaking changes: the accuser speaks to the judges about the woman but he directly addresses the children in v. 4a and the woman in v. 8, turning away from the judges.[9]

V. 16 begins with the same two particles as v. 8 – לָכֵן הִנֵּה – so that it is often taken as the start of a paragraph as well.[10] After the lawsuit of 2:4-15 which ends with a punishment, it is here in v. 16 that the Lord's positive reaction begins. On the other hand, there is no difference between the formal syntax of לָכֵן here in v. 16 and of לָכֵן in vv. 8 and 11. 'En serie anafórica',[11] all three show a syntactic link with what precedes, even though in v. 16, the particle is used 'in response to an objection'.[12] The third person references to Israel continue until v. 18.

At that point, the introductory clause in v. 18a makes it very clear – and more so than in v. 16 – that another paragraph begins.

> And it shall be on that day – says the Lord –
> that *you* will say, 'my husband', and *you* will not call me 'my Baal'.
> (Hos. 2:18)

With a new section heading, WillV and GrNB indeed make a major paragraph division here at v. 18 and not at v. 16.[13] After v. 18, this new paragraph continues with third person references to Israel. The paragraph ends with vv. 21-22, in which Israel is again addressed with second person forms. The next, and final paragraph of this section, vv. 23-25 ('And it shall be on that day ... – says the Lord – '), stands out because of poetical and stylistic reasons.

---

[9] A.P.B. Breytenbach, 'Hosea 2:4-15 teen die achtergrond van Israelitiese regsgebruike', *Acta Theologica* 1 (1996) 24-40, esp. 26-31. Such a device is referred to in rhetoric as *apostrophe* (Ch. Perelman, L. Olbrechts-Tyteca, *The New Rhetoric: A Treatise on Argumentation*, Notre Dame, IN 1971, 178; Y. Gitay, *Prophecy and Persuasion: A Study of Isaiah 40-48* (FThL, 14), Bonn 1981, 148). Crüsemann analyses how this kind of twofold direction of speaking determines the structure of thanksgiving psalms (F. Crüsemann, *Studien zur Formgeschichte von Hymnus und Danklied in Israel* (WMANT, 32), Neukirchen-Vluyn 1969, 225-51, 264, 273-4, 282-4, 309).

[10] Cf. E.R. Wendland, *The Discourse Analysis of Hebrew Prophetic Literature: Determining the Larger Textual Units of Hosea and Joel* (Mellen Biblical Press Series, 40), Lewiston 1995, 39-40 on לָכֵן; F.I. Andersen, D.N. Freedman, *Hosea: A New Translation with Introduction and Commentary* (AncB, 24), Garden City, NY 1980, 235; Breytenbach, 'Hosea 2:4-15', 26, 37-8.

[11] L. Alonso Schökel, *Diccionario bíblico hebreo-español*, Madrid 1994, 392.

[12] C.H.J. van der Merwe *et al.*, *A Biblical Hebrew Reference Grammar* (Biblical Languages: Hebrew, 3), Sheffield 1999, 304, § 40.12.2.

[13] For the abbreviations of Bible translations see the List of Abbreviations at the end of this volume.

Thus, to a very high extent, second person references help to determine the structure of Hos. 2:4-25. In a context of what are mostly third person references, second person references mark the beginning of new paragraphs.

The 𝕲 translation of Hos. 2:4-25 may well have involved such a homogenising translation strategy, a 'Neigung von LXX, anzugleichen'.[14] In a context of third person references, it has a third person reference – instead of 𝕸's second person reference – in v. 8a (τὴν ὁδὸν αὐτῆς 'her way') and in v. 18 (καλέσει 'she shall call', cf. also *vocabit* in the 𝖁). And immediately before the second person references of vv. 21-22 it already has a second person reference at the end of v. 20, instead of 𝕸's third person form at that point.

καὶ κατοικιῶ σε ἐπ' ἐλπίδι
And I will let *you* dwell in hope.

(end of Hos. 2:20 𝕲)

Similarly, the VSyn as well as NAfrV, CEV and GrNB homogenise the pronominal references to Israel by translating, on the one hand, a third person form at the beginning of v. 8 and, on the other hand, second person forms in v. 19 (because of the second person forms in v. 18). More radically, the GNB has homogenised all second person forms in between v. 4a and v. 21 by translating third person forms throughout these verses, thus probably losing impact.[15] While this could have been avoided in English, the translator has no other solution at his disposal in Bassa, a language spoken in Liberia. In a lawsuit, the accused is never spoken to in second person in this language; it would be too face-threatening.[16]

In 8:6, the 𝕲 translates ὁ μόσχος σου, Σαμάρεια 'your calf, O Samaria' instead of 'the calf of Samaria' (עֵגֶל שֹׁמְרוֹן, 𝕸). The 𝕲 thus homogenises the end of v. 6 with v. 5a (עֶגְלֵךְ שֹׁמְרוֹן τὸν μόσχον σου, Σαμάρεια '*your* calf, *O Samaria*'), presumably because the same words are involved.[17]

2.2 Hosea 11

In Hosea 11, the Lord refers to Israel with third person forms in vv. 1-7, expressing his love for Israel in vv. 3-4.

---

[14]Wolff, *Dodekapropheton 1: Hosea*, 56.

[15]The verse numbering of the Hebrew text is followed.

[16]Don Slager, personal communication. In a situation like this, the translator may still find other ways to indicate where in the text the direction of speaking changes.

[17]The GNB does the reverse; it has third person in v. 5 as well as in v. 6.

בְּחַבְלֵי אָדָם אֶמְשְׁכֵם בַּעֲבֹתוֹת אַהֲבָה
I drew *them* with human ties, with cords of love ...
(Hos. 11:4)

But when the same love is expressed again in vv. 8-9, the Lord addresses it in second person (except in v. 9b), reacting with love to the charge that precedes in vv. 5-7.

אֵיךְ אֶתֶּנְךָ אֶפְרַיִם
How can I give *you* up, Ephraim? ...
(Hos. 11:8)

Thus, vv. 8-9 are not only a return to the same subject for the sake of a concentric pattern, but these verses address Israel anew. In the concentric structure of the chapter,[18] vv. 8-9 (second person) are an intensification of vv. 3-4 (third person) rather than merely a repetition. The person shift in vv. 8-9 occurs in the 𝕲 and 𝖁 as well; these versions have not homogenised the address forms to third person.[19]

3 Other Examples from Prophetic Texts

Person shifts in other prophetic books will now be discussed and compared with the above.

3.1 Amos

In Amos 8-9, Israel is mostly referred to with third person forms. Against this, the second person address forms in 8:4, 8:10 and 9:7 stand out. This helps further to divide the rest of these two chapters into sections. The paragraph of 8:4-10 begins and ends with second person forms, addressing Israel anew. And the start of the paragraph of 9:7-10 is indicated by the second person in 9:7a. In Amos 8-9, then, the situation is quite similar to the one in Hosea.

When we look for person shift earlier in the book of Amos, what becomes clear is that the first occurrence of second person forms of address is only in Amos 2:10. After the other peoples (including Judah),

---

[18] J.C. Siebert-Hommes (personal communication; italics mine): son from Egypt (A, v. 1); away from the Lord (B, v. 2); *the Lord's love for Ephraim (C, vv. 3-4)*; refusal to turn (D, v. 5); sword in the city (E, v. 6); refusal to turn (D', v. 7); *the Lord's love for Ephraim (C', vv. 8-9)*; back to the Lord (B', vv. 10a-c); sons from Egypt (A', vv. 10d-11).

[19] This stands in contrast to their homogenisation in v. 3. The 𝔐 in 11:3 refers to the Lord in third (קָחָם עַל־זְרוֹעֹתָיו '*He* took them on *his* arms', v. 3b) as well as first person. Although קָחָם may not be a third person form, the suffix in זְרוֹעֹתָיו is. But the 𝕲 and 𝖁 actually refer to the Lord in first person throughout this line, in harmony with the context: ἀνέλαβον ... ἐπὶ τὸν βραχίονά μου, *portabam ... in brachiis meis* 'I took ... on my arm(s)'. Most modern translations follow this homogenisation, while they keep the second person forms in vv. 8-9.

only Israel is addressed directly. But in the passage about Israel, in 2:6-16, Israel is not directly spoken to immediately. In vv. 6-9, references to Israel are still in third person. The Translator's Handbook already recommends that

> [I]f some way can be found to continue the style of the previous messages, as though God were still talking about someone else, and then switch dramatically to the more direct form later, as the Hebrew does, this may be very effective in many languages ... This would strongly emphasize that although the message begins the same way as the earlier ones, the implications for the hearers are not the same at all.[20]

At first, Israel is treated just like the other peoples, and then gradually it turns out to be different from the others. By way of 'rhetoric of entrapment',[21] the change from third to second person only takes place in vv. 10-13, more to the end of this section, near the climactic rhetorical question in v. 11. The issue that remains, however, is that it does not occur in v. 9 where one might perhaps have expected it (and where many modern translations have it). Thus, the second person address forms are only used when the Lord's direct dealing with Israel becomes the topic; '[T]he spotlight is on the purpose and goal of the Exodus ... and on the present condition of the people.'[22] This applies to the 𝔐 as well as to the ancient versions. In comparison with the climax that follows, v. 9 only provides background information.

וְאָנֹכִי הִשְׁמַדְתִּי אֶת־הָאֱמֹרִי מִפְּנֵיהֶם	But I destroyed the Amorite for *their* sake ...
וְאָנֹכִי הֶעֱלֵיתִי אֶתְכֶם מֵאֶרֶץ מִצְרָיִם	I even brought *you* out of the land of Egypt ...
הַאַף אֵין־זֹאת בְּנֵי יִשְׂרָאֵל נְאֻם־יְהוָה	... Isn't that so, people of Israel, says the Lord.

(Amos 2:9-11)

When translations, e.g., GNB, have 'for *your* sake' in v. 9, this is an interesting instance of (second person) homogenisation.[23] There is, however, one good reason for translating third person in v. 9. The Lord speaks to Amos (about the people) on the one hand, and through

---

[20] J. de Waard, W.A. Smalley, *A Translator's Handbook on the Book of Amos*, New York 1979, 45

[21] R. Alter, *The Art of Biblical Poetry*, New York 1985, 144.

[22] F.I. Andersen, D.N. Freedman, *Amos: A New Translation with Introduction and Commentary* (AncB, 24A), Garden City, NY 1989, 327.

[23] NAfrV, CEV and GrNB have similar translations with second person already here in Amos 2:9.

Amos to the people on the other within one verse. By keeping the third person reference in v. 9 intact, the translation can show this double-edged nature of prophecy more clearly.

Similar to the climax of second person forms in Amos 2:10-13 (within 2:6-16), there are the second person forms in 5:11-12 in the middle of the section of 5:10-13 (on the 'corruption of justice'[24]). Vv. 10 and 13 refer to (different) people in third person. Again, this suggests that in Amos, second person address forms do not usually mark the beginning or end of a paragraph, as is largely the case in Hosea, but they can help to indicate a climax in the text if third person forms occur before and after.

3.2 Zephaniah

Something quite similar occurs in Zephaniah. The structuring role of shifts to second person in a context of third person forms is not as clear as in Hosea, but they do mark turning points in the text.

In Zeph. 1:2-18, the paragraphs of 1:7-10 and 11-18 both start with second person address forms, addressing the inhabitants anew: הַס 'Hush, be silent' (v. 7), הֵילִילוּ 'Howl' (v. 11). The messages of judgment in chapter 1, mostly in third person, lead to a call to repentance in second person in 2:1-3.[25]

After this first part of the book, the messages of doom in Zeph. 2:4–3:8 are mostly in third person again. In 2:5, vocatives and other second person forms occur with הוֹי 'Woe', a macrosyntactic marker (here after the Masoretic *setumah*). In 2:12, at the point where the geographical direction shifts to the south, another shift to second person takes place.

גַּם־אַתֶּם כּוּשִׁים חַלְלֵי חַרְבִּי הֵמָּה

You too, Ethiopians, fallen by my sword are they[26]   (Zeph. 2:12)

The section of 3:1-8, 'the invective-threat',[27] with third person references to the rebellious city of Jerusalem, only addresses her in second

---

[24]P.R. Noble, 'The Literary Structure of Amos: A Thematic Analysis', *JBL* 114 (1995), 209-26, esp. 211.

[25]D.J. Clark, H.A. Hatton, *A Translator's Handbook on the Books of Nahum, Habakkuk, and Zephaniah*, New York 1989, 163.

[26]The phenomenon of a third person pronoun in a modifying clause after a vocative in poetic and prophetic language is discussed in W. Gesenius, *Hebrew Grammar*, ed. E. Kautzsch, 2nd English ed. A.E. Cowley, Oxford 1910, § 144p; and in D.H. Ryou, *Zephaniah's Oracles against the Nations: A Synchronic and Diachronic Study of Zephaniah 2:1–3:8*, dissertation Free University, Amsterdam 1994, 43-4.

[27]B.S. Childs, *Introduction to the Old Testament as Scripture*, London 1979, 459.

person, with an imperative form, in the 'judgment speech'[28] of v. 8, when the Lord turns out to be her accuser in a lawsuit.

לָכֵן חַכּוּ־לִי נְאֻם־יְהוָה לְיוֹם קוּמִי לְעַד כִּי מִשְׁפָּטִי

Therefore wait for me – says the Lord – for the day when I stand up as an accuser,[29] for my decision is ...

(Zeph. 3:8)

Ryou offers an interesting explanation as to why 3:8 is rhetorically climactic.

> ... Yahweh's scenarios of judgment constantly move from one sphere to another. This movement also provides a profound rhetorical effect on the audience/reader: it starts with the all too familiar geographical direction from south to north (2:4), then expands the scope to include more broadened directions, west-east-south-north (2:5-15). At this juncture, attention has suddenly shifted to an unexpected direction, Jerusalem itself [3:1-8]. Thus the rhetorical effect cannot be missed when this shift occurs. This rhetorical device functions to reinforce the severity of guilt and sin on the part of the unexpected addressee, the city Jerusalem. Then in a comprehensive way, Yahweh's judgment is depicted in a sweeping fashion [3:8]: ... Not only Israel and her neighbours are summoned for judgment, but the whole world also will not escape from the fury of Yahweh's anger.[30]

Crucially, it is exactly here in 3:8 that the shift to second person occurs. Although 3:7a contains second person references as well,[31] these are part of embedded speech (or thought), unlike the rest of v. 7, which still refers to the city in third person.[32] It is only in v. 8 that the second person forms are not due to embedded speech.

אָמַרְתִּי אַךְ־תִּירְאִי אוֹתִי תִּקְחִי מוּסָר
וְלֹא־יִכָּרֵת מְעוֹנָהּ כֹּל אֲשֶׁר־פָּקַדְתִּי עָלֶיהָ
אָכֵן הִשְׁכִּימוּ הִשְׁחִיתוּ כֹּל עֲלִילוֹתָם

I said to the city, 'Surely you will fear me and accept correction!'
Then her dwelling would not be cut off, nor all my punishments come upon her.
But they were still eager to act corruptly in all they did. (NIV)
Je disais: Si tu me craignais, Si tu acceptais la correction ...! Sa demeure ne serait pas détruite ... (Segond)

(Zeph. 3:7)

---

[28] Ryou, *Zephaniah's Oracles*, 279.
[29] Reading עֵד, with most translations, following the 𝔊 and 𝔖.
[31] Singular in the 𝔐 and 𝔙, plural in the 𝔊 and 𝔖.
[32] In the rest of v. 7, the 𝔊 has some second person forms as well as third.

Another shift, that of singular to plural, takes place in v. 7, thus 'shifting from a third person feminine singular personification of the city to the third person plural. [V. 8] picks up on this shift and turns to address the same group with a plural command, i.e., the potentially repentant people of Judah, represented by the people of Judah and its leaders.'[33] This helps to establish the connection between v. 7 (third person) and v. 8 (second person).

In Zeph. 3:9-13, 'the promise',[34] the people are referred to in third person, except for vv. 11-12 in the middle. These second person address forms can be seen as climactic, as was the case in Amos 2:10-13 and 5:11-12. Finally, Zephaniah concludes with a passage on redemption and restoration addressing Israel in second person (3:14-20), a situation similar to the second person address forms in 2:1-3 after chapter 1.

Floyd observes that the commands in 1:7, 1:11, 2:1-3, 3:8 and 3:14 mark turning points in the text.[35] As mentioned above, all these are shifts to second person forms of address. It is of interest that the 𝔊 and ᴰ did not homogenise them with the third person forms in their context.

If Israel is addressed in second person throughout 3:14-20, what is one to make of v. 18, which combines both second and third person feminine singular forms, מִמֵּךְ 'from you' and עָלֶיהָ 'on her'? If these forms were simply to refer to the same addressee, Jerusalem, the third person form would seem out of order in comparison with the second person forms in the context. So most modern translations, including NAfrV, NIV and WillV, apply homogenisation here: they replace this third person form with a second person form, so that Jerusalem is indeed addressed in second person throughout the passage.

But do these forms really refer to the same addressee in the Hebrew? The personification of Jerusalem in this passage applies to more than one generation, i.e., both to the city's inhabitants and to their descendants, the younger generation.

> The transgenerational dimension of the figure is ... evident from the way in which 3:18 combines both second and third person feminine singular forms ... Although there is a shift at 3:18 from nonoracular to oracular prophetic speech, direct address of the same group continues. Yahweh speaks to the younger generation about their predecessors. He announces

---

[33] M.H. Floyd, *Minor Prophets, Part 2* (FOTL, 22), Grand Rapids, MI 2000, 234.
[34] Childs, *Introduction*, 459.
[35] Floyd, *Minor Prophets, Part 2*, 169.

that he has removed the dissident group 'from you' (i.e., the daughter) because they were a burden 'on her' (i.e., the mother).[36]

In other words, the shift of person here does not amount to a shift of person while referring to the same participant and should not be understood as such. Some French translations as well as Floyd have actually maintained the third person as well as the second.[37] Floyd's is slightly different from these translations because it does not adhere to the Masoretic accentuation of הָיוּ.

נוּגֵי מִמּוֹעֵד אָסַפְתִּי
מִמֵּךְ הָיוּ
מַשְׂאֵת עָלֶיהָ חֶרְפָּה׃

Je rassemblerai ceux qui sont dans la tristesse,
privés des fêtes solennelles;
ils sont sortis de toi,
et l'opprobre pèse sur eux. (VSyn)

Je rassemble ceux qui étaient privés de fêtes;
ils étaient loin de toi
– honte qui pesait sur Jérusalem. (TOB)

(Zeph. 3:18)

נוּגֵי מִמּוֹעֵד אָסַפְתִּי מִמֵּךְ
הָיוּ מַשְׂאֵת עָלֶיהָ חֶרְפָּה׃

Those from the assembly who were sorrowful I have removed from you; they were a burden on her, a reproach.

(Zeph. 3:18 Floyd)

Interestingly, the rendering of עָלֶיהָ has remained a third person form in the 𝔊 and ʋ: ἐπ' αὐτήν and *super eis*. At this point, only the ѕ has applied homogenisation by translating with a second person form: ܚܠܝܟܝ. By means of the difference between second and third person, the 𝔐 highlights the difference between the generations. It would be interesting if translations could do the same, for example, by keeping that difference in person intact or by replacing a pronoun with a name, as in TOB. The presence of third as well as second person forms in the 𝔐, 𝔊 and ʋ of 3:19 is due to the same transgenerational dimension.

---

[36]Floyd, *Minor Prophets, Part 2*, 238.
[37]Floyd, *Minor Prophets, Part 2*, 237.

3.3 Isaiah

In Isa. 1:5, the poem changes from third person to second person references to Israel. This switch clearly marks the beginning of a new segment. As long as Israel is being denounced in third person in vv. 2-4, the listener might think that these verses refer to others, but in v. 5 he suddenly learns that he is being addressed himself. After the example of Amos 2:10-13, this is another instance of a rhetoric of entrapment. Sweeney mentions the shift to second person plural address form here in this rhetorical question as one of the elements that challenges the audience to change its behaviour, ending their suffering by ending their apostasy.³⁸ By way of homogenisation, the NAfrV, GNB, CEV, and GrNB already have second person forms in Isa. 1:4. The same type of second person entrapment, following third person forms that refer to the same participant and are part of the same passage, occurs in Isa. 2:5 (בֵּית יַעֲקֹב לְכוּ 'O house of Jacob, come'); 2:22; 3:12, 14b-15; 3:25; 8:8; 10:3 (in rhetorical questions as well); 10:22; 14:3-4; 16:1, 7, 9; 19:11, 12; 24:17; 27:12; 30:3; 30:12; 62:2; 65:7.³⁹ All but the last two examples are from First Isaiah.

The issue of person shift has influenced somewhat the analysis of Isa. 3:25 in its context. The women of Jerusalem are still the subject here, but the shift to second person singular is found to be puzzling.⁴⁰ However, in the passage of 3:16-4:1 about the women of Jerusalem, v. 25, at the beginning of a new section in this passage, is a good place for this person shift as part of the rhetoric of entrapment. In 16:1 (שִׁלְחוּ־כַר מֹשֵׁל־אֶרֶץ 'Send lambs to the ruler of the land'), Moab is finally addressed in second person after the pronouncement against Moab has already started in 15:1 in third person. In chapter 19:1-

---

³⁸Sweeney, *Isaiah 1-39*, 76.

³⁹The 𝔐 maintains the same person shifts, with the exception of homogenisation from second to third person in 16:7, and from third to second person in 30:1-4. The 𝔊 applies homogenisation a bit more often: from third to second person in 1:4 before the second person in 1:5; second person in 3:24 and 26 as well as v. 25; from third to second person in 8:7 and 30:1; and, conversely, from second to third person in 65:7 in a context of third person forms. Among modern translations, the GNB gets rid of second person forms in 3:25; 10:22; 14:3-4; 16:7, 9; 27:12; 30:3; and 65:7, thus often applying homogenisation with the third person forms in the context.

⁴⁰'Die Abgrenzung des Abschnittes ist umstritten und mit der Echtheitsfrage verknüpft. Da auch hier [in 3:25-4:1] Gericht über Frauen angekündigt wird, fasst man die Verse vielfach als Fortsetzung der vorhergehenden auf. Aber die Suffixe stehen in 25 in der 2. Pers. sing. fem. ... Vermutlich ist der Anfang des Wortes bei der Kombination mit dem vorhergehenden Abschnitt weggefallen.' (H. Wildberger, *Jesaja, 1. Teilband: Jesaja 1-12* (BK, 10/1), Neukirchen-Vluyn 1972, 146).

15, Egypt is only addressed directly in vv. 11 and 12 in connection with the wise counsellors of Pharaoh, after various other groups of Egyptians have already been referred to in third person.

אֵיךְ תֹּאמְרוּ אֶל־פַּרְעֹה
בֶּן־חֲכָמִים אָנִי ...
אַיָּם אֵפוֹא חֲכָמֶיךָ

How can you say to Pharaoh:
I am one of the sages ...?
Where are now your sages?

(Isa. 19:11b-12a)

In chapter 24, the imperative in v. 15 is probably part of the people's own direct speech, so the people are only addressed directly in v. 17 (פַּחַד וָפַחַת וָפָח עָלֶיךָ יוֹשֵׁב הָאָרֶץ 'Terror and pit and trap upon you, inhabitant of the earth'). In 27:6-13, after third person references to Jacob/Israel, they are not addressed directly before v. 12 (וְאַתֶּם תְּלֻקְּטוּ לְאַחַד אֶחָד בְּנֵי יִשְׂרָאֵל 'You, children of Israel, will be picked up one by one'). In 30:1-5, the Lord addresses the disloyal people only directly in v. 3, in connection with shame and humiliation (וְהָיָה לָכֶם מָעוֹז פַּרְעֹה לְבֹשֶׁת 'The refuge of Pharaoh will be a shame to you'). In 30:8-17, the people are first referred to in third person but then addressed directly in v. 12, precisely at the point where the transgressions are followed by the Lord's punishment (לָכֵן כֹּה אָמַר קְדוֹשׁ יִשְׂרָאֵל יַעַן מָאָסְכֶם בַּדָּבָר הַזֶּה 'Therefore, thus says the Holy One of Israel: because you have rejected this message'). Finally, in 65:1-7, the people are referred to in third person until v. 7 (עֲוֺנֹתֵיכֶם וַעֲוֺנֹת אֲבוֹתֵיכֶם יַחְדָּו 'your sins and your fathers' sins together').

The Song of the Vineyard, Isa. 5:1-7, contains four strophes, in which person shift is at least one of the structuring devices. The particle וְעַתָּה 'and now' (vv. 3 and 5) marks the beginning of the middle two strophes, vv. 3-4 and 5-6. The beginning of these strophes is marked as well by the second person forms that address the inhabitants of Jerusalem as the accuser in a lawsuit.

שִׁפְטוּ־נָא בֵּינִי וּבֵין כַּרְמִי
... you be the judges between me and my vineyard.

(Isa. 5:3)

In the first and last strophe, the beloved – who turns out to be the Lord of Hosts – is referred to in third person.[41] But in the two middle strophes, the beloved is the speaker himself, as he is referred to not with third, but with first person forms.[42] Gitay describes this as 'the

---

[41] In reference to the beloved, the 𝔊 has first person throughout the poem; the ᵴ continues the first person in the last strophe, in v. 7.

[42] D.J. Clark, 'The Song of the Vineyard: Love Lyric or Comic Ode? A Study

turning of the speech to a new person, thus giving life to the new character. Such a device allows the prophet to confront his audience gradually.'[43] This twofold shift of person in reference to the same participant, the beloved, is indeed '[t]he most remarkable structuring principle in this poem'.[44]

In only a few other passages in Isaiah does person shift in reference to the same participant (Israel or Jerusalem) play a structuring role in a similar way, such as 52:1-6. Chapter 59 and 42:18-25 are of interest because the person shifts involve three persons rather than two. Thus, in 42:18-25 the people are addressed directly in vv. 18, 20, 23, referred to in first person in v. 24c (where the prophet identifies with the people), and in third person elsewhere in the passage.

זוּ חָטָאנוּ לוֹ   against whom *we* have sinned (𝔐)
ᾧ ἡμάρτοσαν αὐτῷ   against whom *they* sinned (𝔊)

(Isa. 42:24c)

The 𝔊 is 'due to contextual harmonisation, in this case to an assimilation to the third person plural verbs' that follow.[45] In 59:2-21 the people are referred to in second person (vv. 2-3), third (vv. 4-8), first (vv. 9-13, where the prophet indentifies with the people as well), third (vv. 14-20), and again second person (v. 21).[46]

In terms of frequency, then, person shift in Isaiah is much more important by way of rhetorical entrapment than as a structuring device. The 𝔊 translation of Isaiah applies homogenisation to person shifts in a number of cases, whereas the 𝔙 mostly maintains the person shifts that occur in the 𝔐.

---

of the Oral and Discourse Features of Isaiah 5.1-7', in: E.R. Wendland (ed.), *Discourse Perspectives on Hebrew Poetry in the Scriptures* (UBS.MS, 7), Reading, UK 1994, 131-46, esp. 134.

[43] Y. Gitay, *Isaiah and his Audience: The Structure and Meaning of Isaiah 1-12* (SSN, 30), Assen, The Netherlands 1991, 99.

[44] M.L. Folmer, 'A Literary Analysis of the "Song of the Vineyard" (Is. 5:1-7)', *JEOL* 29 (1985-86), 106-23, esp. 118.

[45] J. de Waard, *A Handbook on Isaiah* (Textual Criticism and the Translator, 1), Winona Lake, IN 1997, 165, who notes that in the 𝔐, 'the prophet on one side expresses his solidarity with the public guilt, and, on the other hand, takes his distance with regard to those who consciously refuse to obey God. Translators will have to express such subtleties without imposing awkward constructions upon the receptor language.' See also M.C.A. Korpel, J.C. de Moor, *The Structure of Classical Hebrew Poetry: Isaiah 40-55* (OTS, 41), Leiden 1998, 123, n. 16.

[46] In these three passages of 52:1-6, 42:18-25 and 59:2-21, the 𝔙 has the same person shifts. The 𝔊 has the same person shifts in 42:18-25 (except for the homogenising third person in v. 24c) and in 59:2-21 (first person in vv. 11b-14). In 52:1-6, the 𝔊 has a shift to second person (instead of the first person form) in v. 5.

3.4 Micah and Ezekiel

For an example of rhetorical entrapment elsewhere, see Mic. 2:1-5 where, after third person references in vv. 1-3a, the direct address in second person only occurs in vv. 3b-5 (where the Lord in first person announces punishment). So it is interesting that this is how Micah's discussion with his opponents begins. The CEV harmonises the third person forms in vv. 1-3a with the second person forms in vv. 3b-5, translating second person throughout.[47]

In Ezek. 23:2-35, the first message concerning Oholah and Oholibah, alias Samaria and Jerusalem (v. 4), they are referred to in third person until v. 21 where a shift to second person takes place. This corresponds with the transition from story to punishment.

It is important to remind ourselves that we are dealing with person shift in reference to the same participant. So the change of grammatical person in Ezek. 46:13-14 does not count as an example. After third person references (to the prince) in 46:12, the people are addressed directly in vv. 13-14 (תַּעֲשֶׂה 'you shall provide'). Translating with a singular third person form, as in the ancient versions, gives the wrong impression that vv. 13-14 are still about the ruler.[48]

3.5 Obadiah

In comparison with the above texts, the situation in Obadiah is quite different. Shift of person plays its part, but hardly in reference to the same participant in the same section. First, the second person plural – קוּמוּ 'Up!' – and third person singular at the end of v. 1 refer to the nations and to Edom, respectively (as in Jer 49:14). Edom is then addressed throughout vv. 2-16 in second person (except for vv. 6 and 7f-8).[49] After that, only third person forms are used in the book's final

---

[47]The 𝔊 maintains the same person shift in this passage. The ʋ and NAfrV, after translating with second person in Mic. 2:1, maintain the third person in vv. 2-3a. The NAfrV then, in reverse, homogenises the second person in v. 3b with the third person in vv. 2-3a!

[48]This is pointed out in W. Zimmerli, *Ezechiel, 2. Teilband: Ezechiel 25–48* (BK, 13/2), Neukirchen-Vluyn ²1979, 1168, 1174. Compare ποιήσει (𝔊), *faciet* (ʋ), and ܐܬܠ ... ܐܬܡܐ ܪܐܡܐ (s).

[49]As the second person form in v. 16a – שְׁתִיתֶם 'you drank' – is plural, it may well refer to Israel, as some modern translations (GrNB, NAfrV, WillV) have made explicit. On the other hand, it is interesting that the Hebrew text as it stands does not indicate a change of subject here and, as some have pointed out, the text refers to Edom with a plural form anyway in v. 6: נֶחְפְּשׂוּ 'they will be ransacked' (G.Ch. Aalders, *Obadja en Jona* (COT), Kampen 1958, 41; S. Romerowski, *Les livres de Joël et d'Abdias* (ComEvB), Vaux-sur-Seine, France 1989, 273; E. Ben Zvi, *A*

section, vv. 17-21, referring to the house of Jacob gaining victory over the house of Esau. Hence, in the negative passage of vv. 2-16, Edom is spoken to directly, whereas in the positive passage of vv. 17-21, no people are addressed directly at all. Thus, this shift of person, from second to third, seems to indicate that the judgment of Edom should be of more immediate concern to the audience than the epilogue.

3.6 Jeremiah

As in Obadiah, person shift does occur in Jeremiah, but only very infrequently in reference to the same participant in the same section. Rather than person shift, it is the many introductory prophetic formulas in Jeremiah that have a structuring function.[50] The person shift examples to be discussed here are thus the exception rather than the rule. And because of the many differences between the 𝔐 and 𝔊 of Jeremiah, one should not allow text-critical issues to interfere with questions concerning person shift in the various versions.[51]

Some instances are like Zeph. 3:18-19 (and, e.g., Ezek. 6:9, 10, 14) in that a transgenerational dimension is involved. In Jer. 3:2-8 and 7:21-26 the second and third person forms refer to the present generation of Israel and their predecessors, respectively. And in 3:14-18; 13:23b-25; 22:24-27; 46:27; and probably 42:16-17 these forms apply, respectively, to the present and future generation. Looking at it this way, the shift from second to third person in, say, 13:24 does not need to be described as 'awkward'.[52]

Historical-Critical Study of the Book of Obadiah (BZAW, 242), Berlin 1996, 180; see also J. Renkema, *Obadja* (COT), Kampen 2000,173-8. (In v. 16, the second person singular forms ἔπιες in the 𝔊 and *bibisti* in the 𝔙 are harmonisations with preceding singular forms.) Throughout the passage, the real audience is not Edom, but the Israelites. The form of the prophecy concerning a foreign nation 'ultimately addresses Israel even though [as here] it is ostensibly addressed to another nation.' (Sweeney, *Isaiah 1-39*, 26).

[50] On the structuring function of prophetic formulas in Jeremiah, see H. Van Dyke Parunak, 'Some Discourse Functions of Prophetic Quotation Formulas in Jeremiah', in: R.D. Bergen (ed.), *Biblical Hebrew and Discourse Linguistics*, Dallas, TX 1994, 489-519.

[51] For this reason, differences with regard to person in 4:1-2; 8:6; 9:9; 10:19-20; 14:17; and 25:3-5 are left out of the discussion. The question whether the 𝔊 represents an older text of 25:3-5 than the 𝔐, is addressed in, e.g., R.P. Carroll, *Jeremiah* (OTL), London 1986, 490-1; W.L. Holladay, *A Commentary on the Book of the Prophet Jeremiah*, vol. 1: Chapters 1-25 (Hermeneia), Philadelphia 1986, 664; W. McKane, *A Critical and Exegetical Commentary on Jeremiah*, vol. 1: Chapters 1-25 (ICC), Edinburgh 1986, 618-623.

[52] Holladay, *Jeremiah 1-25*, 411.

וְהָיָה כִּי תִרְבּוּ וּפְרִיתֶם בָּאָרֶץ בַּיָּמִים הָהֵמָּה נְאֻם־יְהוָה לֹא־יֹאמְרוּ עוֹד אֲרוֹן בְּרִית־יְהוָה
And when you increase and are fertile in the land, in those days
– oracle of the Lord – they shall no longer speak of the ark of the
covenant of the Lord ...

(Jer. 3:16)

In a context of second person forms, the shift to third person in 2:24 (פֶּרֶה 'a wild ass'), 26 (כְּגַנָּב ... 'like a ... thief'); 3:1 (הָאָרֶץ הַהִיא ... אֶת־אִשְׁתּוֹ 'his wife ... that land'); and 15:7 (בְּמִזְרֶה 'with a winnowing fork') may be caused by figurative language in reference to Israel.[53] In the above examples from Jeremiah, the 𝔊 as well as the ⅴ show the same person shifts.[54]

A rare instance of homogenisation in the ⅴ is to be found in 5:31. After third person references to the people, the 𝔐 and 𝔊 shift to second person at the end of the verse (וּמַה־תַּעֲשׂוּ, καὶ τί ποιήσετε 'and what will you do?'); the ⅴ does not (*quid igitur fiet*). In 51:57 (𝔊 28:57), the 𝔊 homogenises the first person reference to the Lord (as found in the 𝔐 and ⅴ) with the third person references to him in the context.[55]

In the 𝔐 (and ⅴ) of 25:3-5, both the prophet and the Lord are involved; the prophet is the speaker and he refers to the Lord in third person. In the 𝔊 the Lord himself is the speaker throughout the passage so that the prophet is not there in the text itself. Thus, already in vv. 3-5 one finds first person forms instead of the third person forms of the 𝔐. This is in harmony with the first person references to the Lord in the rest of the passage (vv. 6-7). A similar phrase in 7:25 may have contributed to this first person homogeneity in the 𝔊. However, this homogeneity does not imply homogenisation, considering the suggestion from a text-critical point of view, that the 𝔊 text of 25:3-5 came before the redaction found in the 𝔐.

וְשָׁלַח יְהוָה אֲלֵיכֶם אֶת־כָּל־עֲבָדָיו הַנְּבִאִים הַשְׁכֵּם וְשָׁלֹחַ
καὶ ἀπέστελλον πρὸς ὑμᾶς τοὺς δούλους μου τοὺς προφήτας ὄρθρου ἀποστέλλων
And *the Lord* (𝔐) / *I* (𝔊) persistently sent to you *his* (𝔐) / *my* (𝔊) servants, the prophets ...

(Jer. 25:4)

---

[53] Compare Ezek. 22:24, where the phrase אַתְּ אֶרֶץ 'you are a land ...' seems to prompt third person references to the people in the passage that follows, and Ezek. 31:2-18, where the comparison with a cedar in Lebanon (אֶרֶז בַּלְּבָנוֹן, v. 3) prompts third person references in the rest of the passage, and where Pharaoh is only addressed directly in vv. 2, 10, and finally 18.

[54] In 7:25, only the 𝔖 homogenises all the person forms, reading only third person forms ('their fathers ... to them'), as in vv. 24-26.

[55] καὶ μεθύσει μέθῃ 'and *he* will make completely drunk' instead of וְהִשְׁכַּרְתִּי (𝔐) and *et inebrabo* (ⅴ).

וָאֶשְׁלַח אֲלֵיכֶם אֶת־כָּל־עֲבָדַי הַנְּבִיאִים יוֹם הַשְׁכֵּם וְשָׁלֹחַ
καὶ ἐξαπέστειλα πρὸς ὑμᾶς πάντας τοὺς δούλους μου τοὺς προφήτας ἡμέρας καὶ ὄρθρου καὶ ἀπέστειλα
... And I daily and persistently sent to you all my servants the prophets

(Jer. 7:25)

4 Concluding Remarks

Against the background of non-face threatening third person forms, second person forms renew the audience's involvement, addressing Israel anew. A brief change of grammatical person – while referring to the same participant – frequently marks the beginning (or end) of a paragraph. In the book of Hosea, person shift serves both to address the people anew, and to indicate the beginning or end of a paragraph. Thus, person shift is an organising principle at least throughout the book of Hosea.

When in Isaiah the people are addressed anew, this often happens by way of rhetorical entrapment. In several other books (Amos, Zephaniah, Micah), person shift renews the audience's attention as well, for example, towards the end of a paragraph, and particularly at central, climactic points in a paragraph, or in the case of Zephaniah in the text of the book as a whole. However, in these books person shift does not function as a text-structuring device in the way it does throughout Hosea. Neither is this the case in Obadiah, Jeremiah, Ezekiel and the prophets that remain. Still, the shifts to second person renew the audience's involvement.

Ancient versions as well as modern translations sometimes show a tendency to homogenise the alternating grammatical persons in a passage. The ancient versions, though, do this more often in Hosea than elsewhere; in other prophetic books these versions, particularly the Vulgate, seem to maintain the person shifts that are there in the Hebrew text. This suggests that, except in Hosea perhaps, these versions wanted to leave person shifts intact and may have recognised their impact.

From a modern translational point of view, homogenising person shifts can be a convincing way of meeting the needs and patterns of receptor languages that lack person shift (or in which person shift may exist, but with a different function). But to significantly reduce the number of person shifts, particularly shifts to second person, might lead to a loss of impact in comparison with the Hebrew text, even though the translation would be easier to understand.

Klaas Spronk *Amsterdam/Kampen – The Netherlands*

Deborah, a Prophetess
The Meaning and Background of Judges 4:4-5

4 וּדְבוֹרָה אִשָּׁה נְבִיאָה אֵשֶׁת לַפִּידוֹת הִיא שֹׁפְטָה אֶת־יִשְׂרָאֵל בָּעֵת הַהִיא 5 וְהִיא יוֹשֶׁבֶת תַּחַת־תֹּמֶר דְּבוֹרָה בֵּין הָרָמָה וּבֵין בֵּית־אֵל בְּהַר אֶפְרָיִם וַיַּעֲלוּ אֵלֶיהָ בְּנֵי יִשְׂרָאֵל לַמִּשְׁפָּט

4 At that time Deborah, a prophetess, wife of Lappidoth, was judging Israel. 5 She used to sit under the palm of Deborah between Ramah and Bethel in the hill country of Ephraim; and the Israelites came up to her for judgment. (NRSV)

This at first sight simple text calls forth a number of questions. Who was Deborah? Was she really a prophetess, as she is called in Judg. 4:4? Or is this title נְבִיאָה an anachronism, as suggested by many scholars?[1] Was she married to a man called Lapidoth or should this word be taken literary: was she a 'woman of torches', or, more freely translated: 'a spirited woman'? Was she a judge like the male judges of this book or is she rightly left out of the list of judges in 1 Sam. 12:11 and Heb. 11:32? Is the palm tree under which she is said to reside named after her or after another woman?

The person of Deborah has attracted much less attention than the song named after her. On the one hand this is due to the scarce biographical information given in Judg. 4:4-5, part of which is usually regarded as secondary; on the other hand there does not seem to be a problem with regard to the historical reliability of the tradition of this woman in this function. In most commentaries she is compared to the female prophetesses of Mari and Emar or related to female seers among ancient, pre-Islamic Arabs.[2] In this paper I want to present a new theory about the person of Deborah and the place given to her as a prophetess within the story of Israel as recounted in the books Judges, Samuel and Kings. I will tentatively suggest some new answers to the questions formulated above. The basis for this is a new interpretation of Judg. 4:5. In my opinion this verse should not be regarded as a disturbing editorial expansion, but rather as an original

---
[1] Cf. R. Albertz, *Religionsgeschichte Israels in alttestamentlicher Zeit* (GAT, 8/1), Göttingen ²1996, 234, n. 27; A.G. Auld, 'Prophets through the Looking Glass: Between Writing and Moses', in: R.P. Gordon (ed.), *"The Place is Too Small for Us": The Israelite Prophets in Recent Scholarship*, Winona Lake 1995, 289-307 (reprinted from *JSOT* 27 [1983], 3-23).

[2] Cf. among others G. Couturier, 'Débora: une autorité politico-religieuse aux origines d'Israël', *SR* 18 (1989), 213-28, esp. 220-2.

part of the story about the deliverance of Israel from Sisera and his mighty army.

Most commentators agree with the literary critical analysis of Judg. 4:4-5 by Wolfgang Richter,[3] which can summarized as follows. Verse 4a, 'And Deborah, a prophetess, the wife of Lapidoth', belongs together with vv. 6-9 about her conversation with Barak to the oldest redactional layer introducing the story of the battle. The second part of v. 4 and v. 5 can be left out without breaking the story line; on the contrary, the information given in vv. 4b-5 seems to make things unnecessarily complicated. Verse 4b, 'she judged Israel at that time', looks like a later addition relating Deborah in a stereotypical manner (according to the way the judges are described in 2:16, 18) to the judges installed by YHWH to rescue Israel. The secondary character is underlined by the use of the unnecessary personal pronoun הִיא at the beginning functioning as a connecting element and by the use of the expression בָּעֵת הַהִיא at the end, which appears to be typical of editorial passages (cf. Judg. 3:29; 12:6; 14:4 and 'on that day' in Judg. 4:23 which is part of the clearly editorial framework). The information given about Deborah in v. 5 is ascribed to a later editor who wished to explain what was said about Deborah in v. 4b using a similar form: just like v. 4b the next verse begins with הִיא, followed by an active participle. The location of Deborah's activities on a place between Ramah and Bethel, in the tribal area of Benjamin, does not accord well with the fact that the events described in the rest of this chapter take place in a region near the northern border of Israel. To this can be added that the remark about the Israelites coming to Deborah for judgement (לְמִשְׁפָּט) seems to indicate a different use of the verb 'to judge': not the political meaning as in v. 4b and the rest of the book of Judges but in the forensic sense of administering justice. As the reason for the assumed expansion of the text it is usually assumed that a later editor related the Deborah of Judg. 4-5 with the woman bearing the same name who was the nurse of Rebecca and who was,

---

[3] W. Richter, *Traditionsgeschichtliche Untersuchungen zum Richterbuch* (BBB, 18), Bonn ²1966, 37-42; cf. also H.-D. Neef, 'Der Sieg Deboras und Baraks über Sisera: Exegetische Beobachtungen zum Aufbau und Werden von Jdc 4,1-24', *ZAW* 101 (1989), 28-49, esp. 38-40, and U. Becker, *Richterzeit und Königtum: Redaktionsgeschichtliche Studien zum Richterbuch* (BZAW, 192), Berlin 1990, 128-130. Most of his observations are not new and can be found also, for instance, with K. Budde, *Das Buch der Richter* (KHC), Tübingen 1897, 34-5, and G.F. Moore, *Critical and Exegetical Commentary on Judges* (ICC), Edinburgh ²1908, 113-4. See of the modern commentaries, amongst others, J. Gray, *Joshua, Judges, Ruth* (NCB), Grand Rapids 1986, 202, and B. Lindars, *Judges 1-5: A New Translation and Commentary*, Edinburgh 1995, 181-4.

as can be read in Gen. 35:8, buried under an oak below Bethel. According to Lindars 'the later editor, knowing the place, has decided that it was the right place for Deborah simply because the name was the same. This was not necessarily due to simple-minded confusion, but was the result of an hermeneutical principle, whereby one passage of scripture is elucidated by reference to another. In this case it furnished the location of Deborah, which was not given in the text.'[4]

This explanation of v. 5 is not in all aspects convincing. If Lindars is right in assuming that a later editor used Gen. 35:8 to fill the gap of information left in Judg. 4, then why did he not cite it properly? In Gen. 35:8 we hear of Rebecca's nurse Deborah being buried 'under the oak below Bethel' and that this oak received on this occasion the name 'oak of weeping' (אַלּוֹן בָּכוּת). Why does the assumed editor not speak in Judg. 4:5 of an oak, but instead of a palm tree or, to be more precise, of תֹּמֶר, using an uncommon vocalization? A commonly accepted bridge between these names was constructed by Richter.[5] He relates both trees to 'the oak of Tabor' (אֵלוֹן תָּבוֹר) mentioned in 1 Sam. 10:3, which is also located in the vicinity of Bethel. This would be according to an old suggestion a corruption of אֵלוֹן דְּבוֹרָה, 'the oak of Deborah'. This does not explain, however, the use of the word תֹּמֶר in stead of the expected אֵלוֹן. According to Lindars[6] the unusual vocalization might indicate 'a different tree from the various kinds of palm (...) it might denote any tree.' Why did the editor not use then, one could ask, the normal word in Hebrew for tree?[7] More to the point seems to be the explanation of this word by Penna[8] as polemically vocalized with the vowels of בֹּשֶׁת, 'shame', indicating that we are dealing here with a pagan cult object. Lindars reports this suggestion, but does not accept it. In my opinion, however, this could very well be a first clue to a better understanding of this verse.[9]

Another problem concerning the view that Judg. 4:5 is the work

---

[4]Lindars, *op. cit.*, 183.

[5]Richter, *op. cit.*, 40; cf. also *HALAT*, 1617.

[6]Lindars, *op. cit.*, 183.

[7]Cf. also B. Halpern, *The First Historians: The Hebrew Bible and History*, San Francisco 1988, 91: 'the substitution of the palm for an oak is not an error that a historian stealing a literary tradition makes. Are trees the same or are they not? (...) the logical explanation for the tradition is that the prose narrator (or a source) knew of a tree named for Deborah; oblivious to the etiology in Genesis 35:8, he assumed the tree commemorated the activity of a major historical figure. In other words, Deborah's location arose from (possibly older) deduction'.

[8]A. Penna, *Giudici e Rut*, Turin 1963; cited by Lindars and also by J.A. Soggin, *Judges* (OTL), London 1981, 64.

[9]Possibly the difficult תֹּמֶר מִקְשָׁה in Jer. 10:5 which describes a pagan idol was also vocalized after בֹּשֶׁת.

of a later editor has to do with the use of the expression לְמִשְׁפָּט. Most commentators agree that it is used in a different way than the verb שפט in v. 4b. It is usually interpreted in the sense of administering justice,[10] but this would be the only place in the book of Judges where it would have this meaning. There are no other examples of people called 'judge' in this book being described as acting in this way. The closest parallel for this would be 1 Sam. 7:15-17,[11] which is usually interpreted as an editorial expansion clarifying Samuel's role as one of the judges.[12] Here we read how Samuel worked as a judge in Israel, but in these verses only the verb שפט is used and not the expression לְמִשְׁפָּט and it is not necessary to think here of other activities than political or sacral.

Becker speaks of the 'altertümlich wirkende Inhalt' of v. 5.[13] Apparently this is caused by the two elements mentioned above: the location and the use of לְמִשְׁפָּט, that can not be simply explained as editorial. His conclusion, however, is: 'ob v. 5 (...) alte Überlieferung enthält, ist kaum zu entscheiden, aber eher unwahrscheinlich: Der Vers erklärt sich gut als Interpretation und Konkretisierung des vorgegebenen, von DtrH formulierten v. 4'.[14] There are, however, too many difficulties in seeing v. 5 simply as a later added clarification of some elements in v. 4 and there is enough reason to consider more seriously the possibility of v. 5 containing the oldest tradition to which v. 4a and v. 4b have been added. It was already suggested by Smend, that contrary to the common scholarly opinion Judg. 4:4b-5 could have been based on a historically reliable tradition. The authority of the prophetess and the place where she resided would explain why according to the song of Deborah the battle against the Canaanites was not restricted to the northern tribes but concerned all tribes of Israel.[15]

Let us look again, in the first place, at the use of לְמִשְׁפָּט in v. 5b. Boling suggests that 'it stands for her decision in response to a particular inquiry'[16] and should be compared to the use of מִשְׁפָּט in

---

[10] Cf. Neef, art. cit., 39; B. Johnson, 'מִשְׁפָּט', ThWAT, Bd. 5, 97, and H. Niehr, 'שפט', ThWAT, Bd. 8, 425.

[11] Cf. Moore, op. cit., 113, and W. Richter, Die Bearbeitungen des 'Retterbuches' in der deuteronomistischen Epoche (BBB 21), Bonn 1964, 123-5.

[12] Cf. P. Kyle McCarter, I Samuel (AncB), Garden City 1980, 147-8.

[13] Becker, op. cit., 129; cf. also Richter, op. cit., 40-41.

[14] Becker, op. cit., 130.

[15] R. Smend, Jahwekrieg und Stämmebund: Erwägungen zur ältesten Geschichte Israels, Göttingen 1963, 42-5: 'Die Mitwirkung der mittelpalästinensischen Stämme ließe sich aus dem Einfluß der in ihrer Mitte wohnenden und dem Wortlaut unserer Stelle nach mit hoher Autorität begabten Frau erklären' (43).

[16] R.G. Boling, Judges (AncB), Garden City 1975, 95; this suggestion is rejected

Judg. 13:12 ('What will be the judgment of the boy?'). It is interesting to note that this inquiry comes from a human, Manoah, and is addressed to a divine messenger. The action described in Judg. 4:5 can be interpreted in the same way: the people of Israel come to Deborah to receive with her help a divine oracle.[17] מִשְׁפָּט would have been used here then in a way comparable to the expression חֹשֶׁן מִשְׁפָּט, 'the breast-piece of judgement' in Exod. 28:15 denoting the place where the priest kept the Urim and Thummim, the means by which an oracle of God could be asked. This use of מִשְׁפָּט can also be related to Ugaritic *mtpt* in the mantic text KTU 1.124.[18] In this text the deified ancestor of the royal family seems to give an answer to a scorcerer, called 'the lord of the great gods', on a question about the fate of an apparently sick boy child. This answer is indicated as his 'judgement' (*mtpt*). We are dealing here with a form of necromancy.[19] Could this also be the background of the situation described in Judg. 4:5? The given location can be interpreted as an indication pointing in this direction. תֹּמֶר דְּבוֹרָה usually translated as the 'palm tree of Deborah', between Ramah and Bethel, can be related to the place south of Bethel where according to Gen. 35:8 Deborah, the nurse of Rebecca, was buried. One can imagine that the tomb of a person honoured as a helper in lifetime could have become a place for consulting the dead. Halpern makes the interesting observation that 'nurse of Deborah' can be interpreted as a subjective genitive: not the woman who nursed Rebecca, but the woman who helped Rebecca by nursing her son, namely Jacob. This suggestion, supported by the timing of her death, would offer an even more likely candidate for this function of postmortal adviser to 'the sons of Israel'.[20] As was remarked earlier, it is not clear how the oak of Gen. 35 turned into a palm tree,

---

by Soggin, *op. cit.*, 64.

[17] This possible meaning is also mentioned by Johnson, *art. cit.*, 96 (with more literature); cf. also D.I. Block, 'Deborah among the Judges: The Perspective of the Hebrew Historian', in: A.R. Millard *et al.* (eds), *Faith, Tradition, and History: Old Testament Historiography in Its Near Eastern Context*, Winona Lake 1994, 229-53, esp. 238-46.

[18] Cf. *TUAT*, Bd. 2, 329-331, and (with a survey of previous research) O. Loretz, 'Nekromantie und Totenevokation in Mesopotamien, Ugarit und Israel', in: B. Janowski *et al.* (eds), *Religionsgeschichtliche Beziehungen zwischen Kleinasien, Nordsyrien und dem Alten Testament* (OBO, 129), Göttingen 1993, 285-318, esp. 289-93; see on the suggested parallel with Judg. 4:5 also M. Dietrich, O. Loretz, *Mantik in Ugarit: Keilalphabetische Texte der Opferschau – Omensammlungen – Nekromantie* (ALASP, 3), Münster 1990, 238.

[19] Cf. K. Spronk, 'Incantations', in: W.G.E. Watson, N. Wyatt (eds), *Handbook of Ugaritic Studies* (HdO), Leiden 1999, 270-86, esp. 284.

[20] Halpern, *op. cit.*, 102, n. 27.

if indeed תֹּמֶר has to be translated this way. Maybe we should not look, as suggested by Richter, at 'the oak of Tabor' of 1 Sam. 10:3, but at Judg. 20:33 referring to a place in the same neighbourhood, north of Gibea and south of Bethel, called Baaltamar (בַּעַל תָּמָר). Its precise location is not known, but it seems to be not too farfetched to assume a relation with תֹּמֶר דְּבוֹרָה. It would offer the solution to the problem of the uncommon vocalization. As was noted by Penna[21] the vowels are probably taken from בֹּשֶׁת 'shame'. This pejorative reference is usually connected with elements of the rejected Baal cult, as can be seen in the names Ishboshet and Mephiboshet replacing the original Ishbaal and Mephibaal.[22] The name of the pagan god Molech, who can be regarded as the chthonic aspect of Baal, representing this god of fertility during his stay in the netherworld,[23] can be explained as a similar distortion of the original *melek*.[24] All this renders it likely that the תֹּמֶר of Judg. 4:5 refers to a place originally connected with some kind of Baal cult like the cult of Baal Peor, which could very well have included necromancy.[25] The name Tomer Deborah can be interpreted then as a combination of an indication of this kind of cult practised there and the name of the venerated ancestor, Deborah, who acted as a spokeswoman of the divine world.[26]

Originally the story of Judges 4 seems to have told of Israelites who suffered under the yoke of a Canaanite king and went to a woman performing necromancy to get advise.[27] The situation would be the

---

[21] See n. 9 above.
[22] Cf. H.D. Galter, 'Bashtu', in: *DDD*[2], 164.
[23] Cf. K. Spronk, *Beatific Afterlife in Ancient Israel and in the Ancient Near East* (AOAT, 219), Neukirchen-Vluyn 1986, 188, 232-3.
[24] Cf. G.C. Heider, 'Molech', *DDD*[2], 581.
[25] Cf. K. Spronk, 'Baal of Peor', *DDD*[2], 147-8.
[26] Because of this location and its probable meaning we can not agree with Block, *art. cit.*, 241-7, that Deborah is presented here as a positive alternative to a degenerate priesthood. His suggestion is based of the interpretation of 1 Sam. 2:12-13 as indicating that the sons of Eli 'did not know YHWH or the oracles of the priests (מִשְׁפַּט הַכֹּהֲנִים)' and on the assumption that 'the demise of the priesthood outdated the ministry of Samuel' (242). Deborah would have been a legitimate alternative to this degenerate priesthood. It is more likely, however, dat מִשְׁפָּט has the same meaning here as in Deut. 18:3, namely the 'due portion' of the offering; cf. Kyle McCarter, *op. cit.*, 78.
[27] According to Lindars, *op. cit.*, 184, the consecutive verb וַיַּעֲלוּ continues the past continuous sense of יוֹשֶׁבֶת. He translates 'they used to come up'. It is more consistent, however, to put וַיַּעֲלוּ on the same level as the *wayyiqtol* forms in vv. 1-3; cf. E. van Wolde, 'Deborah and Ya'el in Judges 4', in: B. Becking, M. Dijkstra (eds), *On Reading Prophetic Texts: Gender Specific and Related Studies in Memory of Fokkelien van Dijk-Hemmes* (BInt.S, 18), Leiden 1996, 283-295, esp. 287.

same then as in 1 Sam. 28, where Saul, threatened by a Philistine army, seeks help from the woman of Endor. She is called 'mistress of a spirit of the dead' (בַּעֲלַת־אוֹב 1 Sam. 28:7). This probably indicates that she had contact with one special person from the realm of the dead acting as an intermediary between her and other spirits of the dead.[28] This is a common feature in ancient and modern spiritistic literature. As in the Ugaritic text referred to above this venerated ancestor is mentioned by name. In KTU 1.124 we hear of Ditanu, in Judg. 4:5 the name is Deborah. Originally the human person performing the necromancy probably remained anonymous, just as the woman of Endor.

As this old story became part of the history of Israel as one nation with one God who leaves no room for any other divine authority this now dubious context of necromancy had to be changed. For this reason the anonymous scorceress and the venerated spirit of a dead person called Deborah were taken together and reformed to Deborah the prophetess.

She was introduced in a manner similar to the presentation of Ehud in Judg. 3:15: 'Ehud, son of Gera, a Benjaminite, a man cripled in his right hand', and of Jephthah in Judg. 11:1: 'And Jephthah, the Gileadite, was a mighty warrior and he was the son of a prostitute and Gilead had sired Jephthah'. So first comes the name and this is followed by some personal information.[29] In the case of Deborah we hear relatively little about her family. Another peculiarity is the reference to her profession. This has no parallel in the otherwise related introductions and thus attracts extra attention. אִשָּׁה נְבִיאָה can be regarded as the counterpart of the אֵשֶׁת בַּעֲלַת־אוֹב; of 1 Sam. 28:7, the woman Saul went to because God did not speak any more through the prophets (1 Sam. 28:6, 15). As was already suggested by Jepsen,[30] the title נְבִיאָה has been given to Deborah in a later stadium. We can add now that this is done to mark and to secure the distinction between the correct and the more dubious ways of making contact with the world of the divine. It is also in line with the observation of Graeme Auld and others about the title נָבִיא as added to the stories of early Israel in a later stage.[31]

---

[28] Cf. Spronk, *op. cit.*, 254; cf. also the title 'lord of the great gods' (*'adn 'ilm rbm*) in the Ugaritic text KTU 1.124 mentioned above. For other parallels from the Ancient Near East see J.C. de Moor, *The Rise of Yahwism: The Roots of Israelite Monotheism* (BEThL, 91A), Leuven ²1997, 101-2, 317-69.

[29] Cf. Richter, *op. cit.*, 12-3, 37.

[30] A. Jepsen, *Nabi: Soziologische Studien zur alttestamentlichen Literatur und Religionsgeschichte*, München 1934, 151, n. 2; cf. also Smend, *op. cit.*, 45.

[31] Cf. Auld, *art. cit.* and 'Prophets and Prophecy in Jeremiah and Kings', *ZAW*

Another remarkable element in the way Deborah is presented here is that we hear nothing of her father or her tribe. Instead, she is said to be אֵשֶׁת לַפִּידוֹת. At first sight this seems to be no more than the indication that Deborah was a married woman: the wife of an otherwise unknown man called Lapidoth. As with Ehud and Jephthah one would expect this information to serve a certain goal. According to Malamat we should compare it to one of the prophetesses mentioned in the Mari letters being called 'the wife of a man'.[32] He assumes that this was done here and also in the case of the prophetess Huldah, 'the wife of Shallum' (2 Kgs 22:14) 'to stress their stability and reliability'.[33] Susan Ackerman sees this less positively as the attempt of a male redactor to 'domesticate' the female cultic functionary Deborah. In Judg. 5 she still appears without this 'woman's customary trapping of a husband'.[34] One can also think, however, of a symbolic meaning of this name, because in the normal plural form לַפִּידִם it can be used as another word for 'lightning', which is the meaning of the name Barak.[35] Some take it as an indication of her character: 'an inflamed and inflaming woman'.[36] When we take a good look at the Hebrew text we note that the first words of v. 4 can be read as a poetic line with אִשָּׁה נְבִיאָה being parallel to אֵשֶׁת לַפִּידוֹת. This is supported by the fact that לַפִּידוֹת has a feminine ending instead of the common masculine. This may be due to the influence of the feminine ending of the parallel נְבִיאָה.[37] For this reason it seems most likely that לַפִּידוֹת

---

96 (1984), 66-82.

[32] aššat awîlim in: *ARM*, T. 13, 114, 8.

[33] A. Malamat, 'Prophecy at Mari', in: Gordon, *op. cit.*, 50-73, esp. 63-4.

[34] S. Ackerman, *Warrior, Dancer, Seductress, Queen: Women in Judges and Biblical Israel* (AncB Reference Library), New York 1998, 108.

[35] Cf. the use of לַפִּידִם in Exod. 20:18; cf. Lindars, *op. cit.*, 182, referring to an idea already found in the commentary of Kimchi that Barak and Lapidoth are one and the same person. A. Bedenbender, 'Biene, Fackel, Blitz: Zur Metaphorik der Namen in der Deborageschichte (Ri 4-5)', *TeKo* 76 (1997), 43-55, esp. 51-2, adds another suggestion: 'als Umkehrung von *lappid esch*, der Feuerfackel' mentioned in Gen. 15:17; Zech. 12:6; and Dan. 10:6.

[36] M. Bal, *Death and Dissymmetry: The Politics of Coherence in the Book of Judges*, Chicago 1988, 209. NEB suggests in a footnote as a possible translation 'spirited woman'. Cf. also the remarks by R. Breuer, *Das Buch der Richter*, Frankfurt a.M. 1922, 35: 'was kümmert uns, nachdem wir wissen, daß Deborah אשה נביאה gewesen ist, wie der Mann hieß, dessen Gattin sie war? Nicht einem obskuren Lapidoth, den Flammen war sie vermählt, die von der Leuchte der Heiligtums strahlen. Und diese Flammen des Heiligtums wurden von ihr in das Herz des Völkes getragen. Was in "jener Zeit" kein Mann vermochte, die Wiedererhebung des Volkes anzubahnen, Debora, dem "Weibe zündender Begeisterung" ist's gelungen.'

[37] Cf. the remark by Van Wolde, *art. cit.*, 287, n.5 (also in 'Ya'el in Judges 4',

denotes Deborah as the counterpart of Barak. On the other hand this name can be regarded as symbolic for her relation with God, as can be derived from the fact that this word is mentioned in descriptions of the theophany in Gen. 15:17, Exod. 20:18 and Ezek. 1:13.

We may now even go one step further and consider the possibility that the name Deborah as used by the later editor is also meant symbolically.[38] Being explicitly introduced here as a prophetess, her name recalls the fact that a prophet is automatically associated in the Old Testament with the word דָּבָר he or she speaks in the name of God (cf. Deut. 18:18 and especially Jer. 18:18: 'the law shall not perish from the priest, nor counsel from the wise, nor the word from the prophet'). In stead of the usual translation with 'bee' דְּבוֹרָה could very well have been associated in the present context with דָּבָר: 'the woman of the word'.[39] This is also supported by the wordplay of the name Deborah with the verb דבר in Judg. 5:12. The prophetess seems to have been named in this first place after the location where she was said to have worked. In this way the editor who was responsible for the careful adaptation of the old tradition described in Judg. 4:5 was able to repress any remaining idea of a relation with a spirit of the dead and necromancy: Deborah was to be regarded as a prophetess and as nothing else.

Verse 4b, 'she judged Israel at that time', can be ascribed to a still later redaction, in which Deborah is given her place among the

---

ZAW 107 [1995], 240-6, esp. 240, n. 4) that the female plural form 'can perhaps be explained from the fact that in this text it is associated with a woman'.

[38] There appear to be relatively many examples of symbolic names in the book of Judges, like Cushan Rishathaim in 3:8, Haroshet-Hagoim in 4:2, Samson, Delilah, and probably also Manoah in Ch. 13-16; cf. also M. Garsiel, 'Homiletic Name-Derivations as a Literary Device in the Gideon Narrative: Judges VI-VIII', *VT* 53 (1993), 302-17.

[39] Cf. K.A. Deurloo, in: H. Blok *et al.*, *Geen koning in die dagen: over het boek Richteren als profetische geschiedschrijving*, Baarn 1982, 37-8; F. van Dijk-Hemmes, *Sporen van vrouwenteksten in de Hebreeuwse Bijbel*, Utrecht 1992, 183; B.-J. Diebner, 'Wann sang Deborah ihr Lied? Überlegungen zu zwei der ältesten Texte des TNK (Ri 4 und 5)', *ACEBT* 14 (1995), 106-30, esp. 114 (he translates the name Deborah as 'Wörtin'). The least one can say about this theory is that it makes more sense than some interpretations based on the translation of the name Deborah with 'bee': (1) the theory by J.G. Williams, 'The Structure of Judges 2.6-16.31', *JSOT* 49 (1991), 77-85, that the book of Judges is constructed according to the cycle of the solar year, in which Deborah ('bee') and Barak ('lightning') appear as 'signs of spring' (83); (2) the 'apicultural' interpretation of Judg. 4–5 by B.A. Asen, 'Deborah, Barak and Bees: *Apis mellifera*, Apiculture and Judges 4–5', *ZAW* 109 (1997), 514-33, reading the story along the lines of the life cycle of a honey bee colony.

judges.⁴⁰ Following the analysis of Richter many scholars assume that v. 4b and v. 5 belong to the same deuteronomistic edition with v. 5b explaining Deborah's work as a judge. Our study may have made clear that it is more likely to see things precisely the other way. The historically more reliable but theologically hard to accept tradition of v. 5 was adapted to the later Yahwistic standards; first by turning the woman mediating divine oracles with the help of necromancy into a prophetess, a woman speaking only the word of YHWH, secondly by placing her in the ranks of the judges. The latter was done despite the fact that she never really acted as a judge and was therefore rightly left out in the list of judges in 1 Sam. 12:11.

All this is admittedly no more than a hypothesis partly based on circumstantial evidence, but there are some clear advantages compared to the older historical critical interpretation. We were able to find some more or less plausible answers to the questions formulated at the beginning about the person of Deborah and her function. The theory presented here may also shed some new light on the ongoing discussion about the relation between Judg. 4 and Judg. 5.⁴¹ It may be worthwhile to look with extra attention at the places in these chapters where Deborah is mentioned by name because of its possible secondary nature. We already noted above the wordplay with the name of Deborah in 5:12:⁴²

עוּרִי עוּרִי דְּבוֹרָה עוּרִי עוּרִי דַּבְּרִי־שִׁיר

Awake, awake, Deborah, awake, awake, utter a song.

This is not the place to go into further detail, but it is interesting to note that the syntactical structure of another verse mentioning Deborah, Jud. 5:7b, causes problems to the interpreter. The verb in the first person is followed directly by the name of Deborah. One

---

⁴⁰See, next to the remarks above about the litery critical analysis of this verse, also K.-D. Schunk, 'Falsche Richter im Richterbuch', in: R. Liwak, S. Wagner (eds), *Prophetie und geschichtliche Wirklichkeit im alten Israel: Festschrift für Siegfried Herrmann*, Stuttgart 1991, 364-70, stating that Deborah and Eli were actual persons made a judge only by the late deuteronomistic redaction.

⁴¹Of the recent literature, cf. Halpern, *op. cit.*, 76-103, and H.-D. Neef, 'Deboraerzählung und Deboralied: Beobachtungen zum Verhältnis von Jdc. IV und V', *VT* 44 (1994), 47-59, defending the theory that Ch. 5 is the eldest and that Ch. 4 depends on it. This widely held view is challenged by A. Caquot, 'Les tribus d'Israel dans la Cantique de Débora (Juges 5,13-17)', *Sem.* 36 (1986), 47-70, and M. Waltisberg, 'Zum Alter der Sprache des Deboraliedes Ri 5', *ZAH* 12 (1999), 218-32. See on this discussion also Van Dijk-Hemmes, *op. cit.*, 191-206, and A. van der Kooij, 'On Male and Female Views in Judges 4 and 5', in: Becking, Dijkstra (eds), *op. cit.*, 135-52.

⁴²Cf. Van der Kooij, *art. cit.*, 145.

would have expected the insertion of the personal pronoun before the name.[43] In another verse speaking of Deborah, Judg. 5:15, there is a problem with the use of the first person as well.[44] In Judg. 5:7 Deborah receives the title 'mother in Israel' (אֵם בְּיִשְׂרָאֵל). Within the song she is contrasted in this way to Sisera's mother (v. 28),[45] but it also seems to relate her to the later prophets Elijah and Elisha, who are both called 'father, chariots and horsmen of Israel' (2 Kgs 2:12; 13:14).[46] Within the theory of the prophetess Deborah as a secondary element one could consider the possibility that like the title 'prophetess' the title 'mother' is added to the text and derived from later traditions about the prophets in Israel.

We may conclude with a general observation about the role of prophets and prophecy in the stories in the books Judges, Samuel and Kings. The proposed interpretation and suggested background of Judg. 4:4-5 can be related to the view that the story of the אִישׁ נָבִיא in Judg. 6:7-10 sent by YHWH to Israel, is a later addition.[47] We seem to be dealing here with a redaction introducing Deborah as an example of all following prophets. This is apparent in the titles given to her and also in her relation to the political leader, which has clear parallels in the later stories about Samuel and Saul,[48] Nathan and David, Elijah and Ahab. In its present form this has to be regarded as literary fiction. The historical reality, which has left its traces in the literary sources, is that ancient Israelite prophecy only gradually and later than suggested in stories like Judg. 4 broke free from the common ancient Near Eastern mantic practices like necromancy.

---

[43] Cf. Lindars, *op. cit.*, 238.

[44] Cf. Van der Kooij, *art. cit.*, 146.

[45] Cf. Bal, *op. cit.*, 206-11, and Lindars, *op. cit.*, 238.

[46] Cf. K. Baltzer, *Die Biographie der Propheten*, Neukirchen-Vluyn 1975, 66, n. 240, and Block, *art. cit.*, 247-8, n. 67.

[47] Cf. A.G. Auld, 'Prophets and Prophecy in Jeremiah and Kings', *ZAW* 96 (1984), 79; cf. also the remark by L.R. Klein, *The Triumph of Irony in the Book of Judges*, Sheffield 1988, 50, about the sending of 'a man, a prophet': 'This recalls 4.4, in which Deborah is introduced as "a woman, a prophetess". The reader is primed for high expectations. If a woman prophetess could be as effective as Deborah, what will "a man, a prophet" be able to achieve?'

[48] Cf. Van der Kooij, *art. cit.*, 141, n. 11 and 12.

Abbreviations

All abbreviations of series, handbooks and journals in this volume are according to: S.M. Schwertner, *Internationales Abkürzungsverzeichnis für Theologie und Grenzgebiete*, Berlin ²1992 (= S.M. Schwertner, *Theologische Realenzyklopädie: Abkürzungsverzeichnis*, Berlin/New York ²1994). In addition the following abbreviations were used.

BInt	Biblical Interpretation (Leiden).
BBR	*Bulletin for Biblical Research* (Winona Lake).
CEV	Contemporary English Version.
ComEvB	Commentaire Évangélique de la Bible (Vaux-sur-Seine).
CurResB	Currents in Research: Biblical Studies (Sheffield).
DCH	D.J.A. Clines (ed.), *The Dictionary of Classical Hebrew*, Sheffield 1993– .
DDD	K. van der Toorn *et al.* (eds.), *Dictionary of Deities and Demons in the Bible*, Leiden 1995; Leiden & Grand Rapids ²1999.
DtIsa	Deutero-Isaiah.
GNB	Good News Bible.
GrNB	Groot Nieuws Bijbel.
HThK.AT	Herder's Theologische Kommentar: Altes Testament (Freiburg i.B.).
JB	Jerusalem Bible.
LV	Leidse Vertaling.
NAfrV	New Afrikaans Version.
NBG	Nieuwe Vertaling (Nederlands Bijbelgenootschap).
NEB	The New English Bible.
NIV	New International Version.
PrIsa	Proto-Isaiah.
REB	The Revised English Bible.
SAA	State Archives of Assyria (Helsinki).
ScrC	Scripture in Context (Lewiston).
Segond	Nouvelle Version Segond Révisée.
SHCANE	Studies in the History and Culture of the Ancient Near East (Leiden).
SV	Statenvertaling.
TOB	Traduction Oecuménique de la Bible.
TrIsa	Trito-Isaiah.
VSyn	Version Synodale.
WBC	Word Biblical Commentary (Waco, TX).
WillV	Willibrordvertaling.
ZAR	*Zeitschrift für Altorientalische und Biblische Rechtsgeschichte* (Wiesbaden).

Index of Authors

AALDERS, G.C. 228
ABBA, R. 201
ABELA x, 1-30
ABMA, R. 69
ACKERMAN, S. 239
ACKERMAN, J.S. 1, 43
ACKROYD, P.R. 46, 51, 114ff.
ALBERTZ, R. 107, 113, 163, 232
ALLEN, L.C. 204
ALONSO SCHÖKEL, L. 1f., 5, 20-23, 79, 217
ALTER, R. 1, 6f., 22, 88, 220
AMIT, Y. 46
ANDERSEN, F.I. 26, 55, 106, 114, 118, 127, 189, 217, 220
AUCKER, W.B. 42
AUGUSTIN, M. 111
AULD, A.G. ix, 5, 31-44, 87f., 91, 107f., 110, 140, 232, 238, 242

BAKHTIN, M. 175
BAL, M. 239, 241
BALTZER, D. 54
BALTZER, K. 57, 67ff., 72, 77, 125, 242
BAR-EFRAT, S. 6f.
BARSTAD, H.M. 86, 107f., 110, 141
BARTELT, A.H. 60
BARTHES, R. 177
BARTON, J. 111
BAUMGARTNER, W. 84
BECKER, U. 232, 235
BECKING, B.E.J.H. 70, 110, 124, 163, 204, 237
BECKWITH, R. 17
BEDENBENDER, A. 239
BEENTJES, P.C. x, 45-53
BEGG, C.T. 46, 49, 120
BEHRENS, A. 106
BEN-DAVID, A. 47
ASEN, B.A. 240
BEN-PORAT, Z. 195
BEN ZVI, E. 6f., 121f., 228
BERGEN, R.D. 229
BERGERHOF, K. 86
BERGES, U. vii, 54-82
BERLIN, A. 7, 11, 13

BETZ, O. 160
BEUKEN, W.A.M. 52, 59, 67, 69, 74
BEYERLIN, W. 125
BICKERMAN, E.J. 1
BIDDLE, M.E. 54, 72
BJØRNDALEN, A.J. 113ff., 117
BLENKINSOPP, J. 2, 30, 69, 75, 89, 137, 171, 173, 201
BLOCK, D.I. 202, 236, 234
BLOK, H. 240
BLUM, E. 106, 166, 173
BOGAERT, P.-M. 87
BOLING, R.G. 235
BOLIN, T.M. 143f., 150ff.
BOSMAN, H.J. 176
BOWEN, N.R. 197
BRAULIK, G.P. 90
BREUER, R. 239
BREYTENBACH, A.P.B. 128, 217
BRENNER, A. 70
BRIGHT, J. 23
BROYLES, C.C. 54, 64
BUDDE, K. 233
BULTMANN, C. vii, 24, 83-93
BURROWS, M. 1, 189

CAQUOT, A. 241
CARLEY, K.W. 205
CARROLL, R.P. x, 23, 86f., 90, 105, 108, 110ff., 144, 160, 176f., 185, 192, 195, 197
CHAPMAN, R.W. 95
CHATMAN, S. 7
CHILDS, B.S. 1, 3, 20, 22, 93, 221, 223
CLARK, D.J. 221, 226
CLEMENTS, R.E. 106, 113
CLINES, D.J.A. 7, 71, 86, 105f., 161, 176
CLUYSENAAR, A. 94
COATS, G.W. 114
COGAN, M. 125
COGGINS, R.J. 46, 122f., 161
COLLINS, T.A. viii, 75, 94-104
CONRADIE, E. 111f.
COOGAN, M.D. 111
COOK, S.L. 201
COOPER, A. 125

Index of Authors

COOTE, R.B.	125	FISCHER, I.	60
COUTURIER, G.	232	FISHBANE, M.	43, 47, 51, 179, 203
COWLEY, A.E.	221	FITZGERALD, A.	57
CRAIG, JR., K.M.	3	FLOYD, M.H.	223f.
CRENSHAW, J.L.	84, 143	FOHRER, G.	54
CROSS, F.M.	69	FOKKELMAN, J.P.	42ff.
CROUCH, W.B.	5, 9, 27	FOLLIS, E.R.	57
CRÜSEMANN, F.	120, 217	FOLMER, M.L.	227
CURTIS, E.L.	51	FONTAINE, C.	70
		FORBES, A.D.	55
DARR, K.P.	66, 201, 209	FRANK, H.T.	1
DAVIES, G.I.	190	FREEDMAN, D.N.	2, 26, 106, 111, 114, 118, 127f., 143, 189, 217, 220
DAVIES, J.	122		
DAVIES, P.R.	2, 5, 7, 16, 49, 71, 86f., 91		
		FRETHEIM, T.E.	6
DAY, J.	152	FRITZ, V.	107
DAY, P.L.	64	FROLOV, S.	2f., 8-13, 21, 28
DEGENAAR, J.J.	112	FUHS, R.M.	183
DEIST, F.E.	107	FULLER, R.	6f.
DESELAERS, P.	79		
DEURLOO, K.A.	240	GALAMBUSH, J	55
DIAMOND, A.R.	83, 85, 87, 90f.	GALIL, G.	124
DIEBNER, B.-J.	240	GALTER, H.D.	237
DIEDRICH, F.	46	GARCIA-TRETO, F.O.	106
DIETRICH, M.	86, 236	GARRONE, D.	88, 106
DIETRICH, W.	124	GARSIEL, M.	240
DIEZ MACHO, A.	79	GERSTENBERGER, E.S.	86
DIJK-HEMMES, F. VAN	16, 70, 240f.	GESENIUS, W.	221
DIJKSTRA, M.	ix, 70, 105-128, 204f., 237	GILBERT, P.	106, 108
		GITAY, Y.	217, 226f.
DILLARD, R.B.	45, 47	GOOD, E.M.	2, 8f., 13
DIRKSEN, P.B.	160	GORDON, P.	8
DOUGLAS, M.	210ff.	GORDON, R.P.	86ff., 138, 141, 171, 232
DOZEMAN, T.B.	170		
DUGUID, I.M.	200f.	GOSSE, B.	61, 123, 125
DUHM, B.	196	GOULDER, M.D.	142, 150
DUKE, R.K.	46, 201	GRABBE, L.L.	201
DURAND, J.-M.	117	GRAHAM, M.P.	159, 169
		GRAY, J.	136, 233
EGO, B.	81	GREEN, B.	7
ELIOT, T.S.	93	GREENBERG, M.	204, 207
EMERTON, J.A.	46, 107, 114	GREIG, A.	153
EMMENDÖRFER, M.	65	GRETHER, O.	5
ESKENAZI, T.C.	46	GROL, H.W.M. VAN	179
ESLINGER, L.M.	87, 106, 108, 176	GROS LOUIS, R.R.	43
EVANS, C.A.	54, 64, 185	GROSS, W.	114, 125
EXUM, J.C.	32, 106, 176	GROVES, J.A.	176
		GRUBER, M.I.	68
FALES, F.M.	86	GRYSON, R.	214
FECHTER, F.	199	GUNNEWEG, A.H.J.	84, 86
FENTON, T.	viii, 129-141		
FISCHER, G.	66, 68	HALPERN, B.	234, 236, 241

Index of Authors

Hals, R.M.	183		Kratz, R.G.	66, 92, 106
Hanson, P.D.	174		Kristeva, J.	120, 175, 177
Harmsen, J.H.	176		Krüger, Th.	106
Harnisch, W.	82		Kuntzmann, R.	46
Harper, W.R.	216		Kuschke, A.	54
Hatton, H.A.	221		Laato, A.	176
Hauser, A.	20		Landes, G.	3
Hausmann, J.	57		Landy, F.	71
Hayes, J.H.	107		Lang, B.	201
Heintz, J.-G.	107		Lategan, B.C.	112
Hermisson, H.-J.	59, 65, 84f., 87f., 90, 160		Leene, H.	vii, ix, 67, 92, 175-198
Hernando, E.	46		Leeuwen, C. van	107, 113f., 117
Herrmann, S.	92, 108, 175, 241		Lemaire, A.	110, 120
Hertzberg, H.W.	196		Lescow, T.	116
Heschel, A.J.	28f.		Levenson, J.D.	201
Hess, R.S.	55		Levin, C.	92, 110
Hoffmeier, J.K.	125		Lichtenberger, H.	81
Holbert, J.C.	2f., 7f., 9, 13, 22		Lincoln, B.	212
Holladay, W.L.	84, 184, 229		Lindblom, J.	159
Holzinger, H.	131		Lindars, B.	233f., 239, 242
House, P.R.	2f., 6f., 176		Liwak, R.	241
Houtman, C.	164, 171		Lohfink, N.	59, 74
Hunter, A.	x, 142		Long, B.O.	105, 114
Israel, F.	88, 106		Loretz, O.	86, 107, 110, 236
Janowski, B.	236		Lubetski, M.	125
Japhet, S.	45, 48, 51		Lucci, L.	57
Jarick, J.	107f.		Lundbom, J.R.	84, 89
Jaruzelska, I.	106, 118		Lust, J.	124, 161
Jepsen, A.	107, 238		Madsen, A.A.	51
Jeremias, J.	106, 111, 113, 117, 119f., 122, 127, 160		Magonet, J.D.	2, 15, 60, 144, 154
			Maier, J.	80
Johnson, B.	235		Malamat, A.	38, 239
Johnstone, W.	viii, 49, 159-174		Marti, K.	107
Jones, B.A.	6		Martin, J.D.	49
Kautzsch, E.	221		Mason, R.	46
Kegler, J.	45f.		Matheus, F.	70
Kelly, B.E.	49		Mathys, H.-P.	76
Kermode, F.	1, 22		May, H.G.	1, 187
Kessler, R.	78		Mayes, A.D.H.	168
Keulen, P.S.F. van	122		McCarter, P.K.	65, 15, 154, 235, 237
King, P.J.	111		McConville, J.G.	201
Klein, L.R.	242		McKane, W.	49, 85, 88-91, 129, 229
Koch, K.	23, 120			
Köckert, M.	92		McKay, H.A.	86, 161
Koenen, K.	73		McKeating, H.	201
Kooij, A. van der	241f.		McKenzie, S.L.	121, 159, 169, 171
Koole, J.L.	72		Mein, A.	ix, 199-213, 206
Korpel, M.C.A.	63, 67, 70, 78, 197, 204, 214, 227		Melugin, R.F.	73, 105

Index of Authors

MERENDINO, R.P. 67, 69
MERWE, C.H.J. VAN DER 217
MEYER, R.   160
MICHEEL, R.   45f.
MILES, JR., J.A.   11
MILGROM, J.   159, 203
MILLARD, A.R.   236
MILLER, J.W.   175, 187
MILLER, P.D.   69
MOMMER, P.   111
MOOR, J.C. DE   x, 67, 78, 89, 105, 105, 107, 142, 179, 198, 215, 231, 238
MOORE, G.F.   232, 235
MOWINCKEL, S.   161
MÜLLER, H.-P.   109
MULDER, M.J.   214
MULKEN, M. VAN   186
MUÑOZ LEON, D.   79
MUSIL, A.   132
MYERS, E.M.   159

NEEF, H.-D.   233, 235, 241
NELSON, R.D.   122, 201, 203, 208f.
NEUMANN, P.K.D. 115
NEUSNER, J.   211
NEWSOME, J.D.   46, 50
NICHOLSON, E.W. 167
NIEHR, H.   235
NIELSEN, K.   120
NISSINEN, M.   86
NOBLE, P.R.   106f., 221
NOGALSKI, J.D.   6, 16ff., 21, 176
NOTH, M.   17, 19, 122, 127

ODELL, M.S.   199f., 205
OESCH, J.M.   26, 57, 78, 214
OGDEN, D.K.   77, 107, 145
OLBRECHTS-TYTECA, L.   217
OLLENBURGER, B.C.   54
OTTO, E.   54, 169
OVERHOLT, TH.W.   106f.

PARPOLA, S.   134
PATTON, C.   200
PAYNE, D   8
PENNA, A.   234
PERELMAN, C.   217
PERLITT, L.   92, 120
PETERSEN, D.L.   5, 46, 203
PFEIFER, G.   106, 118
POHLMANN, K.-F. 83f., 204

POLK, T.   83
POLZIN, R.   37, 40, 43
PORTEOUS, N.W.   54
POSWICK, R.-F.   179
PRAETORIUS, F.   125
PREUSS, H.D.   58
PUGLIATTI, P.   7

RAD, G. VON   3, 22-24, 84f., 120, 205
RAMIREZ, G.   106, 108
REED, W.L.   1
REENEN, P. VAN   186
REGT, L.J. DE   vii-viii, 52, 214-231
REID, S.B.   106
RENAUD, B.   173
RENKEMA, J.   229
RENZ, TH.   55
REVENTLOW, H.G. 111, 205
RHEA, R.   159
RHODES, E.F.   26
RICHARDS, K.H.   46
RICHTER, W.   233ff., 238
RINGGREN, H.   107
RÖMER, T.   41
RÖSEL, M.   55
ROFÉ, A.   87, 91
ROMEROWSKI, S.   228
ROOY, H.F. VAN   46, 105, 198, 215
RUDOLPH, W.   47, 113
RUITEN, J.T.A.G.M. VAN 59
RYOU, D.H.   221f.

SÆBØ, M.   110, 120
SASSON, J.M.   1-3, 5, 14f., 21, 25f., 143f., 146, 150
SAWYER, J.F.A.   70, 122, 181
SCHÄFER-LICHTENBERGER, C. 160
SCHAEFFER, G.E. 50
SCHEARING, L.S.   121, 159, 169, 171
SCHMID, H.   118
SCHMIDT, W.H.   123, 161f.
SCHMITT, J.J.   54, 60, 64, 68
SCHNIEDEWIND, W.M.   46ff., 52f., 159
SCHREINER, J.   191
SCHULTZ, R.L.   187, 195
SCHUNK, K.-D.   23, 111, 241
SCHWARTZ, D.R.   199
SEELIGMANN, I.L. 46
SICRE DIAZ, J.L.   1f., 5, 20f., 23
SIEBERT-HOMMES, J.C.   219

Index of Authors

Simon, U.	40, 43	Wagner, A.	106
Ska, J.L.	6f., 13	Wagner, S.	241
Smalley, W.A.	220	Ward, J.M.	107
Smelik, K.A.D.	42	Watisberg, M.	241
Smend, R.	84, 122, 189, 235, 238	Watson, W.G.E.	89, 142, 214, 236
Smith, D.L.	210-212	Watts, J.D.W.	6, 106, 151, 176
Smith, G.V.	120	Watts, J.W.	3, 6, 142, 176
Snyman, G.F.	47	Weber, R.	214
Söllner, P.	79, 82	Weigl, M.	125
Soggin, J.A.	19, 88, 106, 113, 234f.	Weinberg, J.P.	46
		Weinfeld, M.	124
Sommer, B.D.	159, 176	Weippert, H.	88
Spieckermann, H.	92	Weippert, M.	86
Spronk, K.	vii, 232-242	Welch, A.	111, 128
Spykerboer, H.C.	72	Wellhausen, J.	107, 129
Steck, O.H.	58, 66, 70, 74, 77, 80, 106	Wendland, E.R.	2f., 20, 217, 227
		Wenham, G.J.	55
Steins, G.	189	Wevers, J.W.	185
Sternberg, M.	5, 7f.	Wieringen, A.L.H.M. van	61, 179, 195
Stevenson, K.R.	207f.		
Stoebe, H.J.	127	Wildberger, H.	115, 225
Strassfeld, M.	167	Willi, T.	47
Strübind, K.	46	Williams, J.G.	240
Sweeney, M.A.	60, 73, 200, 215, 225, 229	Williamson, H.G.M.	51, 105f., 108f., 113ff., 117f., 120-3, 125, 127
Talmon, S.	185	Willi-Plein, I.	105
Talstra, E.	176	Willmes, B.	46
Taylor, G.	87, 108	Wilshire, L.E.	70
Then, R.	46	Wilson, R.R.	107
Thiel, W.	111, 160, 175, 191, 196	Wittenberg, G.H.	120
		Wolde, E. van	176, 237, 239
Toorn, K. van der	64f.	Wolff, H.W.	6, 78, 106, 113-7, 120, 123, 143, 181, 189, 216, 218
Trible, Ph. L.	1, 146		
Tucker, G.M.	106		
Tull Willey, P.	65	Wolters, A.	125
		Woude, A.S. van der	105, 113, 181
Uehlinger, C.	125	Wright, D.P.	159
Utzschneider, H.	106	Würthwein, E.	26
Van Dyke Parunak, H.	229	Wyatt, N.	148, 155, 236
Vanoni, G.	25		
Van Seters, J.	169f., 173	Zenger, E.	59, 169
Vaux, R. de	202	Ziegler, J.	214
Vawter, B.	1	Zimmerli, W.	183, 187, 190, 196f., 199, 204f., 208, 228
Veijola, T.	90, 126		
Vermeylen, J.	72, 74, 87		
Vervenne, M.	59, 124, 161	Zobel, H.J.	57
Viberg, Å.	106, 108		
Vieweger, D.	175, 187, 189, 194, 196		
Waard, J. de	220, 227		

Index of Texts

GENESIS

1:1–2:4	167
1:2	149
1:9	147
1:10	147
1:26	145
1:28	145
2:21	14
6:5	154
6:11	154
6:13	154
7:11	149
8	145
8:1-12	145
8:2	149
9:24	188
15:12	14
15:17	239f.
18:20-33	28
20:2	114
20:7	171
28:5	114
30:29	188
32:4	114
32:1-5	118
32:6-8	118
35:8	234, 236
37	153
39-41	153
44:31	155
46:2	36
49:25	149
50:21	65

EXODUS

2:3	148
2:5	148
3:12	163
3:18	163
4:1	163
4:14-16	170
14:9	147
4:16	131
4:21	163
6:2-5	171
7:1	131, 170
7:9	174
9:25	156
10:19	147
11:5	156
11:7	156
12:12	156
12:29	156
13:2	156
13:15	156
13:18	147, 163
14–15	147
14	153
14:16	147
14:22	147
14:29	147
15	62, 145, 147, 150, 153
15:1-13	145, 147
15:2	150
15:2	62
15:4	147
15:5	148ff.
15:8	149
15:13	150
15:14-15	143
15:19	147
15:20-21	171
15:20	39
15:22	147
17:2	173
17:4-7	173
17:8-16	163
18:1-12	172
19–24	162
19–20	164, 167
19:2–20:21	167
19:9	168
19:16–20:21	168
19:16	189
19:18	168
19:19	168f., 189
19:20-25	168, 179
19:20-24	169
19:24	170
19:25	169
20	167
20:1-17	167ff.
20:1	168f.
20:18	168f., 189, 240
20:20	163
20:22–23:33	169
23:10-19	166
23:31	147
24:16-18	169
25:1–31:17	172f.
25:10-22	166
28:15	236
32-34	173
32	164
32:11-14	170, 172f.
32:11	171
32:26-29	173
32:30-35	172
33:1-6	172
33:7-11	172f.
33:11	174
33:12	188
33:13-16	172
34:1-4	164ff., 172
34:2-3	166
34:5-26	166
34:5-9	172
34:5-16	166
34:6-7	25
34:6	146, 148, 150, 154
34:9	121
34:10-28	172
34:11	163
34:17-26	166
34:27-29	164f.
34:29–Num. 10:28	171
34:29	172
35–40	173
37:1-9	166
38:8	36
39:32	173

LEVITICUS

10:10-11	203
16:16	207
16:19	207

NUMBERS

3:10	48
4:14	48
10:11	171
10:28	171
10:29	172

INDEX OF TEXTS

11	172	4:10	168	18	161, 163f., 173
11:2-3	171	4:12	168	18:3	233
11:3	173	4:14	166	18:4	162
11:4	173	4:26	170	18:5	31
11:25-27	171	4:29-30	49	18:9-22	161
11:29	48, 171	4:30	49	18:14-22	160f., 163, 167
12:6	36	4:34	169	18:14	163
14:25	147	4:44	161	18:15	162, 171
16	163f.	5	167	18:16-17	167
16:5-11	164	5:1	170	18:21-22	11, 13
16:5	188	5:5	167, 170	18:16-17	162
16:12	114, 164	5:6-21	167	18:16	163
16:15	164	5:7	161	18:18	126, 162, 171, 240
16:16-23	164	5:9	161	18:20	162, 171
16:25	164	5:31	166	18:21-22	162
16:27-34	164	6:1-3	170	18:22	171
16:30-34	145	6:5	162	22:3	193
16:35	164	8:2	188	23:5	126
20:14	114	8:3	90	26	75
21:4	147	8:7	149	29:1	170
21:21	114	9:7–10:11	171, 173	29:14	88
21:32	114	9:8	173	29:15	188
22:5	114	9:9	171	29:19	123
22:6	188	9:18	171f.	30:15	101
23:12	126	9:22	173f.	31:1	170
23:14	190	9:23	164	33:8	173
23:26	126	9:25–10:11	172	33:10	202
24:1-2	190	9:25	171	33:13	149
24:11	117, 126	9:26-29	173	34	170
24:13	126	10:1-5	164ff.	34:9	173
26:9-11	164	10:1-3	166	34:10	163, 171
33:10	147	10:1	172		
33:11	147	10:2	172	JOSHUA	
		10:3	172	2:1	114
DEUTERONOMY		10:4	166	2:10	147
1–11	163	10:5	172	4:22	147
1:5	161	10:8	172	4:23	147
1:21	164	10:10	171	6:5	189
1:26	164	11:4	147, 169	6:20	189
1:40	147	11:6	164	24:3-4	114
2:1	147	11:26	170	24:6	147
4	170	12–26	169		
4:1	170	13	92, 162f., 173	JUDGES	
4:2	170	13:1	161	2:16	233
4:5	170	13:2-6	160f., 163, 167	2:18	233
4:8	161	13:2	163, 171	3:8	239
4:9-13	168	13:3	161f.	3:15	238
4:9–5:33	167	13:4	163, 171	3:29	233
4:9–5:31	167	13:5	163	4	153, 241
4:9	168	13:6	161f., 163, 171	4:4-5	232-42

4:4	39	3	34, 37-44	14:18	42
4:6-9	233	3:1	34, 37ff., 41	14:44	44
4:23	233	3:2	35, 39	15:10	115
5	153, 241	3:3	35, 40	15:16	41
5:7	241f.	3:7	35	15:29	42
5:12	240f.	3:9	35, 40	16:3	188
5:13-17	241	3:10	35, 40	16:7	40
5:14	242	3:11	43	17:42	40
6:7-10	242	3:12	32	18:1	115
11:12-13	118	3:13	35, 39, 41	18:22	42
11:14-27	118	3:14	36	18:36	42
11:16	147	3:15	35, 40f.	19:20	48
11:28	118	3:17	43	19:23	48
12:6	233	3:18	36, 41	20:13	44
13–16	240	3:19	36, 41	22:18	34
13:12	236	3:20	36, 42	23:10	40
14:4	233	3:21	36, 41, 43	23:11	40
17:20	118	4:4	33	25:22	44
20:33	237	4:14	41	25:39	40
21:17-19	118	4:18	31f.	28:2	188
		4:21	32f.	28:6	238
1 Samuel		4:22	32f.	28:7	238
1:1	41	7:5	33	28:9	188
1:3	31	7:7-14	163	28:15	238
1:6	33	7:15-17	41, 235	31	39
1:7	33	8:1-3	41		
1:8	33	8:6	33	2 Samuel	
1:9	31	8:9	41	2:22	32
1:10	33	8:20	48	2:18	32
1:12	33	8:53	42	3:1	32
1:16	33	8:56	42	3:9	44
1:23	37	9	41	3:18	40
1:27	33	9:1	41	3:35	44
2	31	9:6	41	5:10	36
2:1-10	39	9:8	41	5:11	38
2:1	33	9:9	41, 130	5:12	35
2:6	155	9:15	37, 41	5:20	35, 37
2:10	144	9:18	41	5:24	48
2:11	34	9:19	41	6–7	36
2:12-13	237	9:27	37, 41	6:2	33
2:18	34	9:36	42	6:8	35, 37
2:21	36	10:1-16	159	6:9	36
2:22-25	39	10:3	233, 237	6:14	34
2:23	44	10:5-13	41	6:15	168
2:27-36	44	10:8	188	6:17	35
2:27	43	10:10	42	7	35, 39f., 41
2:28	31	10:16	41	7:2	40
2:29	32	12:11	241	7:4	37-40, 115
2:30	32, 38	12:19	33	7:5	38, 40
2:33	31	13:12	171	7:7	38
2:35	32, 36, 38			7:8-17	126

Index of Texts

7:8	40, 126	9:5	31	2:16	42
7:11	35f.,126	9:26	147	4:33	33
7:13	38	10:2	36	5:15	42
7:14	36	10:10	36	5:17	42
7:17	36, 38f.	10:11	36f.	5:18	42
7:20	35	10:23	36	6:3	42
7:21	35	11:13	41	6:17	33
7:25	33	11:29-39	45	6:18	33
7:27	38	11:32	41	6:31	44
10:12	36	11:34	41	8:10	40
11:20	188	11:36	41	8:12	188
12:1	114	11:38	41	8:13	40, 42
12:30	36	12:22	37, 115	8:19	41
15:10	189	13	116	9	45
15:26	36	13:6	33, 171	9:1-13	118
19:14	44	13:20	115	9:7	42, 121, 124
21-24	43	14	119	9:11	131
22	145	14:7-11	124	9:14	118
23:1	38	14:8	41	9:36	121, 124
24	40	14:10	124	10:10	121
24:2	35	14:18	121	10:30	124
24:10	35f.	14:25	120	11:4	114
24:11	127	15:9-24	47	13:4	171
		15:29	121	13:14	242
1 Kings		16:1-4	124	13:22-25	120
1:41	189	16:1	115	13:23	114, 120
2:5	188	16:3	124	14:2	42
2:9	188	17-18	151	14:8	114
3:5	36	17:2	115	14:23-27	151
3:6	41	17:8	115	14:25-27	120
3:7	34f., 41	18	131	14:25	17-20, 120f., 143
3:9	41	18:1	115		
3:13	32	18:15-19	121	14:13	37
5:15	114	18:36	114	15:12	124
6:11	115	19	154	15:10	127
7:9-11	37	20:22	188	16:8-9	125
8:6	35	21:1	32	17:2-20	124
8:7	35	22	123	17:7-20	124
8:11	32	22:19-23	123	17:13	42, 121, 124
8:16	31	21:17	115	17:21-23	124
8:20	38	21:28	115	17:23	42, 117, 121, 124
8:23-50	35	22	45, 88, 109		
8:25	31	22:5	37	19:15	33
8:26	32	22:7	36	19:34	41
8:28	33	22:19	37	20:4	115
8:29	33, 35	22:25	119	20:6	41
8:30	35			20:12	114
8:35	35	**2 Kings**		21	43
8:59	41	2-9	151	21:1-18	122
8:66	41	2	42	21:6	33
9:2	36	2:12	242	21:7	31

21:8	42f,	3:14-15	225	12:3	59
21:10-15	124f.	3:16–4:1	225	12:6	59, 61
21:10	42f., 121	3:16-17	60	13–23	61
21:12	42	3:18-23	60	14:3-4	225
21:13-14	125	3:18	60	14:14-15	155
22:3	114	3:24	225	15:1	225
22:8	90	3:25–4:1	6, 2251	16:1	64, 225
22:14-20	39	3:25	225	16:7	225
22:14	239	3:26	61, 225	16:9	225
22:16	92	4:3	58	17:10-11	62
22:17	33	4:5	64	18:7	64
22:19	33, 39	5:1-7	226f.	19:1-15	225
24–25	64	5:3-4	226	19:6	148
24:2	42, 121, 124	5:3	54, 56, 226	19:11	225f.
24:4	123	5:5-6	226	19:12	225f.
25:21	117, 124	5:5	188, 226	21:1-10	62, 190
		5:20	101	22:1-4	62
Isaiah		5:24	60	22:4	62, 65
1–39	56-64	6	1-30, 88	22:10	54
1:1–2:5	60	6:1-13	115	22:21	54, 56
1	134	6:9-10	22f.	23:12	64
1:1	54, 56, 61	6:11	22	24:5	60
1:2–4:6	61	6:11-13	23	24:15	226
1:2-9	60	7:1	115	24:17	225f.
1:2-4	225	7:3	115f.	24:23	64
1:2-3	56	7:6	56	26:3	184
1:3	56	7:13	115	27:6-13	226
1:4	56	8:1-4	115	27:12	225f.
1:5-6	57	8:1	116	28:14	54
1:5	57, 225	8:3	116	28:17	125
1:6	57	8:7	225	29:3-6	62
1:8	57, 75, 81	8:8	225	29:8	64
1:9	58	8:14	54	30:1-5	226
1:10	60	8:16	60, 69	30:1-4	225
1:13	135	8:18	64	30:1	225
1:21-26	58	8:20	60	30:3	225f.
1:21	58	9:14-15	181	30:8-17	226
1:27	58	10:3	225	30:9	60
1:29	214	10:10	54	30:12	225f.
2	138, 157	10:11	54	31:4	64
2:1–4:6	60	10:12	64	33	62
2:1	54, 56, 61	10:22	225	33:2	62
2:2-4	59, 73	10:24	61	33:22	62
2:3	60, 63f.	10:32	63f.	3:14	62
2:5	225	11	138	33:17-24	62
2:6-22	60	11:1	62	33:20	62
2:22	225	11:10	62	33:21	62
3:1-3	60	12	59, 61f., 76	33:22	62f.
3:1	54, 56, 60	12:1	61	34	63, 78
3:8	54, 56	12:3-4	61	34:8	62
3:12	181, 225				

Index of Texts

35:3	76	45:13	102	52:1-2	71
35:10	63	45:14-17	66	52:1	71, 73
36–37	63f.	45:14	67	52:2	57, 71, 75
36:2	54	45:15	67	52:3	71
36:7	54, 56	46–47	67	52:5	71, 227
36:20	54	46:13	54, 67	52:7	66, 71
37:10	54	47	67	52:8	71
37:14	63	47:1-15	72	52:9	64, 71
37:20	63	47:1	57, 64	53	57
37:22-23	81	48:1-2	67	53:4	57
37:22	57	48:1	67	53:5	57, 185
37:23	63	48:2	67	53:7	66
37:24-25	64	48:12	182	53:10	69, 73
37:31-32	64	49–55	57, 70, 78	54-55	71
37:31	56	49–52	81	54	70
37:32	56, 64	49	66	54:1	61, 71, 76
38	145	49:6	66	54:2	62
38:4	115	49:13	64	54:3	71, 74
38:9	57	49:14-26	67ff.	54:4-7	63
39:1	114	49:14-20	68	54:13	69
40–66	54, 65	49:14	67f., 71	54:17	69, 72
40–55	55, 64-72, 74, 81	49:15	68	55	72
40–52	64	49:21-26	68	55:1-5	72
40:1-11	64	49:21	68	55:1-3	72f.
40:1-2	65	49:24	69	55:3-5	72
40:2	63, 66	49:25-26	69	56–66	55, 72-5
40:6-8	71	49:25	71	55–59	73
40:9-11	65f.	50:1-3	69	56:4-5	76
40:9	61, 66, 73f.	50:1	63, 66	57	185
40:11	68	50:2	69	57:6-13	72
41:2-3	102	50:4-9	69	57:6-13	72
41:25	102	50:4	69	57:7	72
41:27	66	50:9	69	57:13b3	73
42	66	50:10-11	69	57:19	184
42:1	59	50:10	70, 81	57:21	182
42:4	60	51–52	73	59:2-21	227
42:18-25	227	51:1-11	70	59:2-3	227
42:18	227	51:1	70	59:4-8	227
42:20	214, 227	51:3	64, 71, 74	59:9-13	227
42:24	227	51:4	60	59:11-14	227
42:23	227	51:7	60	59:14-20	227
42:24	60	51:10	149	59:20-21	58, 74
42:21	60	51:11	71	59:20	54, 73
44:3	147	51:12-16	73	59:21	73f., 82, 227
44:26	54	51:12	64, 71	60–62	62, 71f., 74
44:28	54, 64, 66, 102	51:16-17	73	60:1-3	73
45:1-3	102	51:16	71, 73	60:6	66
45:1	64, 66	51:17-23	71	60:7	72
45:11-13	66	51:19	64	60:9	72
45:13-15	65	52:1-6	226f.	60:13	72

60:14	71	4:9-10	91	9:18	75
60:19-20	73	4:10	181f.	10:5	233
60:21-22	73	4:11	65	10:19-20	229
60:21	73f.	4:19	189ff.	11:1	115
61	66, 74, 82	4:21	189ff.	11:11	92, 189
61:1	66, 74	4:31	57, 75	12:1	83
61:2	62	5:3	85	12:5	92
61:3	71, 74	5:27	193f.	12:12	182
61:4	71, 74	5:31	230	13:6	116
61:7	74	6	185f., 190, 191f., 198	13:20	67
61:9	74			13:23-25	229
61:11	74f.	6:1	191	13:24	229
62:1	71, 74	6:2	58, 75	14:1–15:9	43, 185
62:12	225	6:9-15	175, 177-187	14:9	90
62:6-7	75	6:12-15	185, 192	14:13-16	180, 187
62:7	62, 76	6:12	194	14:13	178, 182
62:9	75	6:14	177f., 181f., 184f.	14:14	176, 178, 180
62:11	57, 62, 71, 75			14:15	176, 180
61:12	75	6:16-21	187-92	14:17	65, 229
63:1-6	78	6:16	188, 192	14:19	75, 181
63:13	149	6:16-21	92, 175	15	83-93
63:16	56	6:17	188f., 191f.	15:1-4	43
64:7	56	6:18	185	15:1	43, 171
65:1-7	226	6:19	189, 194	15:4	43
65:7	225f.	6:23	58, 75	15:7	230
		6:26	65, 92	15:10-21	84, 86
JEREMIAH		7:1	115	15:10-12	87
1	88, 92f., 161	7:10	88, 90	15:12	91
1:7	57	7:11	90	15:15-19	87-91, 93
1:14	116	7:12	43	15:15	85, 87, 90, 188
1:18-19	90, 92	7:14	43, 90	15:16	85, 89f., 93
2:5-13	92	7:16	171	15:17	87, 90, 92
2:5-9	92	7:21-26	229	15:18	83, 92
2:8	91	7:24-26	230	15:19	85, 87ff., 91f.
2:18	56	7:25	230f.	15:20	90, 92
2:13	92	7:30	90	17:6	59
2:19	188	8:4-7	92f.	17:12-18	83
2:23	188	8:6	229	17:14-18	91
2:24	230	8:10-13	175	17:15	84, 91
2:26	230	8:10-12	185	17:16	91
2:32	63	8:11	65, 177f., 181f., 184f,	17:18	189
3:2-8	229			18	195
3:13	188	8:15	181	18:1	115
3:14-18	229	8:19	65, 75	18:18-23	175, 192-96
3:14	63, 75	8:21-23	92	18:18	9, 123, 193-6, 202, 240
3:16	230	8:21	65		
4:1-2	229	8:22	65	18:20	85, 88
4:5-8	92	8:23	65	18:20-21	194
4:5	190f.	9:6	65	18:21	194
4:6	75, 92	9:9	229	18:22	123, 193-6
4:8	92				

Index of Texts

19:1	195	28	109, 161, 197	36	116
19:3	43, 189	28:6-8	162	36:1	115
19:15	189	28:8-9	162	36:7	80
20	91	28:9	176, 178, 182	36:27	115
20:7-18	83	28:12	115	36:31	189
20:7-13	91	28:15	176, 189	37:6	115
20:7-9	24, 91	28:16	119, 162	39:16	189
20:7	92	29	159, 197	40:1	115
20:8	85, 92	29:1	195	41:5	43
20:9	91	29:9	176, 180	42:7	115
20:14	83	29:13-14	49	42:14	189
21:1	115	29:14	49	42:16-17	229
22:24-27	229	29:24-32	117	42:17	189
23	9, 181, 197	29:26-27	117	43:2	176, 180
23:9-40	159	29:26	131, 174	43:8	115
23:9	85	29:30	115	44:1	115
23:9-32	91	29:31	176, 180	44:2	189
23:12	189	29:32	162	45:5	189
23:13	178, 180	30–31	68	46:27	229
23:16	176	30:1	115	49:7	194f.
23:17	85, 178, 182	30:5	182	49:14	228
23:18	88	30:17	75	49:21	147
23:19	178	31:6	51, 75	49:37	189
23:21	176, 178, 180	31:7-14	72	50:5	75
23:22	88	31:10	188	60:6	181
23:25	163	31:12	75	50:28	75
23:26	176	31:15	68, 149	51:10	75
23:30-32	178f.	31:16-17	68	51:24	75
23:30	176, 178	31:16	51f.	51:35	75
23:31	176, 178	31:23-25	72	51:57	230
23:32	176, 178, 180	31:23	68	51:64	189
24:3	116	31:34	188		
25:1	115	32:1	115	**Ezekiel**	
25:3-5	229f.	32:30	178	1–5	199
25:4	230	32:31	178	1:1	36, 199f.
25:6-7	230	32:32	178	1:3	199
25:29	90	32:34	90	1:13	240
25:35	194	32:26	115	2:8–3:3	87-91
26	116, 118	32:42	189	2:8–3:2	200
26:4-5	90	33:6	185	3	190, 192
26:6	43	33:26	114	3:16-24	118
26:9	43	34:1	115	3:16-21	175, 190, 192
26:16-18	116	34:8	115	3:25	118
26:18	75, 116	34:12	115	4:4-6	200
26:19	171	34:15	90	4:13-15	212
27–28	159, 162	35:1	115	4:9-17	204
27	161	35:4	135	4:9-15	200
27:9	163	35:12	115	4:13	204
27:15	176, 180	35:15	121	4:14	205
28-29	197	35:17	189	4:15	205
				5:1	200

6:9	229	23:21	228	43:7	207
6:10	229	23:30	206	43:10	207
6:14	229	24:13	206	43:18-27	202
7	196, 202	24:15-18	201	44:6-8	209
7:23-27	175, 192-96	26:19	149	44:9-28	202
7:24	193-6	27	151, 154	44:9	209
7:25	181	27:4	149	44:10-14	208
7:26	193-6, 202	27:25	149	44:23	202f., 207
8	211	27:26	149	44:24	202
8:1	201	27:27	149	46:2-9	202
8:3	36	28:2	149	46:11-15	202
11:55	181	28:9	181f.	46:12	228
11:15	73	31:2-18	230	46:13-14	228
11:24	181	31:2	230	46:19-21	202
12:21-25	176	31:3	230	47	59, 62, 209
13	176, 18, 184-187, 195, 197	31:4	149	**HOSEA**	
		31:10	230	1–3	63
		31:18	230	1:2	116
13:1-16	175, 177-187, 197	33	188, 190f., 192, 198	1:4	124
				2	16
13:3-5	184	33:1-9	175, 187-92	2:4-25	215-8
13:5	181, 184	33:2-6	191	2:4-15	217
13:6-7	184	33:2	188f., 194	2:4-7	215f.
13:6	180ff.	33:4	188f.	2:4	215f., 218
13:7	178, 181f.	33:5	188f.	2:8-17	216
13:8-9	180	33:7-9	191	2:8-9	216
13:9	197	33:7	188f., 191	2:8	216ff.
13:10	180ff., 184	33:8	188, 191	2:11	216
13:15	184	33:9	191	2:15	215
13:16	181	33:24	73	2:16	216ff.
13:17-23	197	35:5	194	2:18-22	216
14:1-11	176	36	207	2:18	215-8
14:1	201	36:16-38	206	2:19-20	216
20:1	201	36:17-18	206	2:20	218
20:7	206	36:20	206	2:21-22	216ff.
20:18	206	36:25	206f.	2:21	218
20:30	206	36:29	206f.	2:23-25	216f.
20:32-44	206	36:33	207	2:23	215
20:43	206	37:1	181	2:25	216
22	202f.	37:23	206f.	3:1	116
22:3	206	38:17	121	3:4	51
22:4	206	40–48	55, 202, 206f., 209, 211	3:5	52
22:15	206			5:14	102
22:24	230	40:2	36, 208	8:1	189
22:25-29	203	40:4	206	8:5	218
22:26	203, 208	40:5	208	8:6	218
22:28	178, 180ff.	42:13-14	202	9:7-8	190
23	63	42:20	208	9:7	132
23:2-35	228	43–46	206	9:8	189
23:4	228	43:3	36	11:1-9	218f.
23:7	206				

Index of Texts

11:1-7	218	4:4	100	7:13	114
11:3-4	218f.	4:11	100, 104	7:14-16	139
11:3	219	4:12	99, 104	7:14-15	118
11:4	219	4:13	98ff., 104	7:14	7, 108
11:5-7	219	5:4-5	104	7:15	116, 125
11:8-9	219	5:5	117	7:16	114, 119
11:8	219	5:6	97	7:17	114, 119, 124
11:9	219	5:7	100, 104	8-9	219
13:7-8	102	5:8-9	98	8:1-2	125
		5:8	99, 101, 104	8:1-3	105
JOEL		5:10-13	221	8:4-10	105
2:1	75	5:10	221	8:4	219
2:15	75	5:11-12	221, 223	8:8	99, 104, 128
2:23	75	5:13	221	8:9-10	128
3:5	75	5:14-15	101	8:9	101, 104
4:16	75	5:14	104	8:10	101, 104, 219
4:17	75	5:15	101	9	96f.
4:21	75	5:16-17	99	9:1-4	96
		5:17	103	9:1	98, 103
AMOS		5:18-20	96, 101	9:3	96, 103
1-9	99	5:18	99, 101	9:5-6	98f.
1:1	95f., 98, 128	5:19	96, 103	9:5	104, 128
1:2	75, 95, 99, 103f.	5:21-24	134	9:7-10	219
1:3–2:5	94	5:27	117, 124	9:7	125, 219
1:5	125	6:1	75	9:11-15	103
2:2	189	6:7	124		
2:6-16	220f.	6:11	97f., 103	**OBADIAH**	
2:6-9	220	6:12	101, 104	1	228
2:6	71	7-8	112	2-16	228f.
2:9-11	220	7	94, 97, 112f.,	6	228
2:9	220		119, 123, 126f.	7-8	228
2:10-13	220f., 223, 225	7:1–8:3	105	9-14	78
2:10	219	7:1-17	114	16	228
2:11	220	7:1-16	114	17-21	229
2:14	96, 194	7:1-8	115	17	75
2:16	96	7:1-3	105	21	75
3:1	95, 103	7:2	123		
3:2	100	7:4-6	105	**JONAH**	
3:3-6	96, 100	7:4	149	1	146, 154
3:4	95, 103	7:7-8	97, 105, 113	1:1-3	4, 9, 14, 19, 29,
3:6-7	190	7:9-17	105-28		157
3:7	88, 95, 121,	7:9	103, 113f., 116,	1:1-2	158
	123, 125		124, 127	1:1	5, 7f., 17ff., 115
3:8	95, 103	7:10-17	113f., 116	1:2	6, 10f., 29
3:9	51	7:10-17		1:3	6, 12, 15, 27,
3:12	95, 103	7:10	117		158
3:14-15	97	7:11	114, 119, 124,	1:4-16	13
3:14	98, 103		127	1:4	10, 158
3:15	103	7:12-13	119	1:5	14, 157
4	99	7:12	114, 126	1:6	15
4:3	97, 117			1:7-12	146

1:9	14, 19, 28, 147, 156	4:7	15	1:7-10	221
1:10	14f.	4:8	27f.	1:7	221, 223
1:12	14	4:9	14, 16	1:11-18	221
1:14	15	4:10-11	2ff., 16, 28f.	1:11	221, 223
1:14	147	4:11	156	2:1-3	221, 223
1:15-16	156			2:4–3:8	221
1:15	152	**Micah**		2:4	222
1:16	146	1:9	181	2:5-15	222
2	2, 4, 14, 142-58	1:13	75	2:5	221
2:2	4, 6, 15, 18	1:14	67	2:12	221
2:3-10	20f., 144, 152f., 153	1:16	67	3:1-8	221
		2:1-5	228	3:3-4	203
2:3	152, 158	2:1-3	228	3:7	222f.
2:4-8	152	2:1	228	3:8	222f.
2:4	148f.	2:2-3	228	3:9-13	223
2:5	150, 158	2:3-5	228	3:11-12	223
2:6	148	2:3	228	3:14-20	223
2:7	150, 158	2:8-9	181	3:14-15	76
2:8	150	2:10	67	3:14	75, 223
2:9-10	152	3:3	181	3:16-20	76
2:9	146, 150	3:5	178, 180f.	3:16-17	76
2:10	146, 150, 158	3:8	181	3:16	75
2:11	147	3:9-11	116	3:17	76
3	9, 154	3:10	75	3:18-19	229
3:1–4:4	13, 27	3:11	202	3:18	216, 223f.
3:1-3	157	3:12	75, 116	3:19	76, 224
3:1	26	4	157		
3:2	26	4:2	75	**Haggai**	
3:3	26, 143, 156	4:7	75	1:1	115
3:4	26, 29	4:8-13	75		
3:5-8	26	4:8	75	**Zechariah**	
3:6	157	4:10	62, 75	1:1	115
3:9	14, 26	4:11	75	1:8	148
3:10–4:4	12	4:13	75	1:14	75
3:10–4:1	27	7:1-13	78	1:17	75
3:10	15, 25f., 156, 158	7:7-13	75, 78	2:11	62, 75f.
		7:7	78, 190	2:14	75f.
4	9, 154	7:8-10	78	7	76
4:1-3	158	7:8	78	7:1	115
4:1	15, 26	7:9	78, 80	8:2	75
4:2-3	14f., 26	7:10	78	8:3	75
4:2	10ff., 24ff., 27-29, 146, 154, 156f.	7:11-13	78	8:10	51f., 182
		7:18-20	148	9:9	75f.
		7:19	148	9:13	75f.
4:3	14, 26, 27f.			10:11	148
4:4	15, 27f., 26	**Habakkuk**		12:6	239
4:5-11	15, 27	2:1	190	13:2-6	159
4:5	12, 27	3:10	149	14:5	111, 128
4:6	15			14:8	62
4:6-8	27	**Zephaniah**			
		1:2-18	221	**Psalms**	
				1	59

Index of Texts

5:4	190	78:15	149	21:27	135
8:9	145	84–86	142	23:29-35	214
18	145, 152, 154	87–89	142	23:31	214
30:4	155	87	59	23:34	149
33:7	149	87:7	59	25:18	37
36:7	149	88:7	148	29:18	37
37:9	73	95:5	147	30:19	149
37:11	73	98:6	189		
37:22	73	99:6	43	**Ruth**	
37:29	73	104:6	149	1:17	44
37:34	73	105	150		
38:4	182	105:9	114	**Qohelet**	
40:9	90	106:7	147	3:19	156
42–49	142	106:9	147, 149	3:21	156
42:8	149	106:22	147		
46	62	107–150	142	**Lamentations**	
46:5-7	76	107	145f., 150, 154	1:1	58, 61
46:5	62	107:22	146	1:4	61
46:9-11	76	107:23-32	145f.	1:5	78
47:6	189	107:23-30	146	1:8	78
48	62	107:24	148f.	1:13	57
48:3-8	76	107:26	149	1:17	78
50	131f., 139, 142	118:14	62	1:21	78
51-72	142	132	153	2:1	58
55	145, 153, 157f.	135:6	149	2:4	58
55:7	157f.	136:13	147	2:8	58, 61
55:8	157	136:15	147	2:11	62, 65
55:9	157f.	139	20	2:13	58, 62
55:10-12	157f.	139:7-10	403	2:15	78
55:13-15	157f.	142:5	194	2:16	78
55:16	157f.	148:7	149	2:18	58, 61
55:17-20	157f.			2:21	61
55:24	157f.	**Job**		3	68, 78, 82
63:11	193	7:9	155	3:21	78, 80
66:6	147	11:20	193	3:24	78, 80
68:8	48	28	143	3:31-33	78
68:23	148	28:14	149	3:48	62, 65
69	145f., 152, 154	38:16	149	4:1	58, 61
69:2-4	145	38:30	149	4:3	65
69:2-3	146	39:24	189	4:4	61
69:3	146, 148	41:16	150	4:6	65
69:14-19	146	41:23	148f.	4:10	65
69:14-16	145	41:24	149	4:12-13	159
69:16	146, 148			4:13	174
71:20	149	**Proverbs**		4:21	78
73–83	142	3:20	149	5:16	78
73	153	8:24	149	5:17	78
76:7	14	8:27	149		
77:17	149	8:28	149	**Daniel**	
78	150	15:8	135	8:19	188
		21:3	135	10:6	239
				10:7	36

10:8	36	1:10	35	18:7	45
10:9	14	1:11	35	18:9	45
10:16	36	1:12	32. 35	18:11	45
		3:6	37	18:12	45
Ezra		5–7	168	18:17	45
1:1-4	66	5:14	32, 168	18:18	37
1:5-11	66	6	168	18:21	45
9:11	121	6:14-39	35	18:22	45
		6:20	33	19:2	48
Nehemiah		6:21	33	20:14	46f., 49, 53
4:14	189	6:42	40	20:17	49
5	71	7:1-2	168	20:20	45
6:14	109	7:12	36	20:37	45
9	145	9:1	37	21:12	45
9:9-11	145, 147, 150	9:2	115	24:19	45
9:9	147	9:9	37	24:10	46
9:11	147f.	9:10	37	24:20	48, 50, 53
		9:22	36	25:15	45
1 Chronicles		9:298	45	25:14-16	116
10	39	11:2	37	25:16	45
11:9	36	12:5	45, 50	26:22	45f.
12:19	184	12:15	45	28:9	45, 48
12:19	46, 48, 53	13:22	45	28:16	114
14:15	48	14-15	49	29:25	45, 127
15:27	34	14:2–15:15	47	30:6	114
15:28	189	14:3	50	30:18	33
16:16	114	14:5	50	32:9	114
16:22	45	14:6	50	32:16	40
17	36, 41	14:9	48	32:20	33, 45
17:1	45	14:11-12	47	32:24	33
17:3	38	14:15	47	32:32	45f.
17:15	32, 37, 38	15:1-7	47f.	33:13	33
17:25	33	15:1	46, 49, 53	34:8	114
17:3	37	15:2	48-51	34:27	38
19:13	36	15:3-7	52	35:15	127
20:2	36	15:3-6	48, 50-53	35:18	45
21:8	35f.	15:3	51	35:21	53
21:9	127	15:4	49f., 52	35:25	46
22:8	115	15:5	51f., 182	36:10	114
22:18	49	15:7	48, 51f.	36:12	45
23:2–26:32	160	15:8	45	36:16	45, 53
25:1	45, 160, 171	15:9	49		
25:2	45	15:12	49	**Baruch**	
25:3	45	15:13	49	4–5	82
25:5	127	15:15	49f., 52	4:5–5:9	79
27	160	16:7-10	47	4:8	79
28:9	49f.	18	45	4:9-29	79
29:18	114	18:4	37	4:12-13	79
29:29	45, 127	18:5	45	4:18	80
		18:6	36, 45	4:21-26	80
2 Chronicles				4:22	80
1:7	36				

4:25	80	10:55	81	13:11	79
4:28	80			13:16	79
4:29	80	1 Maccabees			
		14:41	80	Luke	
4 Ezra		Sirach		10:29	1
9–10	80–2	48:18	56	John	
9:26–10:59	80	48:24	56	19:11	119
9:41–10:4	80	Tobit		Hebrews	
10:6	80	13	78f., 82	11:32	232
10:21-23	81	13:2	79		
10:24	81	13:5	79	Revelation	
10:25-28	81	13:10	79	21:1-2	82
10:44	81				

ERRATA

p. 46, n. 11: deuteronomistischen en > deuteronomistischen und

p. 222, restore n. 30 as follows: Ryou, Zephaniah's Oracles, 282.

www.ingramcontent.com/pod-product-compliance
Lightning Source LLC
Chambersburg PA
CBHW021836220426
43663CB00005B/280